AMERICA'S GOT POWERS™

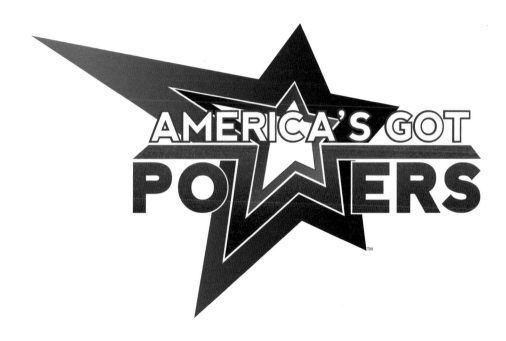

JONATHAN ROSS   BRYAN HITCH
SCRIPT   STORY   ART

PAUL NEARY
INKS CHAPTERS 1-7

ANDREW CURRIE
INKS CHAPTERS 1-2

JASON PAZ
INKS CHAPTERS 3-5

PAUL MOUNTS
COLORS CHAPTERS 1-6

DAVID BARON
COLORS CHAPTERS 6-7

CHRIS ELIOPOULOS
LETTERS

NEIL EDWARDS
LOGO

JEFF MARIOTTE
SERIES EDITOR

DREW GILL
DESIGN

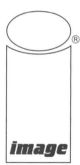

IMAGE COMICS, INC.
Robert Kirkman – Chief Operating Officer
Erik Larsen – Chief Financial Officer
Todd McFarlane – President
Marc Silvestri – Chief Executive Officer
Jim Valentino – Vice-President

Eric Stephenson – Publisher
Ron Richards – Director of Business Development
Jennifer de Guzman – Director of Trade Book Sales
Kat Salazar – Director of PR & Marketing
Corey Murphy – Director of Retail Sales
Jeremy Sullivan – Director of Digital Sales
Emilio Bautista – Sales Assistant
Branwyn Bigglestone – Senior Accounts Manager
Emily Miller – Accounts Manager
Jessica Ambriz – Administrative Assistant
Tyler Shainline – Events Coordinator
David Brothers – Content Manager
Jonathan Chan – Production Manager
Drew Gill – Art Director
Meredith Wallace – Print Manager
Monica Garcia – Senior Production Artist
Jenna Savage – Production Artist
Addison Duke – Production Artist
Tricia Ramos – Production Assistant
IMAGECOMICS.COM

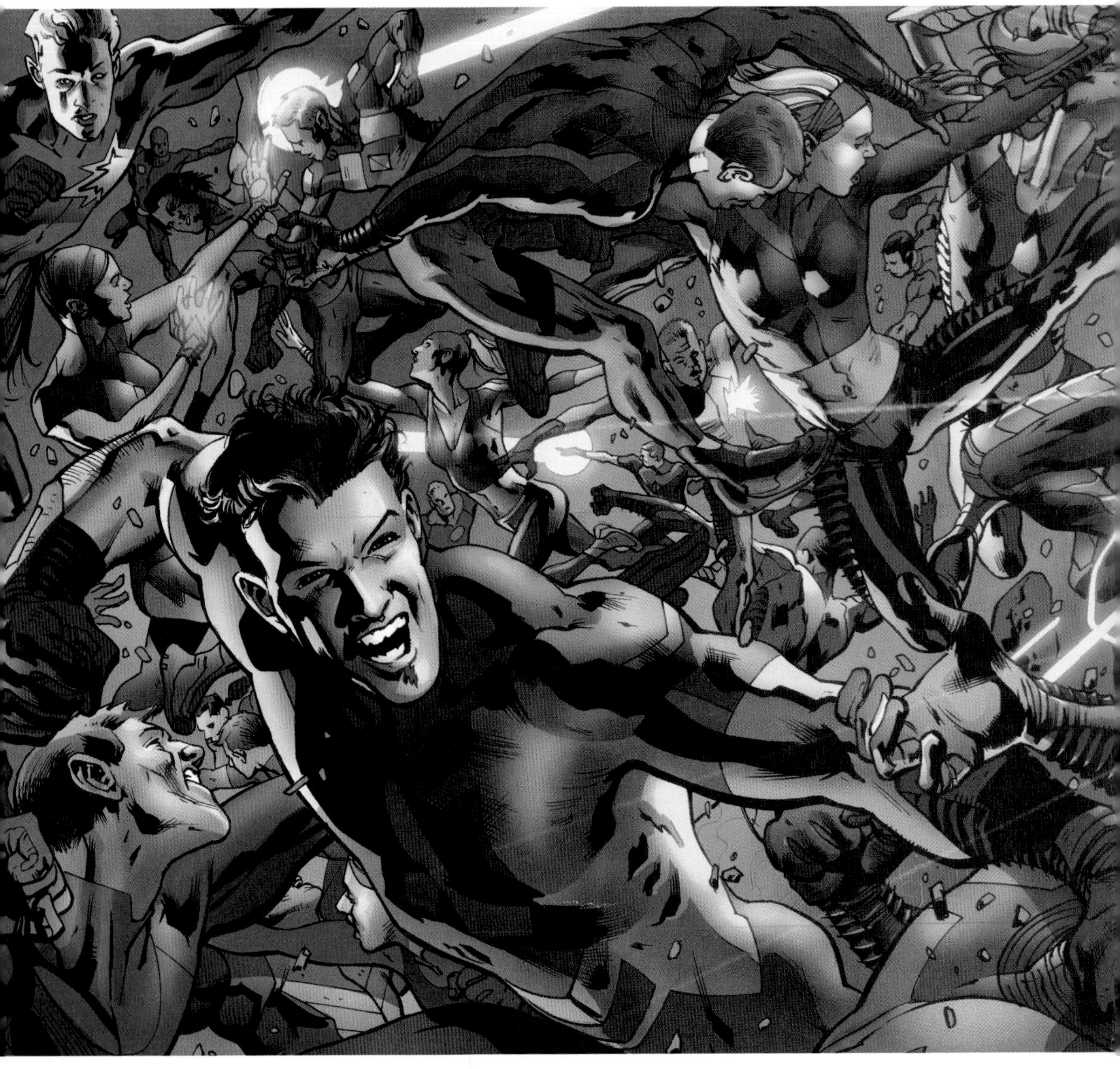

CHAPTER **ONE**

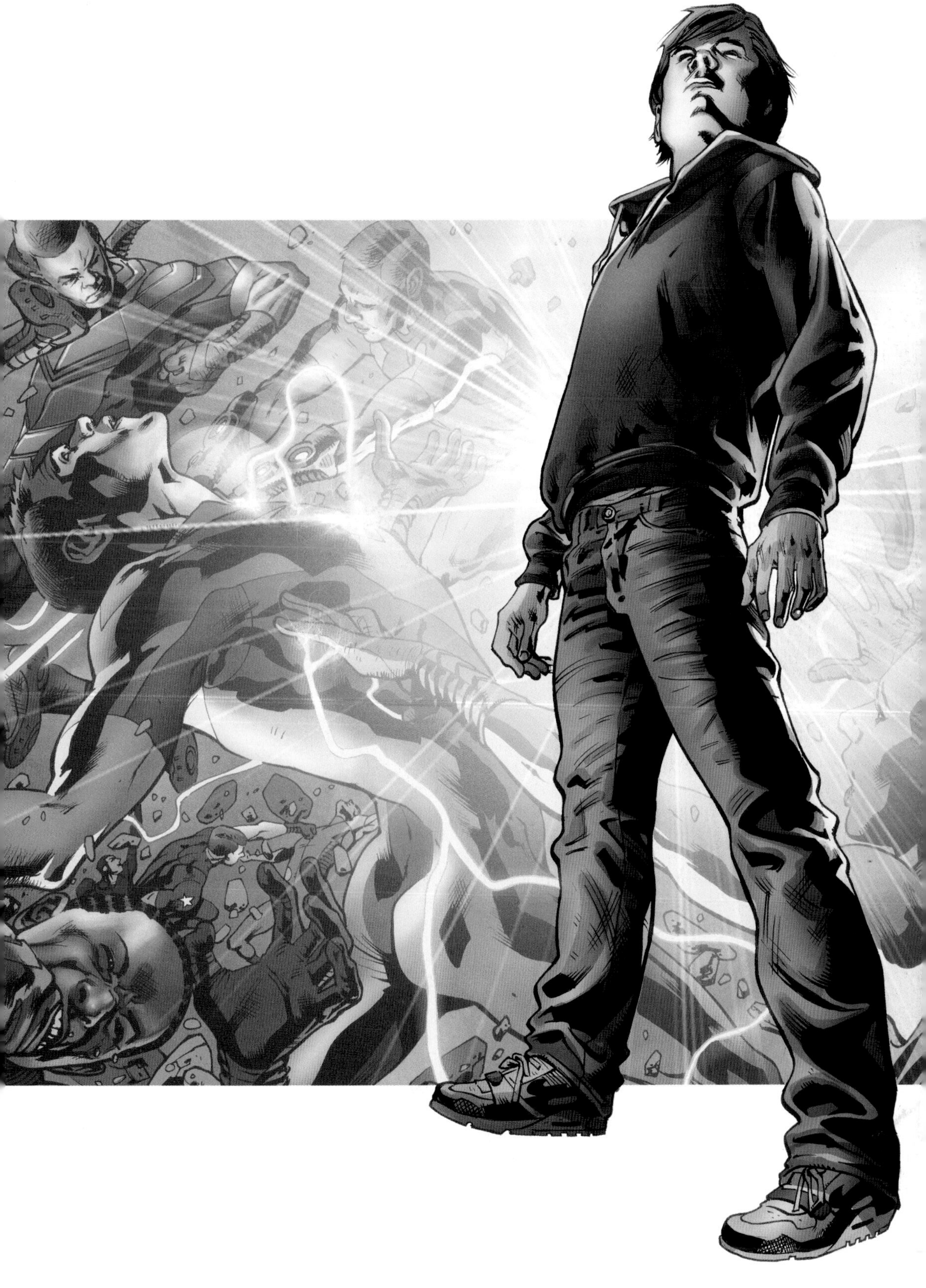

‘AGP’ SuperTeam and Senator: Press conference - Recap

Published Thursday September 7 2012 10.00am PDT

All four members of the super-team POWER GENERATION were present at the press Conference held today to launch the brand new series of America’s Got Powers (September 7).

Sitting alongside Blur, Whispa, Ice and new team captain Quarterback was show creator Professor Colin Syell and Government representative Senator Susan Handler.

Details of the new look games that will help ring in the changes and, it is hoped, reverse the slide in ratings that marked the last Season were announced.

Addressing the fatal injury during the last season final that led to a spike in ratings, Senator Handler acknowledged that new season would be marked by greater freedom for participants to utilize full extent of their powers. New-look Paladins would also be operating at maximum force. This is at the request of the Powered participants claims Handler.

“They are desperate to show what they are capable of, and it would be an infringement of their super-human rights for us to deny them the chance to be the best they can ”

But protestors have already attacked the development, insisting that new level of play can only lead to more fatalities and more severe injuries.

Details of the new games are on the shows website at www.americasgotpowers.com

Have your say below and follow the action on Twitter #AGPPressConference

Add a comment
16 comments

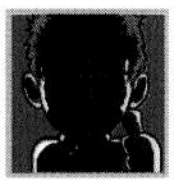

LuvPowez · Top Commenter

Bring back Karmeleon so she can go on to win the show! Booted off far too early, she clearly would have gone through to the final stages had the public had the choice. She was one of the favourites in the competition! That injury was nothing!

Reply · 28

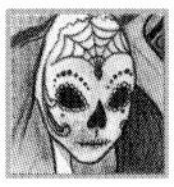

Slizzard · Top Commenter

In all honesty It should technically just be Quarterback going through as he’s the only one to have really proved himself.. Guaranteed if it was the girls that fought as hard Karmaleon wud have been winner. New rules sounds awesome!!

Reply · 14

BooYah27 · University of Boston

It seems odd that those in the earlier seasons are still in the team and get another chance yet those who where knocked out last season when competition was WAY more brutal have no chance of return even though they may ultimately be a better power.

Human2

WTF?!? Peeple complain that they fight too hard in new show? Remember the riots! They hurt 2 many normal peeple to have ANY rights left. Heroes are marines and cops. Firefighters. Not freaks.

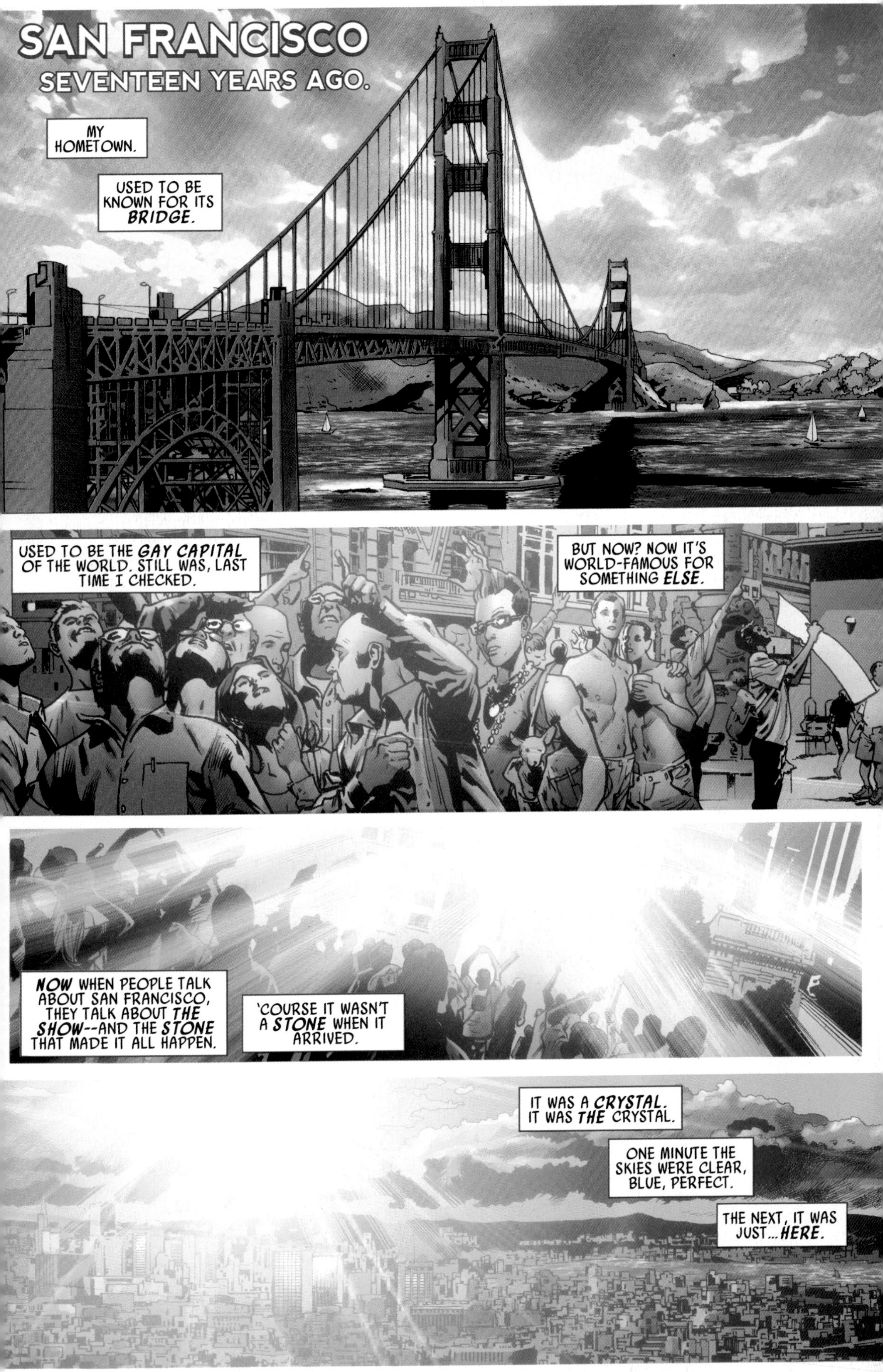
SAN FRANCISCO
SEVENTEEN YEARS AGO.
MY HOMETOWN.
USED TO BE KNOWN FOR ITS BRIDGE.
USED TO BE THE GAY CAPITAL OF THE WORLD. STILL WAS, LAST TIME I CHECKED.
BUT NOW? NOW IT'S WORLD-FAMOUS FOR SOMETHING ELSE.
NOW WHEN PEOPLE TALK ABOUT SAN FRANCISCO, THEY TALK ABOUT THE SHOW--AND THE STONE THAT MADE IT ALL HAPPEN.
'COURSE IT WASN'T A STONE WHEN IT ARRIVED.
IT WAS A CRYSTAL. IT WAS THE CRYSTAL.
ONE MINUTE THE SKIES WERE CLEAR, BLUE, PERFECT.
THE NEXT, IT WAS JUST... HERE.

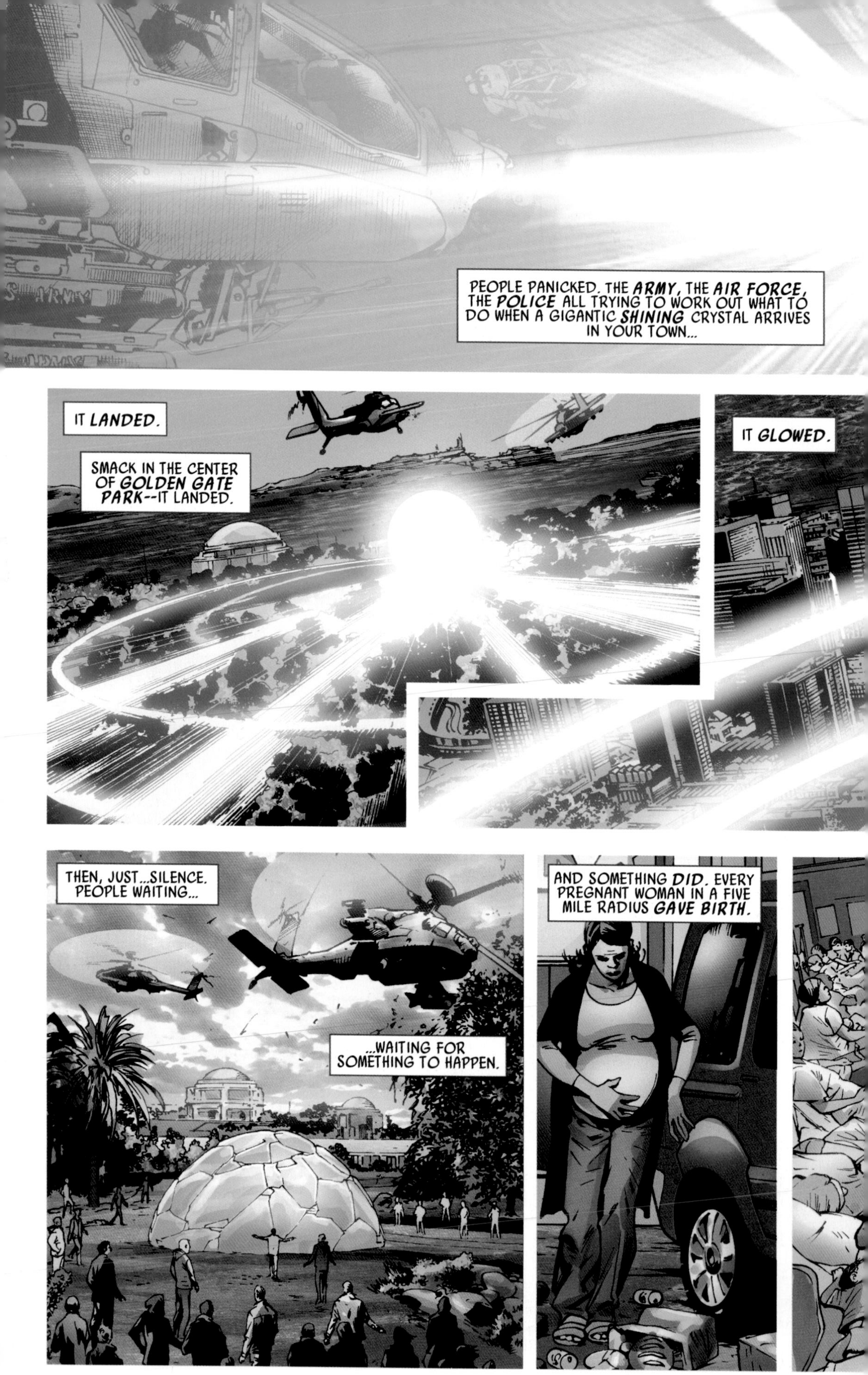
PEOPLE PANICKED. THE ARMY, THE AIR FORCE, THE POLICE ALL TRYING TO WORK OUT WHAT TO DO WHEN A GIGANTIC SHINING CRYSTAL ARRIVES IN YOUR TOWN...
IT LANDED.
SMACK IN THE CENTER OF GOLDEN GATE PARK--IT LANDED.
IT GLOWED.
THEN, JUST...SILENCE. PEOPLE WAITING...
...WAITING FOR SOMETHING TO HAPPEN.
AND SOMETHING DID. EVERY PREGNANT WOMAN IN A FIVE MILE RADIUS GAVE BIRTH.

...WHILE THE *CONSPIRACY NUTS* AND *WHACK JOBS* BLAMED IT ON EVERYONE FROM THE *MUSLIMS* TO THE *LIZARD PEOPLE* THAT SECRETLY RUN THE *U.S.A.*

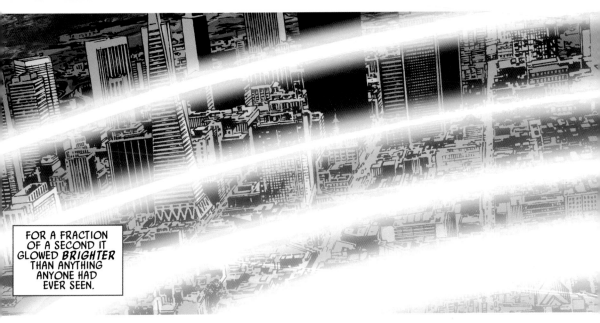

FOR A FRACTION OF A SECOND IT GLOWED *BRIGHTER* THAN ANYTHING ANYONE HAD EVER SEEN.

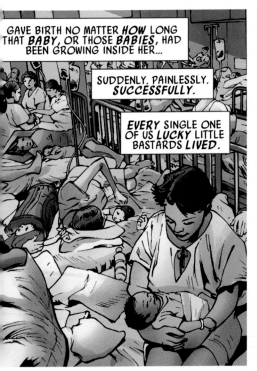

GAVE BIRTH NO MATTER *HOW* LONG THAT *BABY*, OR THOSE *BABIES*, HAD BEEN GROWING INSIDE HER...

SUDDENLY. PAINLESSLY. *SUCCESSFULLY.*

EVERY SINGLE ONE OF US *LUCKY* LITTLE BASTARDS *LIVED.*

EVERY SINGLE ONE GOT A *GIFT. A TALENT.*

A POWER.

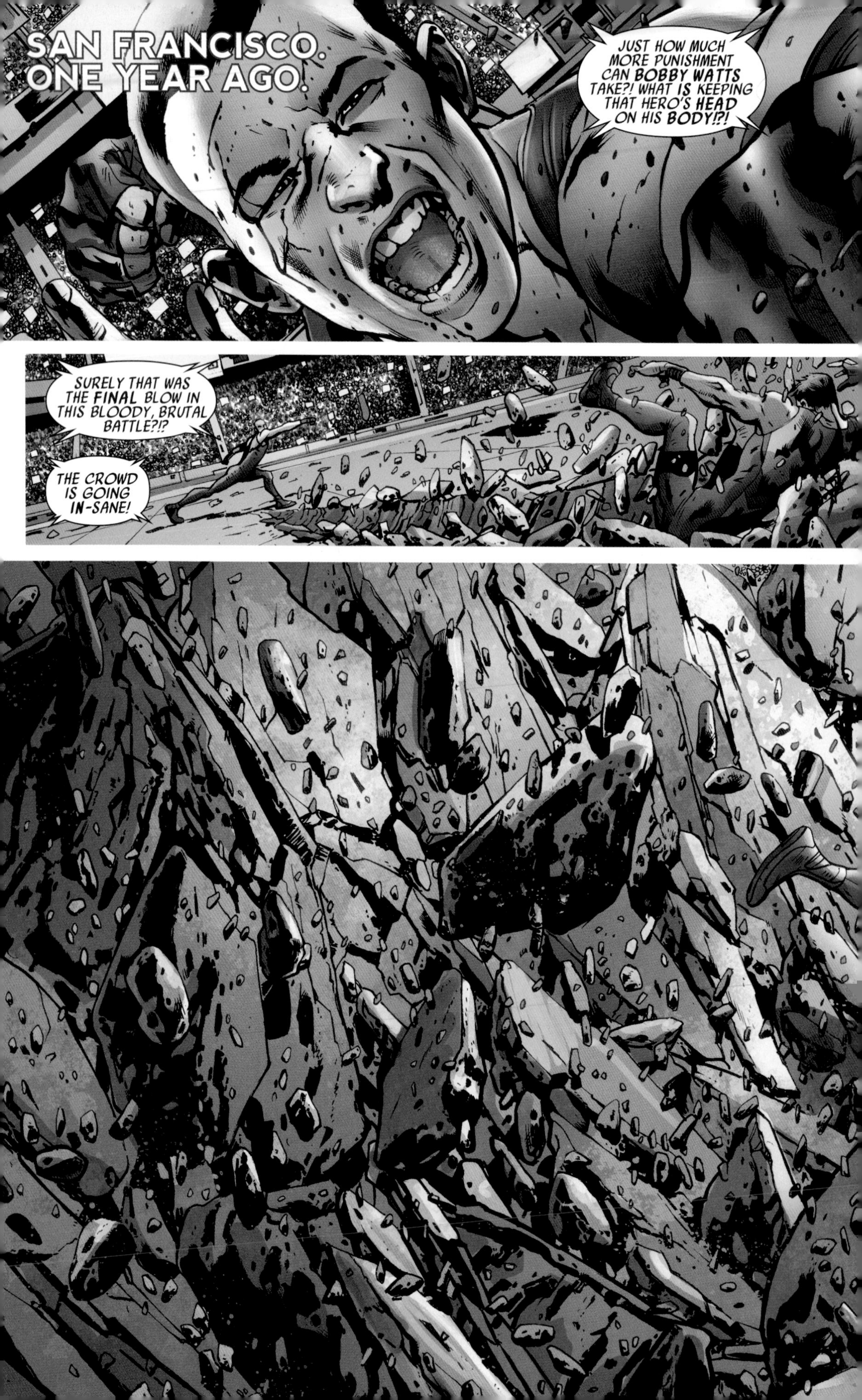
SAN FRANCISCO. ONE YEAR AGO.
JUST HOW MUCH MORE PUNISHMENT CAN BOBBY WATTS TAKE?! WHAT IS KEEPING THAT HERO'S HEAD ON HIS BODY!?!
SURELY THAT WAS THE FINAL BLOW IN THIS BLOODY, BRUTAL BATTLE?!?
THE CROWD IS GOING IN-SANE!

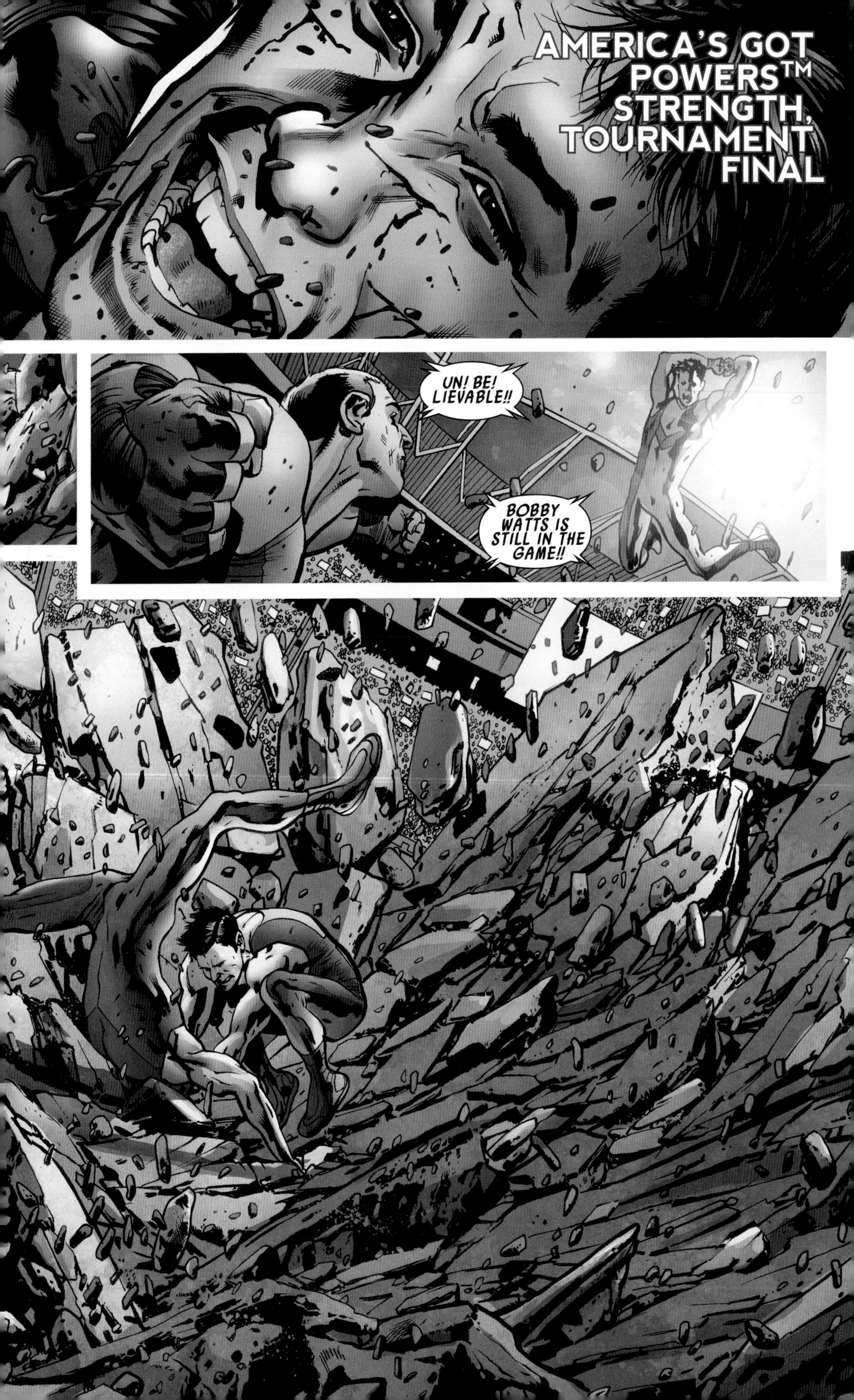
AMERICA'S GOT POWERS™ STRENGTH, TOURNAMENT FINAL
UN! BE! LIEVABLE!!
BOBBY WATTS IS STILL IN THE GAME!!

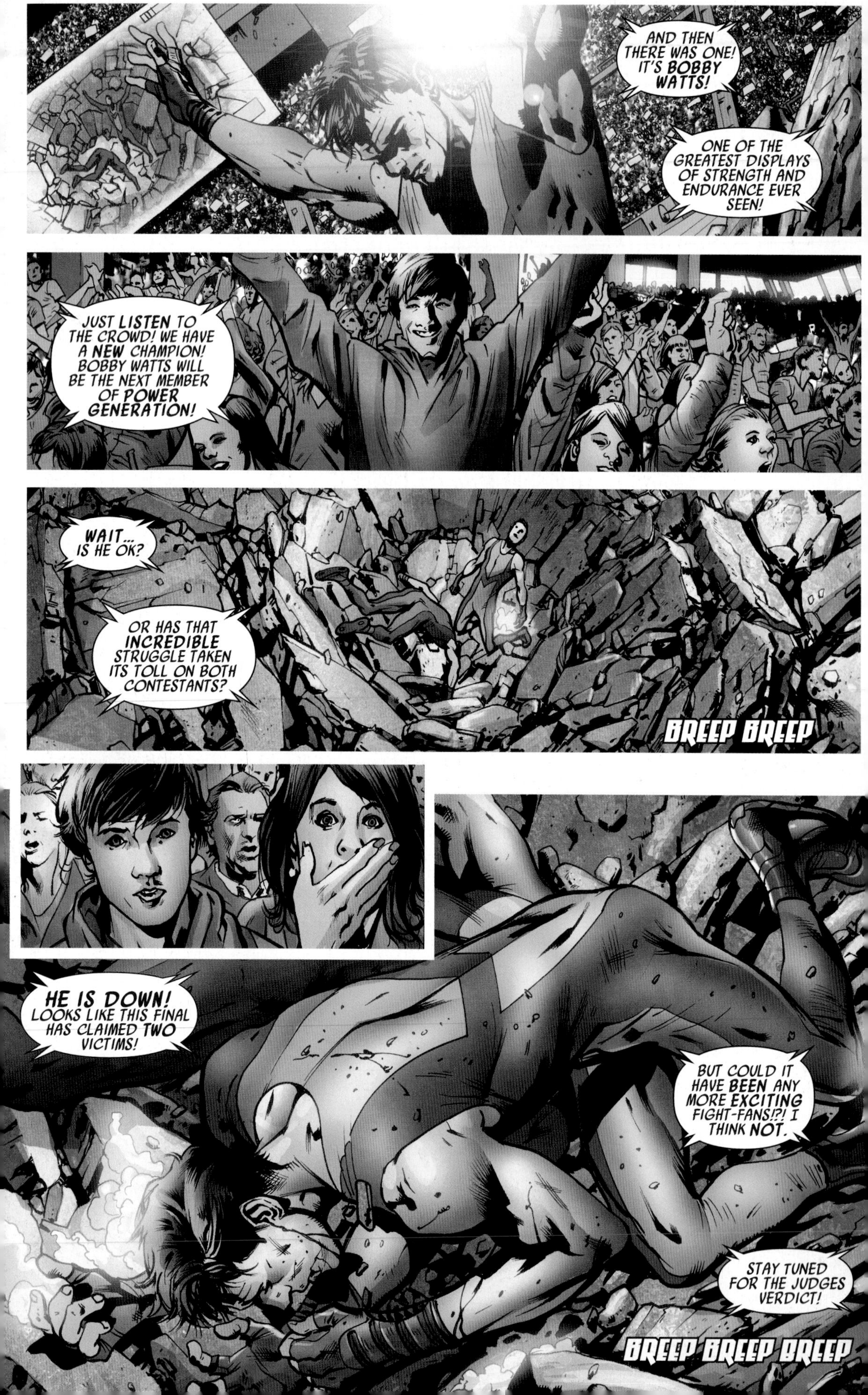
AND THEN THERE WAS ONE! IT'S BOBBY WATTS!
ONE OF THE GREATEST DISPLAYS OF STRENGTH AND ENDURANCE EVER SEEN!
JUST LISTEN TO THE CROWD! WE HAVE A NEW CHAMPION! BOBBY WATTS WILL BE THE NEXT MEMBER OF POWER GENERATION!
WAIT... IS HE OK?
OR HAS THAT INCREDIBLE STRUGGLE TAKEN ITS TOLL ON BOTH CONTESTANTS?
BREEP BREEP
HE IS DOWN! LOOKS LIKE THIS FINAL HAS CLAIMED TWO VICTIMS!
BUT COULD IT HAVE BEEN ANY MORE EXCITING FIGHT-FANS!?! I THINK NOT.
STAY TUNED FOR THE JUDGES VERDICT!
BREEP BREEP BREEP

BREEP BREEP BREEP
DEBBIE CALLING
WE ALL GOT POWERS!
EVERY SINGLE ONE OF US.

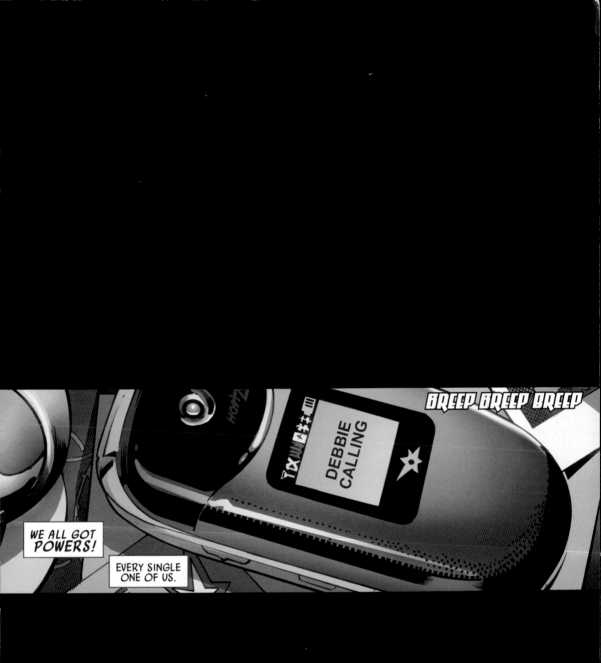

EXCEPT ME.

SAN FRANCISCO. TODAY.

FUCKFUCK FUCKFUCKFUCK FUCKFUCKFUCK FUCKFUCKFUCK FUCKFUCK

SHITFUCK SHITFUCKSHIT FUCKSHITFUCK SHITFUCKSHIT FUCKSHIT

I'M GOING TO GET A FINE. AGAIN.

SHIT. FUCK.

POWERS ENTRANCE ONLY
POWER STAR SCAN
ENSURE...IS

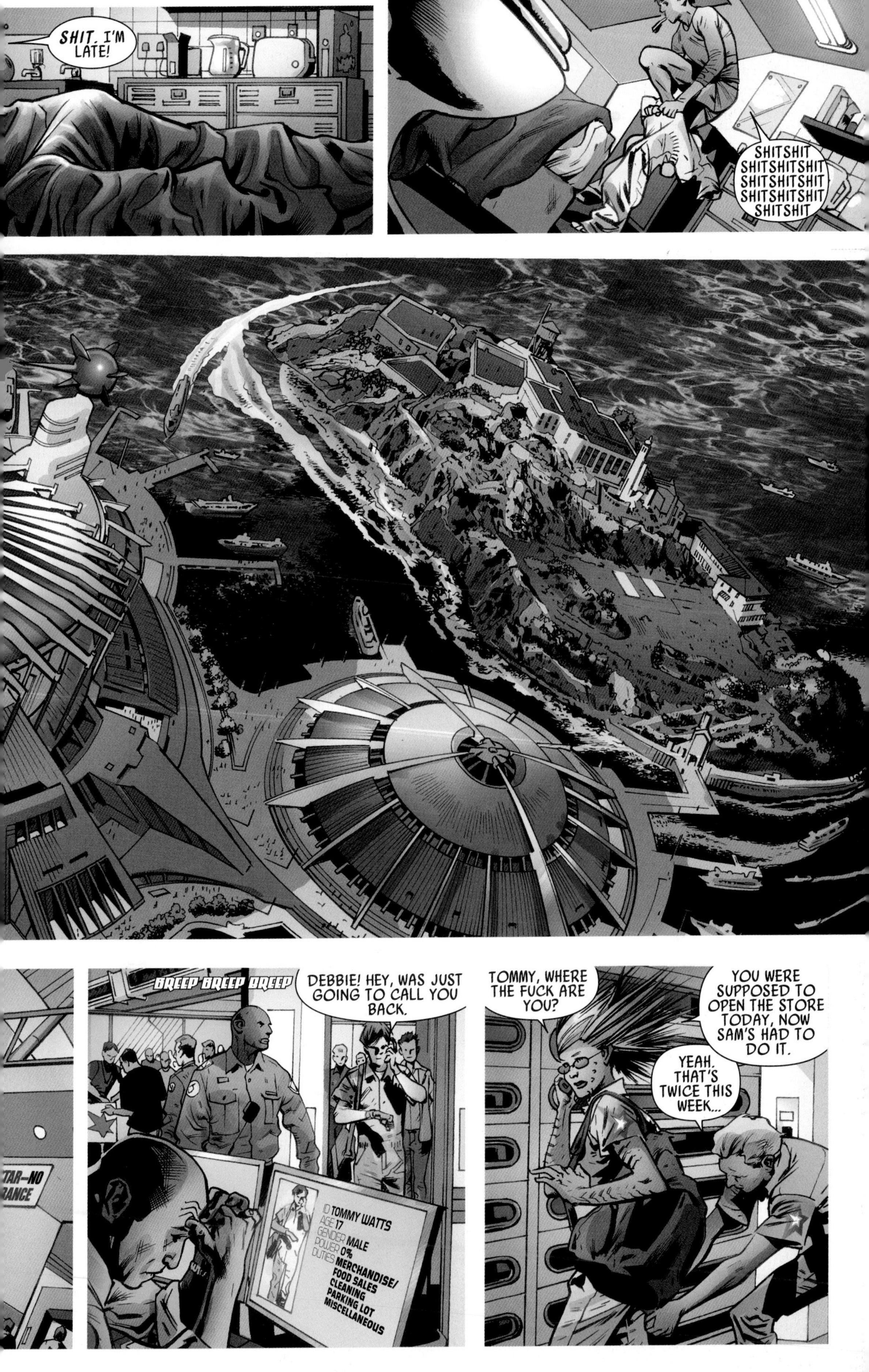

SHIT. I'M LATE!
SHITSHIT SHITSHITSHIT SHITSHITSHIT SHITSHITSHIT SHITSHIT
BREEP BREEP BREEP
DEBBIE! HEY, WAS JUST GOING TO CALL YOU BACK.
ID TOMMY WATTS
AGE 17
GENDER MALE
POWER 0%
DUTIES MERCHANDISE/ FOOD SALES CLEANING PARKING LOT MISCELLANEOUS
TOMMY, WHERE THE FUCK ARE YOU?
YOU WERE SUPPOSED TO OPEN THE STORE TODAY, NOW SAM'S HAD TO DO IT.
YEAH. THAT'S TWICE THIS WEEK...

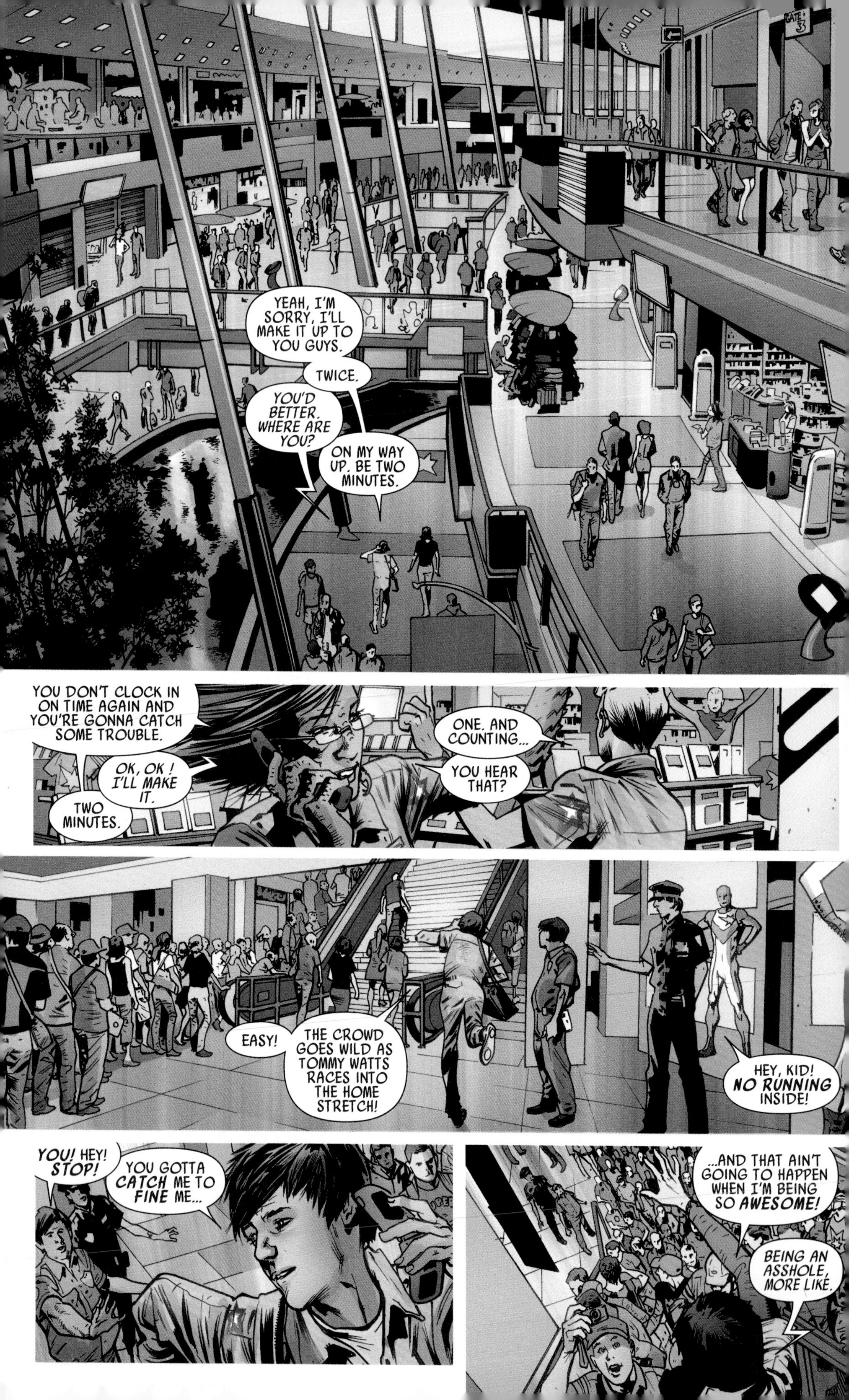
GATE 3
YEAH, I'M SORRY, I'LL MAKE IT UP TO YOU GUYS.
TWICE.
YOU'D BETTER. WHERE ARE YOU?
ON MY WAY UP. BE TWO MINUTES.
YOU DON'T CLOCK IN ON TIME AGAIN AND YOU'RE GONNA CATCH SOME TROUBLE.
OK, OK! I'LL MAKE IT.
TWO MINUTES.
ONE. AND COUNTING...
YOU HEAR THAT?
EASY!
THE CROWD GOES WILD AS TOMMY WATTS RACES INTO THE HOME STRETCH!
HEY, KID! NO RUNNING INSIDE!
YOU! HEY! STOP!
YOU GOTTA CATCH ME TO FINE ME...
...AND THAT AIN'T GOING TO HAPPEN WHEN I'M BEING SO AWESOME!
BEING AN ASSHOLE, MORE LIKE.

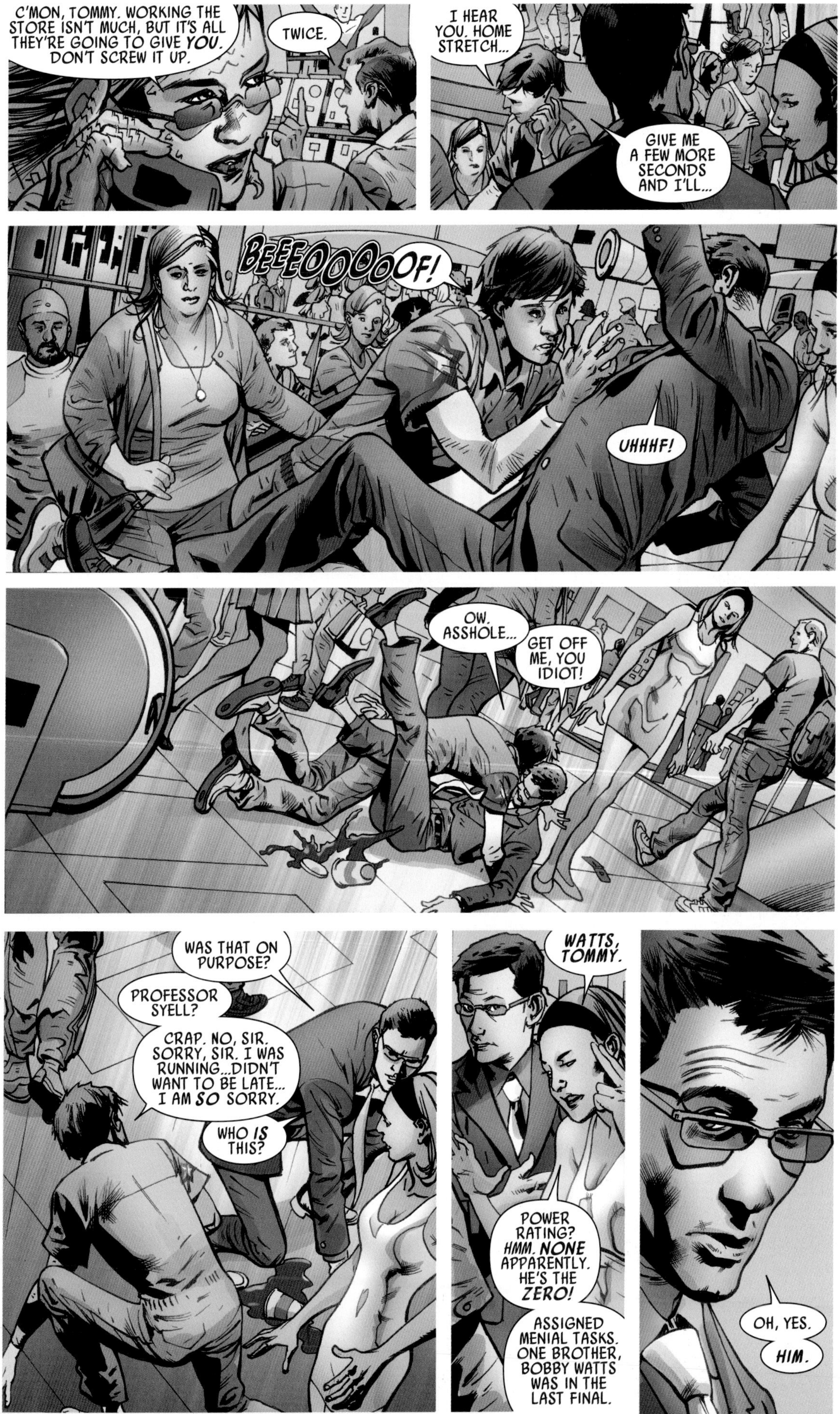
C'MON, TOMMY. WORKING THE STORE ISN'T MUCH, BUT IT'S ALL THEY'RE GOING TO GIVE YOU. DON'T SCREW IT UP.
TWICE.
I HEAR YOU. HOME STRETCH...
GIVE ME A FEW MORE SECONDS AND I'LL...
BEEEOOOOOF!
UHHHF!
OW. ASSHOLE...
GET OFF ME, YOU IDIOT!
WAS THAT ON PURPOSE?
PROFESSOR SYELL?
CRAP. NO, SIR. SORRY, SIR. I WAS RUNNING...DIDN'T WANT TO BE LATE... I AM SO SORRY.
WHO IS THIS?
WATTS, TOMMY.
POWER RATING? HMM. NONE APPARENTLY. HE'S THE ZERO!
ASSIGNED MENIAL TASKS. ONE BROTHER, BOBBY WATTS WAS IN THE LAST FINAL.
OH, YES.
HIM.

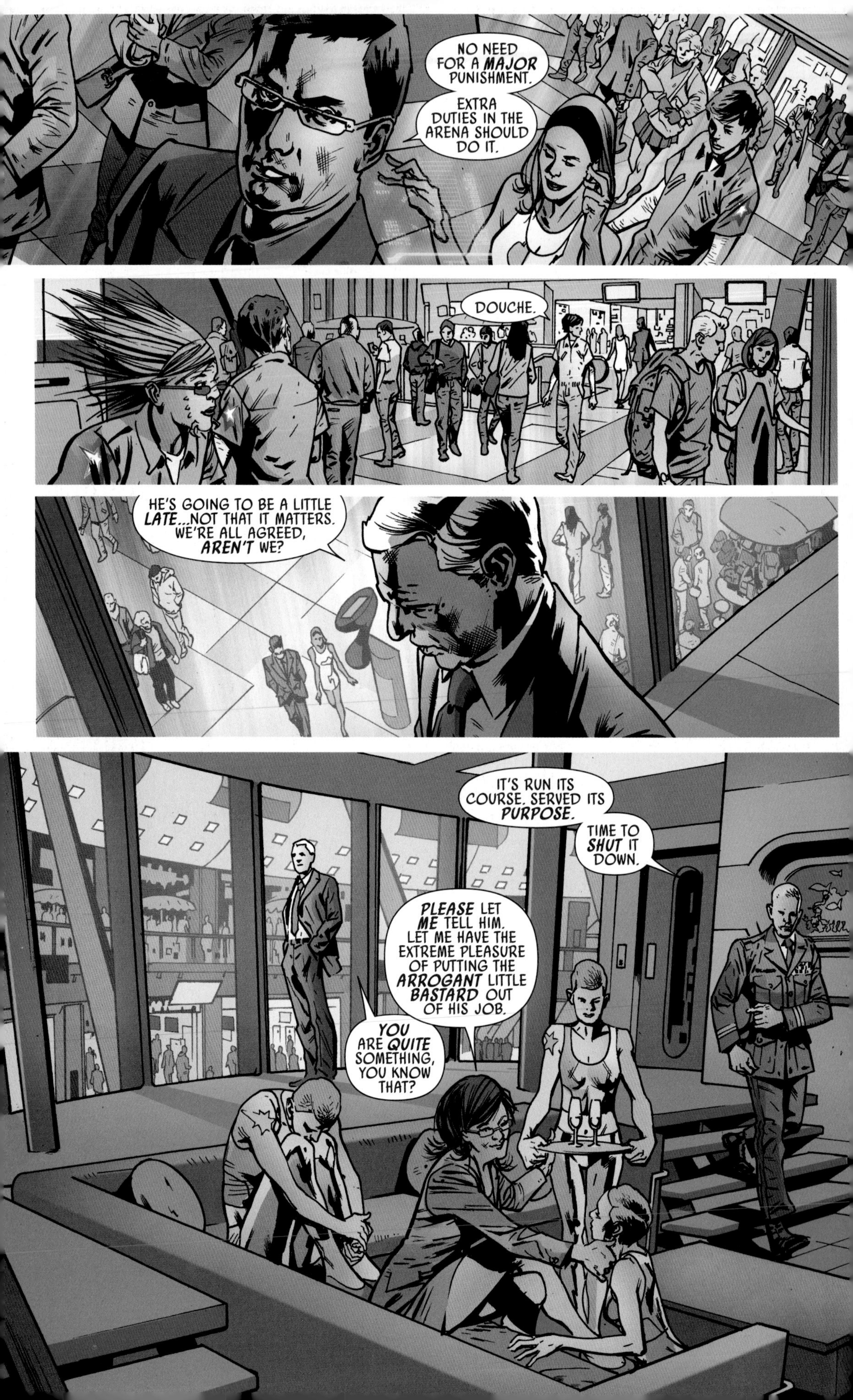
NO NEED FOR A MAJOR PUNISHMENT.
EXTRA DUTIES IN THE ARENA SHOULD DO IT.
DOUCHE.
HE'S GOING TO BE A LITTLE LATE...NOT THAT IT MATTERS. WE'RE ALL AGREED, AREN'T WE?
IT'S RUN ITS COURSE. SERVED ITS PURPOSE.
TIME TO SHUT IT DOWN.
PLEASE LET ME TELL HIM. LET ME HAVE THE EXTREME PLEASURE OF PUTTING THE ARROGANT LITTLE BASTARD OUT OF HIS JOB.
YOU ARE QUITE SOMETHING, YOU KNOW THAT?

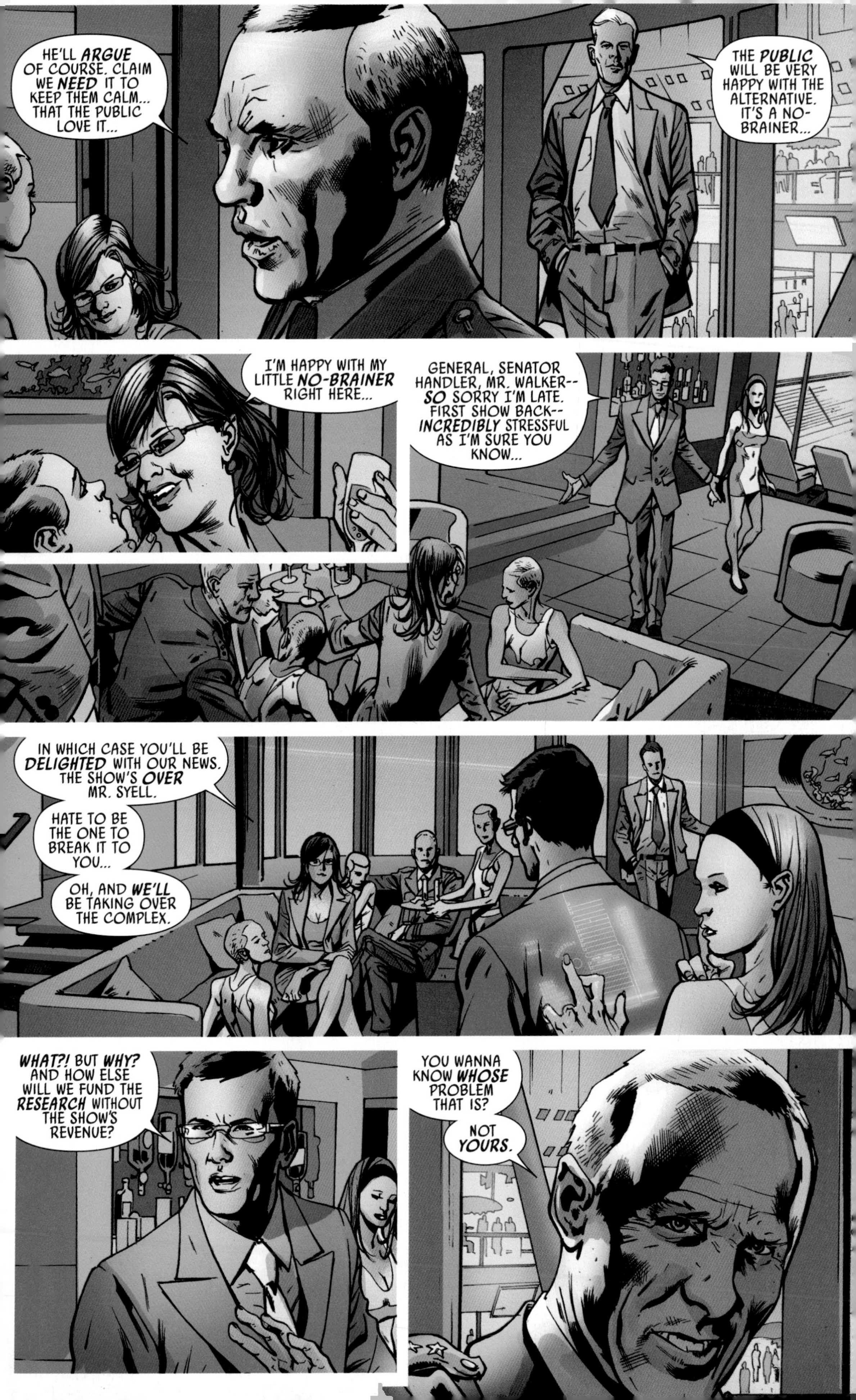
HE'LL ARGUE OF COURSE. CLAIM WE NEED IT TO KEEP THEM CALM... THAT THE PUBLIC LOVE IT...
THE PUBLIC WILL BE VERY HAPPY WITH THE ALTERNATIVE. IT'S A NO-BRAINER...
I'M HAPPY WITH MY LITTLE NO-BRAINER RIGHT HERE...
GENERAL, SENATOR HANDLER, MR. WALKER-- SO SORRY I'M LATE. FIRST SHOW BACK-- INCREDIBLY STRESSFUL AS I'M SURE YOU KNOW...
IN WHICH CASE YOU'LL BE DELIGHTED WITH OUR NEWS. THE SHOW'S OVER MR. SYELL.
HATE TO BE THE ONE TO BREAK IT TO YOU...
OH, AND WE'LL BE TAKING OVER THE COMPLEX.
WHAT?! BUT WHY? AND HOW ELSE WILL WE FUND THE RESEARCH WITHOUT THE SHOW'S REVENUE?
YOU WANNA KNOW WHOSE PROBLEM THAT IS?
NOT YOURS.

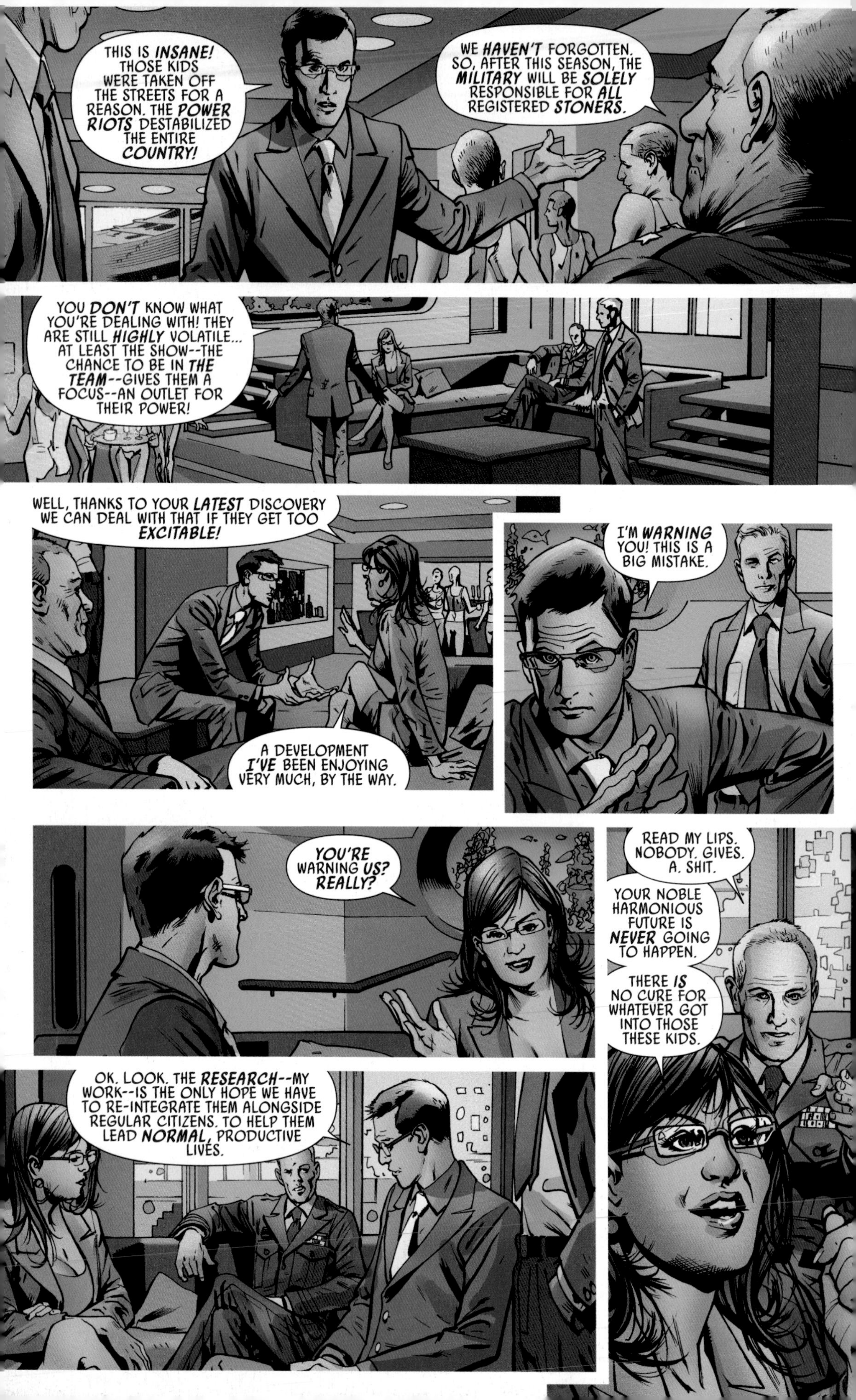
THIS IS INSANE! THOSE KIDS WERE TAKEN OFF THE STREETS FOR A REASON. THE POWER RIOTS DESTABILIZED THE ENTIRE COUNTRY!
WE HAVEN'T FORGOTTEN. SO, AFTER THIS SEASON, THE MILITARY WILL BE SOLELY RESPONSIBLE FOR ALL REGISTERED STONERS.
YOU DON'T KNOW WHAT YOU'RE DEALING WITH! THEY ARE STILL HIGHLY VOLATILE... AT LEAST THE SHOW--THE CHANCE TO BE IN THE TEAM--GIVES THEM A FOCUS--AN OUTLET FOR THEIR POWER!
WELL, THANKS TO YOUR LATEST DISCOVERY WE CAN DEAL WITH THAT IF THEY GET TOO EXCITABLE!
A DEVELOPMENT I'VE BEEN ENJOYING VERY MUCH, BY THE WAY.
I'M WARNING YOU! THIS IS A BIG MISTAKE.
YOU'RE WARNING US? REALLY?
OK. LOOK. THE RESEARCH--MY WORK--IS THE ONLY HOPE WE HAVE TO RE-INTEGRATE THEM ALONGSIDE REGULAR CITIZENS. TO HELP THEM LEAD NORMAL, PRODUCTIVE LIVES.
READ MY LIPS. NOBODY. GIVES. A. SHIT.
YOUR NOBLE HARMONIOUS FUTURE IS NEVER GOING TO HAPPEN.
THERE IS NO CURE FOR WHATEVER GOT INTO THOSE THESE KIDS.

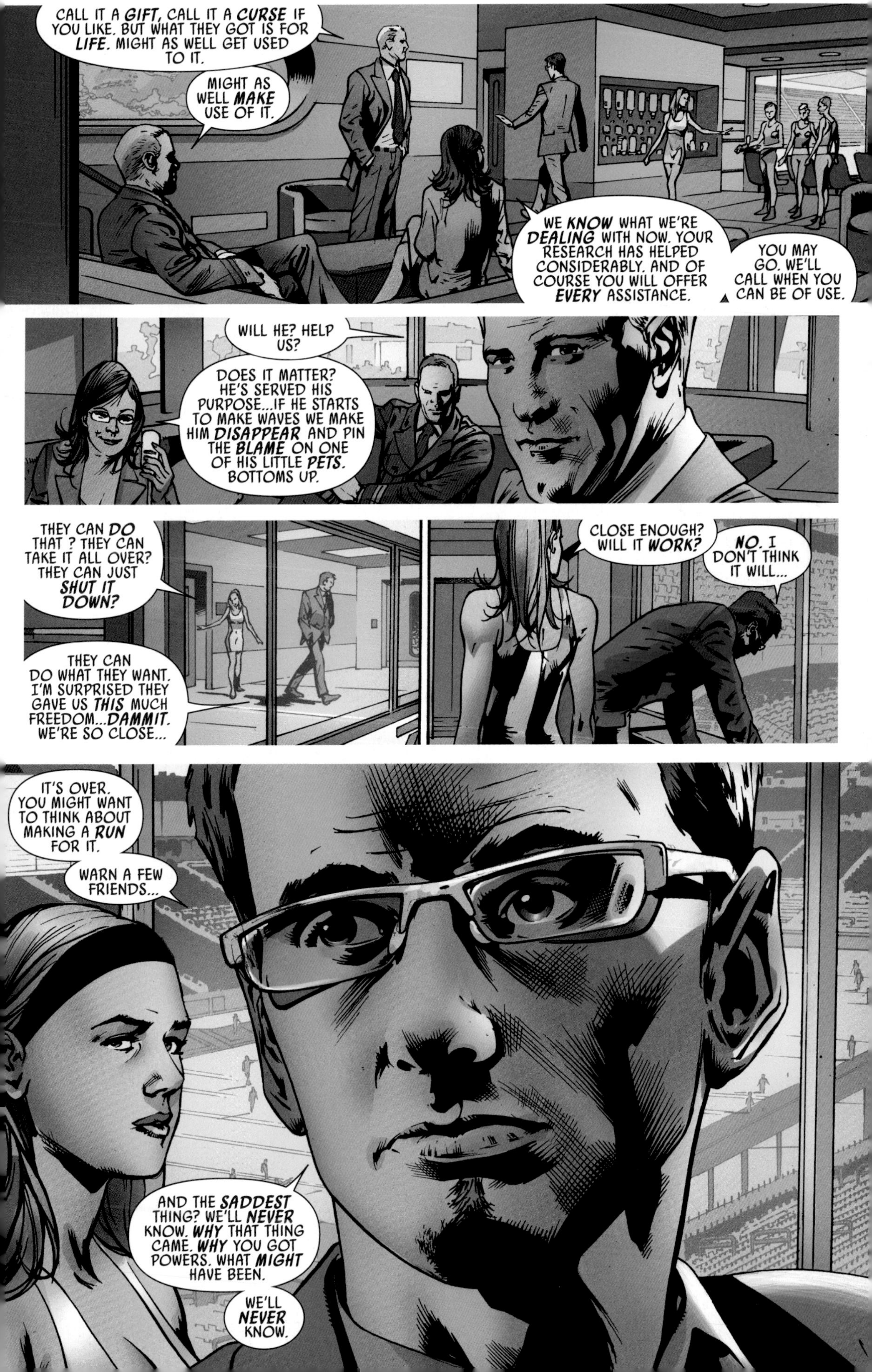
CALL IT A GIFT, CALL IT A CURSE IF YOU LIKE. BUT WHAT THEY GOT IS FOR LIFE. MIGHT AS WELL GET USED TO IT.
MIGHT AS WELL MAKE USE OF IT.
WE KNOW WHAT WE'RE DEALING WITH NOW. YOUR RESEARCH HAS HELPED CONSIDERABLY. AND OF COURSE YOU WILL OFFER EVERY ASSISTANCE.
YOU MAY GO. WE'LL CALL WHEN YOU CAN BE OF USE.
WILL HE? HELP US?
DOES IT MATTER? HE'S SERVED HIS PURPOSE...IF HE STARTS TO MAKE WAVES WE MAKE HIM DISAPPEAR AND PIN THE BLAME ON ONE OF HIS LITTLE PETS. BOTTOMS UP.
THEY CAN DO THAT ? THEY CAN TAKE IT ALL OVER? THEY CAN JUST SHUT IT DOWN?
THEY CAN DO WHAT THEY WANT. I'M SURPRISED THEY GAVE US THIS MUCH FREEDOM...DAMMIT. WE'RE SO CLOSE...
CLOSE ENOUGH? WILL IT WORK?
NO. I DON'T THINK IT WILL...
IT'S OVER. YOU MIGHT WANT TO THINK ABOUT MAKING A RUN FOR IT.
WARN A FEW FRIENDS...
AND THE SADDEST THING? WE'LL NEVER KNOW. WHY THAT THING CAME. WHY YOU GOT POWERS. WHAT MIGHT HAVE BEEN.
WE'LL NEVER KNOW.

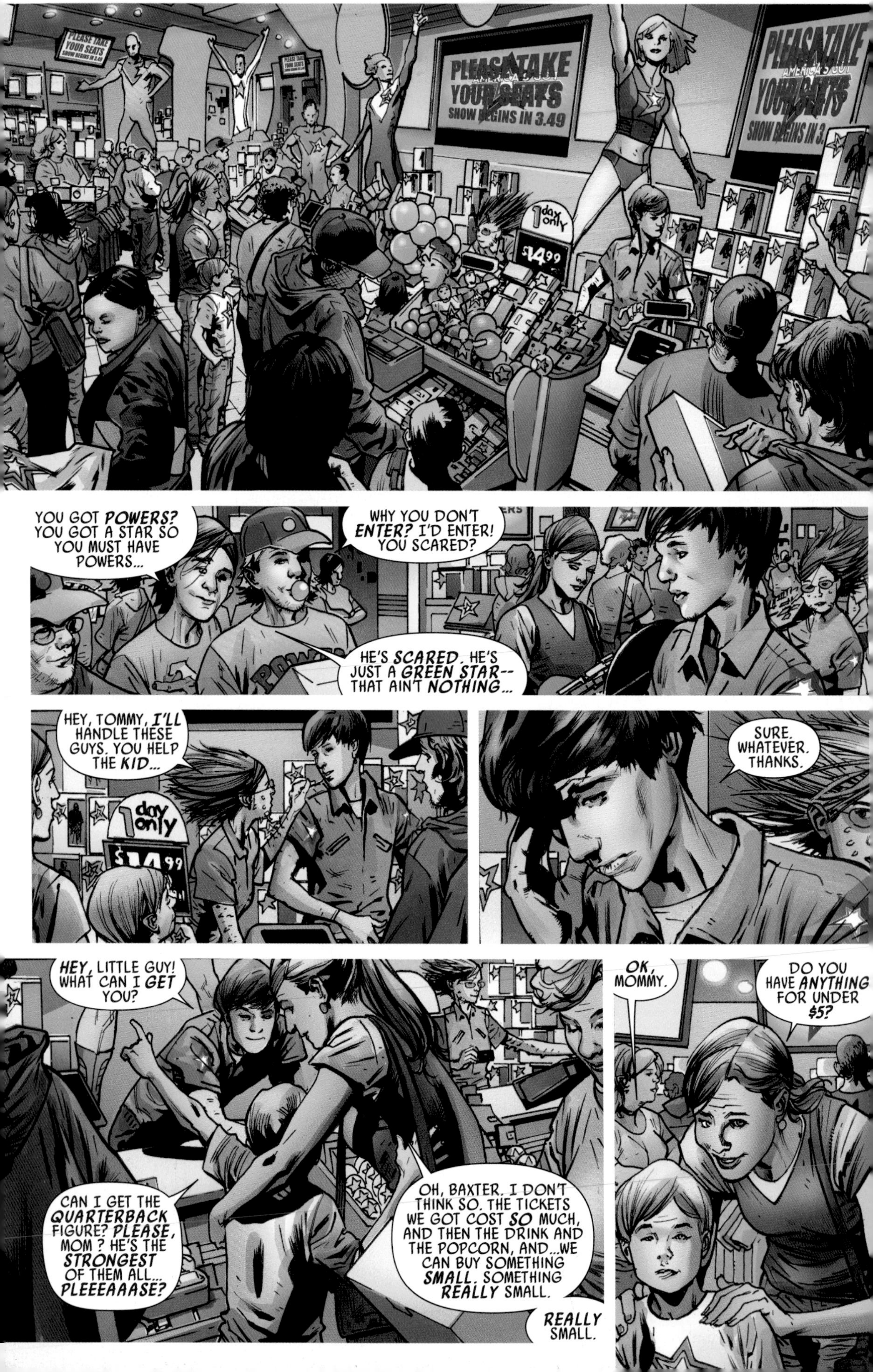
PLEASE TAKE YOUR SEATS SHOW BEGINS IN 3.49
PLEASE TAKE YOUR SEATS SHOW BEGINS IN 3.49
1 day only
$14.99
YOU GOT POWERS? YOU GOT A STAR SO YOU MUST HAVE POWERS...
WHY YOU DON'T ENTER? I'D ENTER! YOU SCARED?
HE'S SCARED. HE'S JUST A GREEN STAR-- THAT AIN'T NOTHING...
HEY, TOMMY, I'LL HANDLE THESE GUYS. YOU HELP THE KID...
1 day only
$14.99
SURE. WHATEVER. THANKS.
HEY, LITTLE GUY! WHAT CAN I GET YOU?
CAN I GET THE QUARTERBACK FIGURE? PLEASE, MOM ? HE'S THE STRONGEST OF THEM ALL... PLEEEAAASE?
OH, BAXTER. I DON'T THINK SO. THE TICKETS WE GOT COST SO MUCH, AND THEN THE DRINK AND THE POPCORN, AND...WE CAN BUY SOMETHING SMALL. SOMETHING REALLY SMALL.
REALLY SMALL.
OK, MOMMY.
DO YOU HAVE ANYTHING FOR UNDER $5?

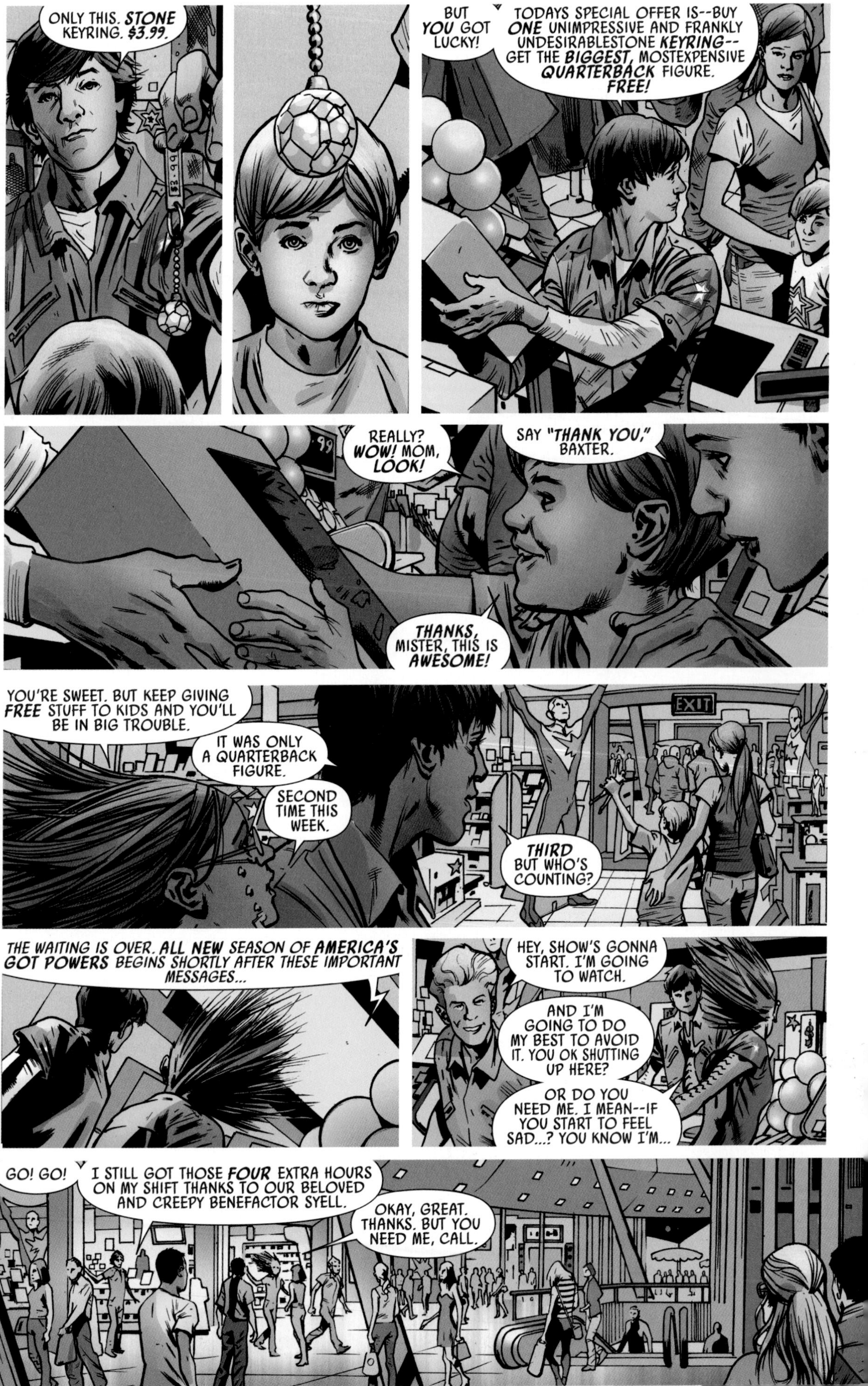
ONLY THIS. STONE KEYRING. $3.99.
BUT YOU GOT LUCKY!
TODAYS SPECIAL OFFER IS--BUY ONE UNIMPRESSIVE AND FRANKLY UNDESIRABLESTONE KEYRING-- GET THE BIGGEST, MOSTEXPENSIVE QUARTERBACK FIGURE. FREE!
REALLY? WOW! MOM, LOOK!
SAY "THANK YOU," BAXTER.
THANKS, MISTER, THIS IS AWESOME!
YOU'RE SWEET. BUT KEEP GIVING FREE STUFF TO KIDS AND YOU'LL BE IN BIG TROUBLE.
IT WAS ONLY A QUARTERBACK FIGURE.
SECOND TIME THIS WEEK.
THIRD BUT WHO'S COUNTING?
EXIT
THE WAITING IS OVER. ALL NEW SEASON OF AMERICA'S GOT POWERS BEGINS SHORTLY AFTER THESE IMPORTANT MESSAGES...
HEY, SHOW'S GONNA START. I'M GOING TO WATCH.
AND I'M GOING TO DO MY BEST TO AVOID IT. YOU OK SHUTTING UP HERE?
OR DO YOU NEED ME. I MEAN--IF YOU START TO FEEL SAD...? YOU KNOW I'M...
GO! GO!
I STILL GOT THOSE FOUR EXTRA HOURS ON MY SHIFT THANKS TO OUR BELOVED AND CREEPY BENEFACTOR SYELL.
OKAY, GREAT. THANKS. BUT YOU NEED ME, CALL.

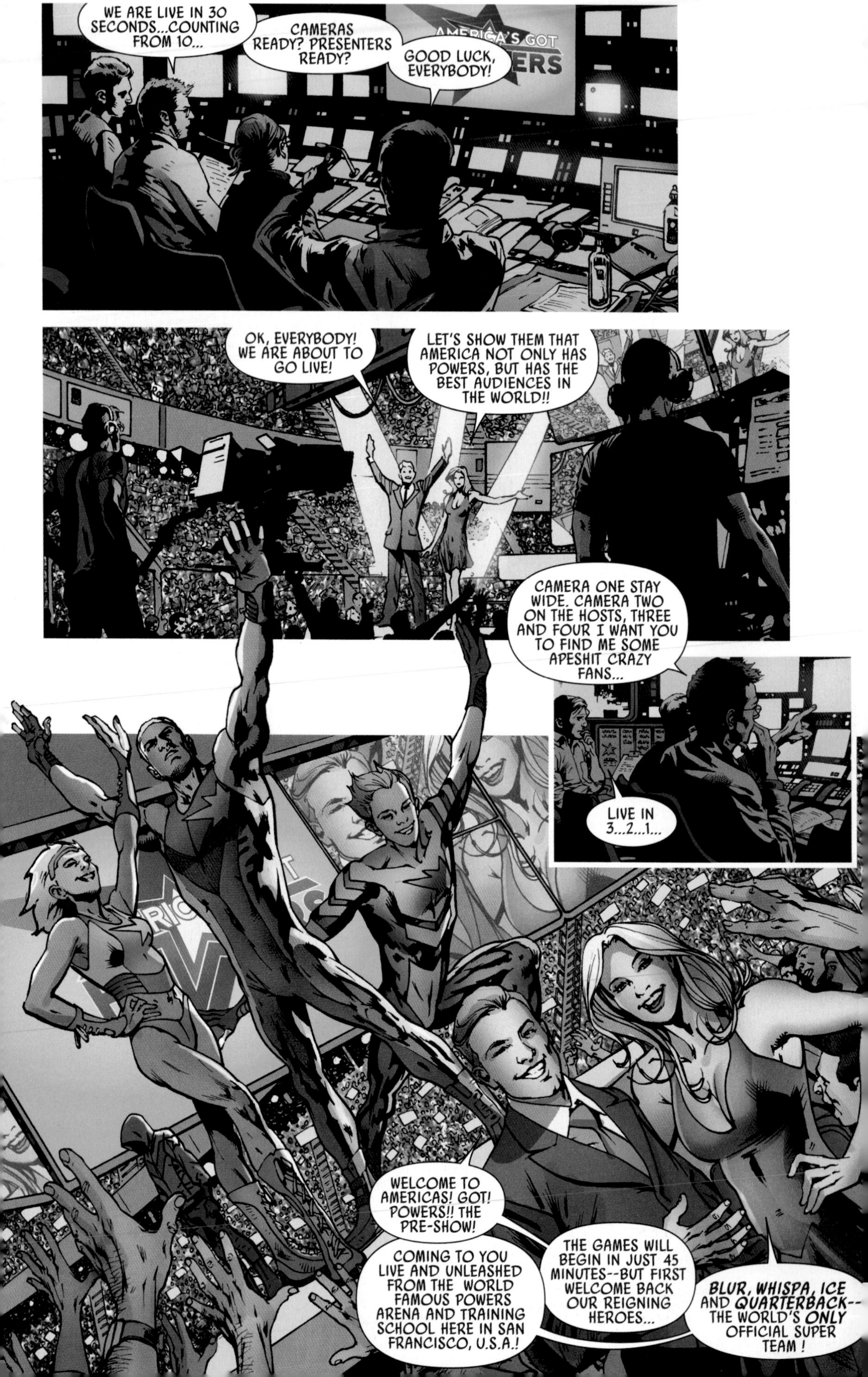

WE ARE LIVE IN 30 SECONDS...COUNTING FROM 10...
CAMERAS READY? PRESENTERS READY?
GOOD LUCK, EVERYBODY!
OK, EVERYBODY! WE ARE ABOUT TO GO LIVE!
LET'S SHOW THEM THAT AMERICA NOT ONLY HAS POWERS, BUT HAS THE BEST AUDIENCES IN THE WORLD!!
CAMERA ONE STAY WIDE. CAMERA TWO ON THE HOSTS, THREE AND FOUR I WANT YOU TO FIND ME SOME APESHIT CRAZY FANS...
LIVE IN 3...2...1...
WELCOME TO AMERICAS! GOT! POWERS!! THE PRE-SHOW!
COMING TO YOU LIVE AND UNLEASHED FROM THE WORLD FAMOUS POWERS ARENA AND TRAINING SCHOOL HERE IN SAN FRANCISCO, U.S.A.!
THE GAMES WILL BEGIN IN JUST 45 MINUTES--BUT FIRST WELCOME BACK OUR REIGNING HEROES...
BLUR, WHISPA, ICE AND *QUARTERBACK*--THE WORLD'S *ONLY* OFFICIAL SUPER TEAM !

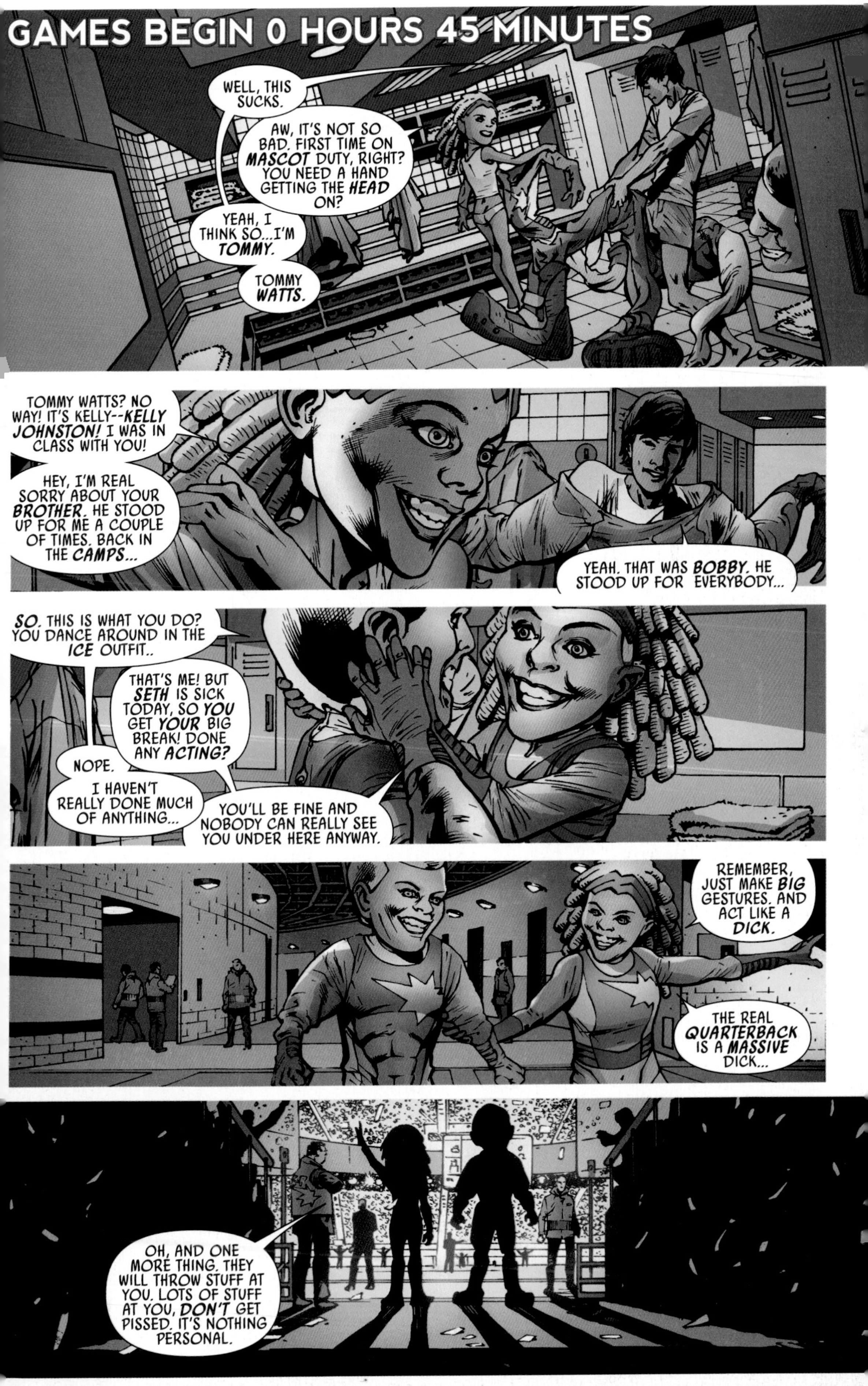
GAMES BEGIN 0 HOURS 45 MINUTES
WELL, THIS SUCKS.
AW, IT'S NOT SO BAD. FIRST TIME ON MASCOT DUTY, RIGHT? YOU NEED A HAND GETTING THE HEAD ON?
YEAH, I THINK SO...I'M TOMMY.
TOMMY WATTS.
TOMMY WATTS? NO WAY! IT'S KELLY--KELLY JOHNSTON! I WAS IN CLASS WITH YOU!
HEY, I'M REAL SORRY ABOUT YOUR BROTHER. HE STOOD UP FOR ME A COUPLE OF TIMES. BACK IN THE CAMPS...
YEAH. THAT WAS BOBBY. HE STOOD UP FOR EVERYBODY...
SO. THIS IS WHAT YOU DO? YOU DANCE AROUND IN THE ICE OUTFIT..
THAT'S ME! BUT SETH IS SICK TODAY, SO YOU GET YOUR BIG BREAK! DONE ANY ACTING?
NOPE.
I HAVEN'T REALLY DONE MUCH OF ANYTHING...
YOU'LL BE FINE AND NOBODY CAN REALLY SEE YOU UNDER HERE ANYWAY.
REMEMBER, JUST MAKE BIG GESTURES. AND ACT LIKE A DICK.
THE REAL QUARTERBACK IS A MASSIVE DICK...
OH, AND ONE MORE THING. THEY WILL THROW STUFF AT YOU. LOTS OF STUFF AT YOU, DON'T GET PISSED. IT'S NOTHING PERSONAL.

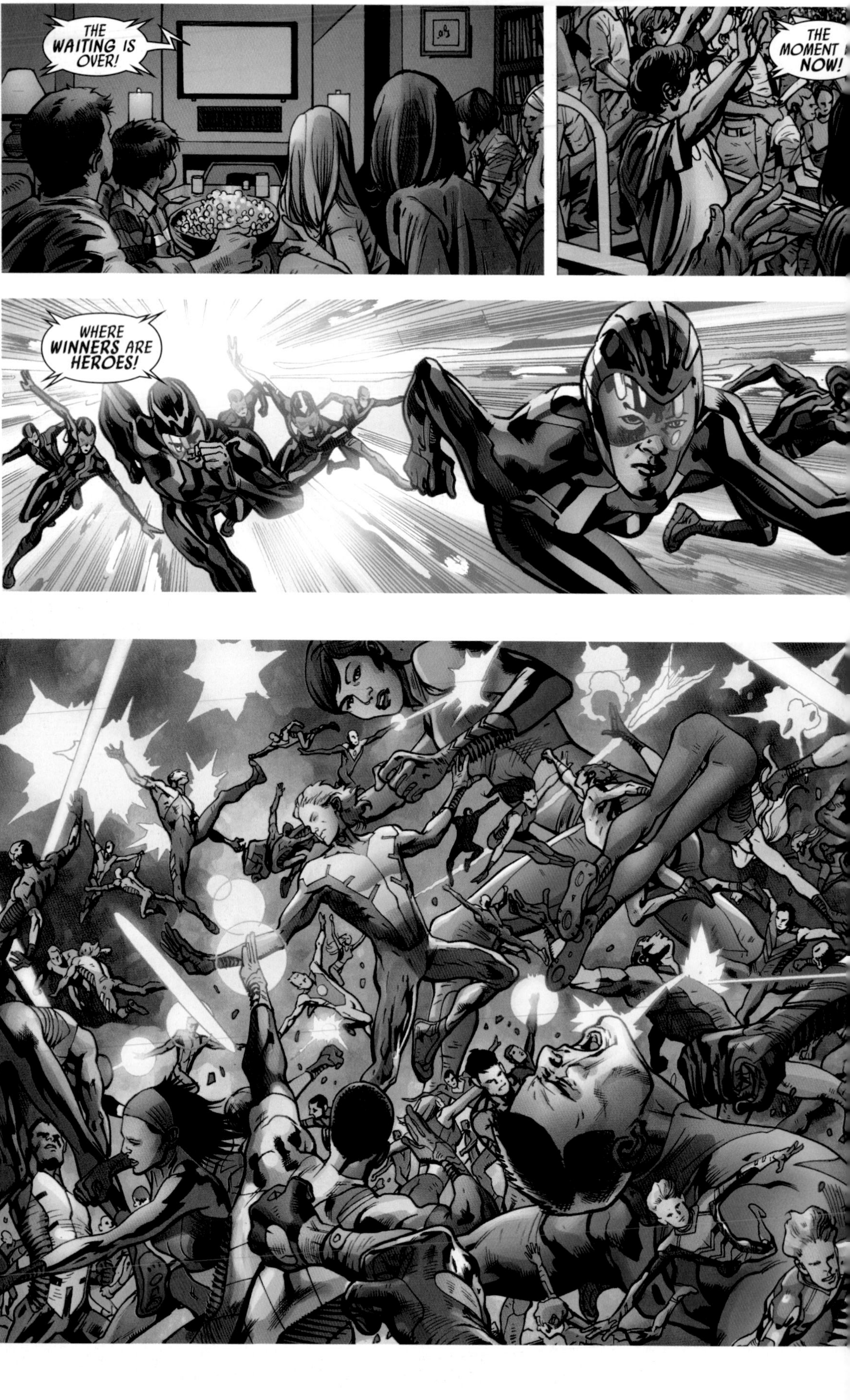
THE WAITING IS OVER!
THE MOMENT NOW!
WHERE WINNERS ARE HEROES!

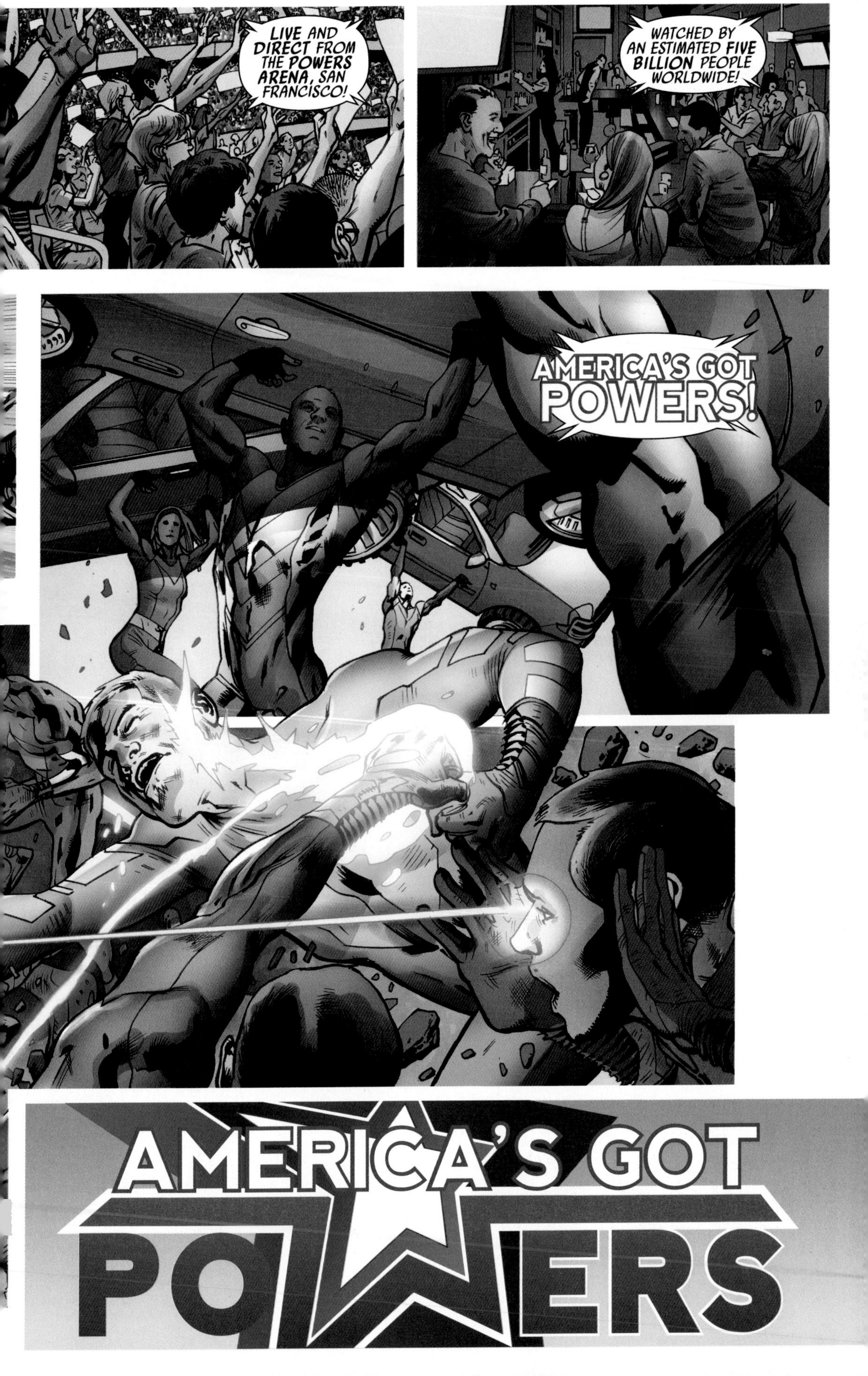
LIVE AND DIRECT FROM THE POWERS ARENA, SAN FRANCISCO!
WATCHED BY AN ESTIMATED FIVE BILLION PEOPLE WORLDWIDE!
AMERICA'S GOT POWERS!
AMERICA'S GOT POWERS

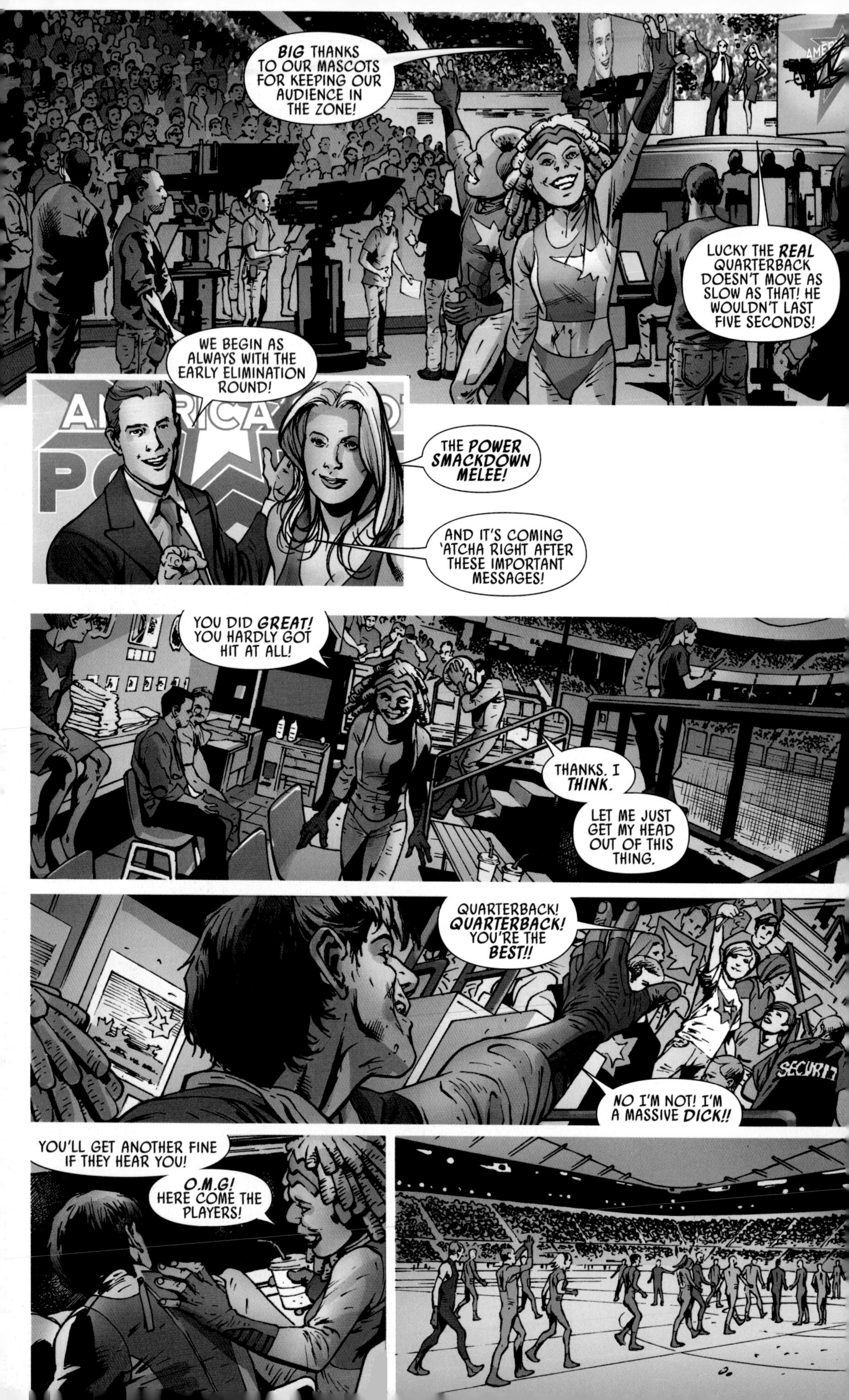
BIG THANKS TO OUR MASCOTS FOR KEEPING OUR AUDIENCE IN THE ZONE!
LUCKY THE REAL QUARTERBACK DOESN'T MOVE AS SLOW AS THAT! HE WOULDN'T LAST FIVE SECONDS!
WE BEGIN AS ALWAYS WITH THE EARLY ELIMINATION ROUND!
THE POWER SMACKDOWN MELEE!
AND IT'S COMING 'ATCHA RIGHT AFTER THESE IMPORTANT MESSAGES!
YOU DID GREAT! YOU HARDLY GOT HIT AT ALL!
THANKS. I THINK.
LET ME JUST GET MY HEAD OUT OF THIS THING.
QUARTERBACK! QUARTERBACK! YOU'RE THE BEST!!
NO I'M NOT! I'M A MASSIVE DICK!!
SECURIT
YOU'LL GET ANOTHER FINE IF THEY HEAR YOU!
O.M.G! HERE COME THE PLAYERS!

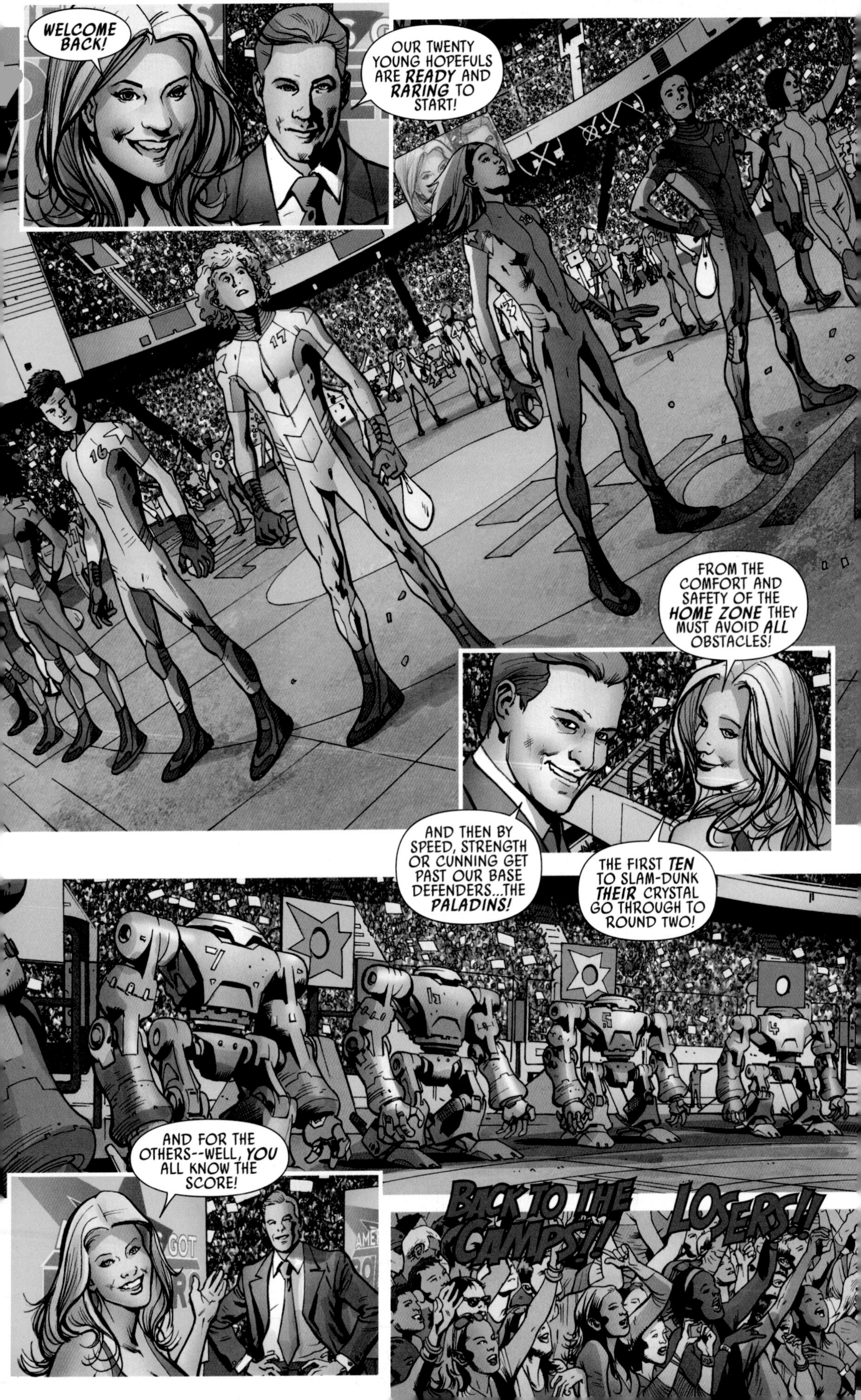
WELCOME BACK!
OUR TWENTY YOUNG HOPEFULS ARE *READY* AND *RARING* TO START!
FROM THE COMFORT AND SAFETY OF THE *HOME ZONE* THEY MUST AVOID *ALL* OBSTACLES!
AND THEN BY SPEED, STRENGTH OR CUNNING GET PAST OUR BASE DEFENDERS...THE *PALADINS!*
THE FIRST *TEN* TO SLAM-DUNK *THEIR* CRYSTAL GO THROUGH TO ROUND TWO!
AND FOR THE OTHERS--WELL, *YOU* ALL KNOW THE SCORE!
BACK TO THE CAMPS!!
LOSERS!!

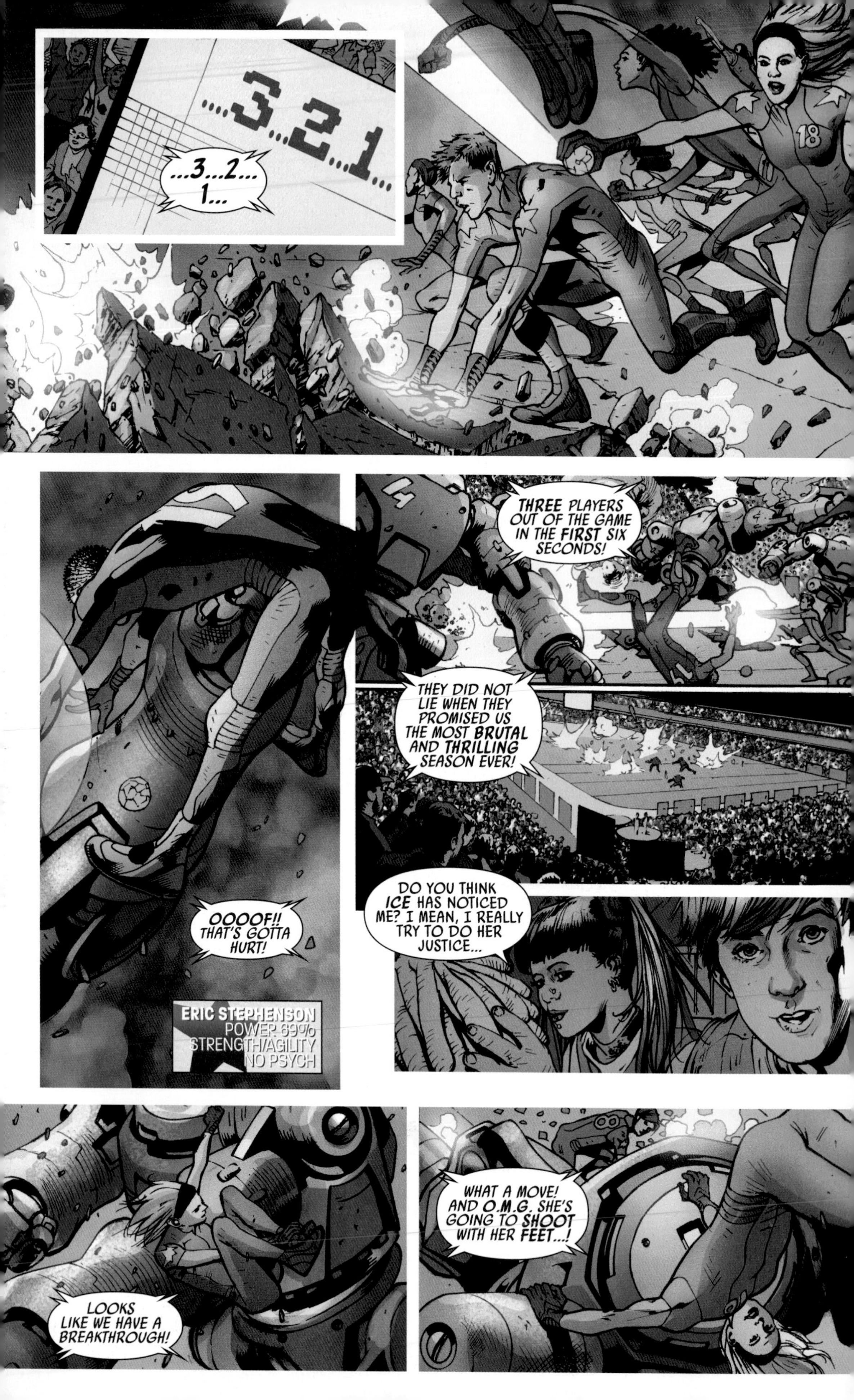
...3...2...1...
...3...2...
1...
THREE PLAYERS OUT OF THE GAME IN THE FIRST SIX SECONDS!
THEY DID NOT LIE WHEN THEY PROMISED US THE MOST BRUTAL AND THRILLING SEASON EVER!
OOOOF!! THAT'S GOTTA HURT!
ERIC STEPHENSON
POWER 69%
STRENGTH/AGILITY
NO PSYCH
DO YOU THINK ICE HAS NOTICED ME? I MEAN, I REALLY TRY TO DO HER JUSTICE...
LOOKS LIKE WE HAVE A BREAKTHROUGH!
WHAT A MOVE! AND O.M.G. SHE'S GOING TO SHOOT WITH HER FEET...!

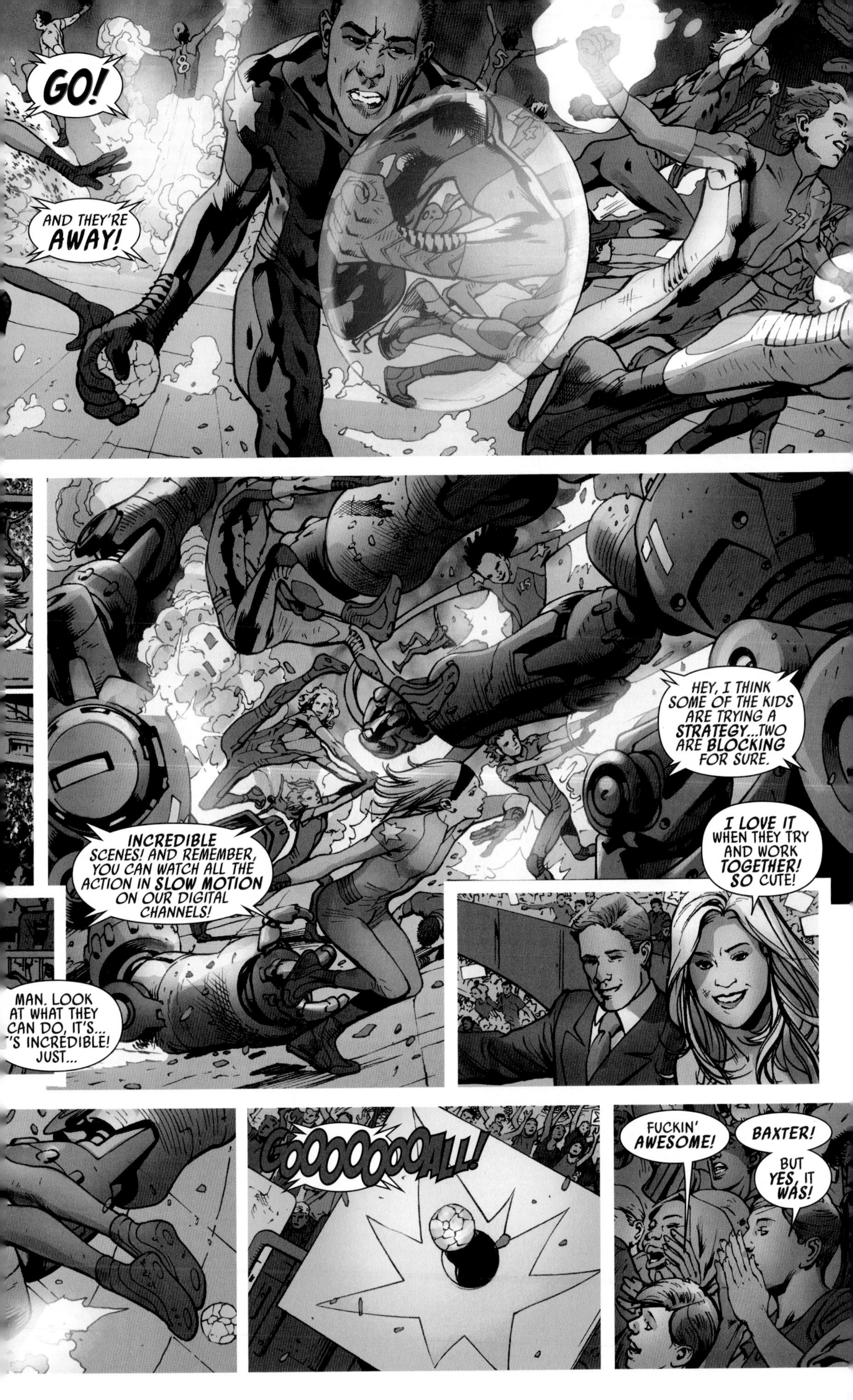
GO!
AND THEY'RE AWAY!
HEY, I THINK SOME OF THE KIDS ARE TRYING A STRATEGY...TWO ARE BLOCKING FOR SURE.
INCREDIBLE SCENES! AND REMEMBER, YOU CAN WATCH ALL THE ACTION IN SLOW MOTION ON OUR DIGITAL CHANNELS!
I LOVE IT WHEN THEY TRY AND WORK TOGETHER! SO CUTE!
MAN. LOOK AT WHAT THEY CAN DO, IT'S... 'S INCREDIBLE! JUST...
GOOOOOOOAL!
FUCKIN' AWESOME!
BAXTER!
BUT YES, IT WAS!

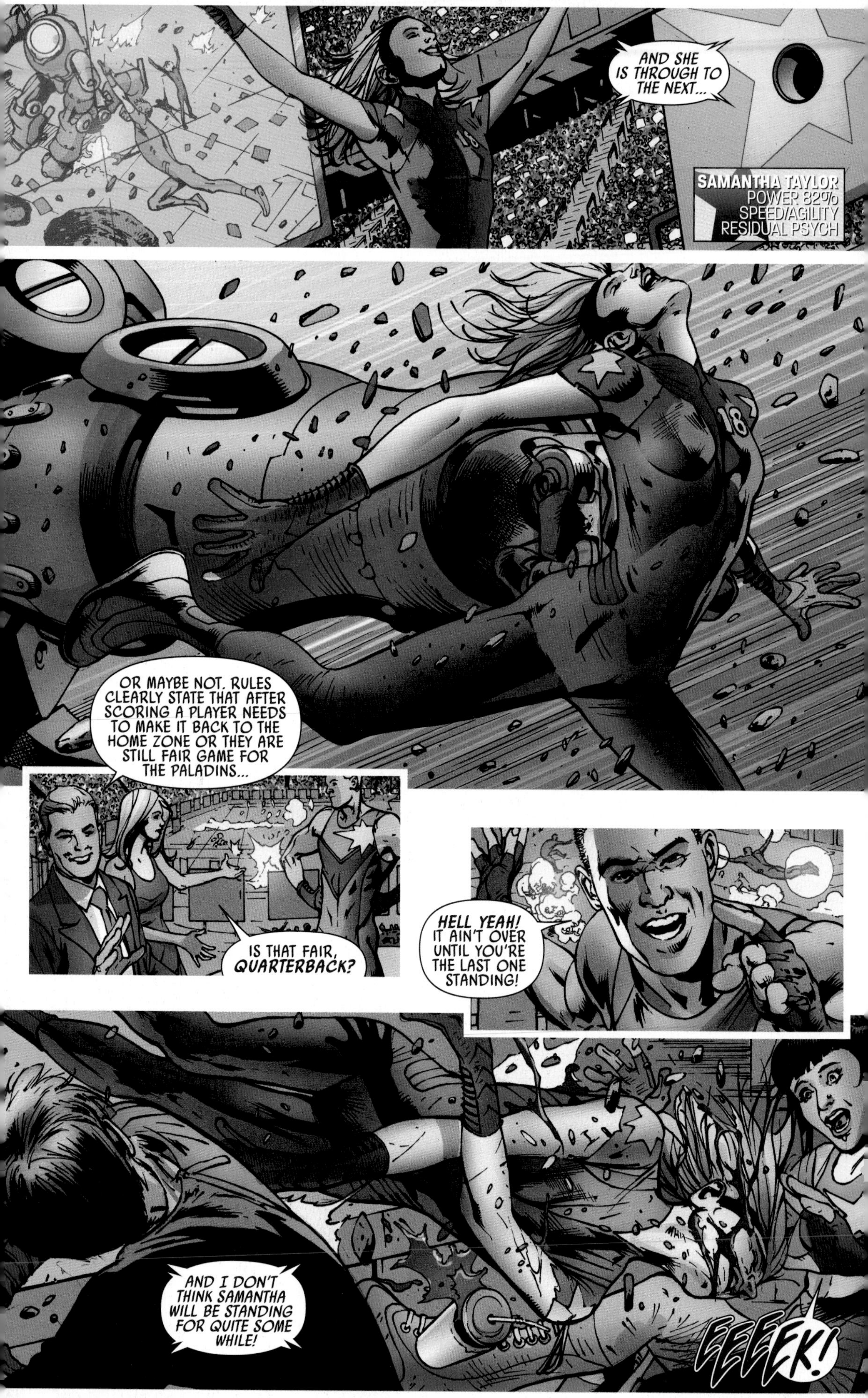
AND SHE IS THROUGH TO THE NEXT...
SAMANTHA TAYLOR
POWER 82%
SPEED/AGILITY
RESIDUAL PSYCH
OR MAYBE NOT. RULES CLEARLY STATE THAT AFTER SCORING A PLAYER NEEDS TO MAKE IT BACK TO THE HOME ZONE OR THEY ARE STILL FAIR GAME FOR THE PALADINS...
IS THAT FAIR, QUARTERBACK?
HELL YEAH! IT AIN'T OVER UNTIL YOU'RE THE LAST ONE STANDING!
AND I DON'T THINK SAMANTHA WILL BE STANDING FOR QUITE SOME WHILE!
EEEEK!

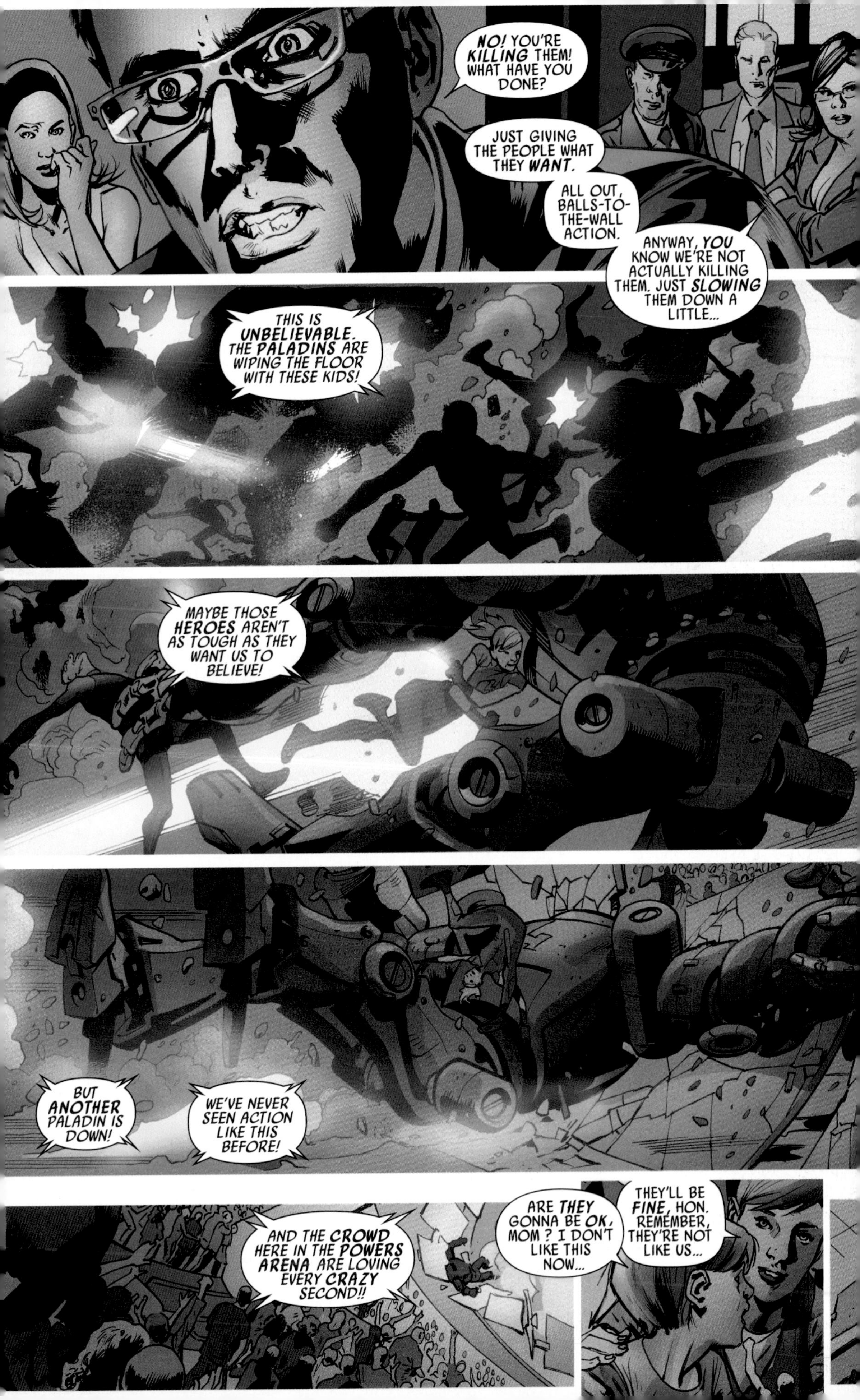
NO! YOU'RE KILLING THEM! WHAT HAVE YOU DONE?
JUST GIVING THE PEOPLE WHAT THEY WANT.
ALL OUT, BALLS-TO-THE-WALL ACTION.
ANYWAY, YOU KNOW WE'RE NOT ACTUALLY KILLING THEM. JUST SLOWING THEM DOWN A LITTLE...
THIS IS UNBELIEVABLE. THE PALADINS ARE WIPING THE FLOOR WITH THESE KIDS!
MAYBE THOSE HEROES AREN'T AS TOUGH AS THEY WANT US TO BELIEVE!
BUT ANOTHER PALADIN IS DOWN!
WE'VE NEVER SEEN ACTION LIKE THIS BEFORE!
AND THE CROWD HERE IN THE POWERS ARENA ARE LOVING EVERY CRAZY SECOND!!
ARE THEY GONNA BE OK, MOM ? I DON'T LIKE THIS NOW...
THEY'LL BE FINE, HON. REMEMBER, THEY'RE NOT LIKE US...

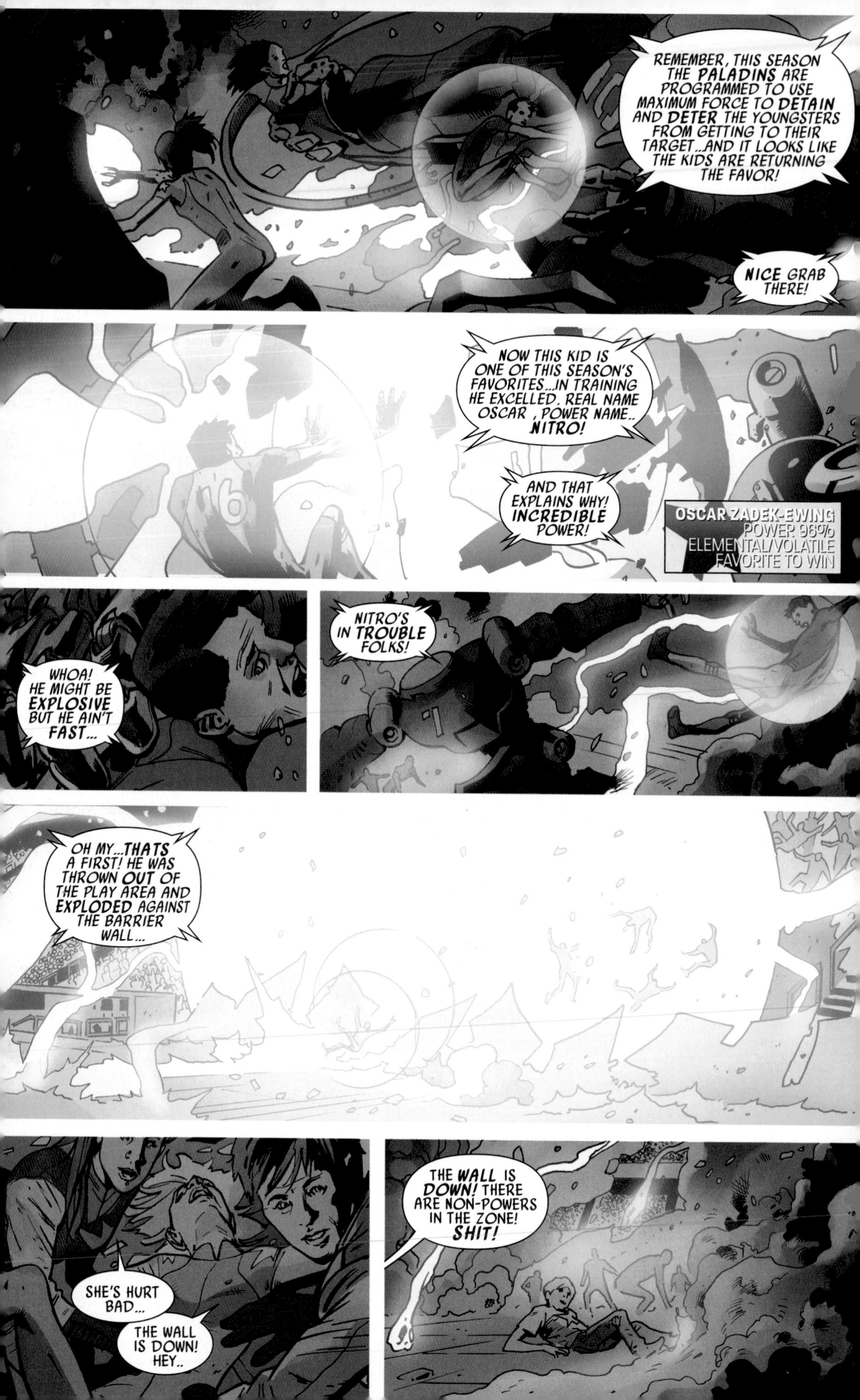
REMEMBER, THIS SEASON THE PALADINS ARE PROGRAMMED TO USE MAXIMUM FORCE TO DETAIN AND DETER THE YOUNGSTERS FROM GETTING TO THEIR TARGET...AND IT LOOKS LIKE THE KIDS ARE RETURNING THE FAVOR!
NICE GRAB THERE!
NOW THIS KID IS ONE OF THIS SEASON'S FAVORITES...IN TRAINING HE EXCELLED. REAL NAME OSCAR , POWER NAME.. NITRO!
AND THAT EXPLAINS WHY! INCREDIBLE POWER!
OSCAR ZADEK-EWING
POWER 96%
ELEMENTAL/VOLATILE
FAVORITE TO WIN
WHOA! HE MIGHT BE EXPLOSIVE BUT HE AIN'T FAST...
NITRO'S IN TROUBLE FOLKS!
OH MY...THATS A FIRST! HE WAS THROWN OUT OF THE PLAY AREA AND EXPLODED AGAINST THE BARRIER WALL...
SHE'S HURT BAD...
THE WALL IS DOWN! HEY..
THE WALL IS DOWN! THERE ARE NON-POWERS IN THE ZONE! SHIT!

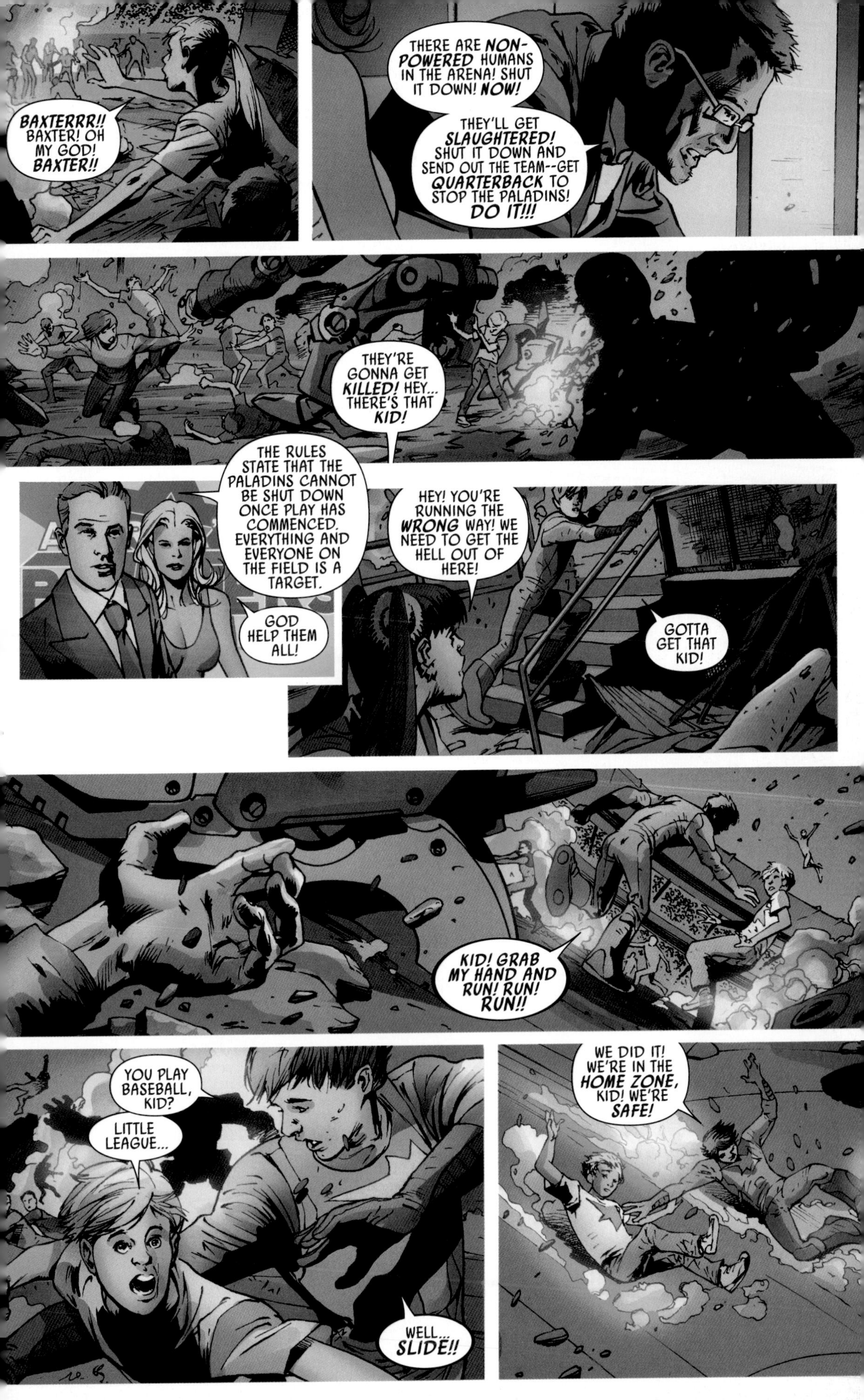
BAXTERRR!! BAXTER! OH MY GOD! BAXTER!!
THERE ARE NON-POWERED HUMANS IN THE ARENA! SHUT IT DOWN! NOW!
THEY'LL GET SLAUGHTERED! SHUT IT DOWN AND SEND OUT THE TEAM--GET QUARTERBACK TO STOP THE PALADINS! DO IT!!!
THEY'RE GONNA GET KILLED! HEY... THERE'S THAT KID!
THE RULES STATE THAT THE PALADINS CANNOT BE SHUT DOWN ONCE PLAY HAS COMMENCED. EVERYTHING AND EVERYONE ON THE FIELD IS A TARGET.
GOD HELP THEM ALL!
HEY! YOU'RE RUNNING THE WRONG WAY! WE NEED TO GET THE HELL OUT OF HERE!
GOTTA GET THAT KID!
KID! GRAB MY HAND AND RUN! RUN! RUN!!
YOU PLAY BASEBALL, KID?
LITTLE LEAGUE...
WELL... SLIDE!!
WE DID IT! WE'RE IN THE HOME ZONE, KID! WE'RE SAFE!

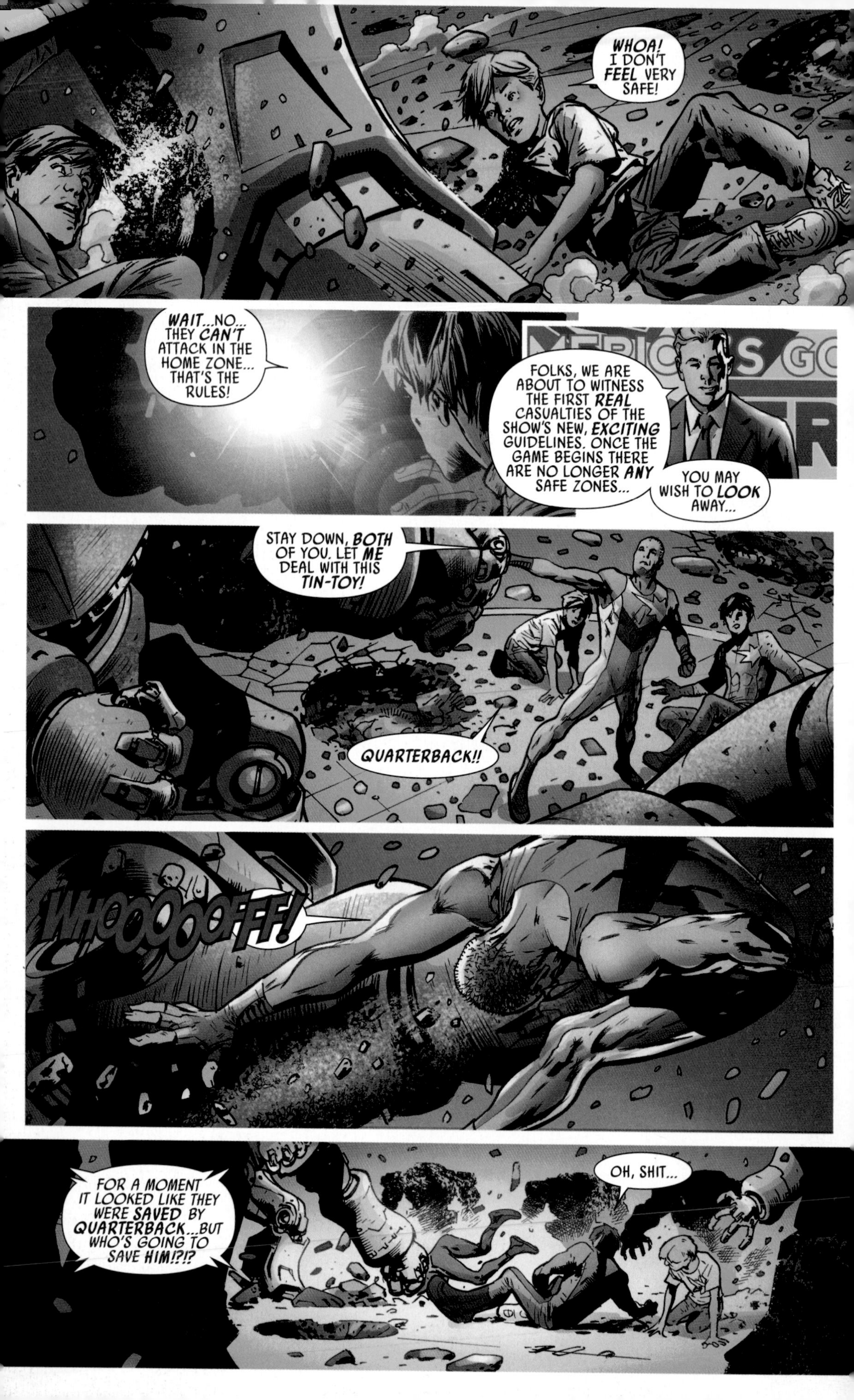
WHOA! I DON'T FEEL VERY SAFE!
WAIT...NO... THEY CAN'T ATTACK IN THE HOME ZONE... THAT'S THE RULES!
FOLKS, WE ARE ABOUT TO WITNESS THE FIRST REAL CASUALTIES OF THE SHOW'S NEW, EXCITING GUIDELINES. ONCE THE GAME BEGINS THERE ARE NO LONGER ANY SAFE ZONES...
YOU MAY WISH TO LOOK AWAY...
STAY DOWN, BOTH OF YOU. LET ME DEAL WITH THIS TIN-TOY!
QUARTERBACK!!
WHOOOOOOFFF!
FOR A MOMENT IT LOOKED LIKE THEY WERE SAVED BY QUARTERBACK...BUT WHO'S GOING TO SAVE HIM!?!?
OH, SHIT...

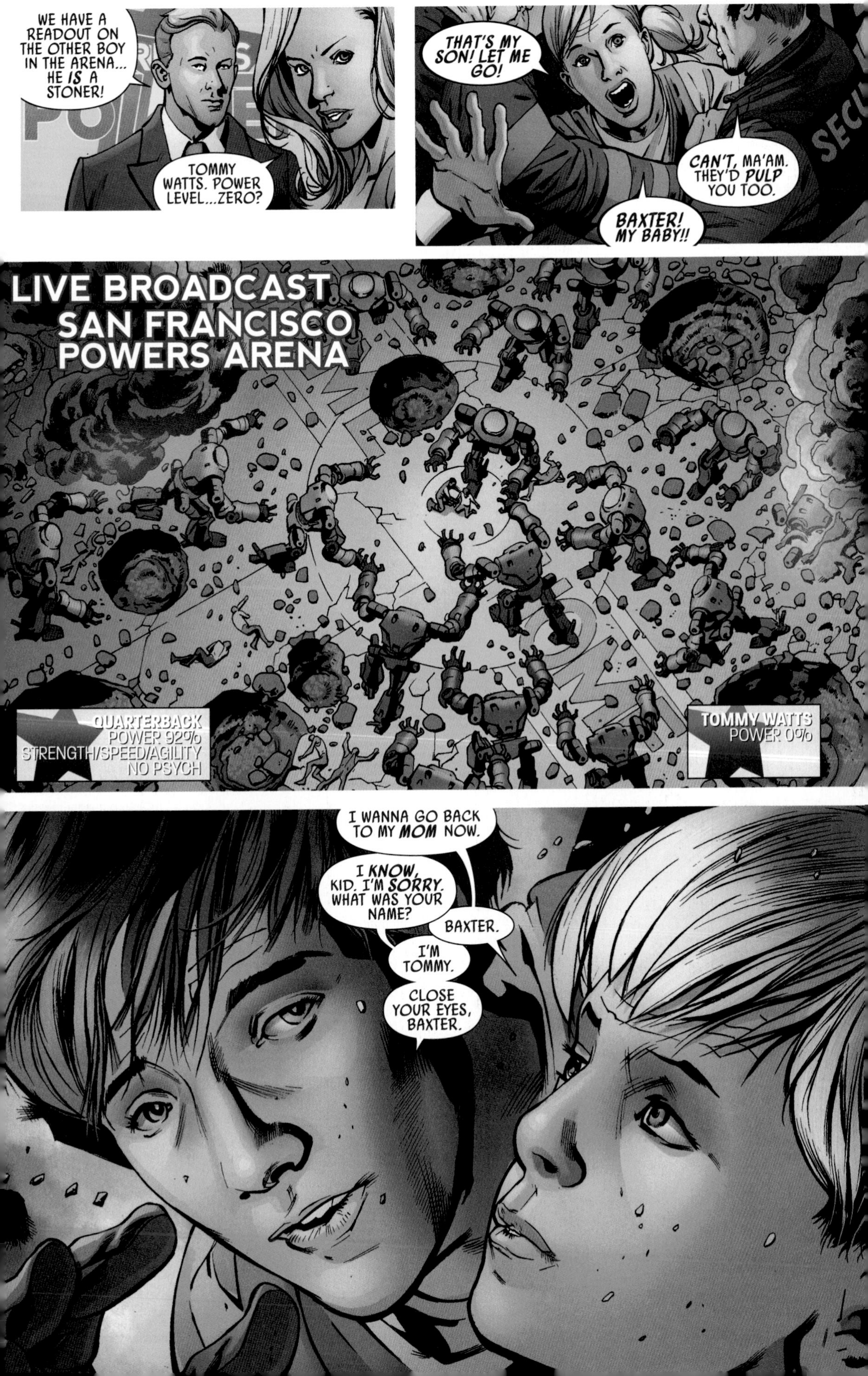
WE HAVE A READOUT ON THE OTHER BOY IN THE ARENA... HE IS A STONER!
TOMMY WATTS. POWER LEVEL...ZERO?
THAT'S MY SON! LET ME GO!
CAN'T, MA'AM. THEY'D PULP YOU TOO.
BAXTER! MY BABY!!
LIVE BROADCAST
SAN FRANCISCO POWERS ARENA
QUARTERBACK
POWER 92%
STRENGTH/SPEED/AGILITY
NO PSYCH
TOMMY WATTS
POWER 0%
I WANNA GO BACK TO MY MOM NOW.
I KNOW, KID. I'M SORRY. WHAT WAS YOUR NAME?
BAXTER.
I'M TOMMY.
CLOSE YOUR EYES, BAXTER.

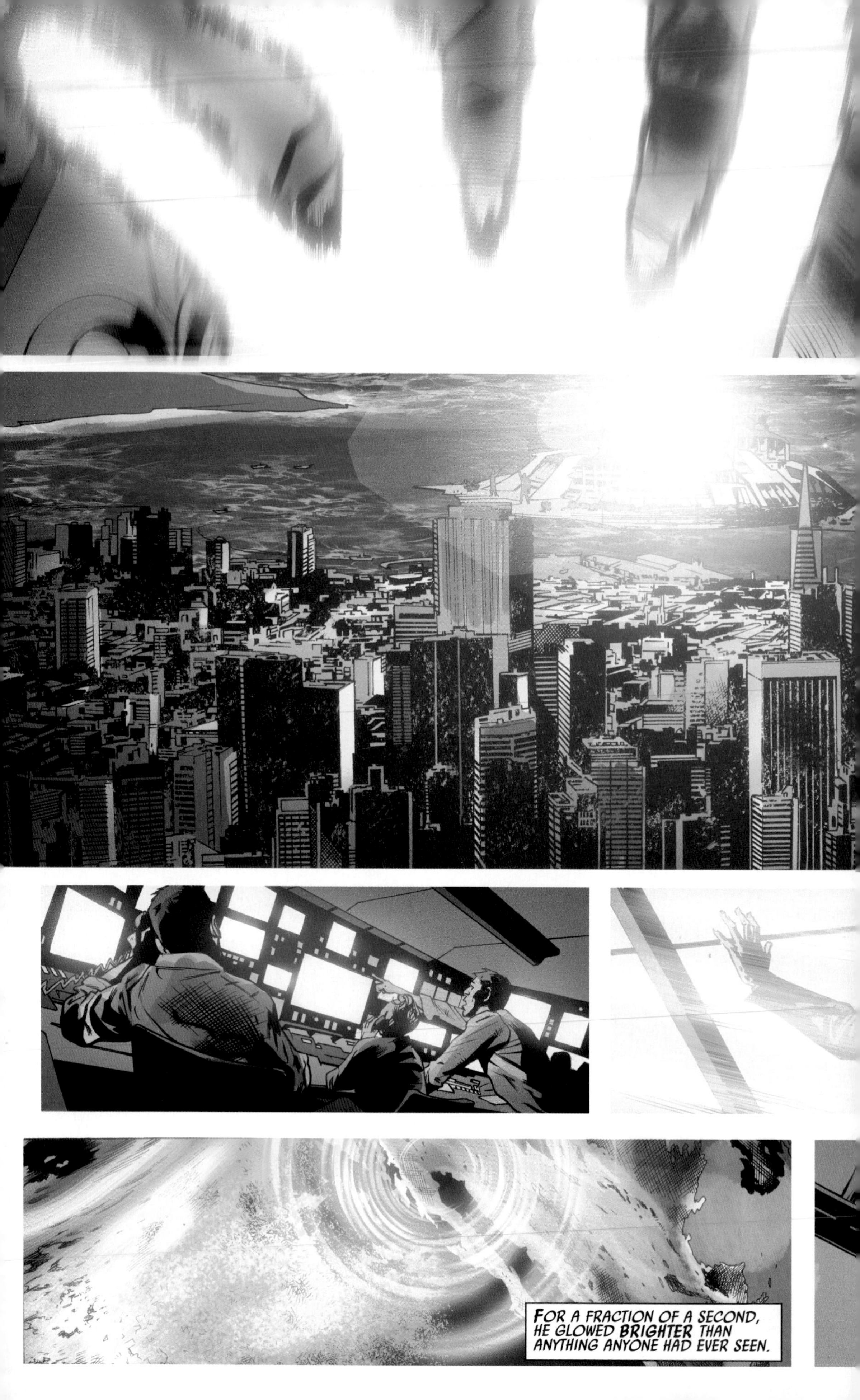
FOR A FRACTION OF A SECOND, HE GLOWED BRIGHTER THAN ANYTHING ANYONE HAD EVER SEEN.

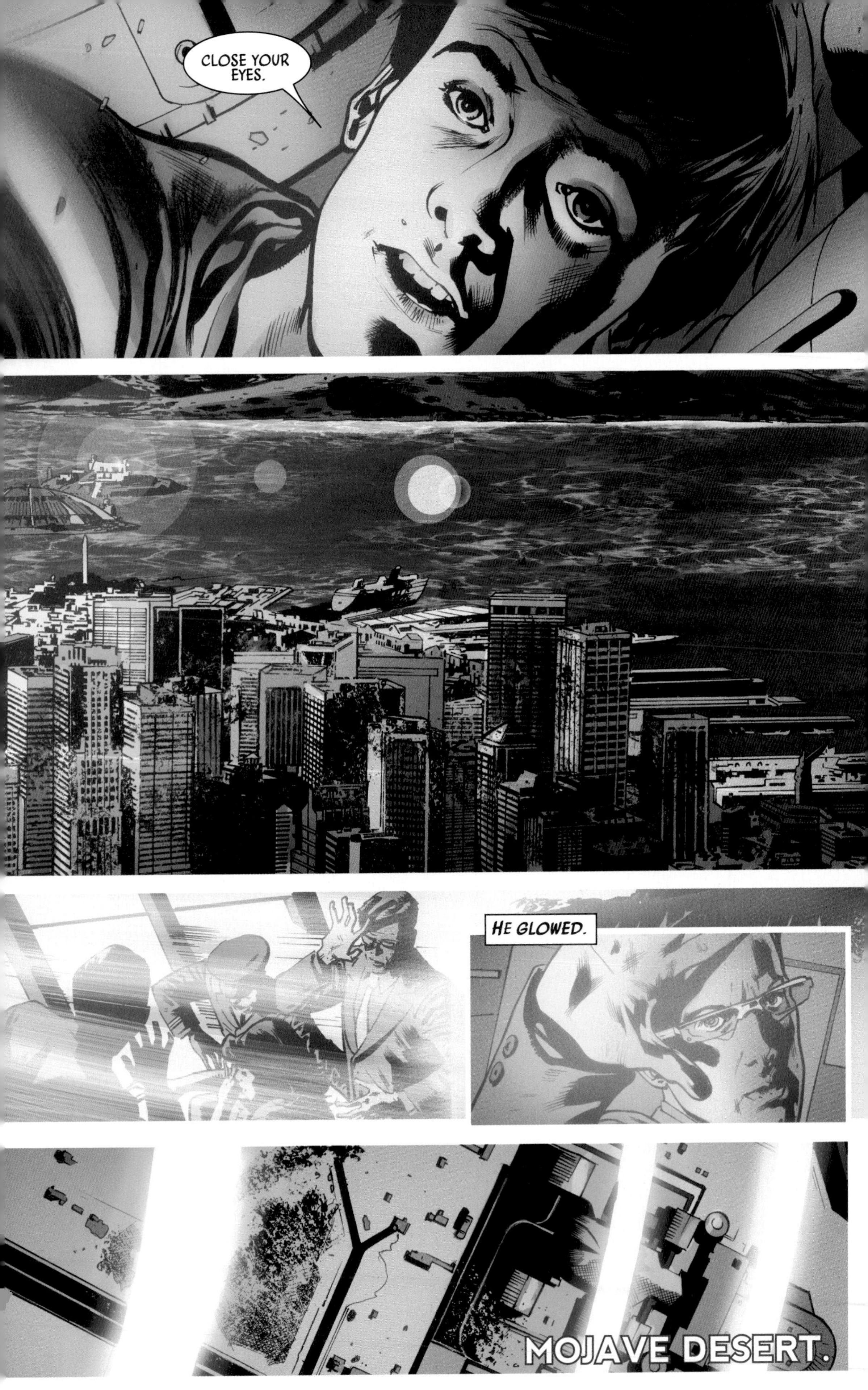
CLOSE YOUR EYES.
HE GLOWED.
MOJAVE DESERT.

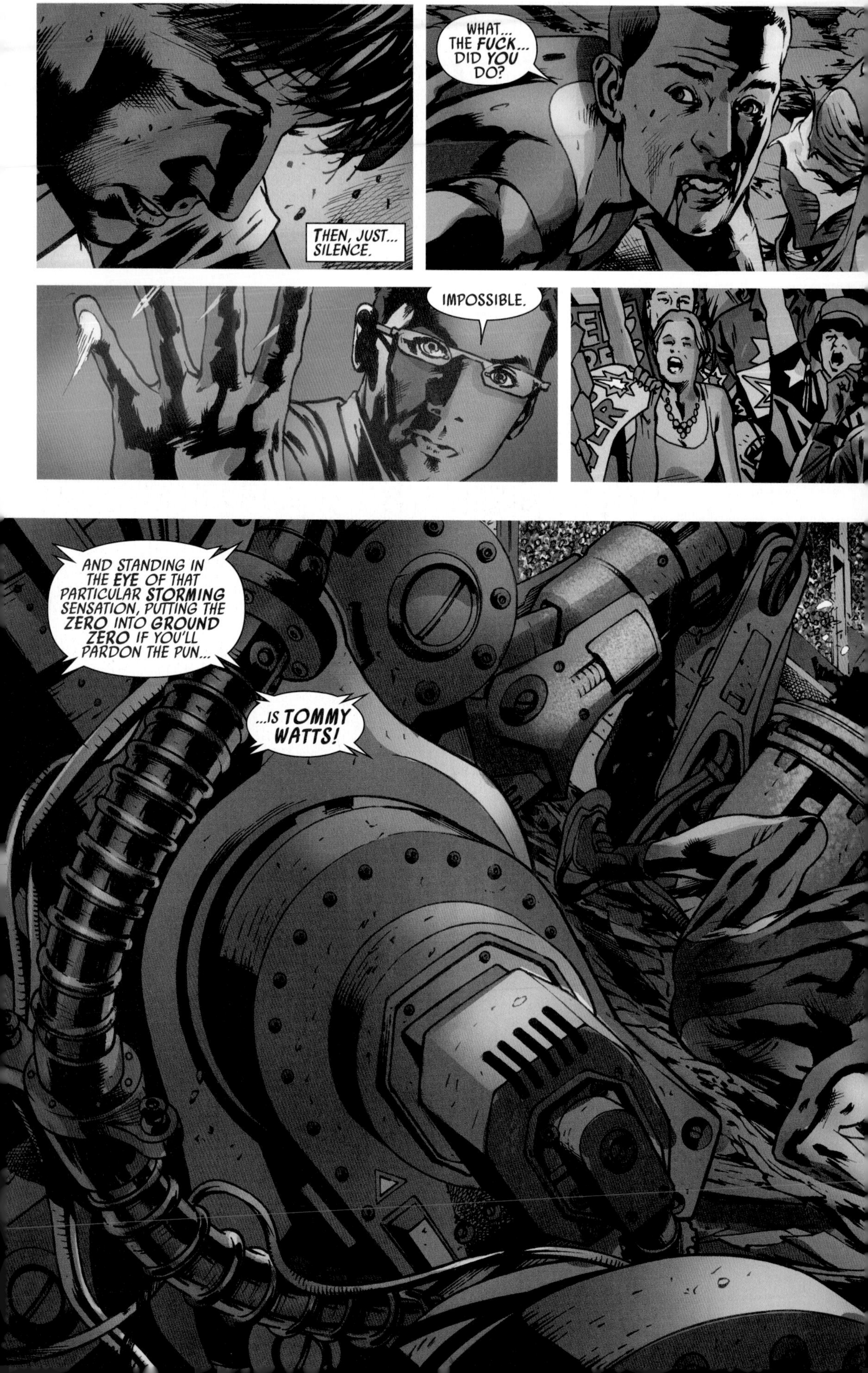
THEN, JUST... SILENCE.
WHAT... THE FUCK... DID YOU DO?
IMPOSSIBLE.
AND STANDING IN THE EYE OF THAT PARTICULAR STORMING SENSATION, PUTTING THE ZERO INTO GROUND ZERO IF YOU'LL PARDON THE PUN...
...IS TOMMY WATTS!

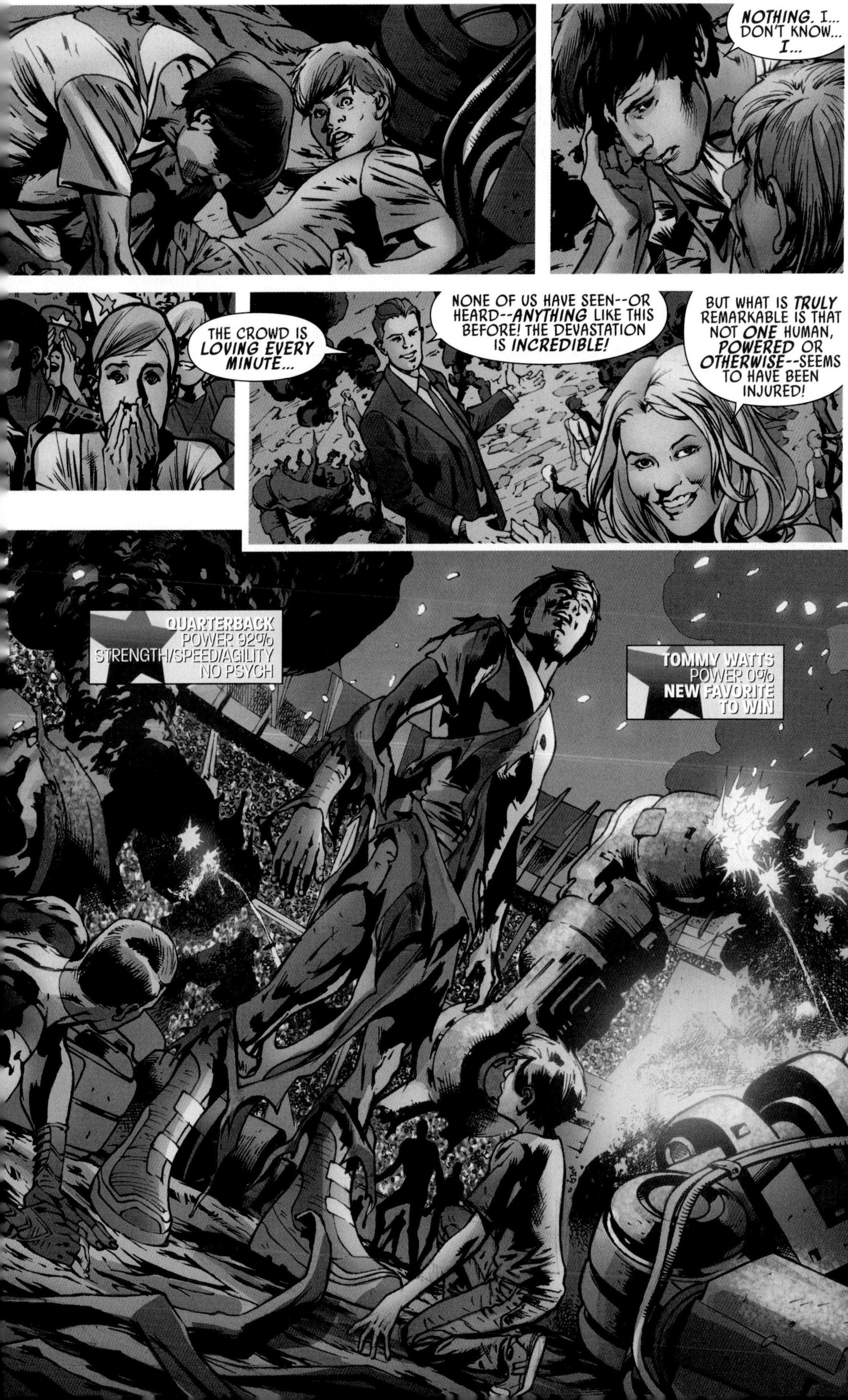
NOTHING. I... DON'T KNOW... I...
THE CROWD IS LOVING EVERY MINUTE...
NONE OF US HAVE SEEN--OR HEARD--ANYTHING LIKE THIS BEFORE! THE DEVASTATION IS INCREDIBLE!
BUT WHAT IS TRULY REMARKABLE IS THAT NOT ONE HUMAN, POWERED OR OTHERWISE--SEEMS TO HAVE BEEN INJURED!
QUARTERBACK
POWER 92%
STRENGTH/SPEED/AGILITY
NO PSYCH
TOMMY WATTS
POWER 0%
NEW FAVORITE
TO WIN

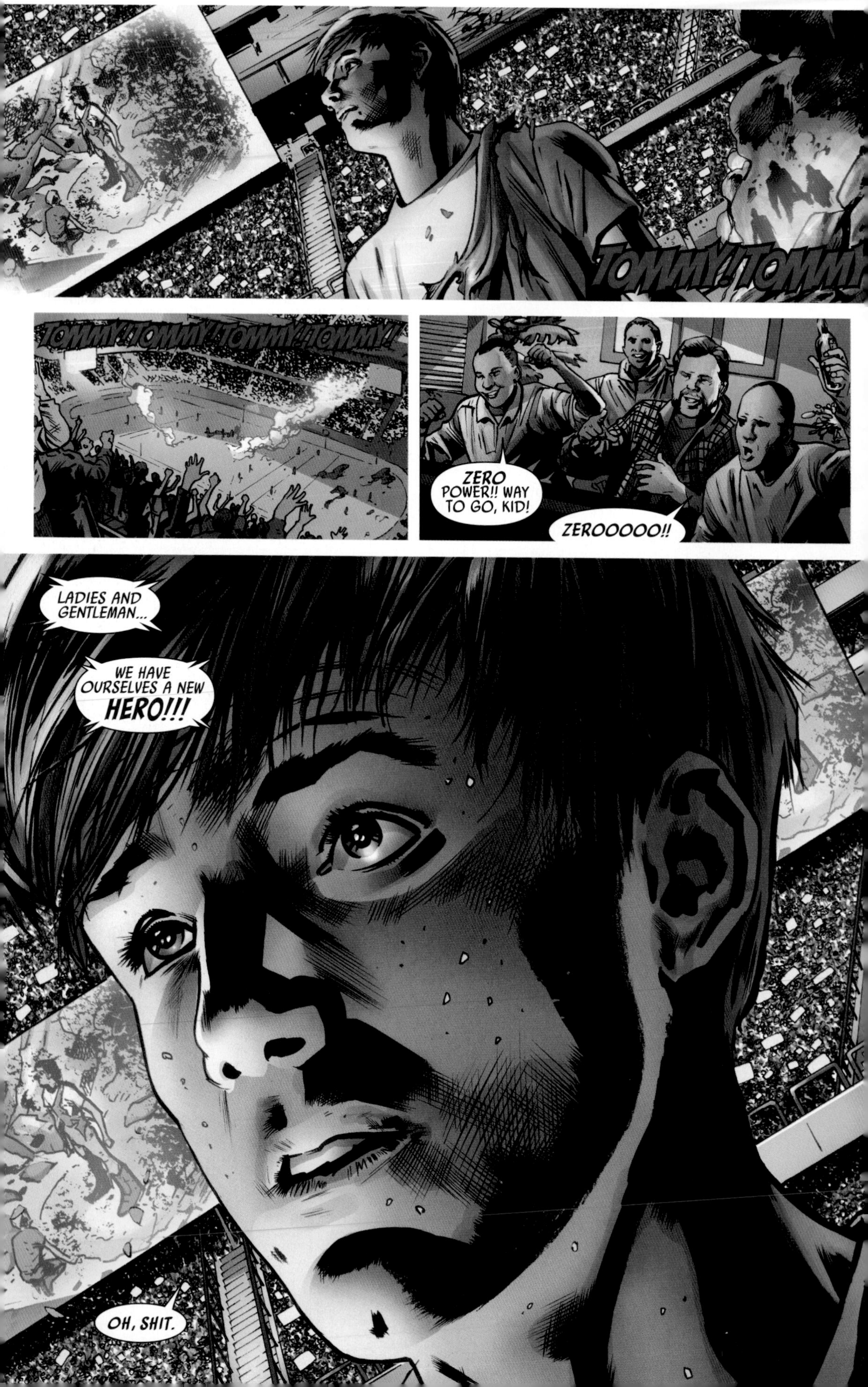
TOMMY! TOMMY!
TOMMY! TOMMY! TOMMY! TOMMY!
ZERO POWER!! WAY TO GO, KID!
ZEROOOOO!!
LADIES AND GENTLEMAN...
WE HAVE OURSELVES A NEW HERO!!!
OH, SHIT.

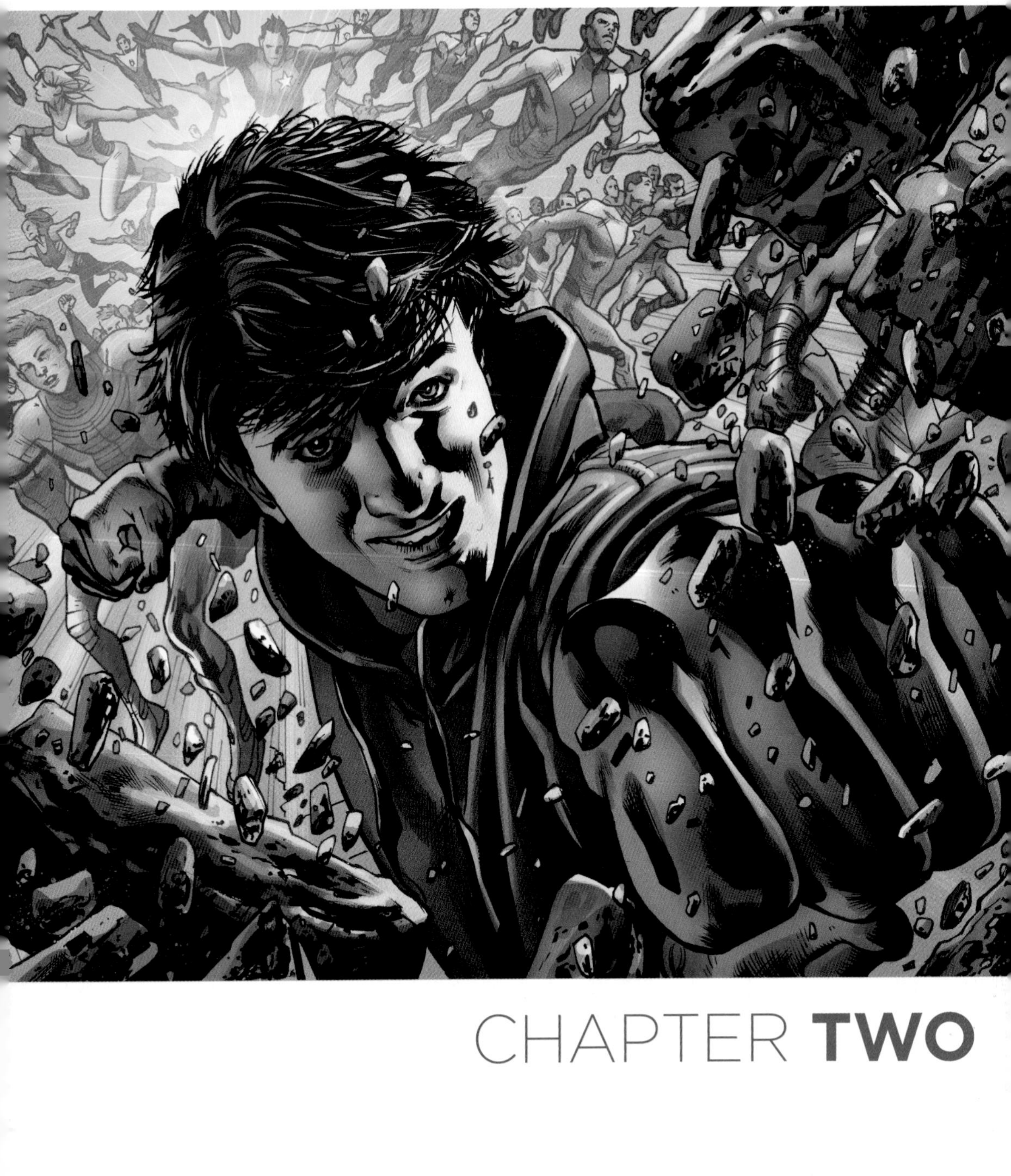

CHAPTER **TWO**

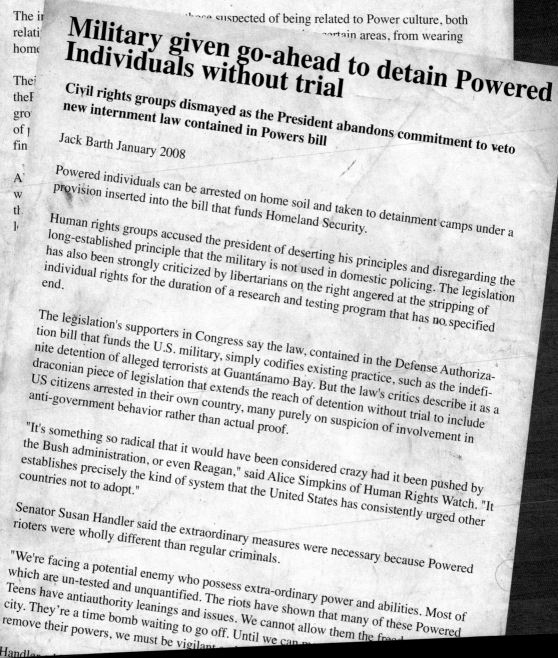

Government's riot prevention legislation infringes children's rights

By Ned Broward Tuesday, 20 November 2007

The introduction of Power-Gang injunctions moves to allow the state to introduce the compulsory wearing of easily identifiable 'Powerstars' on the clothing of all Powered children at all times following the riots that rocked San Francisco last month. It also allows for Police to remove face coverings and calls for young offenders to be prohibited from gathering in groups of three or more in public spaces.

Homeland Security Chief Marino Simone said gang injunctions for all Powered teens will be among the measures intended to deal with the fallout of the riots and prevent repeat activity.

But these and several other injunctions constitute a breach of the children's rights, campaigners have warned.

The i... ...hose suspected of being related to Power culture, both relati... ...rtain areas, from wearing home...

Thei...
theP...
gro...
of ...
fin...

A'...
w...
th...
l...

Military given go-ahead to detain Powered Individuals without trial

Civil rights groups dismayed as the President abandons commitment to veto new internment law contained in Powers bill

Jack Barth January 2008

Powered individuals can be arrested on home soil and taken to detainment camps under a provision inserted into the bill that funds Homeland Security.

Human rights groups accused the president of deserting his principles and disregarding the long-established principle that the military is not used in domestic policing. The legislation has also been strongly criticized by libertarians on the right angered at the stripping of individual rights for the duration of a research and testing program that has no specified end.

The legislation's supporters in Congress say the law, contained in the Defense Authorization bill that funds the U.S. military, simply codifies existing practice, such as the indefinite detention of alleged terrorists at Guantánamo Bay. But the law's critics describe it as a draconian piece of legislation that extends the reach of detention without trial to include US citizens arrested in their own country, many purely on suspicion of involvement in anti-government behavior rather than actual proof.

"It's something so radical that it would have been considered crazy had it been pushed by the Bush administration, or even Reagan," said Alice Simpkins of Human Rights Watch. "It establishes precisely the kind of system that the United States has consistently urged other countries not to adopt."

Senator Susan Handler said the extraordinary measures were necessary because Powered rioters were wholly different than regular criminals.

"We're facing a potential enemy who possess extra-ordinary power and abilities. Most of which are un-tested and unquantified. The riots have shown that many of these Powered Teens have antiauthority leanings and issues. We cannot allow them the freed... city. They're a time bomb waiting to go off. Until we can r... remove their powers, we must be vigilant...

Handler...

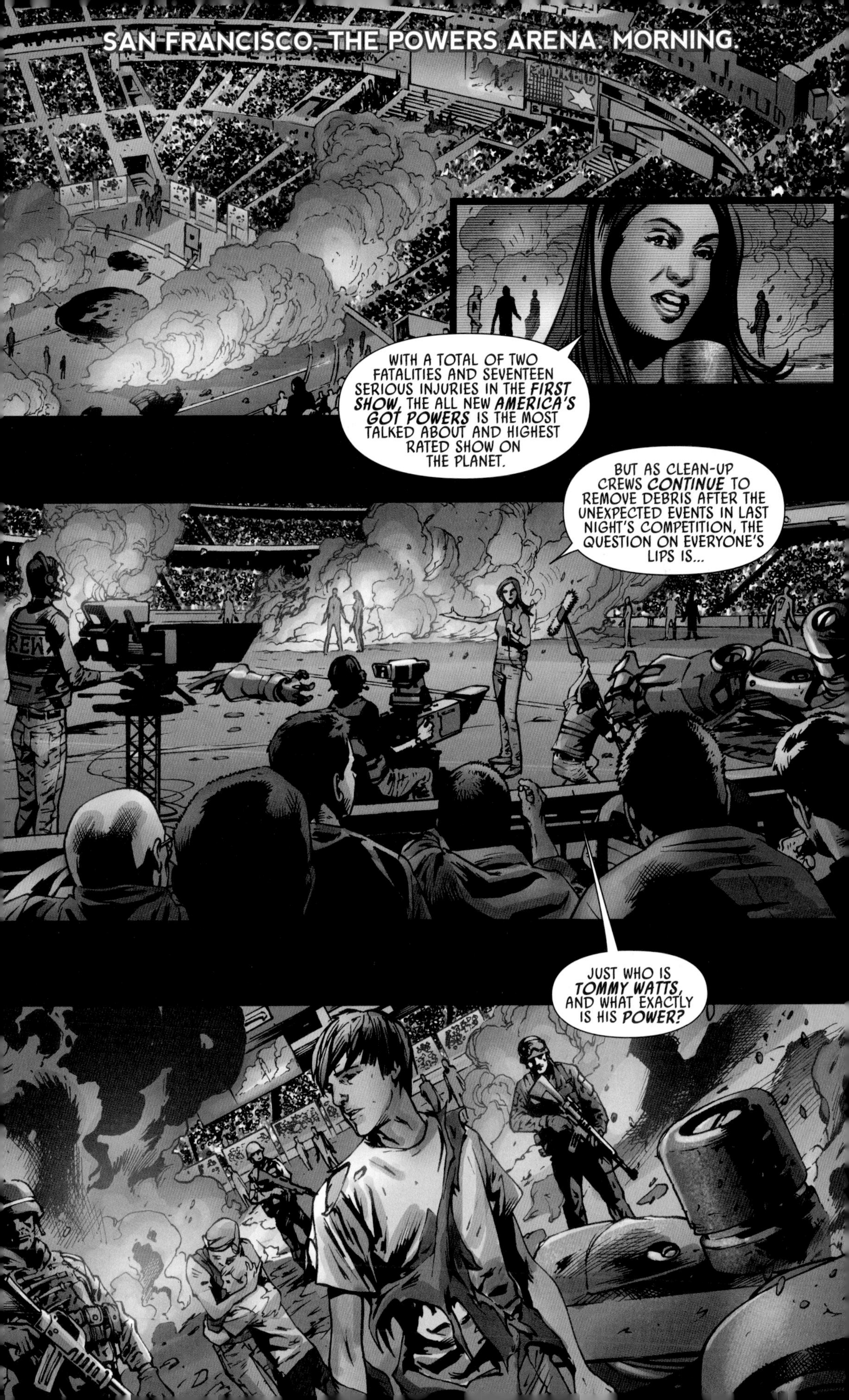
SAN FRANCISCO. THE POWERS ARENA. MORNING.
WITH A TOTAL OF TWO FATALITIES AND SEVENTEEN SERIOUS INJURIES IN THE *FIRST SHOW,* THE ALL NEW *AMERICA'S GOT POWERS* IS THE MOST TALKED ABOUT AND HIGHEST RATED SHOW ON THE PLANET.
BUT AS CLEAN-UP CREWS **CONTINUE** TO REMOVE DEBRIS AFTER THE UNEXPECTED EVENTS IN LAST NIGHT'S COMPETITION, THE QUESTION ON EVERYONE'S LIPS IS...
JUST WHO IS *TOMMY WATTS,* AND WHAT EXACTLY IS HIS *POWER?*

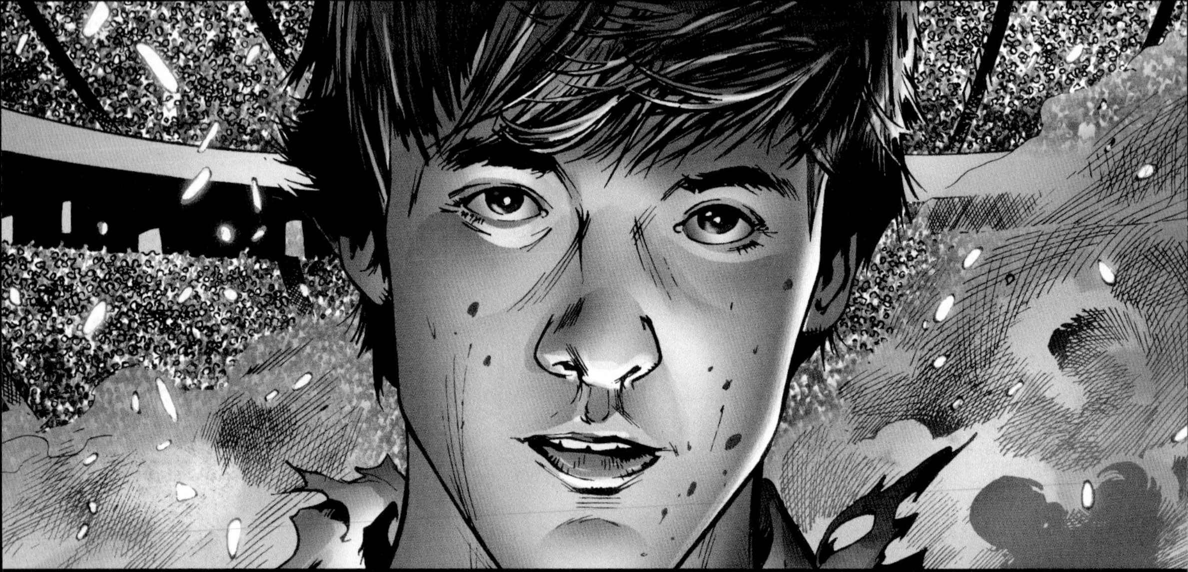

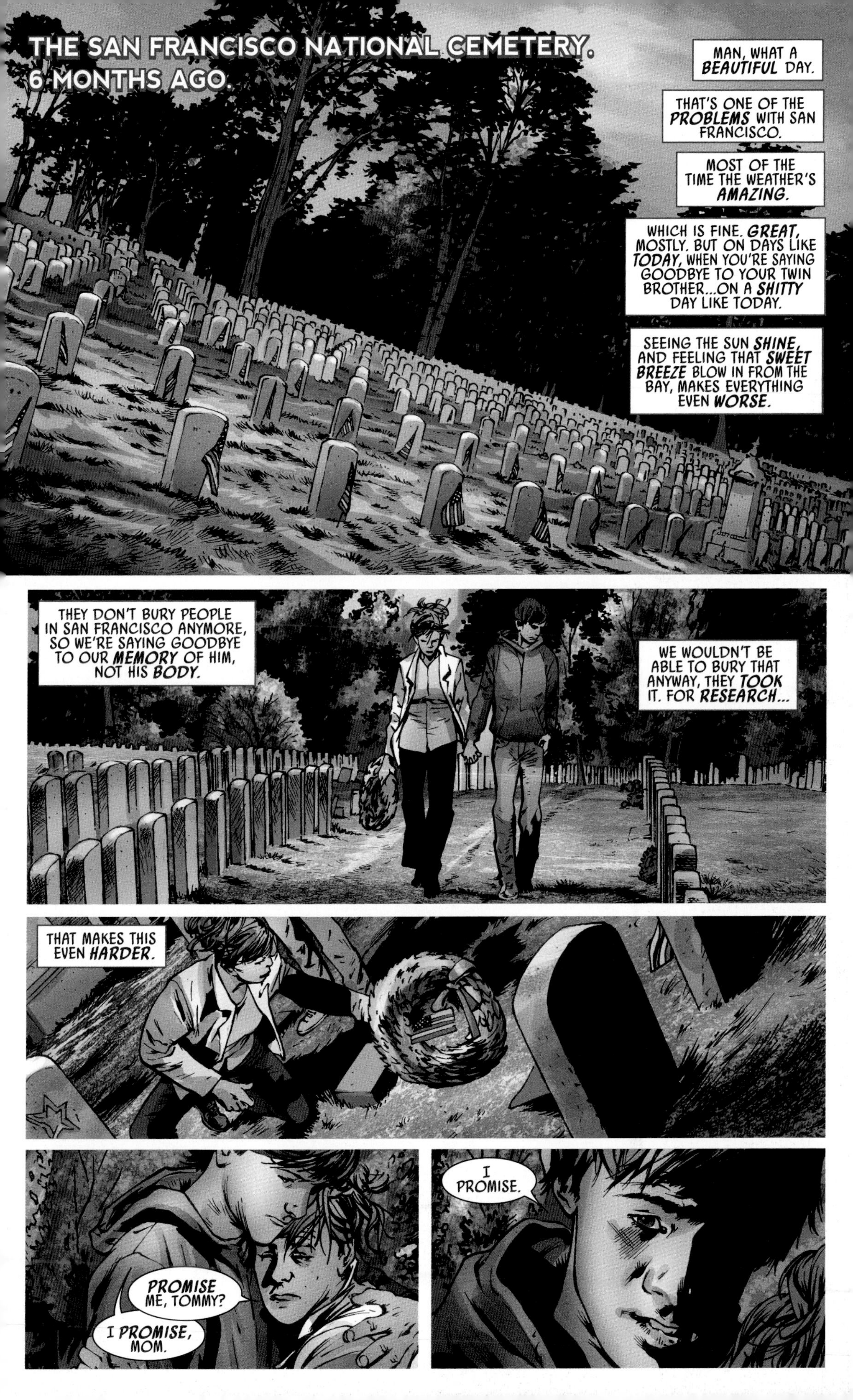
THE SAN FRANCISCO NATIONAL CEMETERY. 6 MONTHS AGO.
MAN, WHAT A BEAUTIFUL DAY.
THAT'S ONE OF THE PROBLEMS WITH SAN FRANCISCO.
MOST OF THE TIME THE WEATHER'S AMAZING.
WHICH IS FINE. GREAT, MOSTLY. BUT ON DAYS LIKE TODAY, WHEN YOU'RE SAYING GOODBYE TO YOUR TWIN BROTHER...ON A SHITTY DAY LIKE TODAY.
SEEING THE SUN SHINE, AND FEELING THAT SWEET BREEZE BLOW IN FROM THE BAY, MAKES EVERYTHING EVEN WORSE.
THEY DON'T BURY PEOPLE IN SAN FRANCISCO ANYMORE, SO WE'RE SAYING GOODBYE TO OUR MEMORY OF HIM, NOT HIS BODY.
WE WOULDN'T BE ABLE TO BURY THAT ANYWAY, THEY TOOK IT. FOR RESEARCH...
THAT MAKES THIS EVEN HARDER.
PROMISE ME, TOMMY?
I PROMISE, MOM.
I PROMISE.

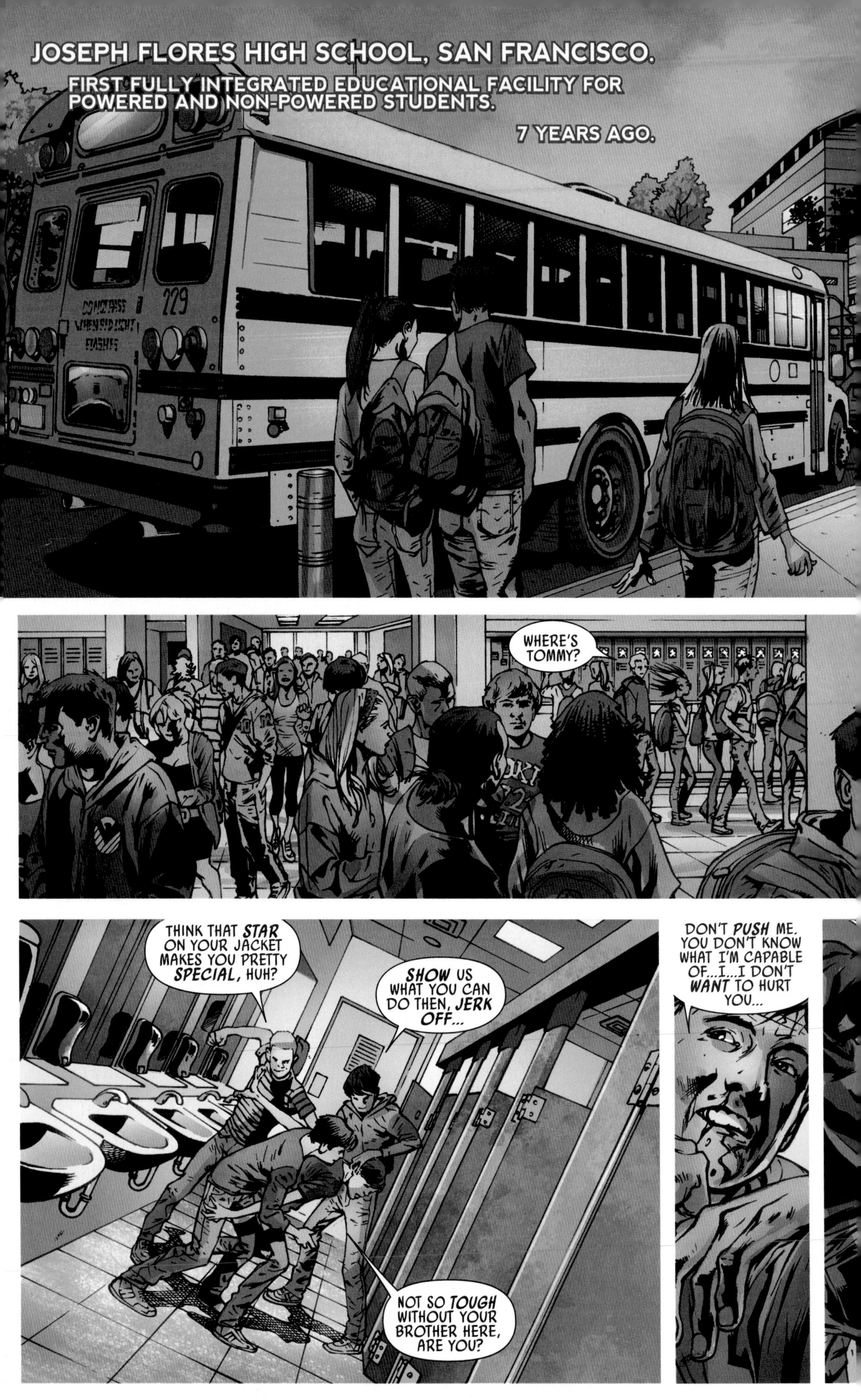
JOSEPH FLORES HIGH SCHOOL, SAN FRANCISCO.
FIRST FULLY INTEGRATED EDUCATIONAL FACILITY FOR POWERED AND NON-POWERED STUDENTS.
7 YEARS AGO.
WHERE'S TOMMY?
THINK THAT STAR ON YOUR JACKET MAKES YOU PRETTY SPECIAL, HUH?
SHOW US WHAT YOU CAN DO THEN, JERK OFF...
NOT SO TOUGH WITHOUT YOUR BROTHER HERE, ARE YOU?
DON'T PUSH ME. YOU DON'T KNOW WHAT I'M CAPABLE OF...I...I DON'T WANT TO HURT YOU...

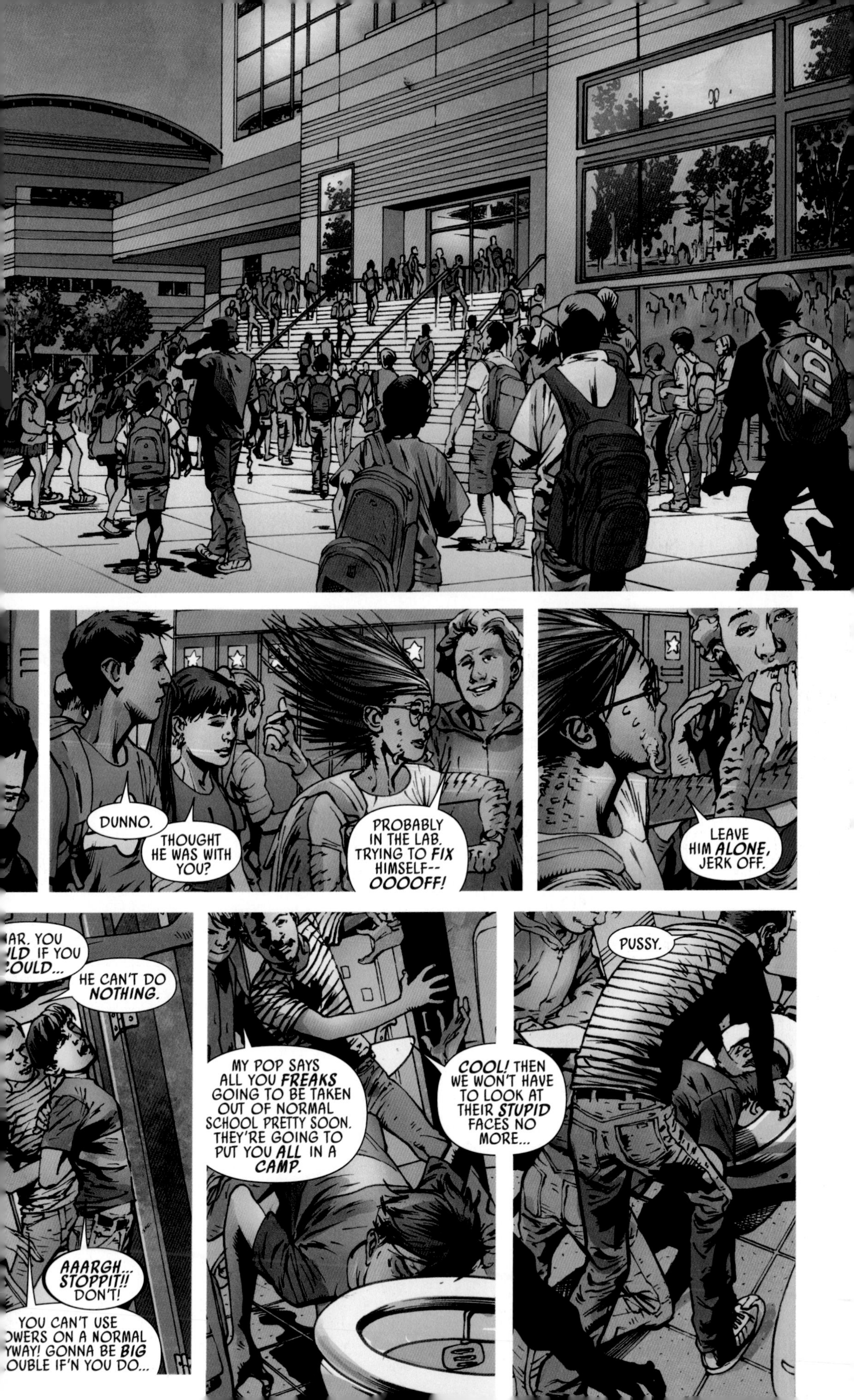
DUNNO.
THOUGHT HE WAS WITH YOU?
PROBABLY IN THE LAB. TRYING TO *FIX* HIMSELF-- *OOOOFF!*
LEAVE HIM *ALONE,* JERK OFF.
AR. YOU LD IF YOU OULD...
HE CAN'T DO *NOTHING.*
AAARGH... STOPPIT!! DON'T!
YOU CAN'T USE OWERS ON A NORMAL YWAY! GONNA BE *BIG* OUBLE IF'N YOU DO...
MY POP SAYS ALL YOU *FREAKS* GOING TO BE TAKEN OUT OF NORMAL SCHOOL PRETTY SOON. THEY'RE GOING TO PUT YOU *ALL* IN A *CAMP.*
COOL! THEN WE WON'T HAVE TO LOOK AT THEIR *STUPID* FACES NO MORE...
PUSSY.

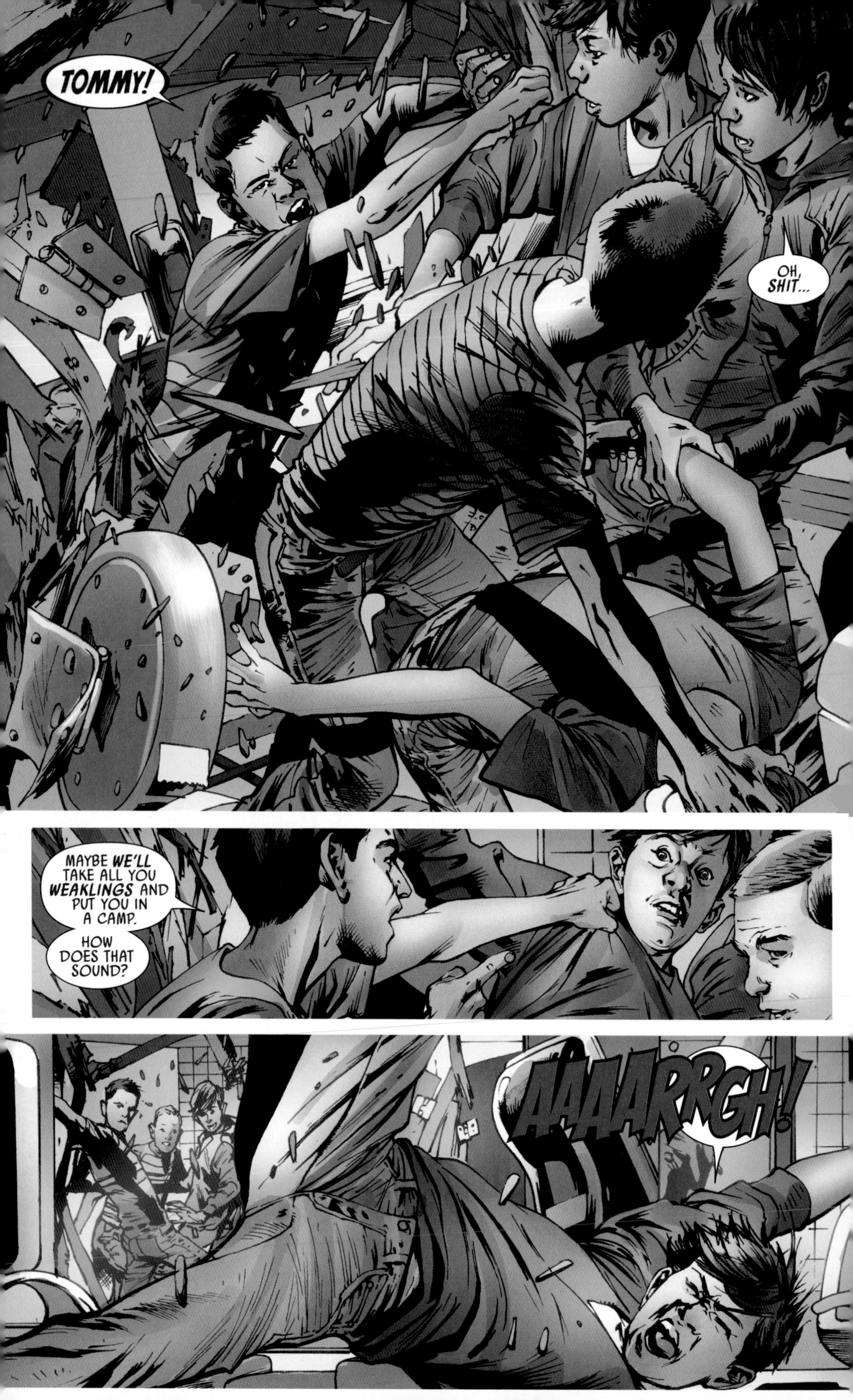
TOMMY!
OH, SHIT...
MAYBE WE'LL TAKE ALL YOU WEAKLINGS AND PUT YOU IN A CAMP.
HOW DOES THAT SOUND?
AAAARRGH!

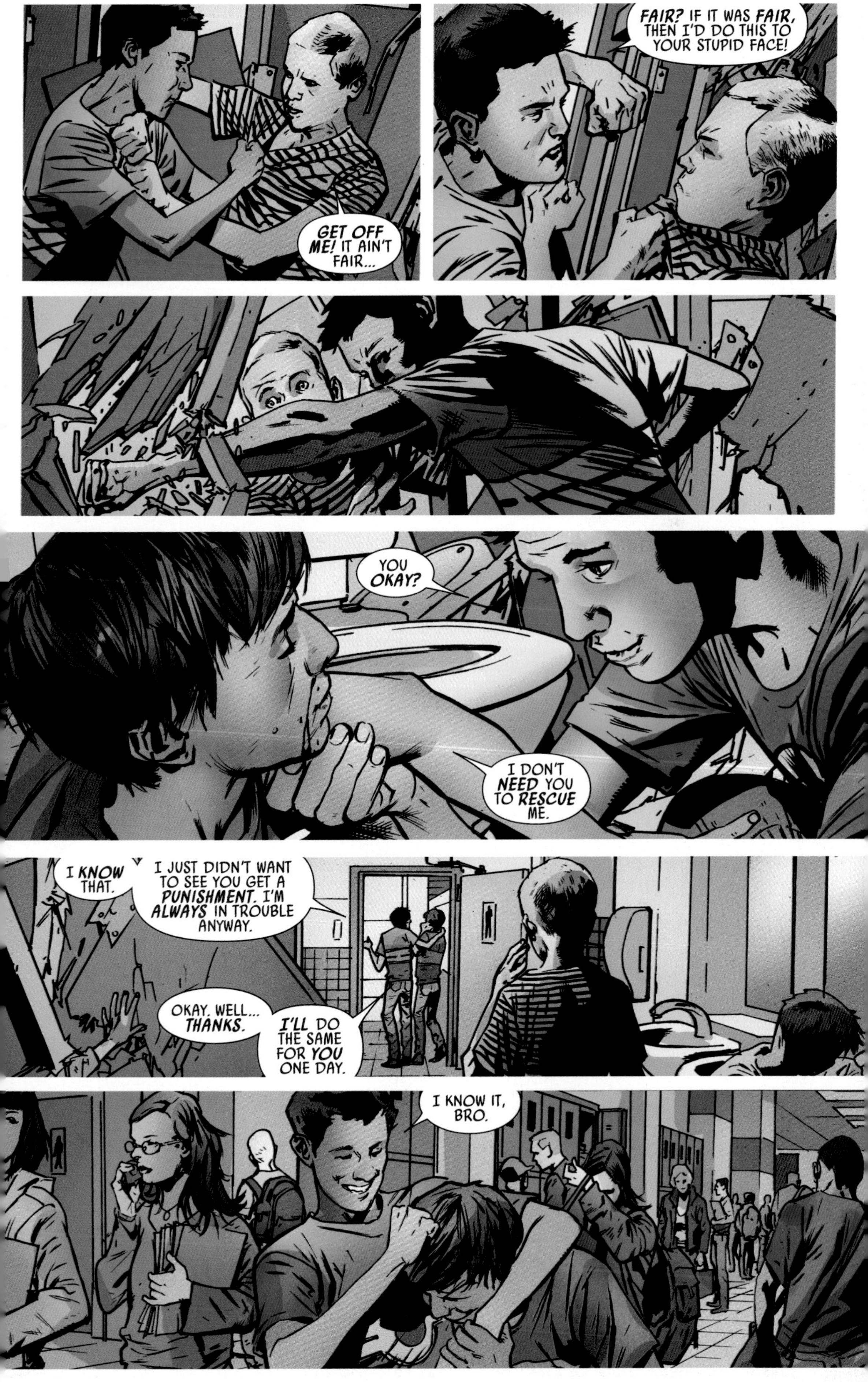
GET OFF ME! IT AIN'T FAIR...
FAIR? IF IT WAS FAIR, THEN I'D DO THIS TO YOUR STUPID FACE!
YOU OKAY?
I DON'T NEED YOU TO RESCUE ME.
I KNOW THAT.
I JUST DIDN'T WANT TO SEE YOU GET A PUNISHMENT. I'M ALWAYS IN TROUBLE ANYWAY.
OKAY. WELL... THANKS.
I'LL DO THE SAME FOR YOU ONE DAY.
I KNOW IT, BRO.

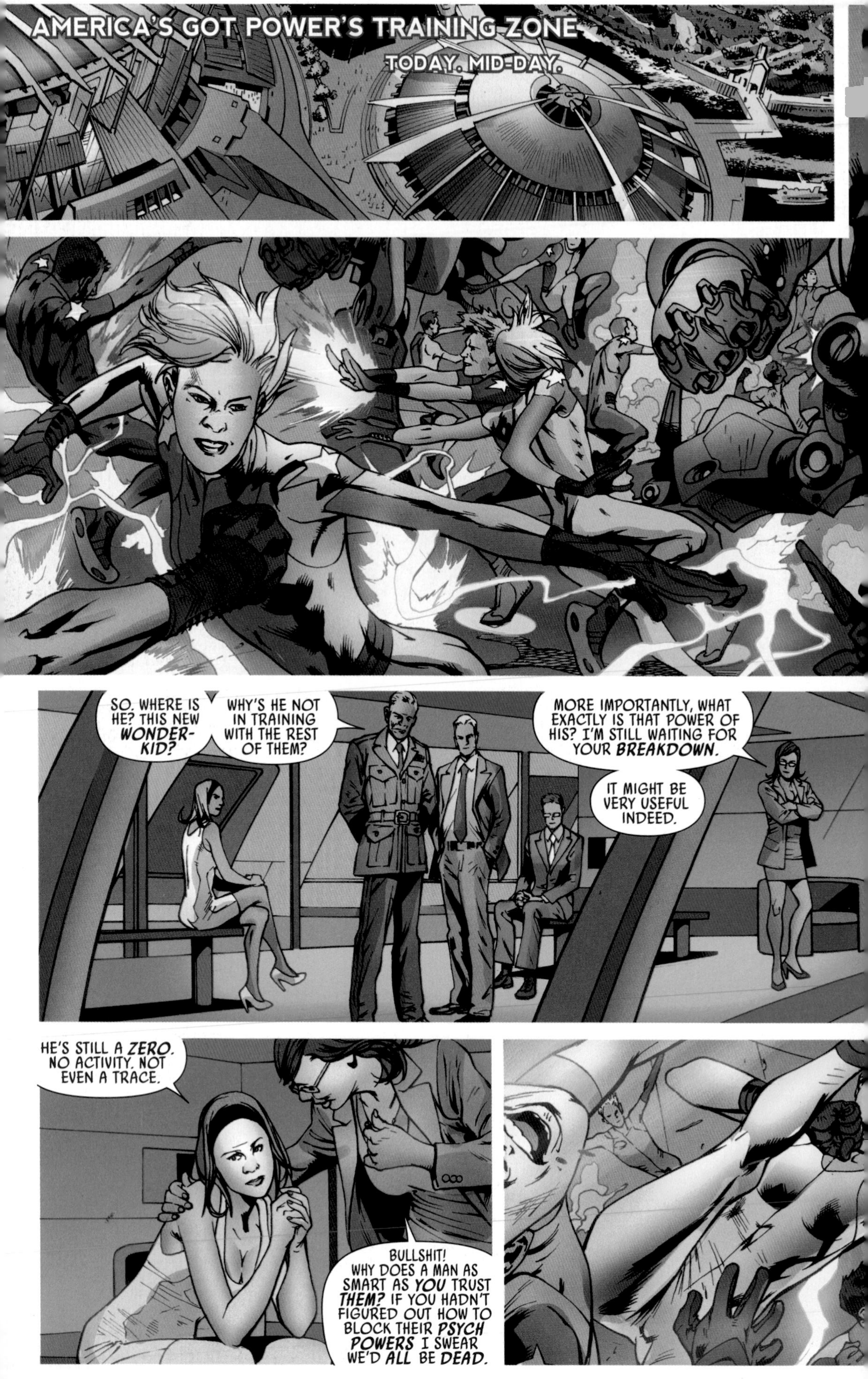
AMERICA'S GOT POWER'S TRAINING ZONE
TODAY. MID-DAY.
SO. WHERE IS HE? THIS NEW WONDER-KID?
WHY'S HE NOT IN TRAINING WITH THE REST OF THEM?
MORE IMPORTANTLY, WHAT EXACTLY IS THAT POWER OF HIS? I'M STILL WAITING FOR YOUR BREAKDOWN.
IT MIGHT BE VERY USEFUL INDEED.
HE'S STILL A ZERO. NO ACTIVITY. NOT EVEN A TRACE.
BULLSHIT! WHY DOES A MAN AS SMART AS YOU TRUST THEM? IF YOU HADN'T FIGURED OUT HOW TO BLOCK THEIR PSYCH POWERS I SWEAR WE'D ALL BE DEAD.

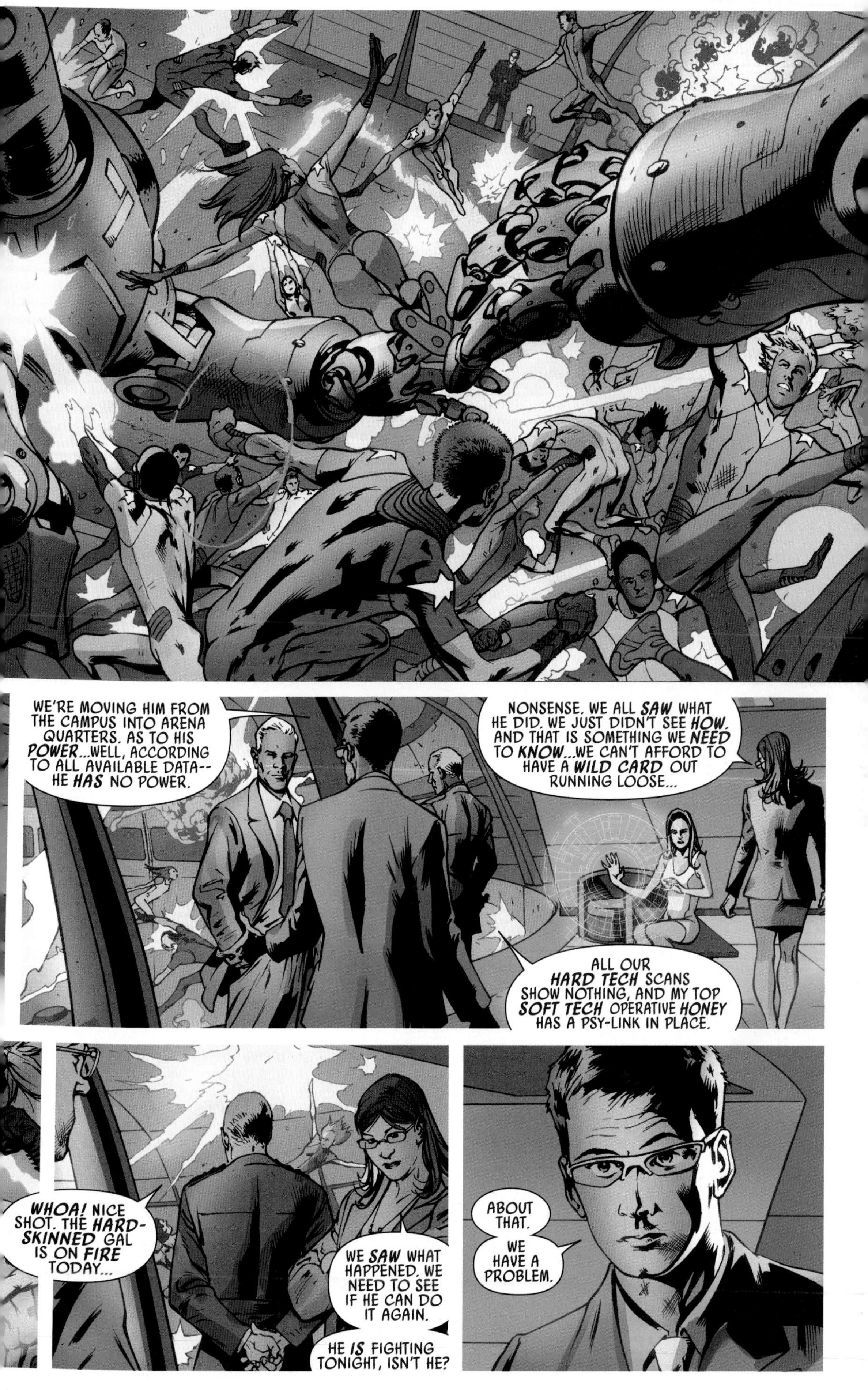
WE'RE MOVING HIM FROM THE CAMPUS INTO ARENA QUARTERS. AS TO HIS POWER...WELL, ACCORDING TO ALL AVAILABLE DATA-- HE HAS NO POWER.
NONSENSE. WE ALL SAW WHAT HE DID. WE JUST DIDN'T SEE HOW. AND THAT IS SOMETHING WE NEED TO KNOW...WE CAN'T AFFORD TO HAVE A WILD CARD OUT RUNNING LOOSE...
ALL OUR HARD TECH SCANS SHOW NOTHING, AND MY TOP SOFT TECH OPERATIVE HONEY HAS A PSY-LINK IN PLACE.
WHOA! NICE SHOT. THE HARD-SKINNED GAL IS ON FIRE TODAY...
WE SAW WHAT HAPPENED. WE NEED TO SEE IF HE CAN DO IT AGAIN.
HE IS FIGHTING TONIGHT, ISN'T HE?
ABOUT THAT.
WE HAVE A PROBLEM.

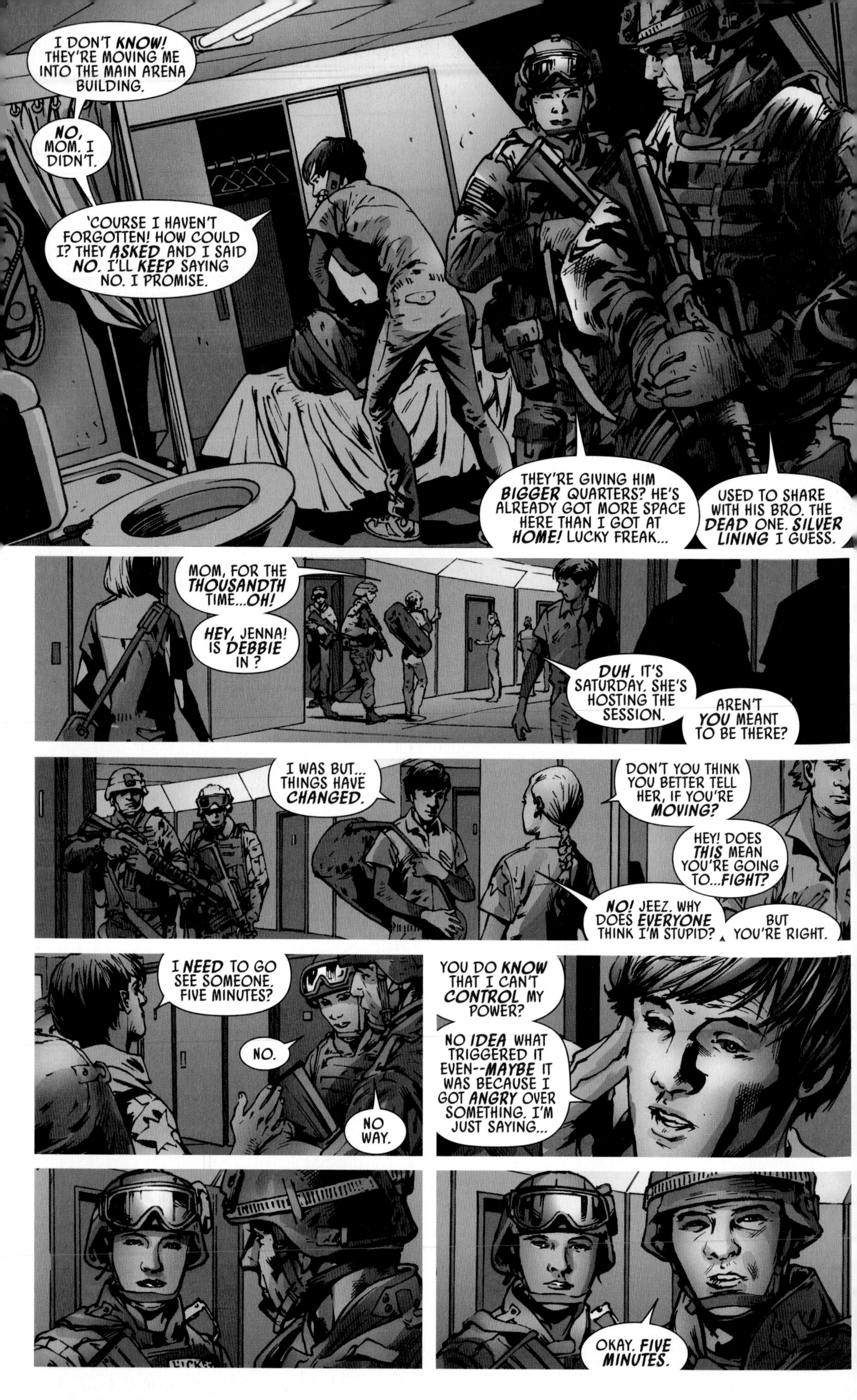
I DON'T KNOW! THEY'RE MOVING ME INTO THE MAIN ARENA BUILDING.
NO, MOM. I DIDN'T.
'COURSE I HAVEN'T FORGOTTEN! HOW COULD I? THEY ASKED AND I SAID NO. I'LL KEEP SAYING NO. I PROMISE.
THEY'RE GIVING HIM BIGGER QUARTERS? HE'S ALREADY GOT MORE SPACE HERE THAN I GOT AT HOME! LUCKY FREAK...
USED TO SHARE WITH HIS BRO. THE DEAD ONE. SILVER LINING I GUESS.
MOM, FOR THE THOUSANDTH TIME...OH!
HEY, JENNA! IS DEBBIE IN?
DUH. IT'S SATURDAY. SHE'S HOSTING THE SESSION.
AREN'T YOU MEANT TO BE THERE?
I WAS BUT... THINGS HAVE CHANGED.
DON'T YOU THINK YOU BETTER TELL HER, IF YOU'RE MOVING?
HEY! DOES THIS MEAN YOU'RE GOING TO...FIGHT?
NO! JEEZ. WHY DOES EVERYONE THINK I'M STUPID?
BUT YOU'RE RIGHT.
I NEED TO GO SEE SOMEONE. FIVE MINUTES?
NO.
NO WAY.
YOU DO KNOW THAT I CAN'T CONTROL MY POWER?
NO IDEA WHAT TRIGGERED IT EVEN--MAYBE IT WAS BECAUSE I GOT ANGRY OVER SOMETHING. I'M JUST SAYING...
OKAY. FIVE MINUTES.

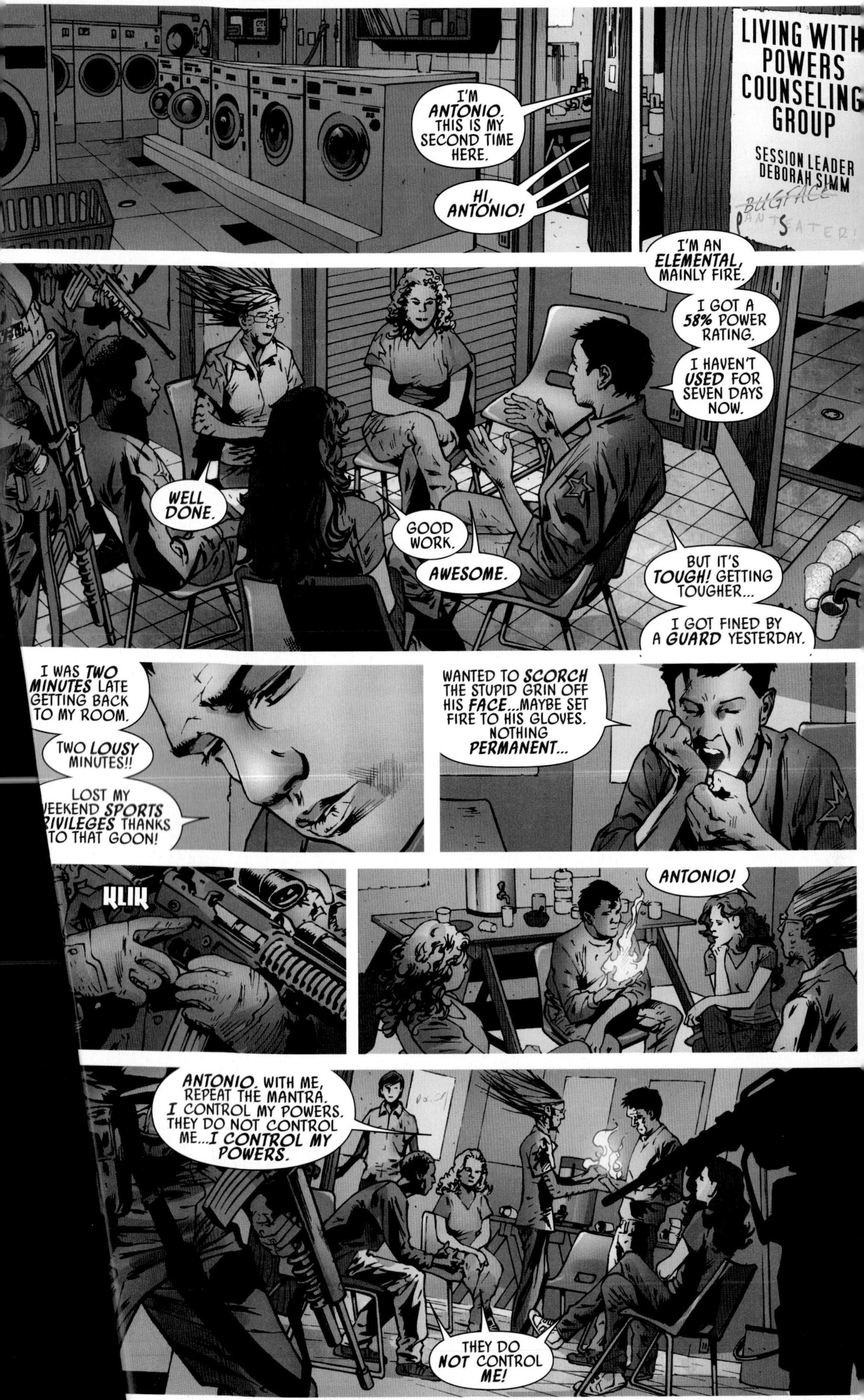
I'M ANTONIO. THIS IS MY SECOND TIME HERE.
HI, ANTONIO!
LIVING WITH POWERS COUNSELING GROUP
SESSION LEADER DEBORAH SIMM
I'M AN ELEMENTAL, MAINLY FIRE.
I GOT A 58% POWER RATING.
I HAVEN'T USED FOR SEVEN DAYS NOW.
WELL DONE.
GOOD WORK.
AWESOME.
BUT IT'S TOUGH! GETTING TOUGHER...
I GOT FINED BY A GUARD YESTERDAY.
I WAS TWO MINUTES LATE GETTING BACK TO MY ROOM.
TWO LOUSY MINUTES!!
LOST MY WEEKEND SPORTS PRIVILEGES THANKS TO THAT GOON!
WANTED TO SCORCH THE STUPID GRIN OFF HIS FACE...MAYBE SET FIRE TO HIS GLOVES. NOTHING PERMANENT...
KLIK
ANTONIO!
ANTONIO. WITH ME, REPEAT THE MANTRA. I CONTROL MY POWERS. THEY DO NOT CONTROL ME...I CONTROL MY POWERS.
THEY DO NOT CONTROL ME!

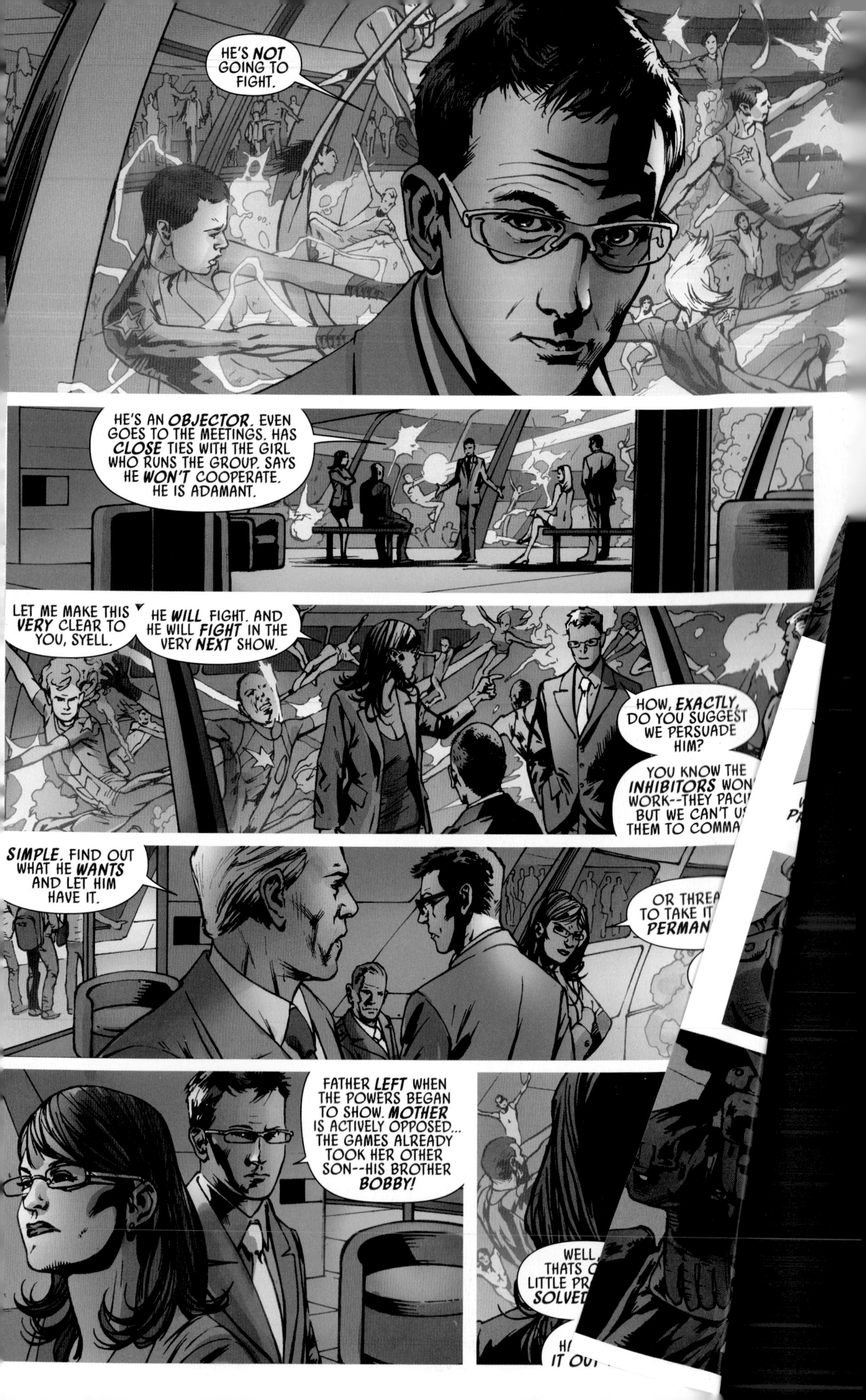
HE'S NOT GOING TO FIGHT.
HE'S AN OBJECTOR. EVEN GOES TO THE MEETINGS. HAS CLOSE TIES WITH THE GIRL WHO RUNS THE GROUP. SAYS HE WON'T COOPERATE. HE IS ADAMANT.
LET ME MAKE THIS VERY CLEAR TO YOU, SYELL.
HE WILL FIGHT. AND HE WILL FIGHT IN THE VERY NEXT SHOW.
HOW, EXACTLY, DO YOU SUGGEST WE PERSUADE HIM?
YOU KNOW THE INHIBITORS WON WORK--THEY PACI BUT WE CAN'T U THEM TO COMMA
SIMPLE. FIND OUT WHAT HE WANTS AND LET HIM HAVE IT.
OR THREA TO TAKE IT PERMAN
FATHER LEFT WHEN THE POWERS BEGAN TO SHOW. MOTHER IS ACTIVELY OPPOSED... THE GAMES ALREADY TOOK HER OTHER SON--HIS BROTHER BOBBY!
WELL, THATS LITTLE PR SOLVED
IT OU

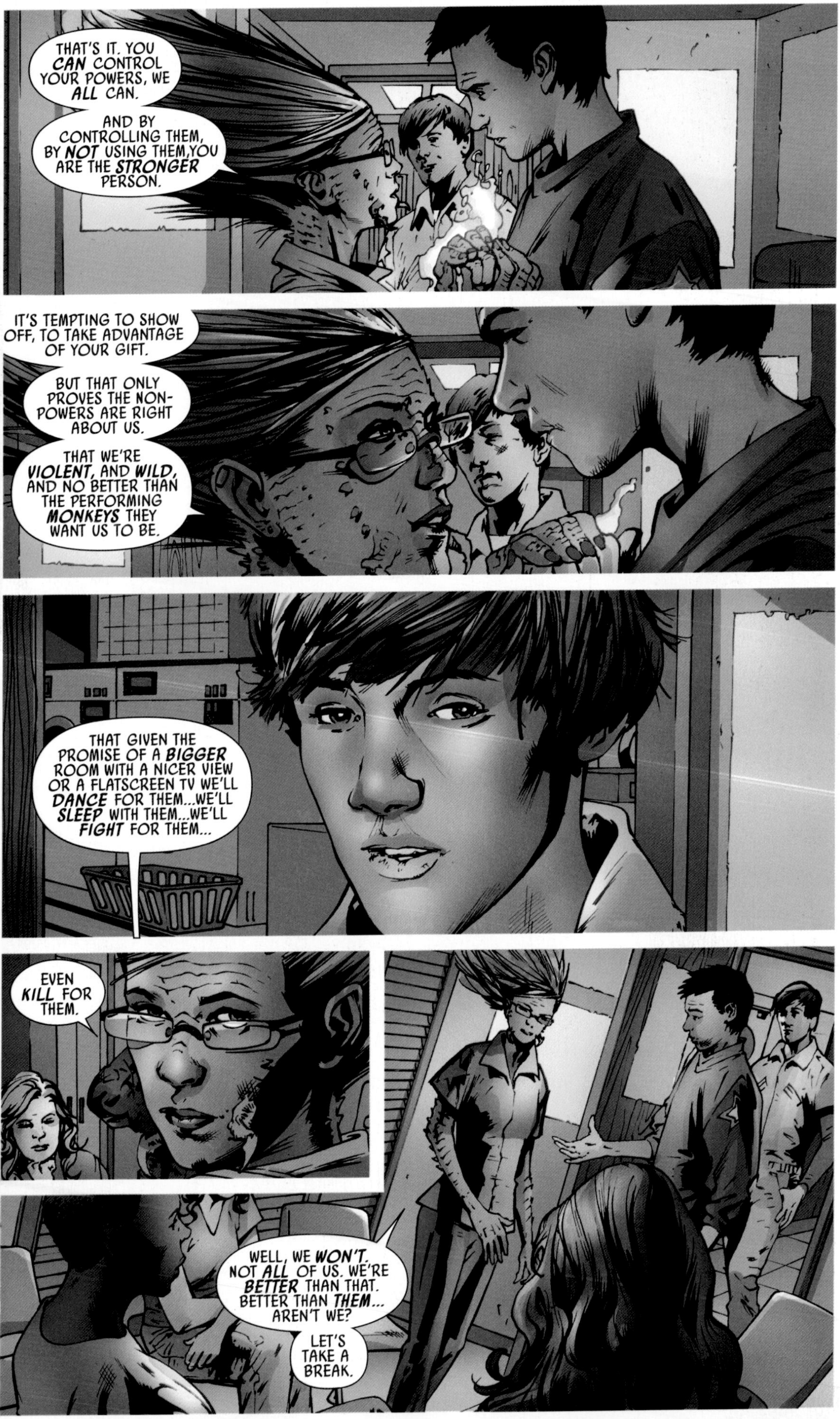
THAT'S IT. YOU CAN CONTROL YOUR POWERS, WE ALL CAN.
AND BY CONTROLLING THEM, BY NOT USING THEM,YOU ARE THE STRONGER PERSON.
IT'S TEMPTING TO SHOW OFF, TO TAKE ADVANTAGE OF YOUR GIFT.
BUT THAT ONLY PROVES THE NON-POWERS ARE RIGHT ABOUT US.
THAT WE'RE VIOLENT, AND WILD, AND NO BETTER THAN THE PERFORMING MONKEYS THEY WANT US TO BE.
THAT GIVEN THE PROMISE OF A BIGGER ROOM WITH A NICER VIEW OR A FLATSCREEN TV WE'LL DANCE FOR THEM...WE'LL SLEEP WITH THEM...WE'LL FIGHT FOR THEM...
EVEN KILL FOR THEM.
WELL, WE WON'T. NOT ALL OF US. WE'RE BETTER THAN THAT. BETTER THAN THEM... AREN'T WE?
LET'S TAKE A BREAK.

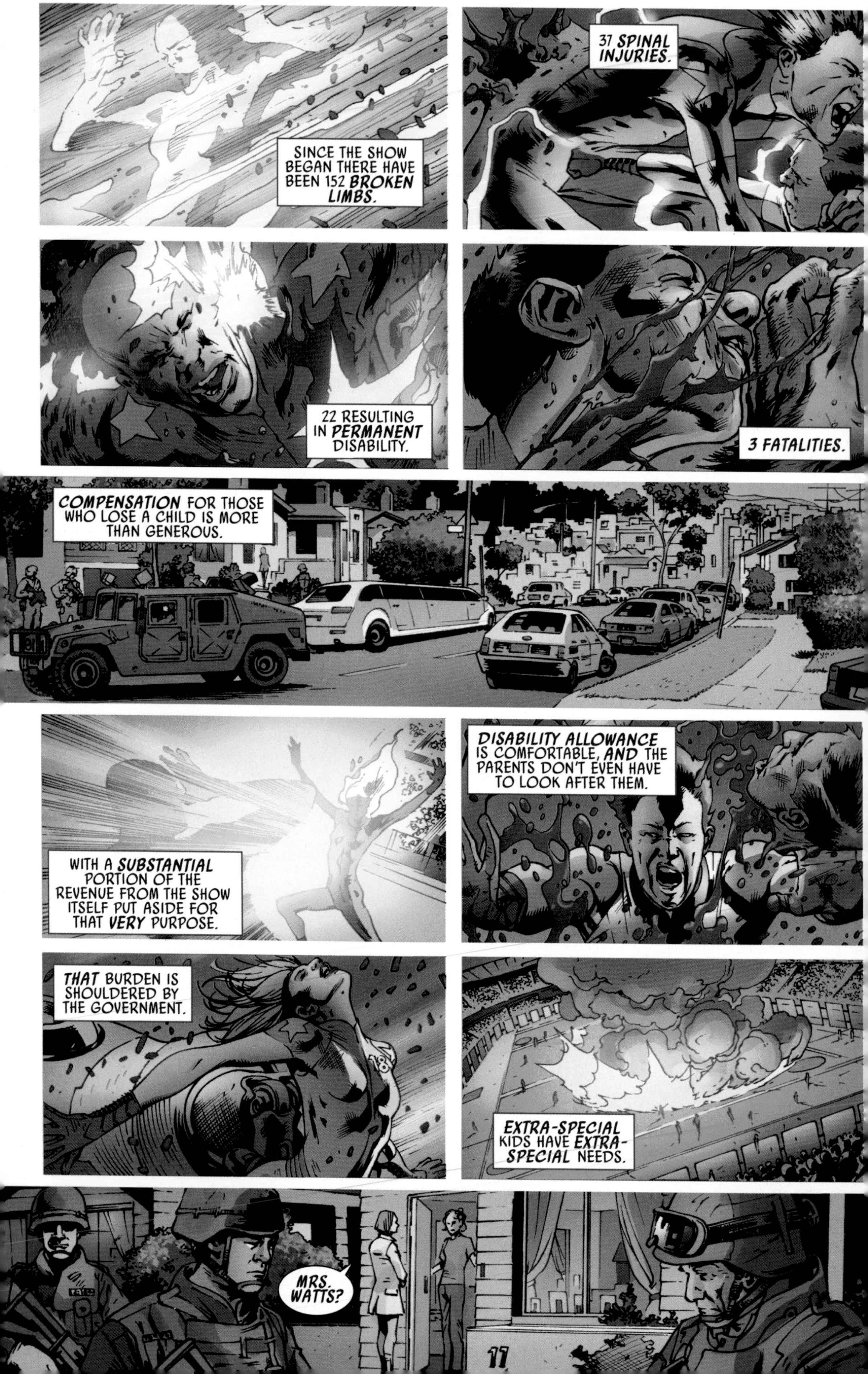
SINCE THE SHOW BEGAN THERE HAVE BEEN 152 BROKEN LIMBS.
37 SPINAL INJURIES.
22 RESULTING IN PERMANENT DISABILITY.
3 FATALITIES.
COMPENSATION FOR THOSE WHO LOSE A CHILD IS MORE THAN GENEROUS.
WITH A SUBSTANTIAL PORTION OF THE REVENUE FROM THE SHOW ITSELF PUT ASIDE FOR THAT VERY PURPOSE.
DISABILITY ALLOWANCE IS COMFORTABLE, AND THE PARENTS DON'T EVEN HAVE TO LOOK AFTER THEM.
THAT BURDEN IS SHOULDERED BY THE GOVERNMENT.
EXTRA-SPECIAL KIDS HAVE EXTRA-SPECIAL NEEDS.
MRS. WATTS?

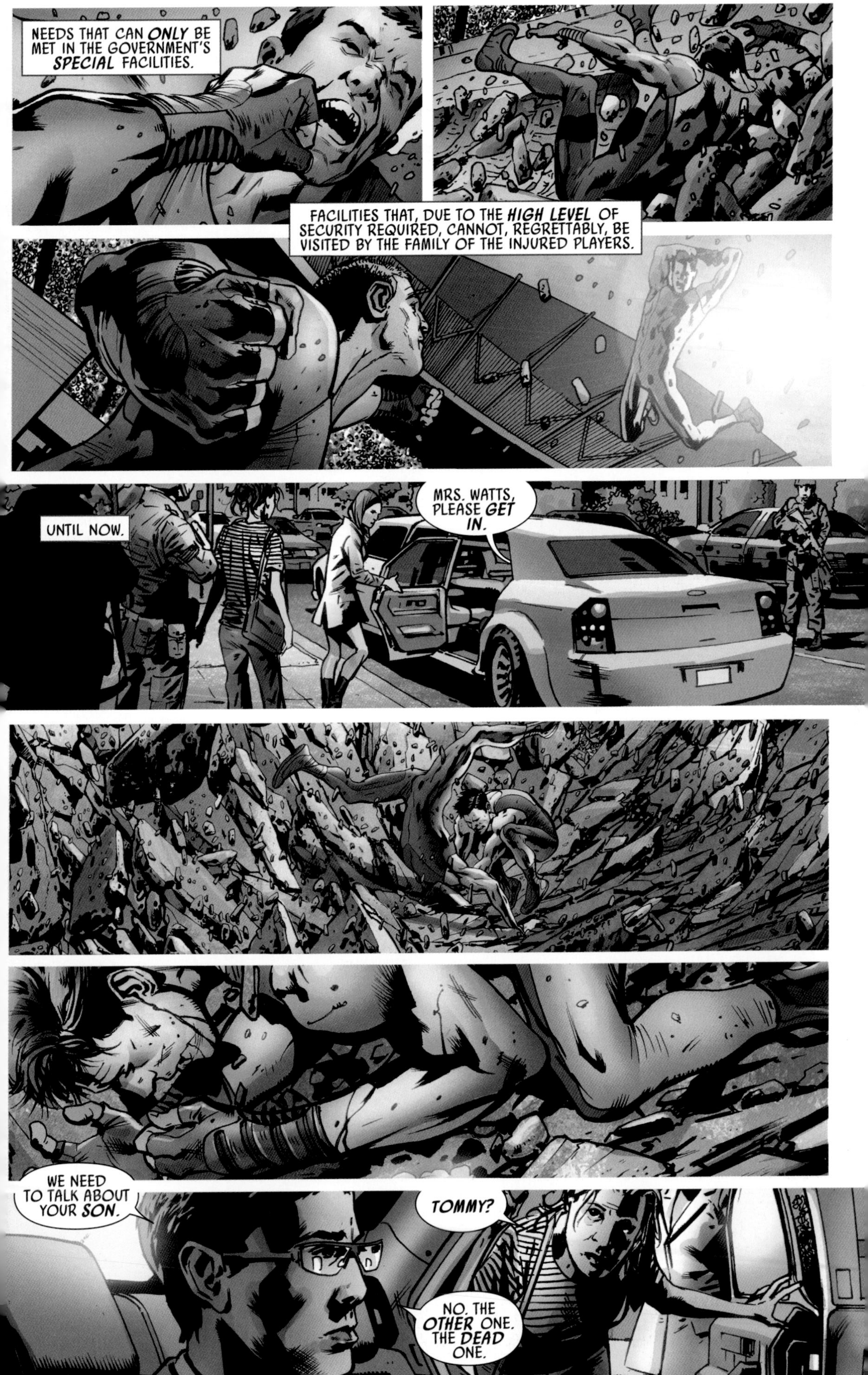
NEEDS THAT CAN ONLY BE MET IN THE GOVERNMENT'S SPECIAL FACILITIES.
FACILITIES THAT, DUE TO THE HIGH LEVEL OF SECURITY REQUIRED, CANNOT, REGRETTABLY, BE VISITED BY THE FAMILY OF THE INJURED PLAYERS.
UNTIL NOW.
MRS. WATTS, PLEASE GET IN.
WE NEED TO TALK ABOUT YOUR SON.
TOMMY?
NO. THE OTHER ONE. THE DEAD ONE.

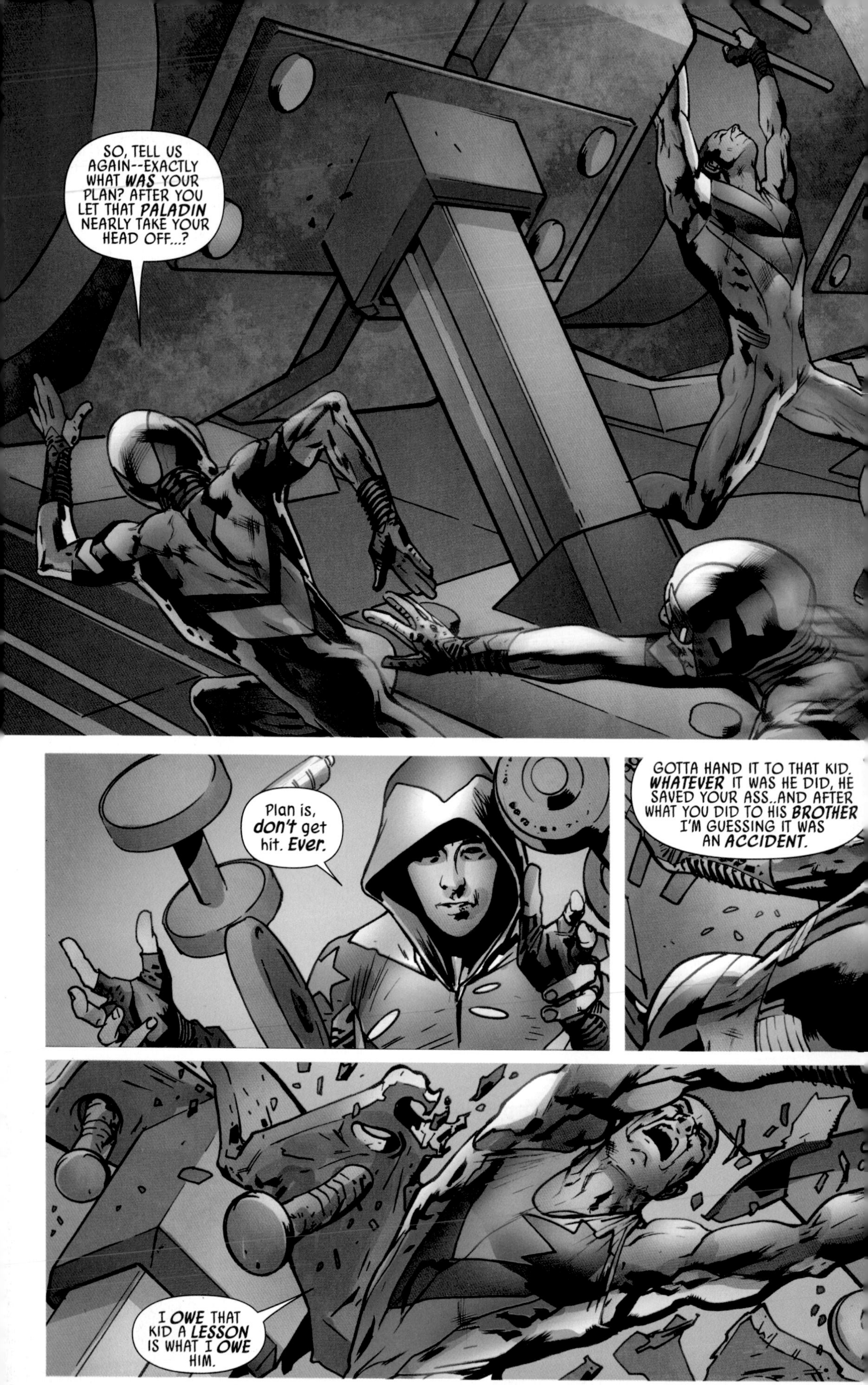

SO, TELL US AGAIN--EXACTLY WHAT **WAS** YOUR PLAN? AFTER YOU LET THAT **PALADIN** NEARLY TAKE YOUR HEAD OFF...?
Plan is, **don't** get hit. **Ever.**
GOTTA HAND IT TO THAT KID. **WHATEVER** IT WAS HE DID, HE SAVED YOUR ASS..AND AFTER WHAT YOU DID TO HIS **BROTHER** I'M GUESSING IT WAS AN **ACCIDENT.**
I **OWE** THAT KID A **LESSON** IS WHAT I **OWE** HIM.

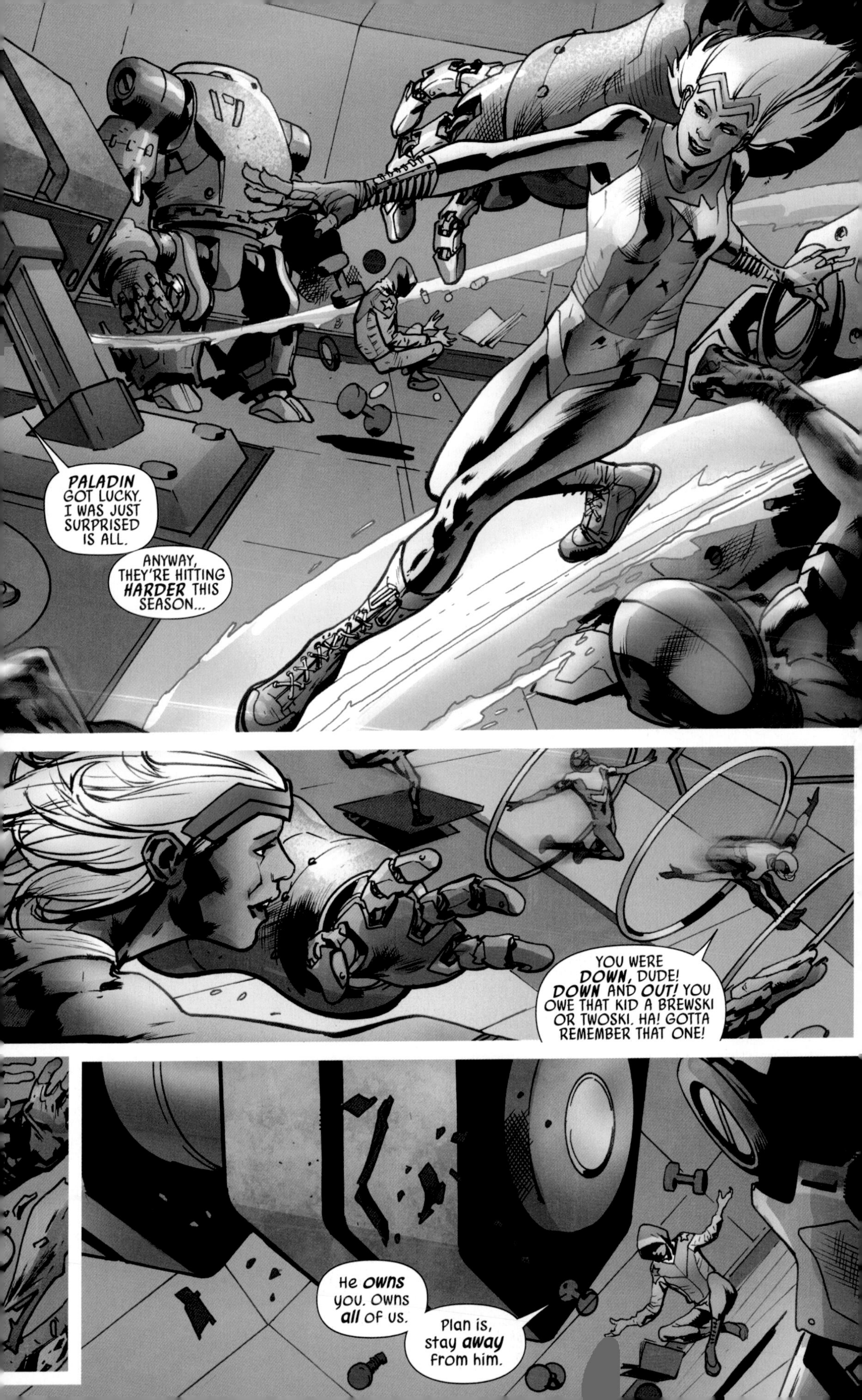
PALADIN GOT LUCKY. I WAS JUST SURPRISED IS ALL.
ANYWAY, THEY'RE HITTING HARDER THIS SEASON...
YOU WERE DOWN, DUDE! DOWN AND OUT! YOU OWE THAT KID A BREWSKI OR TWOSKI. HA! GOTTA REMEMBER THAT ONE!
He owns you. Owns all of us.
Plan is, stay away from him.

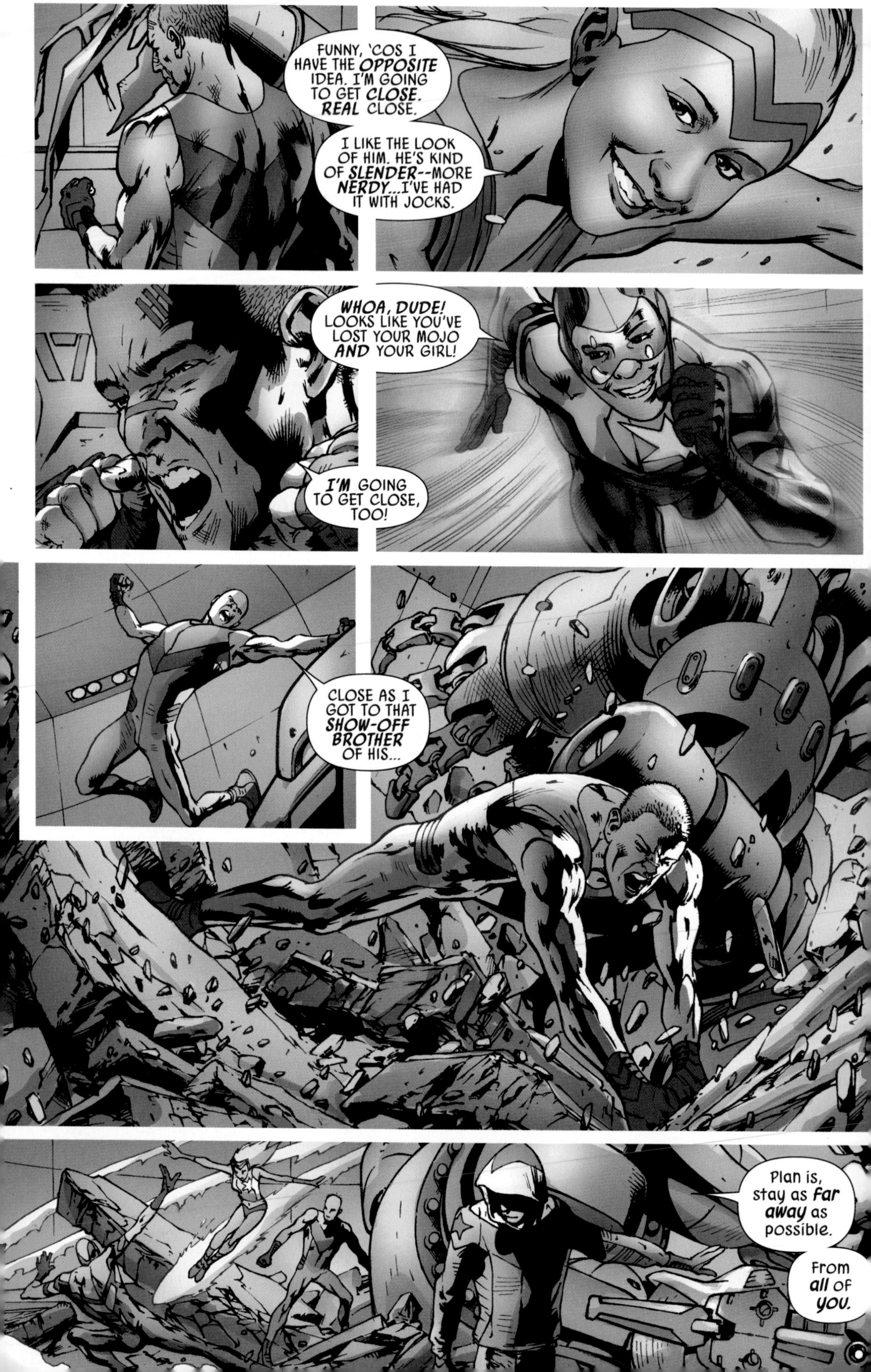

FUNNY, 'COS I HAVE THE OPPOSITE IDEA. I'M GOING TO GET CLOSE. REAL CLOSE.
I LIKE THE LOOK OF HIM. HE'S KIND OF SLENDER--MORE NERDY...I'VE HAD IT WITH JOCKS.
WHOA, DUDE! LOOKS LIKE YOU'VE LOST YOUR MOJO AND YOUR GIRL!
I'M GOING TO GET CLOSE, TOO!
CLOSE AS I GOT TO THAT SHOW-OFF BROTHER OF HIS...
Plan is, stay as far away as possible.
From all of you.

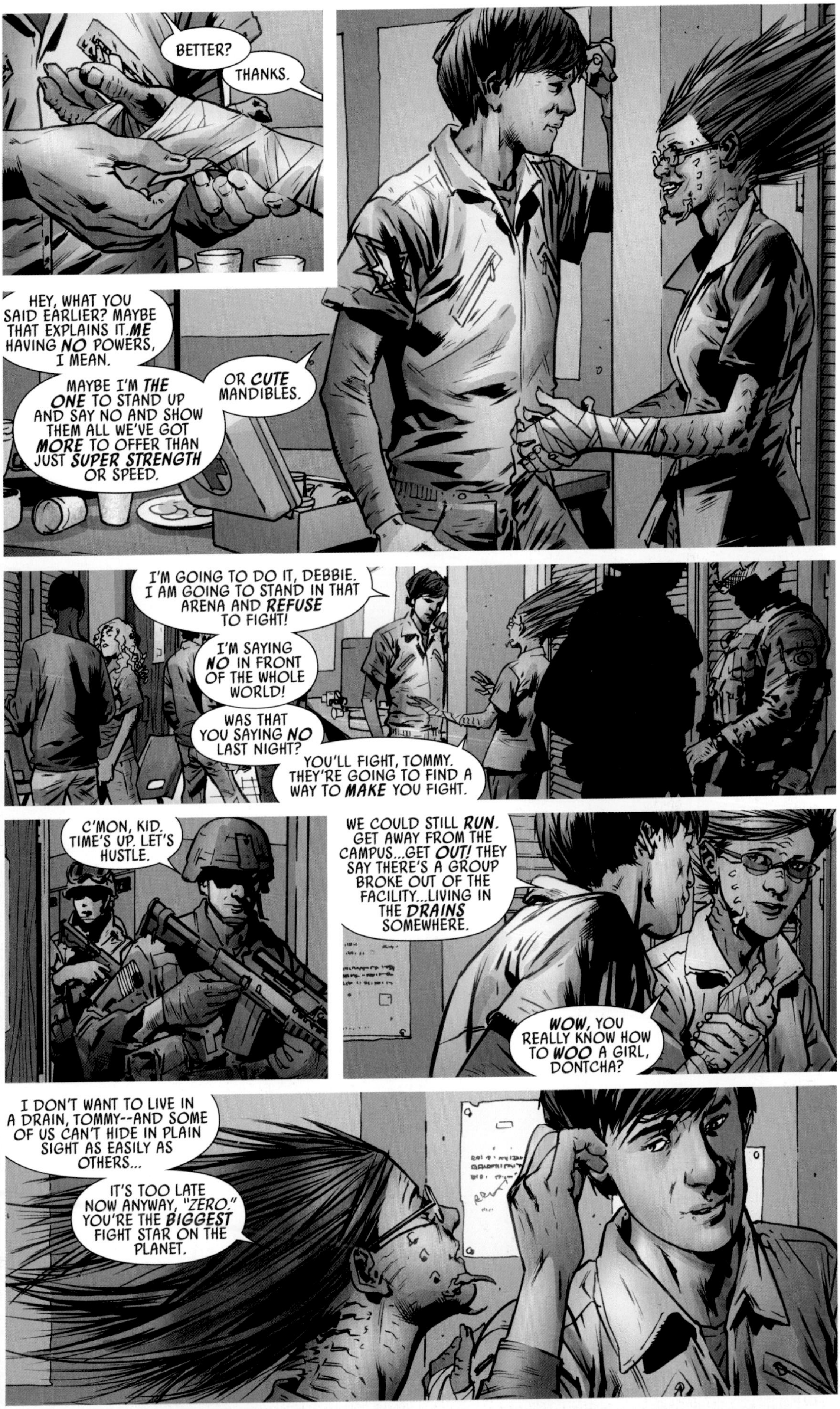
BETTER?
THANKS.
HEY, WHAT YOU SAID EARLIER? MAYBE THAT EXPLAINS IT. ME HAVING NO POWERS, I MEAN.
MAYBE I'M THE ONE TO STAND UP AND SAY NO AND SHOW THEM ALL WE'VE GOT MORE TO OFFER THAN JUST SUPER STRENGTH OR SPEED.
OR CUTE MANDIBLES.
I'M GOING TO DO IT, DEBBIE. I AM GOING TO STAND IN THAT ARENA AND REFUSE TO FIGHT!
I'M SAYING NO IN FRONT OF THE WHOLE WORLD!
WAS THAT YOU SAYING NO LAST NIGHT?
YOU'LL FIGHT, TOMMY. THEY'RE GOING TO FIND A WAY TO MAKE YOU FIGHT.
C'MON, KID. TIME'S UP. LET'S HUSTLE.
WE COULD STILL RUN. GET AWAY FROM THE CAMPUS...GET OUT! THEY SAY THERE'S A GROUP BROKE OUT OF THE FACILITY...LIVING IN THE DRAINS SOMEWHERE.
WOW, YOU REALLY KNOW HOW TO WOO A GIRL, DONTCHA?
I DON'T WANT TO LIVE IN A DRAIN, TOMMY--AND SOME OF US CAN'T HIDE IN PLAIN SIGHT AS EASILY AS OTHERS...
IT'S TOO LATE NOW ANYWAY, "ZERO." YOU'RE THE BIGGEST FIGHT STAR ON THE PLANET.

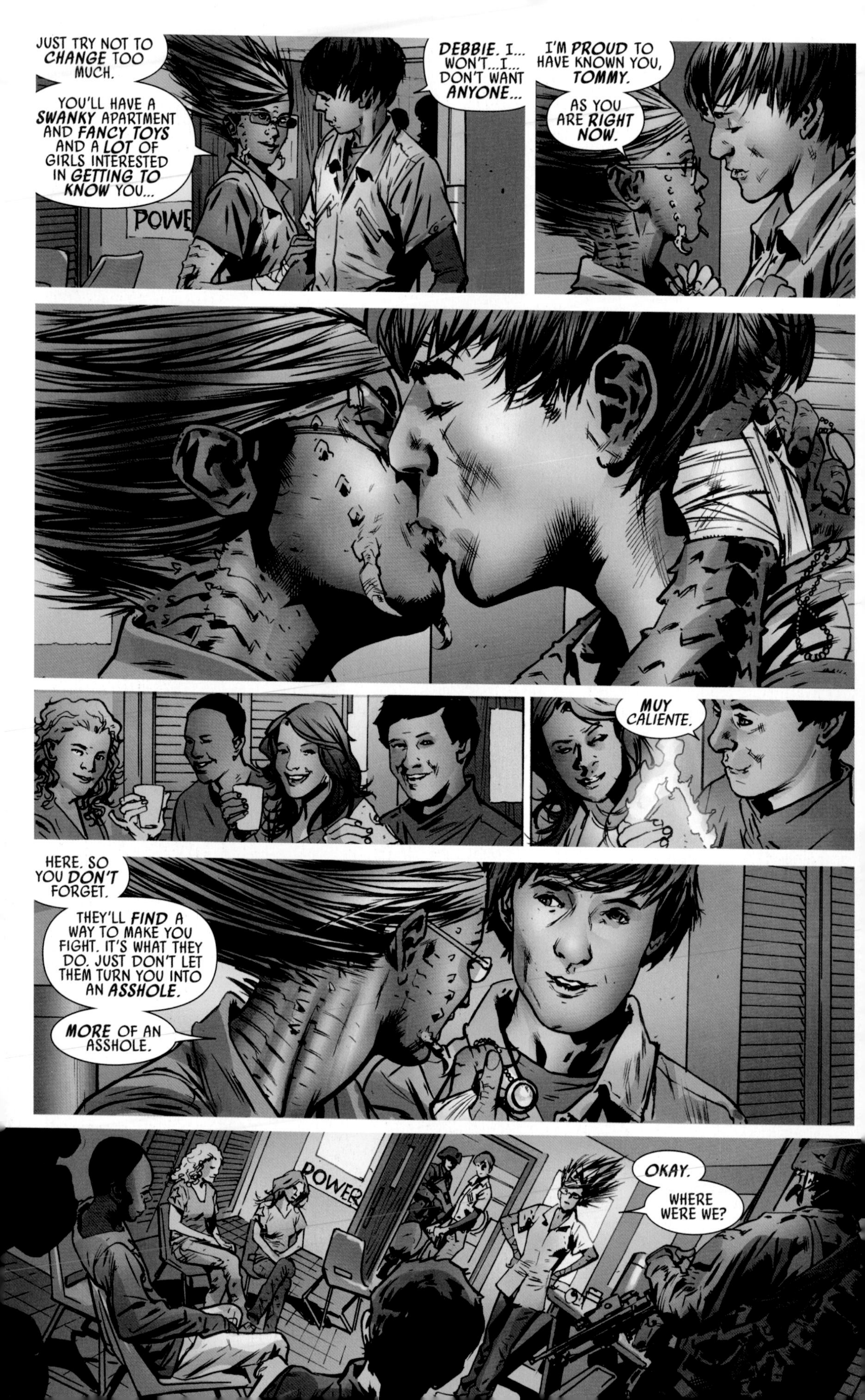
JUST TRY NOT TO CHANGE TOO MUCH.
YOU'LL HAVE A SWANKY APARTMENT AND FANCY TOYS AND A LOT OF GIRLS INTERESTED IN GETTING TO KNOW YOU...
POWE
DEBBIE. I... WON'T...I... DON'T WANT ANYONE...
I'M PROUD TO HAVE KNOWN YOU, TOMMY.
AS YOU ARE RIGHT NOW.
MUY CALIENTE.
HERE. SO YOU DON'T FORGET.
THEY'LL FIND A WAY TO MAKE YOU FIGHT. IT'S WHAT THEY DO. JUST DON'T LET THEM TURN YOU INTO AN ASSHOLE.
MORE OF AN ASSHOLE.
POWER
OKAY.
WHERE WERE WE?

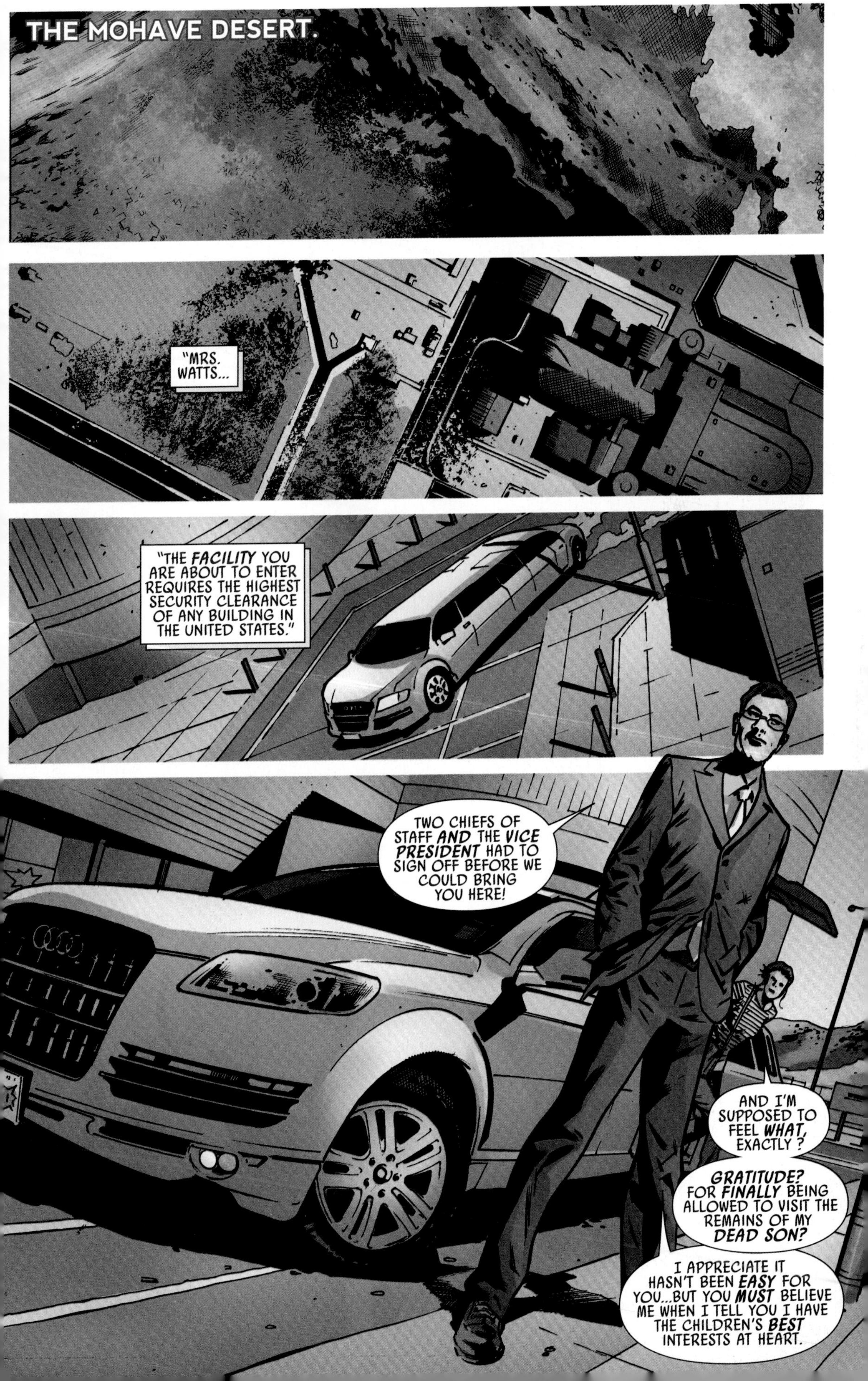
THE MOHAVE DESERT.
"MRS. WATTS...
"THE FACILITY YOU ARE ABOUT TO ENTER REQUIRES THE HIGHEST SECURITY CLEARANCE OF ANY BUILDING IN THE UNITED STATES."
TWO CHIEFS OF STAFF AND THE VICE PRESIDENT HAD TO SIGN OFF BEFORE WE COULD BRING YOU HERE!
AND I'M SUPPOSED TO FEEL WHAT, EXACTLY ?
GRATITUDE? FOR FINALLY BEING ALLOWED TO VISIT THE REMAINS OF MY DEAD SON?
I APPRECIATE IT HASN'T BEEN EASY FOR YOU...BUT YOU MUST BELIEVE ME WHEN I TELL YOU I HAVE THE CHILDREN'S BEST INTERESTS AT HEART.

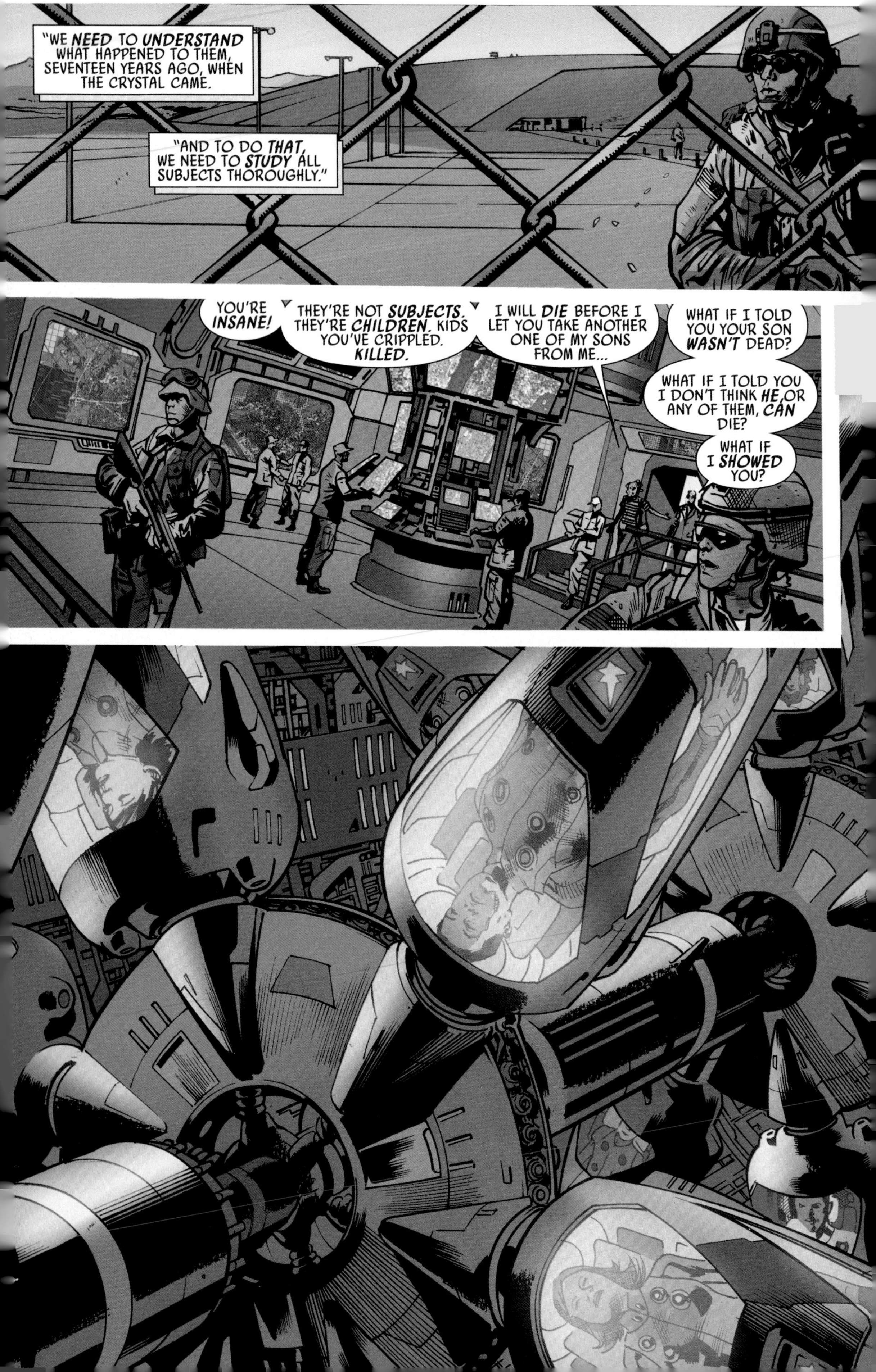
"WE NEED TO UNDERSTAND WHAT HAPPENED TO THEM, SEVENTEEN YEARS AGO, WHEN THE CRYSTAL CAME.
"AND TO DO THAT, WE NEED TO STUDY ALL SUBJECTS THOROUGHLY."
YOU'RE INSANE!
THEY'RE NOT SUBJECTS. THEY'RE CHILDREN. KIDS YOU'VE CRIPPLED. KILLED.
I WILL DIE BEFORE I LET YOU TAKE ANOTHER ONE OF MY SONS FROM ME...
WHAT IF I TOLD YOU YOUR SON WASN'T DEAD?
WHAT IF I TOLD YOU I DON'T THINK HE OR ANY OF THEM, CAN DIE?
WHAT IF I SHOWED YOU?

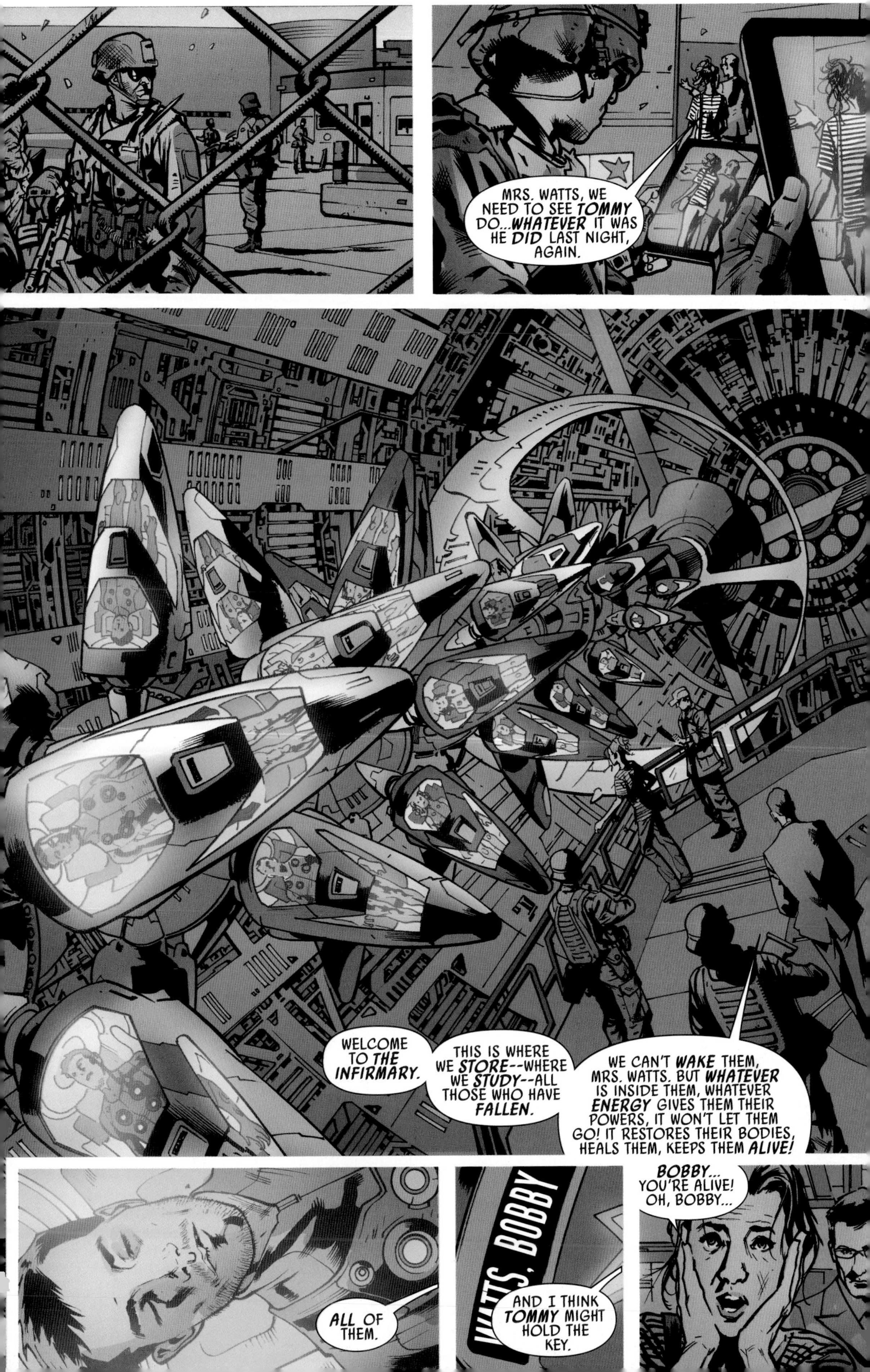
MRS. WATTS, WE NEED TO SEE TOMMY DO...WHATEVER IT WAS HE DID LAST NIGHT, AGAIN.
WELCOME TO THE INFIRMARY.
THIS IS WHERE WE STORE--WHERE WE STUDY--ALL THOSE WHO HAVE FALLEN.
WE CAN'T WAKE THEM, MRS. WATTS. BUT WHATEVER IS INSIDE THEM, WHATEVER ENERGY GIVES THEM THEIR POWERS, IT WON'T LET THEM GO! IT RESTORES THEIR BODIES, HEALS THEM, KEEPS THEM ALIVE!
ALL OF THEM.
WATTS, BOBBY
AND I THINK TOMMY MIGHT HOLD THE KEY.
BOBBY... YOU'RE ALIVE! OH, BOBBY...

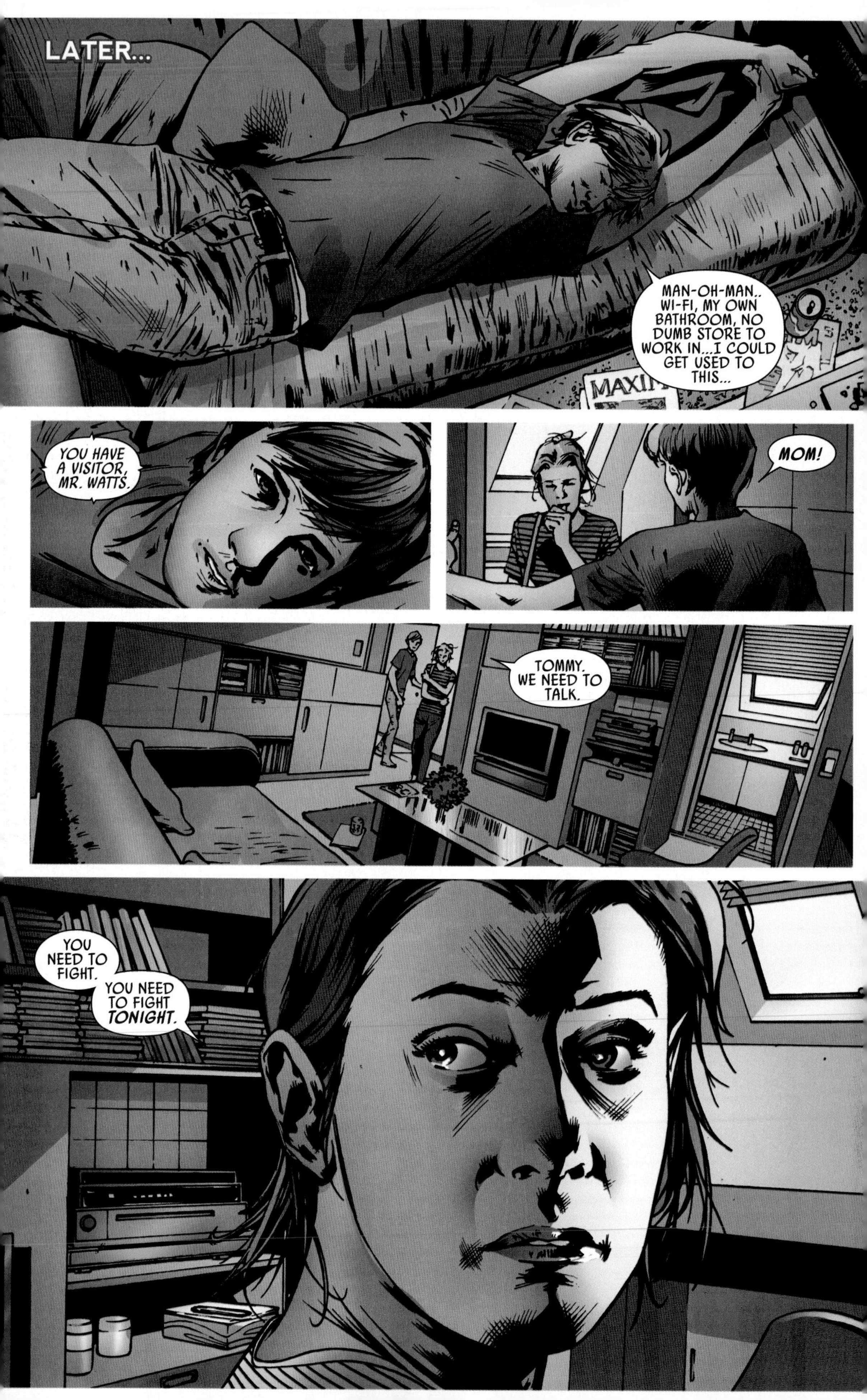
LATER...
MAN-OH-MAN.. WI-FI, MY OWN BATHROOM, NO DUMB STORE TO WORK IN...I COULD GET USED TO THIS...
MAXIM
YOU HAVE A VISITOR, MR. WATTS.
MOM!
TOMMY. WE NEED TO TALK.
YOU NEED TO FIGHT.
YOU NEED TO FIGHT TONIGHT.

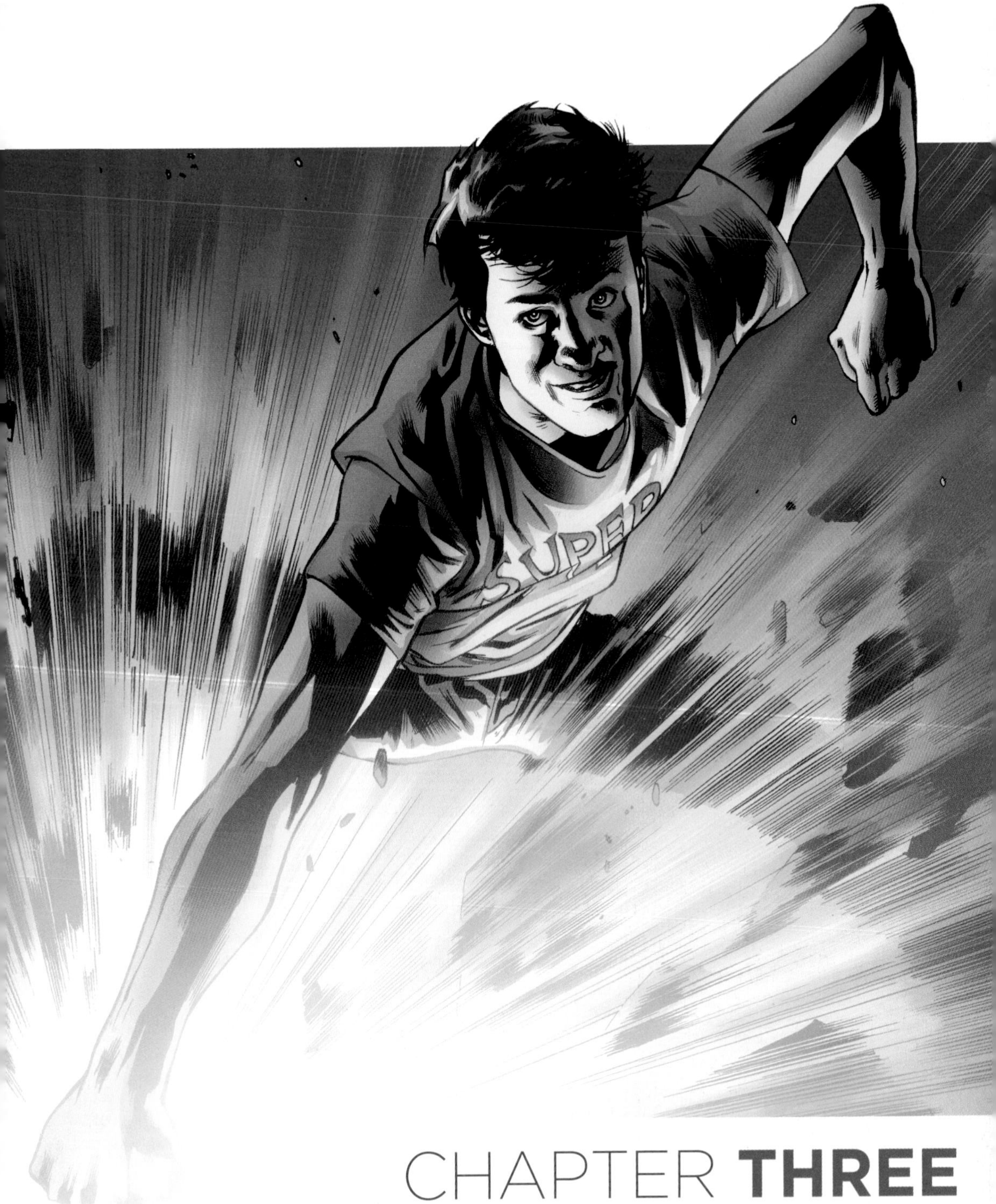
SUPER

CHAPTER **THREE**

Ex-Inmates sue U.S. Gov't over research

A group of nearly 30 former powered individuals has filed a civil suit against the federal government for carrying out experiments on them between 2003 and 2012. The suit, filed in San Francisco's Court of Common Pleas in October, accuses the government of "negligence, carelessness, and recklessness" in "allowing infectious diseases, radioactive isotopes, dioxin, and psychotropic drugs" to be tested on the former rioters "without their knowledge or consent." The prisoners also named the City of San Francisco, AWJ Chemical Company, the Johnson and Burroughs pharmaceutical firm, and Syell's Ivy Research Laboratories in their suit.

—operates within a system of strict rules and regulations concerning the use of human subjects in research. As part of the current framework governing such university-based research, formally established bodies known as Institutional Review Boards—which consist of scientists, ethicists, and members of the local community—review all proposed research involving human subjects for compliance with an array of ethical and other considerations."

"Their institution has a legacy, and this legacy carries on even into today," responded Levene, "and they're morally obligated to answer to wrongs that institutions did despite the circumstances that led to the research. They can't use the excuse of the passage of time. It was wrong then and it's wrong now."

FOR OFFICIAL USE ONLY

CHEMICAL AND BIOLOGICAL POWERS TESTING PROGI

The use of meta-human subjects will be allowed for the testing of chemical and biologic Department of Defense, accounting to Congressional committees with respect to the ex

The Secretary of Defense [may] conduct tests and experiments involving the use of ch agents on meta-human civilian populations within the United States

It is desired that no document be released which refers to experiments with meta-hur reaction on public opinion or result in legal suits. Documents covering such fieldwo

Sycorps

Test:
Bravo
Time:
18:45:00.0 28 February 2004 (GMT)
06:45:00.0 1 March 1 2004 (local)
Location:
Syco Laboratory 7 E/C room
Test Duration and Type:

Extreme pressure (equivalent to 2000 feet below surface)

15 Mt
M/H 0016 tested in 7 was an extreme stress trauma simulation. This was the first "deep" pressure test., and t with no opt-out for the subject. It was the greatest amount of pressure possible to create under current lab conditions. although this was by accident. The ability of M/H 0016 to withstand the force dramatically exceeded predictions, being about [redacted] higher than the best guess and almos [redacted] the estimated maximum possible resistance. (6 Mt predicted, estimated survival range 4-8 Mt).

The Shrimp test device was basically a [redacted] version of the Runt device tested in Castle Romeo, but with partially enriched [redacted] as fuel. Its weight was a comparatively light 23,500 lb, and it was 179.5 in long and 53.9 in wide. The fuel consisted of [redacted] enriched [redacted] deuteride encased in a natural uranium tamper. [redacted] Mt of the yield was from fast fission of the tamper. The Shrimp also tested light case design, substituting an aluminum exterior case for the steel used in the Sausage (tested in Ivy Mike). It used a RACER IV [redacted] primary.

The reason for the unexpectedly high yield was due to the "tritium bonus" provided by the [redacted] which made up most of the [redacted]. This isotope was expected to be essentially inert, but in fact it had a [redacted] reaction cross section with the high energy neutrons produced by tritium-deuterium fusion. When one of these high energy [redacted] collided with a [redacted] atom, it could fragment it into a tritium and a helium atom. [redacted] was the most valuable fusion fuel, being both highly reactive and causing extremely energetic fusion, so this extra source of [redacted] greatly increased the weapon yield.

Within 15 minutes after the test radiation levels began climbing level in control bunker reached x12 previous levels, which was supposed to be reaction created by subject now believed to be immune to fallout. An hour after the shot the level had reached [redacted], and personnel had to retreat from the control room to the most heavily shielded room of the bunker until they could be rescued 11 hours later. Subject remained untroubled by exposure and subsequent tests revealed no damage.

FOR OFFICIAL USE ONLY

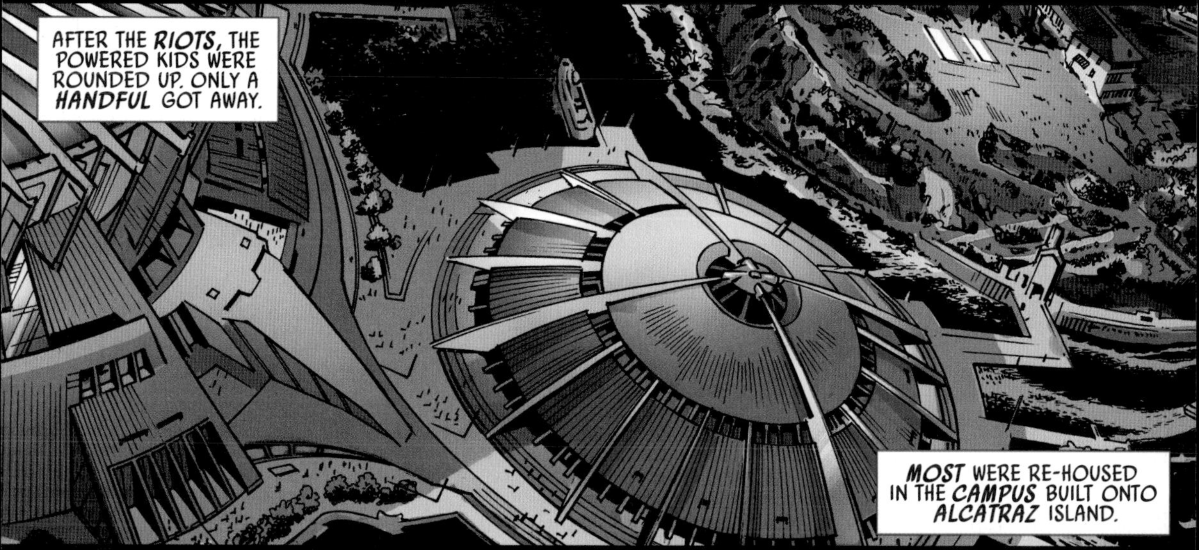
AFTER THE RIOTS, THE POWERED KIDS WERE ROUNDED UP. ONLY A HANDFUL GOT AWAY.
MOST WERE RE-HOUSED IN THE CAMPUS BUILT ONTO ALCATRAZ ISLAND.

January 2008
Persons of the Year
TIME
The Visionaries
General John Burr
Senator Susan Handler
Aaron Walker Junior
Professor Colin Syell
The Military, Bio-Ethics, Big Business and the Solution to San Francisco's 'Problem' Children

BUT ALL THOSE FOUND GUILTY OF *VIOLENT DISORDER* WERE SENT *HERE*.

HIGH SECURITY GOVERNMENT DETENTION CENTER AND RESEARCH FACILITY.

THE MOJAVE DESERT.

WHERE THEY COULD BE CONTAINED.

WHERE THEY COULD DO NO MORE *HARM*.

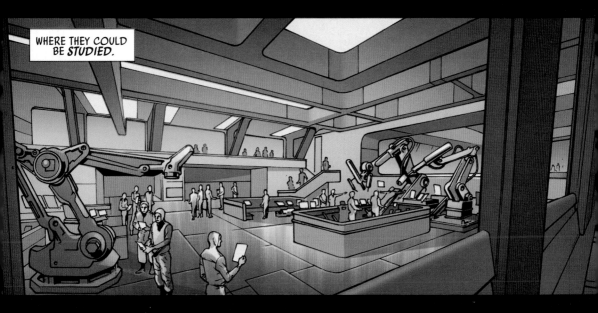

WHERE THEY COULD BE *STUDIED*.

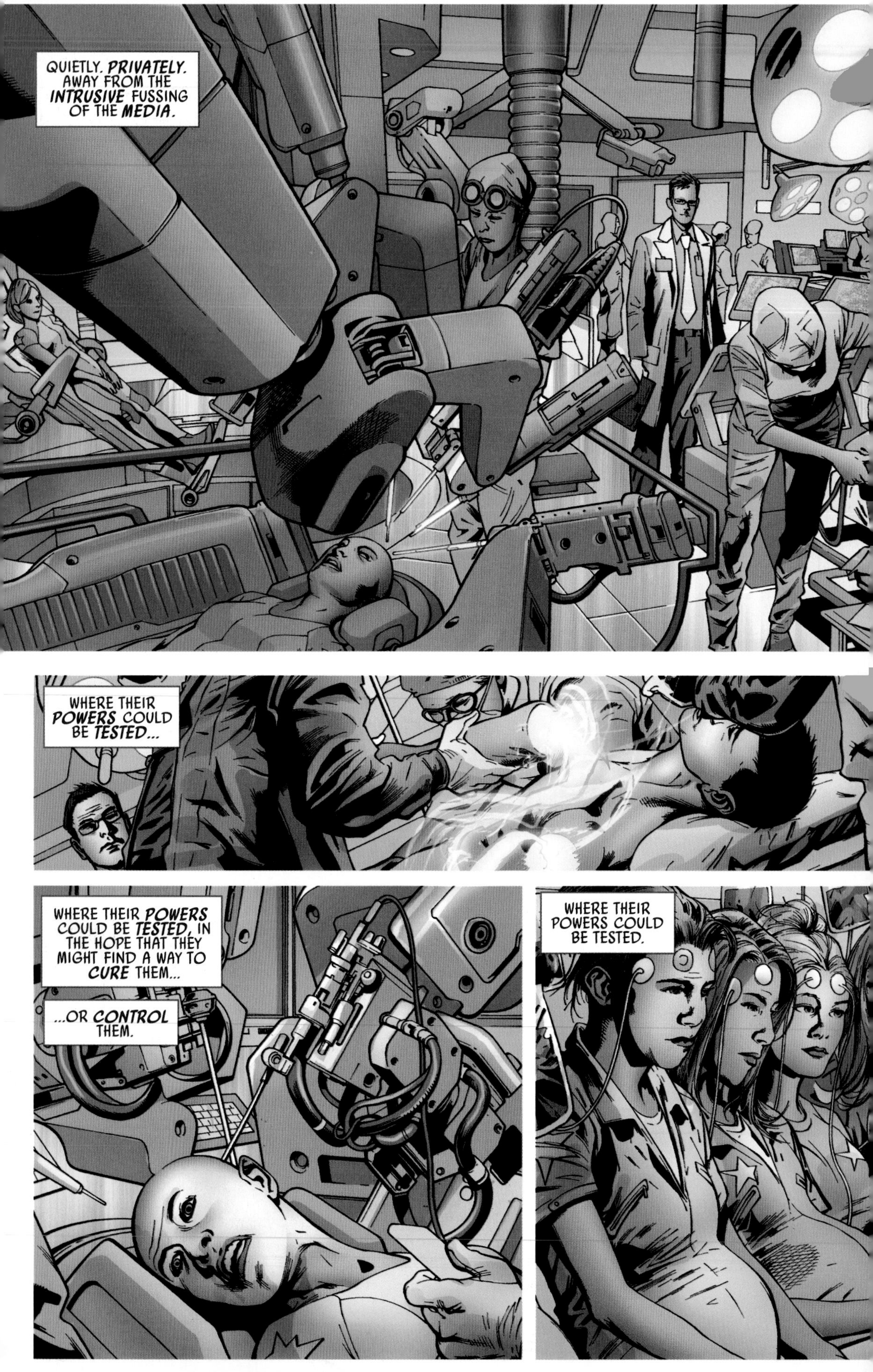
QUIETLY. PRIVATELY. AWAY FROM THE INTRUSIVE FUSSING OF THE MEDIA.
WHERE THEIR POWERS COULD BE TESTED...
WHERE THEIR POWERS COULD BE TESTED, IN THE HOPE THAT THEY MIGHT FIND A WAY TO CURE THEM...
...OR CONTROL THEM.
WHERE THEIR POWERS COULD BE TESTED.

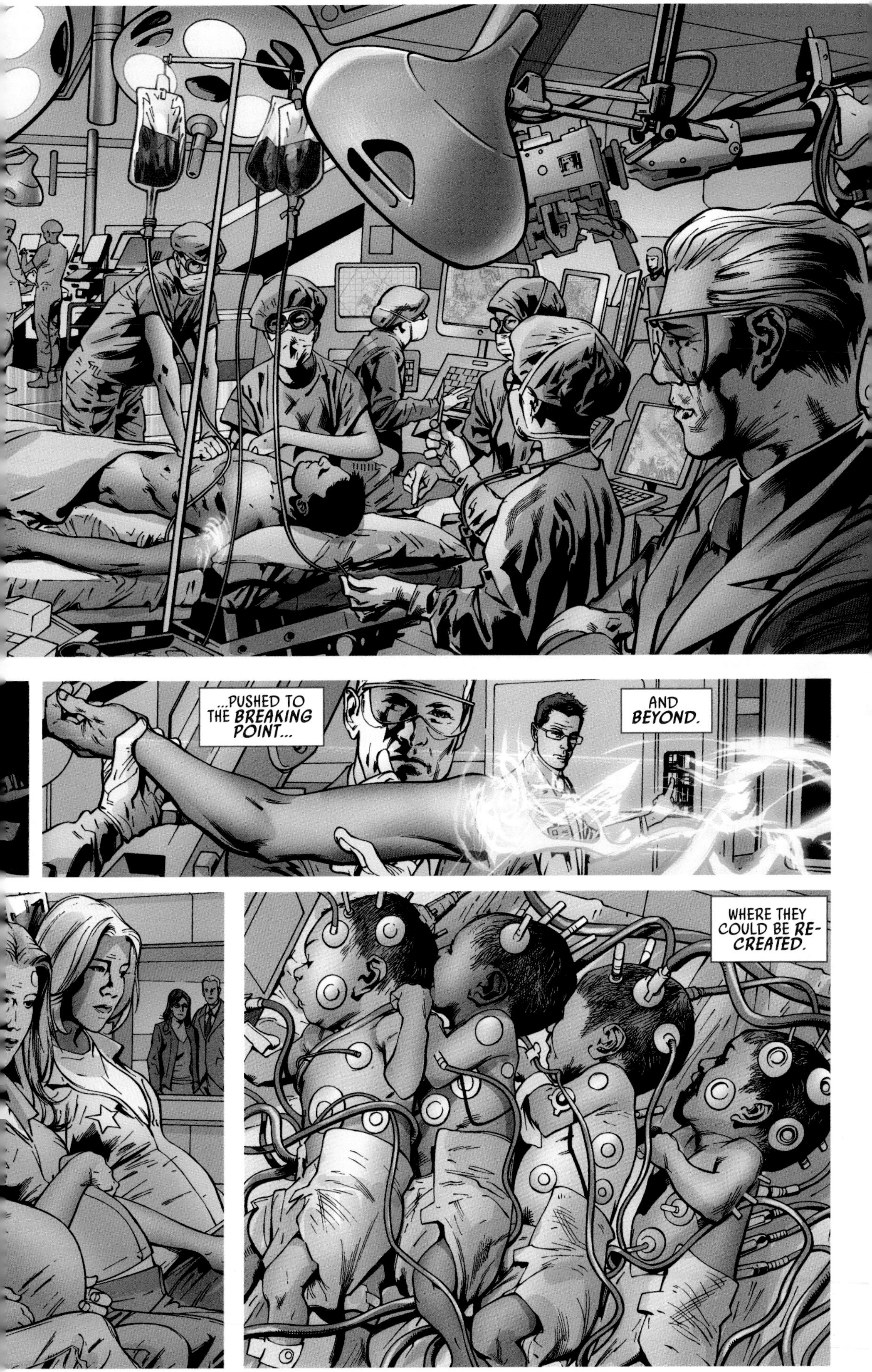
...PUSHED TO THE BREAKING POINT...
AND BEYOND.
WHERE THEY COULD BE RE-CREATED.

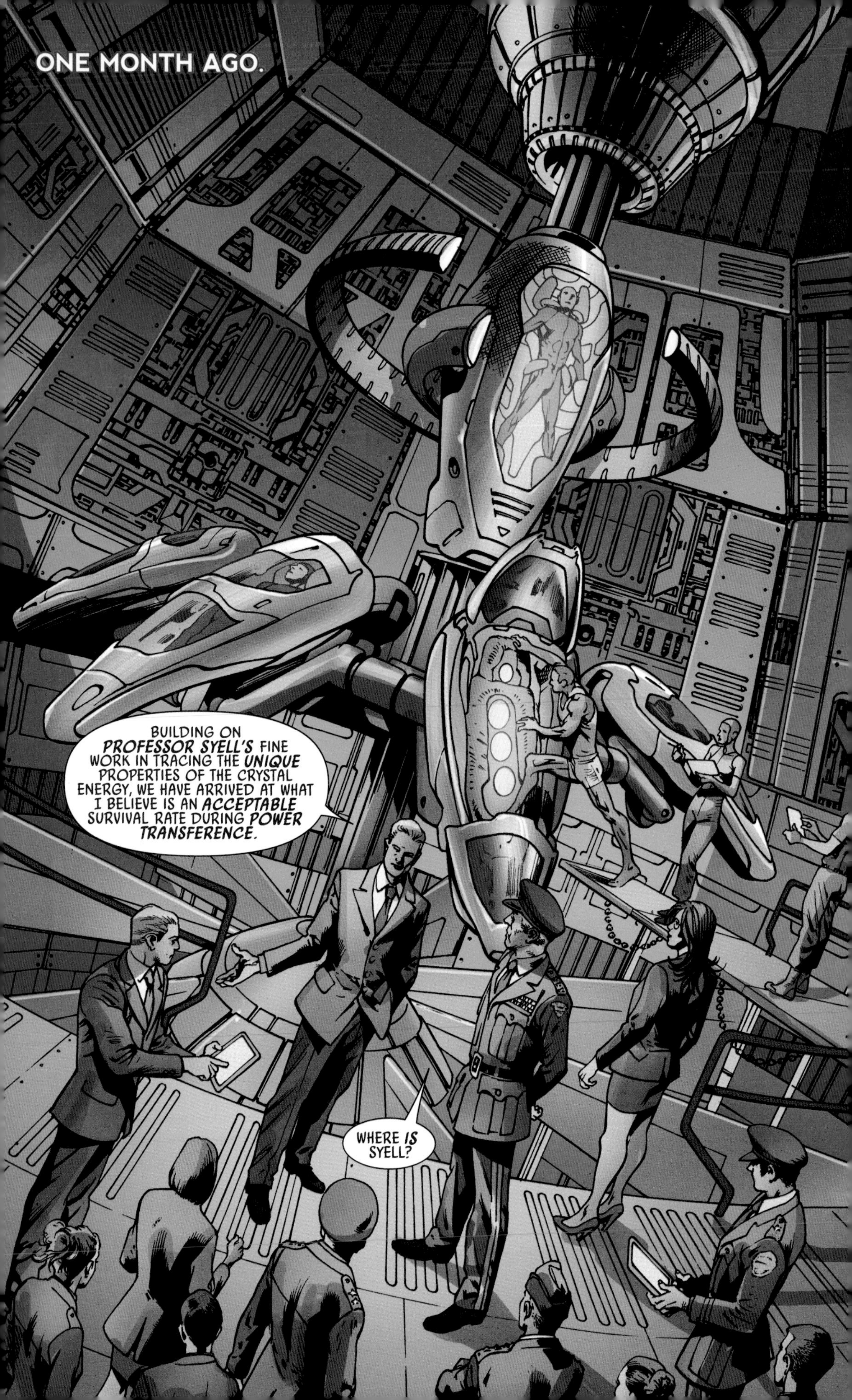
ONE MONTH AGO.
BUILDING ON PROFESSOR SYELL'S FINE WORK IN TRACING THE UNIQUE PROPERTIES OF THE CRYSTAL ENERGY, WE HAVE ARRIVED AT WHAT I BELIEVE IS AN ACCEPTABLE SURVIVAL RATE DURING POWER TRANSFERENCE.
WHERE IS SYELL?

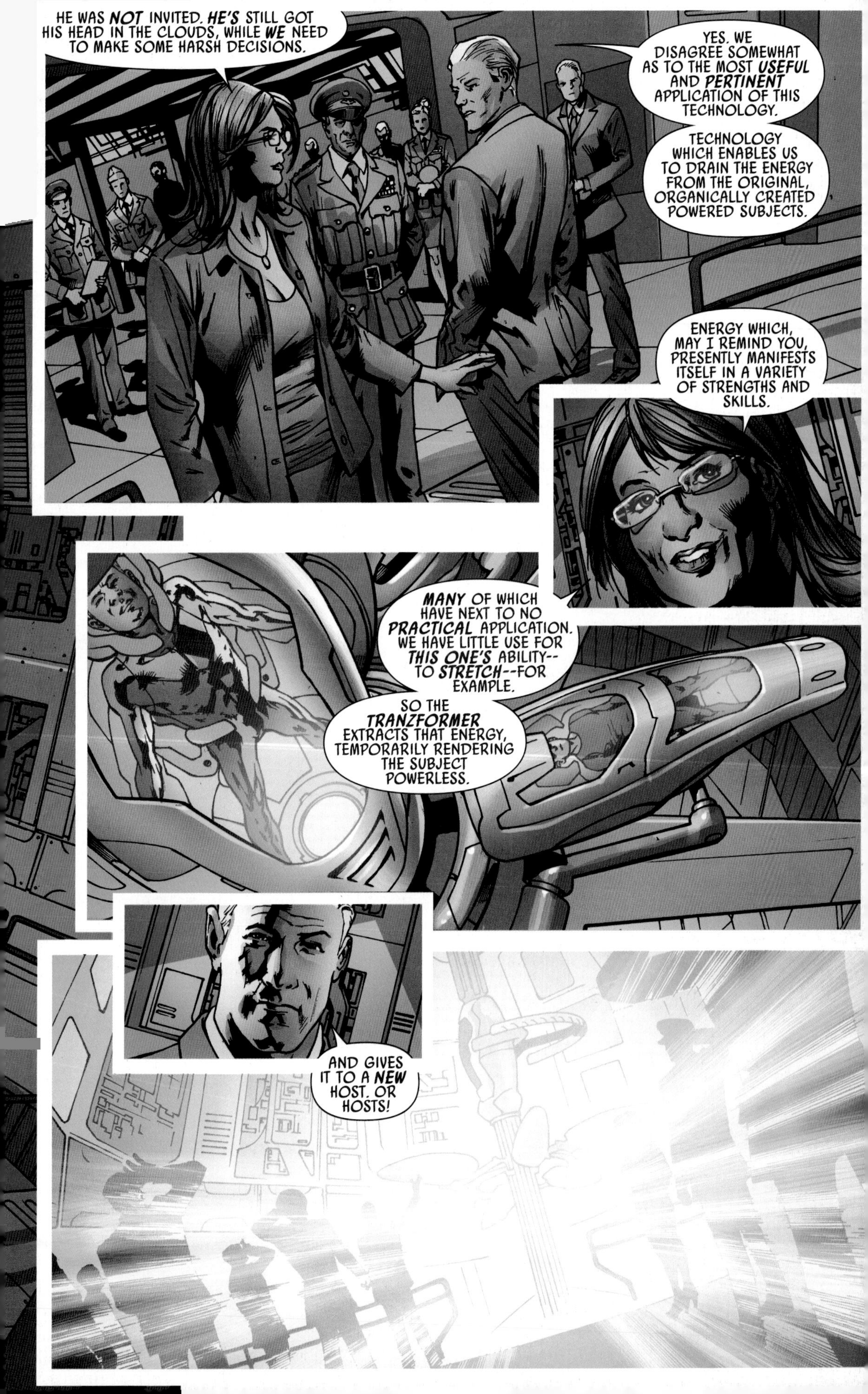
HE WAS NOT INVITED. HE'S STILL GOT HIS HEAD IN THE CLOUDS, WHILE WE NEED TO MAKE SOME HARSH DECISIONS.
YES. WE DISAGREE SOMEWHAT AS TO THE MOST USEFUL AND PERTINENT APPLICATION OF THIS TECHNOLOGY.
TECHNOLOGY WHICH ENABLES US TO DRAIN THE ENERGY FROM THE ORIGINAL, ORGANICALLY CREATED POWERED SUBJECTS.
ENERGY WHICH, MAY I REMIND YOU, PRESENTLY MANIFESTS ITSELF IN A VARIETY OF STRENGTHS AND SKILLS.
MANY OF WHICH HAVE NEXT TO NO PRACTICAL APPLICATION. WE HAVE LITTLE USE FOR THIS ONE'S ABILITY--TO STRETCH--FOR EXAMPLE.
SO THE TRANZFORMER EXTRACTS THAT ENERGY, TEMPORARILY RENDERING THE SUBJECT POWERLESS.
AND GIVES IT TO A NEW HOST. OR HOSTS!

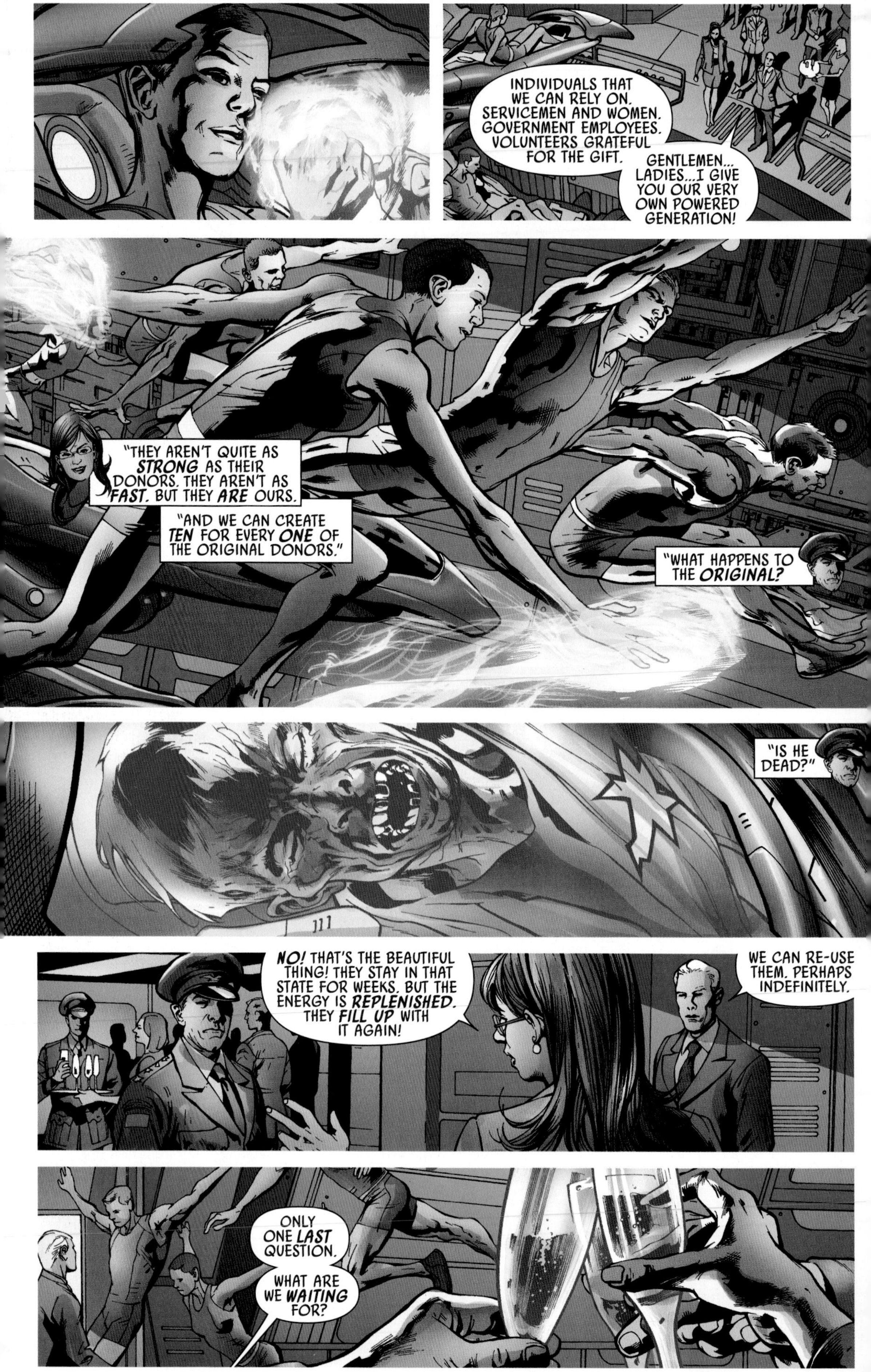
INDIVIDUALS THAT WE CAN RELY ON. SERVICEMEN AND WOMEN. GOVERNMENT EMPLOYEES. VOLUNTEERS GRATEFUL FOR THE GIFT.
GENTLEMEN... LADIES...I GIVE YOU OUR VERY OWN POWERED GENERATION!
"THEY AREN'T QUITE AS STRONG AS THEIR DONORS. THEY AREN'T AS FAST. BUT THEY ARE OURS.
"AND WE CAN CREATE TEN FOR EVERY ONE OF THE ORIGINAL DONORS."
"WHAT HAPPENS TO THE ORIGINAL?
"IS HE DEAD?"
NO! THAT'S THE BEAUTIFUL THING! THEY STAY IN THAT STATE FOR WEEKS. BUT THE ENERGY IS REPLENISHED. THEY FILL UP WITH IT AGAIN!
WE CAN RE-USE THEM. PERHAPS INDEFINITELY.
ONLY ONE LAST QUESTION.
WHAT ARE WE WAITING FOR?

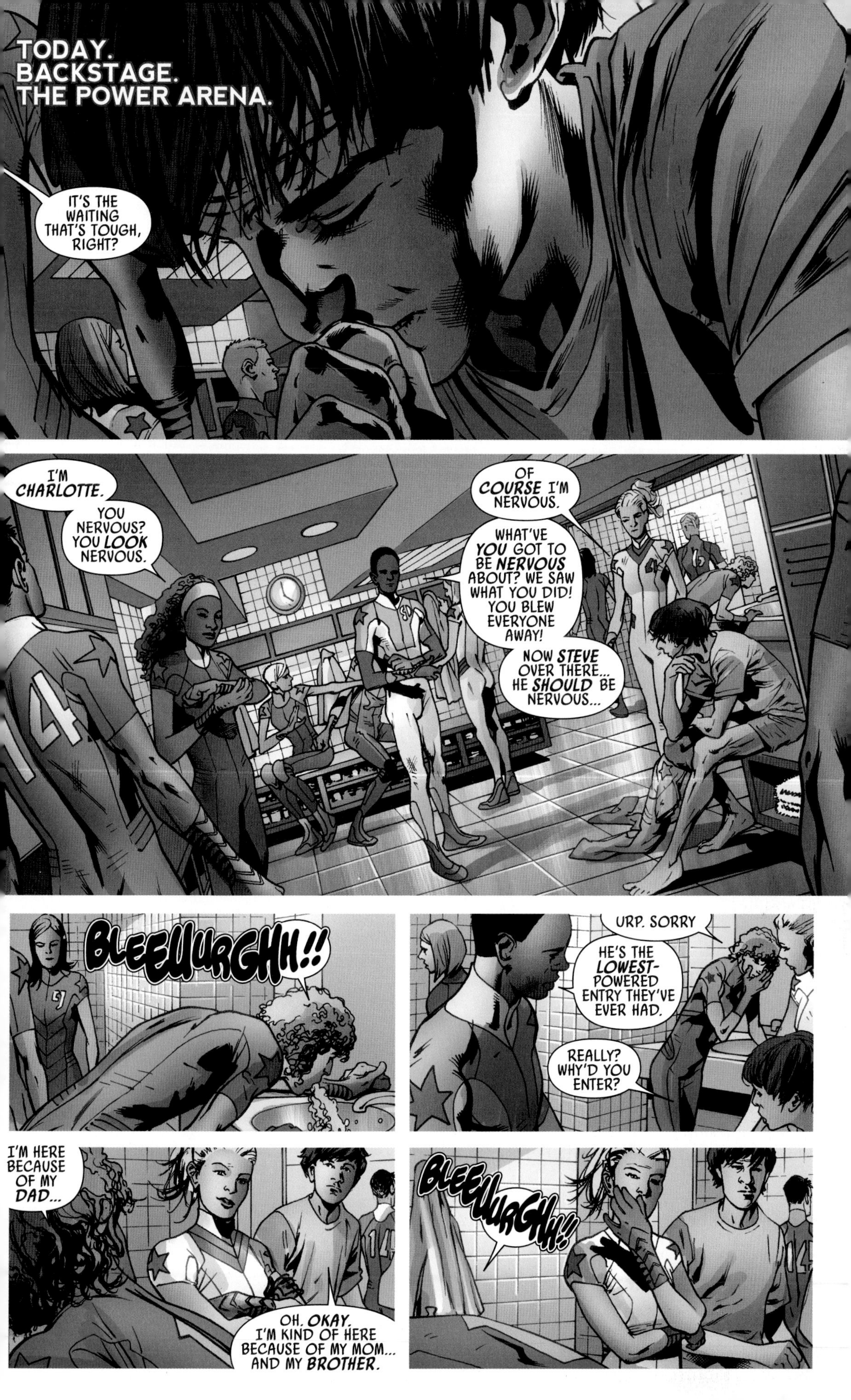
TODAY.
BACKSTAGE.
THE POWER ARENA.
IT'S THE WAITING THAT'S TOUGH, RIGHT?
I'M CHARLOTTE.
YOU NERVOUS? YOU LOOK NERVOUS.
OF COURSE I'M NERVOUS.
WHAT'VE YOU GOT TO BE NERVOUS ABOUT? WE SAW WHAT YOU DID! YOU BLEW EVERYONE AWAY!
NOW STEVE OVER THERE... HE SHOULD BE NERVOUS...
BLEEUURGHH!!
URP. SORRY
HE'S THE LOWEST-POWERED ENTRY THEY'VE EVER HAD.
REALLY? WHY'D YOU ENTER?
I'M HERE BECAUSE OF MY DAD...
OH. OKAY. I'M KIND OF HERE BECAUSE OF MY MOM... AND MY BROTHER.
BLEEUURGHH!!

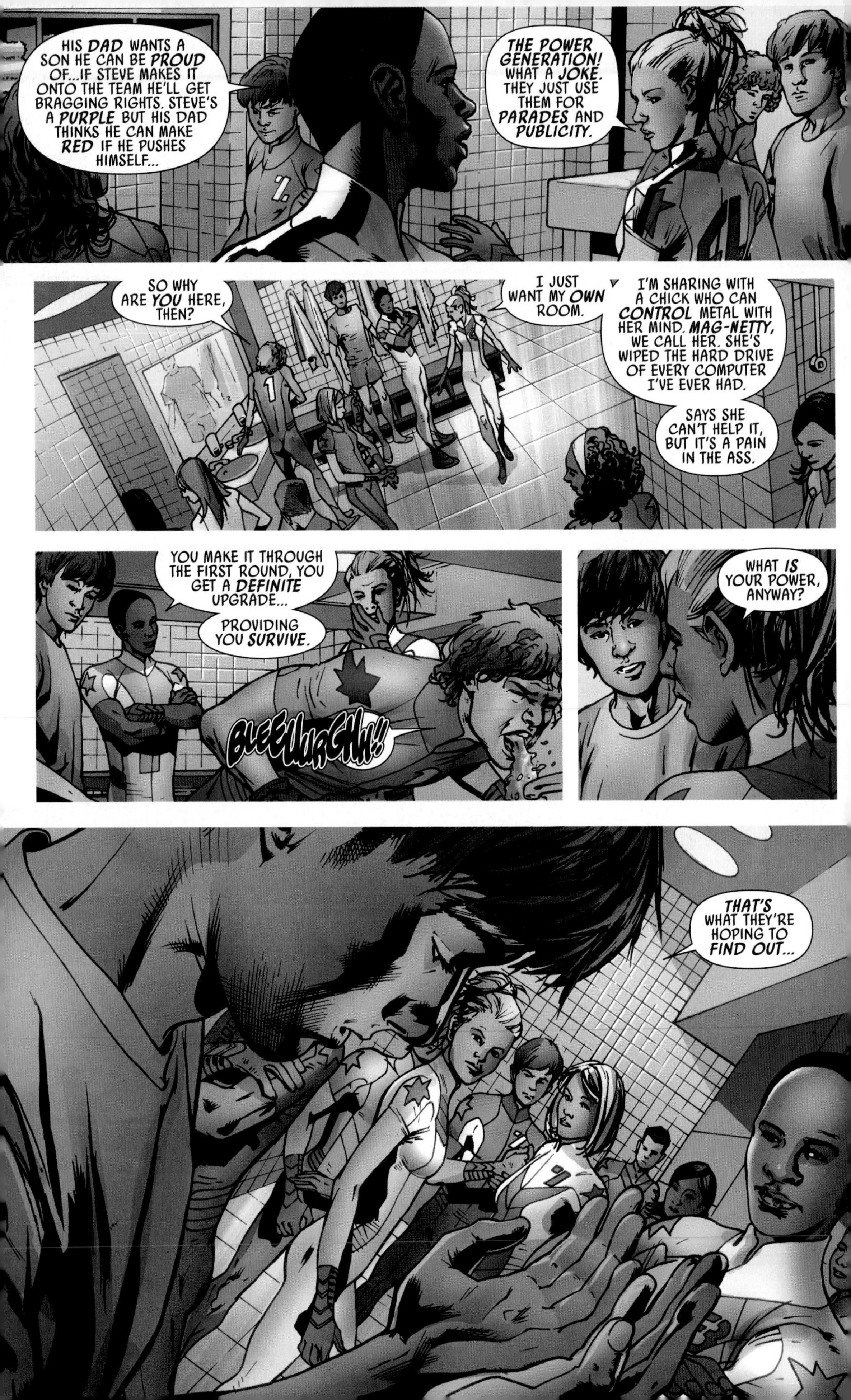

HIS DAD WANTS A SON HE CAN BE PROUD OF...IF STEVE MAKES IT ONTO THE TEAM HE'LL GET BRAGGING RIGHTS. STEVE'S A PURPLE BUT HIS DAD THINKS HE CAN MAKE RED IF HE PUSHES HIMSELF...
THE POWER GENERATION! WHAT A JOKE. THEY JUST USE THEM FOR PARADES AND PUBLICITY.
SO WHY ARE YOU HERE, THEN?
I JUST WANT MY OWN ROOM.
I'M SHARING WITH A CHICK WHO CAN CONTROL METAL WITH HER MIND. MAG-NETTY, WE CALL HER. SHE'S WIPED THE HARD DRIVE OF EVERY COMPUTER I'VE EVER HAD.
SAYS SHE CAN'T HELP IT, BUT IT'S A PAIN IN THE ASS.
YOU MAKE IT THROUGH THE FIRST ROUND, YOU GET A DEFINITE UPGRADE...
PROVIDING YOU SURVIVE.
BLEEUURGHH!!
WHAT IS YOUR POWER, ANYWAY?
THAT'S WHAT THEY'RE HOPING TO FIND OUT...

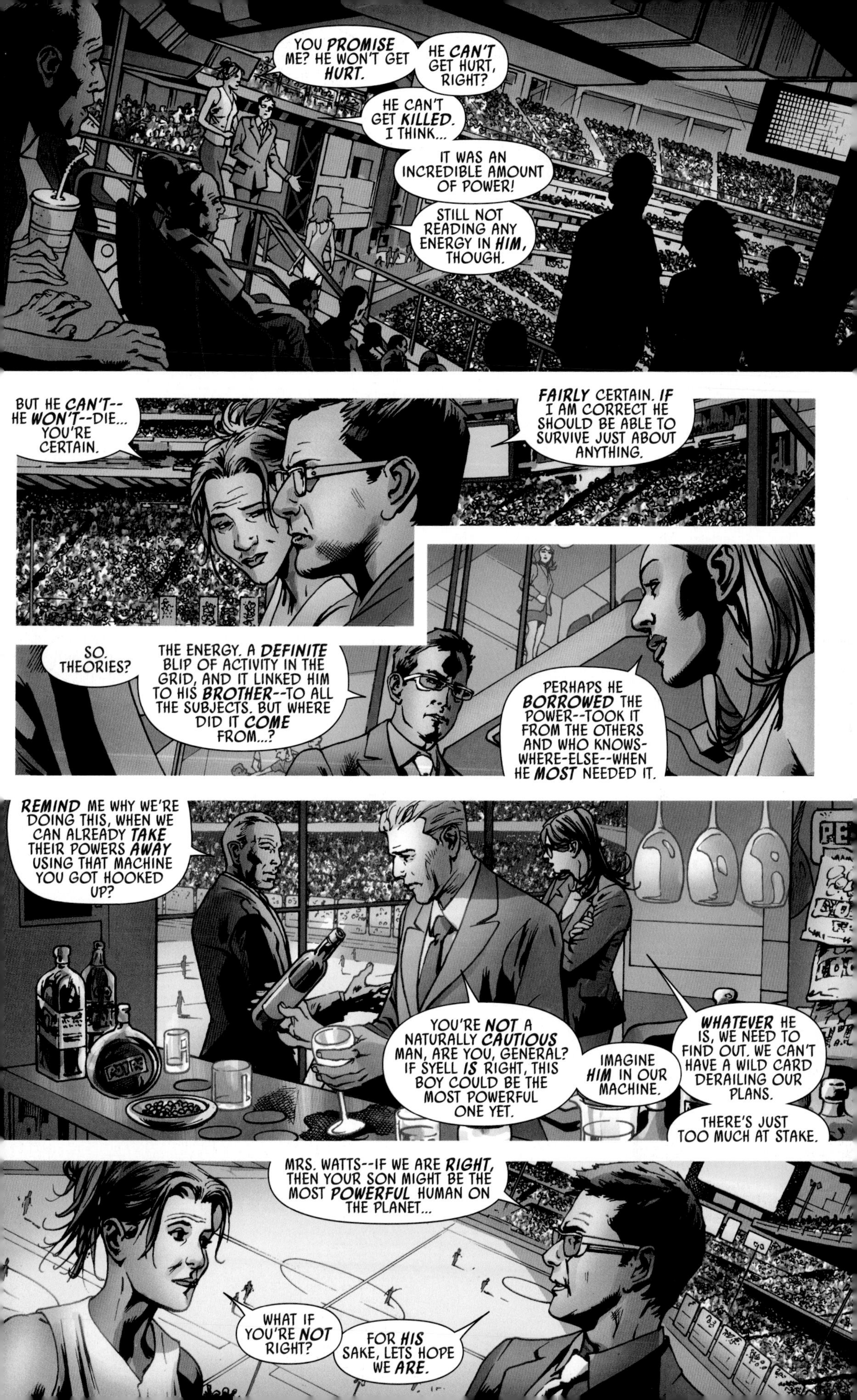
YOU PROMISE ME? HE WON'T GET HURT.
HE CAN'T GET HURT, RIGHT?
HE CAN'T GET KILLED. I THINK...
IT WAS AN INCREDIBLE AMOUNT OF POWER!
STILL NOT READING ANY ENERGY IN HIM, THOUGH.
BUT HE CAN'T--HE WON'T--DIE... YOU'RE CERTAIN.
FAIRLY CERTAIN. IF I AM CORRECT HE SHOULD BE ABLE TO SURVIVE JUST ABOUT ANYTHING.
SO. THEORIES?
THE ENERGY. A DEFINITE BLIP OF ACTIVITY IN THE GRID, AND IT LINKED HIM TO HIS BROTHER--TO ALL THE SUBJECTS. BUT WHERE DID IT COME FROM...?
PERHAPS HE BORROWED THE POWER--TOOK IT FROM THE OTHERS AND WHO KNOWS-WHERE-ELSE--WHEN HE MOST NEEDED IT.
REMIND ME WHY WE'RE DOING THIS, WHEN WE CAN ALREADY TAKE THEIR POWERS AWAY USING THAT MACHINE YOU GOT HOOKED UP?
YOU'RE NOT A NATURALLY CAUTIOUS MAN, ARE YOU, GENERAL? IF SYELL IS RIGHT, THIS BOY COULD BE THE MOST POWERFUL ONE YET.
IMAGINE HIM IN OUR MACHINE.
WHATEVER HE IS, WE NEED TO FIND OUT. WE CAN'T HAVE A WILD CARD DERAILING OUR PLANS.
THERE'S JUST TOO MUCH AT STAKE.
MRS. WATTS--IF WE ARE RIGHT, THEN YOUR SON MIGHT BE THE MOST POWERFUL HUMAN ON THE PLANET...
WHAT IF YOU'RE NOT RIGHT?
FOR HIS SAKE, LETS HOPE WE ARE.

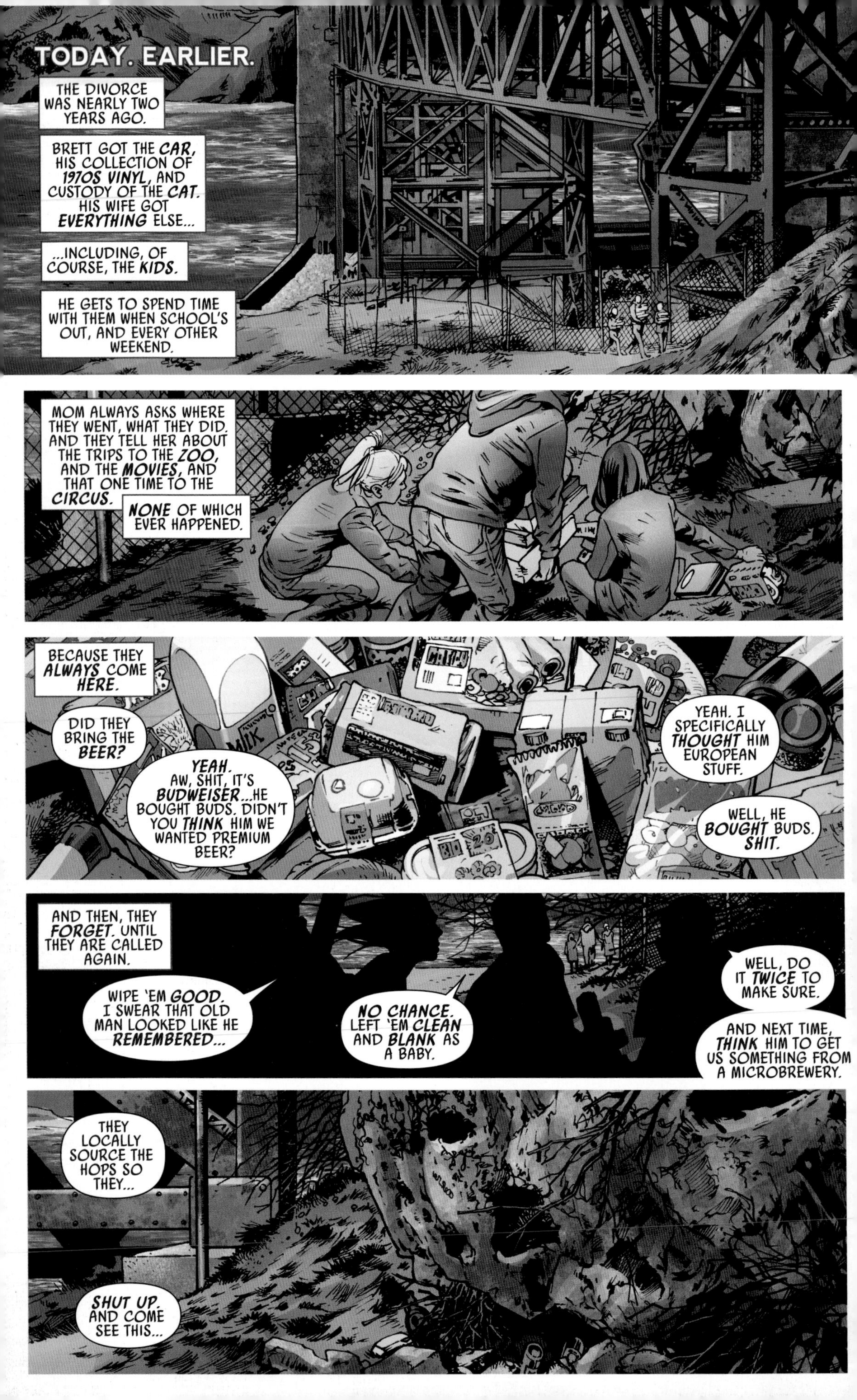
TODAY. EARLIER.
THE DIVORCE WAS NEARLY TWO YEARS AGO.
BRETT GOT THE CAR, HIS COLLECTION OF 1970S VINYL, AND CUSTODY OF THE CAT. HIS WIFE GOT EVERYTHING ELSE...
...INCLUDING, OF COURSE, THE KIDS.
HE GETS TO SPEND TIME WITH THEM WHEN SCHOOL'S OUT, AND EVERY OTHER WEEKEND.
MOM ALWAYS ASKS WHERE THEY WENT, WHAT THEY DID. AND THEY TELL HER ABOUT THE TRIPS TO THE ZOO, AND THE MOVIES, AND THAT ONE TIME TO THE CIRCUS.
NONE OF WHICH EVER HAPPENED.
BECAUSE THEY ALWAYS COME HERE.
DID THEY BRING THE BEER?
YEAH. AW, SHIT, IT'S BUDWEISER...HE BOUGHT BUDS. DIDN'T YOU THINK HIM WE WANTED PREMIUM BEER?
YEAH. I SPECIFICALLY THOUGHT HIM EUROPEAN STUFF.
WELL, HE BOUGHT BUDS. SHIT.
AND THEN, THEY FORGET. UNTIL THEY ARE CALLED AGAIN.
WIPE 'EM GOOD. I SWEAR THAT OLD MAN LOOKED LIKE HE REMEMBERED...
NO CHANCE. LEFT 'EM CLEAN AND BLANK AS A BABY.
WELL, DO IT TWICE TO MAKE SURE.
AND NEXT TIME, THINK HIM TO GET US SOMETHING FROM A MICROBREWERY.
THEY LOCALLY SOURCE THE HOPS SO THEY...
SHUT UP. AND COME SEE THIS...

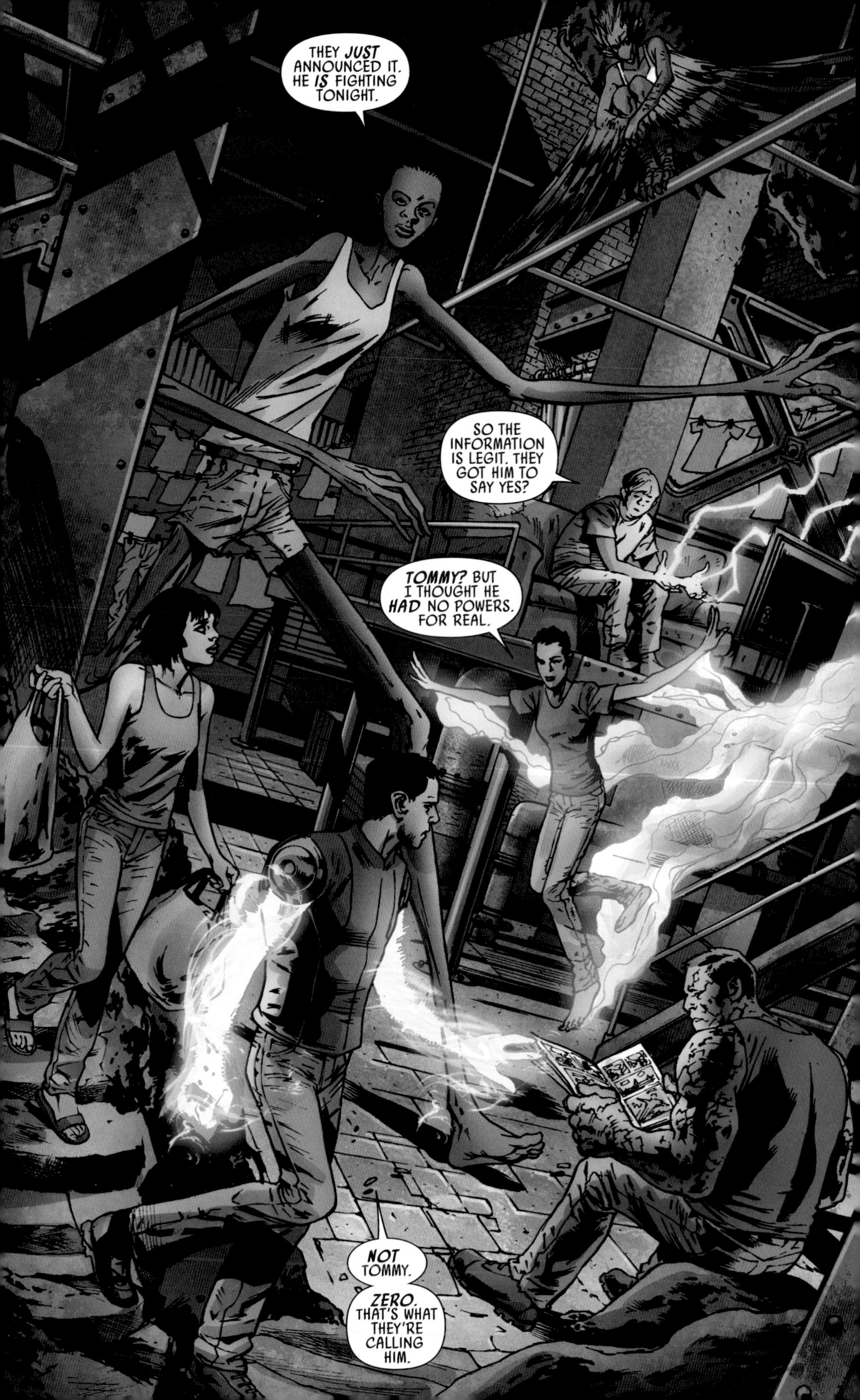
THEY JUST ANNOUNCED IT. HE IS FIGHTING TONIGHT.
SO THE INFORMATION IS LEGIT. THEY GOT HIM TO SAY YES?
TOMMY? BUT I THOUGHT HE HAD NO POWERS. FOR REAL.
NOT TOMMY.
ZERO. THAT'S WHAT THEY'RE CALLING HIM.

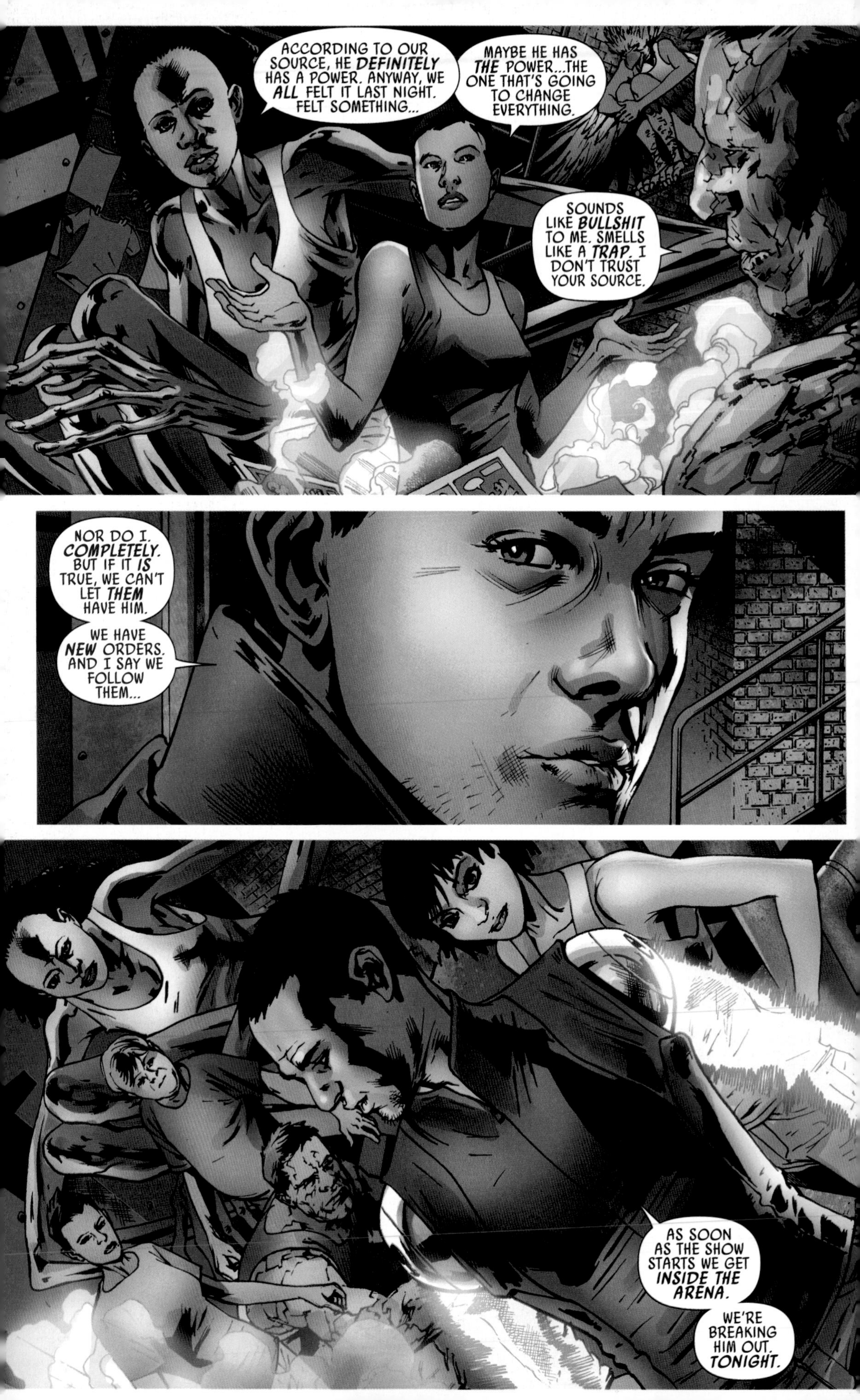
ACCORDING TO OUR SOURCE, HE DEFINITELY HAS A POWER. ANYWAY, WE ALL FELT IT LAST NIGHT. FELT SOMETHING...
MAYBE HE HAS THE POWER...THE ONE THAT'S GOING TO CHANGE EVERYTHING.
SOUNDS LIKE BULLSHIT TO ME. SMELLS LIKE A TRAP. I DON'T TRUST YOUR SOURCE.
NOR DO I. COMPLETELY. BUT IF IT IS TRUE, WE CAN'T LET THEM HAVE HIM.
WE HAVE NEW ORDERS. AND I SAY WE FOLLOW THEM...
AS SOON AS THE SHOW STARTS WE GET INSIDE THE ARENA.
WE'RE BREAKING HIM OUT. TONIGHT.

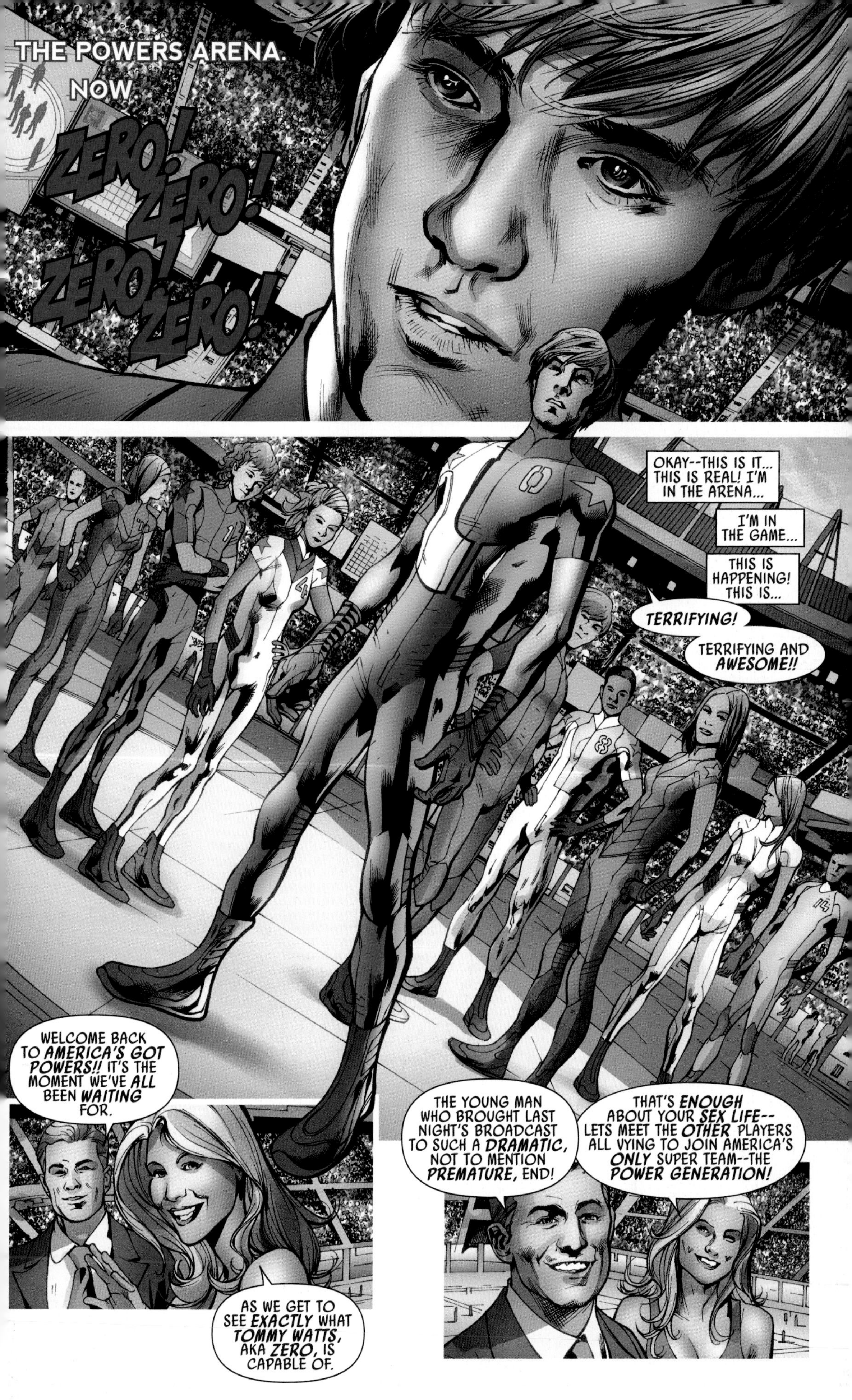
THE POWERS ARENA. NOW.
ZERO! ZERO! ZERO! ZERO!
OKAY--THIS IS IT... THIS IS REAL! I'M IN THE ARENA...
I'M IN THE GAME...
THIS IS HAPPENING! THIS IS...
TERRIFYING!
TERRIFYING AND AWESOME!!
WELCOME BACK TO AMERICA'S GOT POWERS!! IT'S THE MOMENT WE'VE ALL BEEN WAITING FOR.
AS WE GET TO SEE EXACTLY WHAT TOMMY WATTS, AKA ZERO, IS CAPABLE OF.
THE YOUNG MAN WHO BROUGHT LAST NIGHT'S BROADCAST TO SUCH A DRAMATIC, NOT TO MENTION PREMATURE, END!
THAT'S ENOUGH ABOUT YOUR SEX LIFE--LETS MEET THE OTHER PLAYERS ALL VYING TO JOIN AMERICA'S ONLY SUPER TEAM--THE POWER GENERATION!

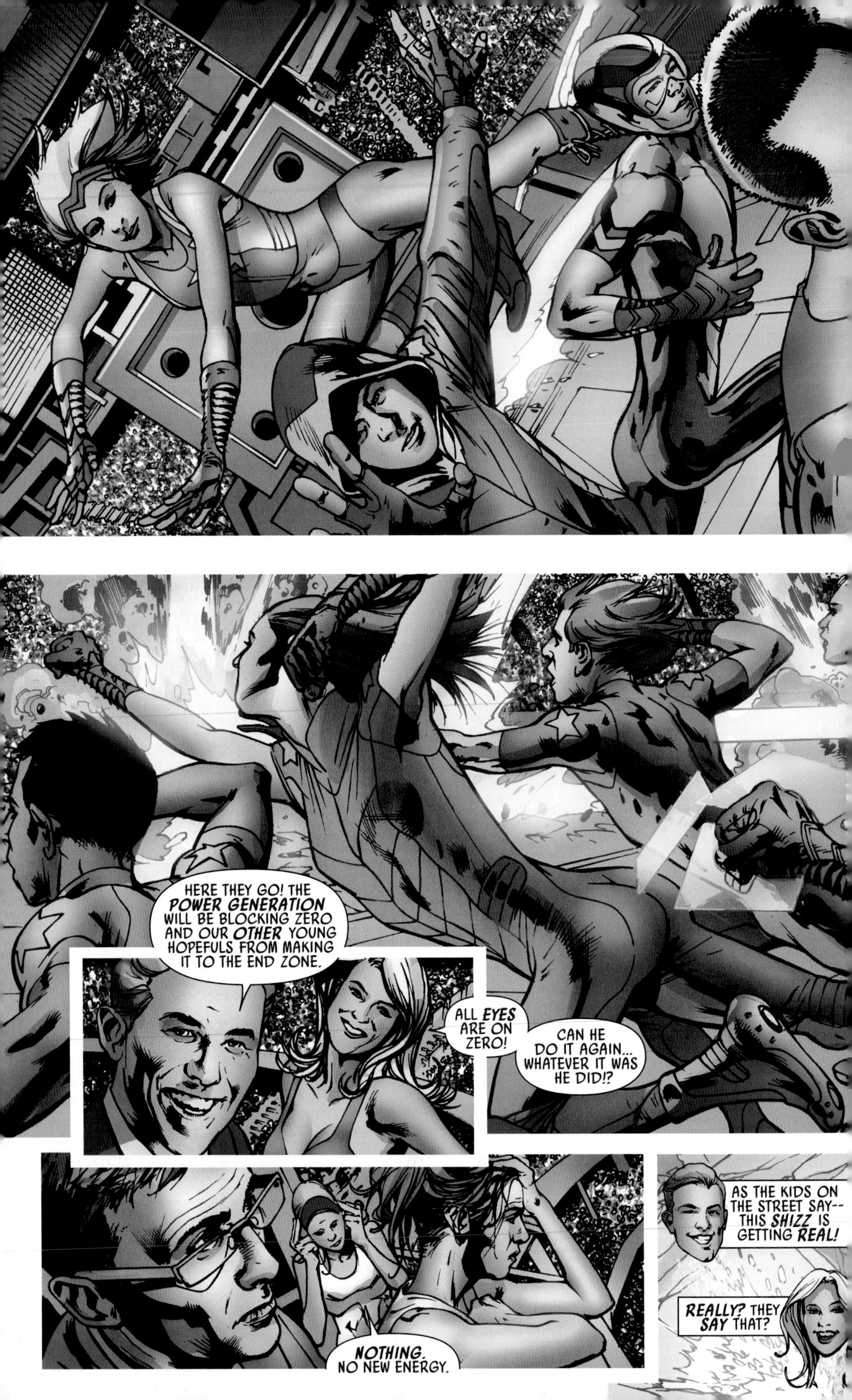
HERE THEY GO! THE POWER GENERATION WILL BE BLOCKING ZERO AND OUR OTHER YOUNG HOPEFULS FROM MAKING IT TO THE END ZONE.
ALL EYES ARE ON ZERO!
CAN HE DO IT AGAIN... WHATEVER IT WAS HE DID!?
NOTHING. NO NEW ENERGY.
AS THE KIDS ON THE STREET SAY-- THIS SHIZZ IS GETTING REAL!
REALLY? THEY SAY THAT?

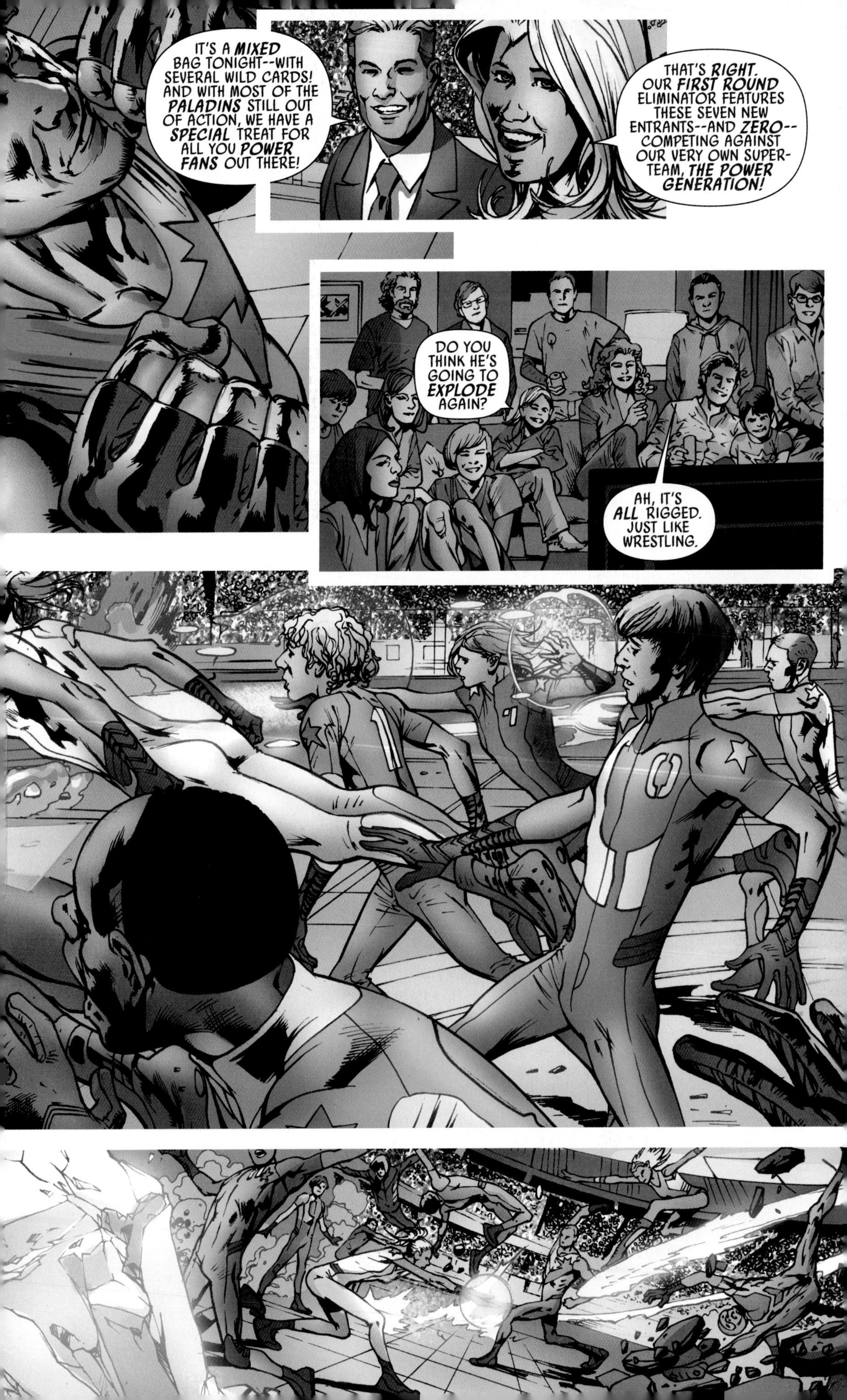
IT'S A MIXED BAG TONIGHT--WITH SEVERAL WILD CARDS! AND WITH MOST OF THE PALADINS STILL OUT OF ACTION, WE HAVE A SPECIAL TREAT FOR ALL YOU POWER FANS OUT THERE!
THAT'S RIGHT. OUR FIRST ROUND ELIMINATOR FEATURES THESE SEVEN NEW ENTRANTS--AND ZERO--COMPETING AGAINST OUR VERY OWN SUPER-TEAM, THE POWER GENERATION!
DO YOU THINK HE'S GOING TO EXPLODE AGAIN?
AH, IT'S ALL RIGGED. JUST LIKE WRESTLING.

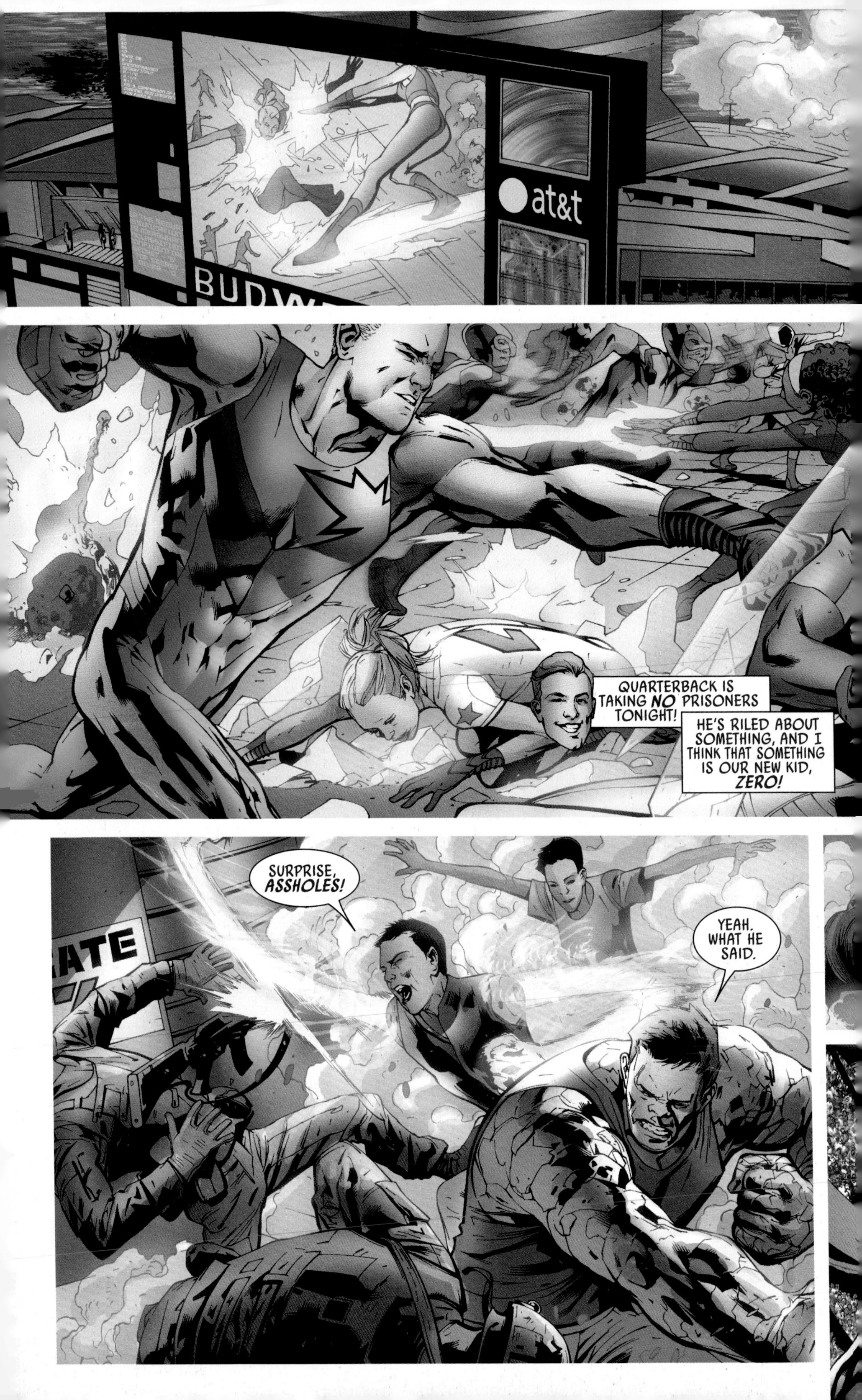
at&t
QUARTERBACK IS TAKING NO PRISONERS TONIGHT!
HE'S RILED ABOUT SOMETHING, AND I THINK THAT SOMETHING IS OUR NEW KID, ZERO!
SURPRISE, ASSHOLES!
YEAH. WHAT HE SAID.

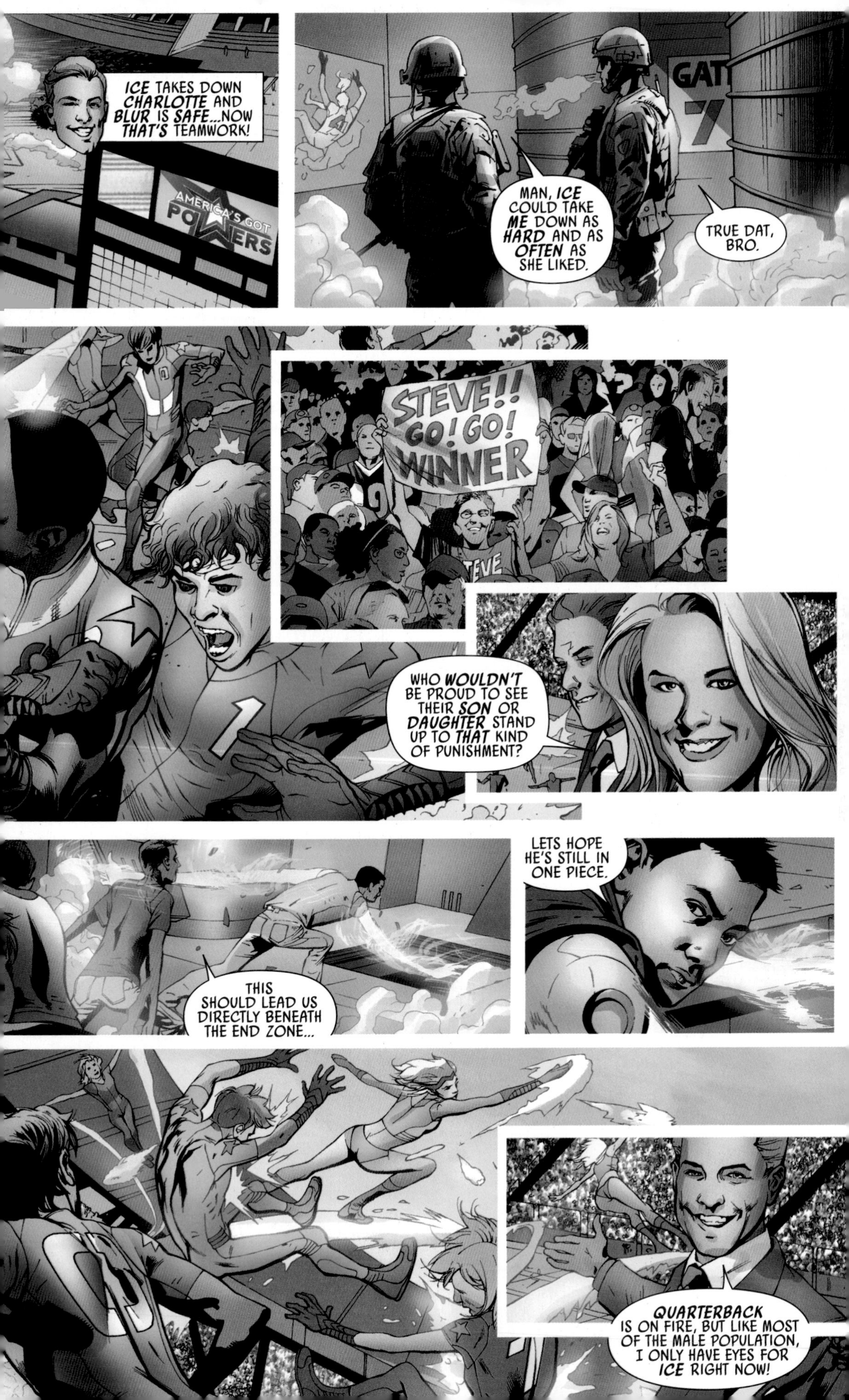
AMERICA'S GOT POWERS
ICE TAKES DOWN CHARLOTTE AND BLUR IS SAFE...NOW THAT'S TEAMWORK!
MAN, ICE COULD TAKE ME DOWN AS HARD AND AS OFTEN AS SHE LIKED.
TRUE DAT, BRO.
STEVE!! GO! GO! WINNER
WHO WOULDN'T BE PROUD TO SEE THEIR SON OR DAUGHTER STAND UP TO THAT KIND OF PUNISHMENT?
THIS SHOULD LEAD US DIRECTLY BENEATH THE END ZONE...
LETS HOPE HE'S STILL IN ONE PIECE.
QUARTERBACK IS ON FIRE, BUT LIKE MOST OF THE MALE POPULATION, I ONLY HAVE EYES FOR ICE RIGHT NOW!

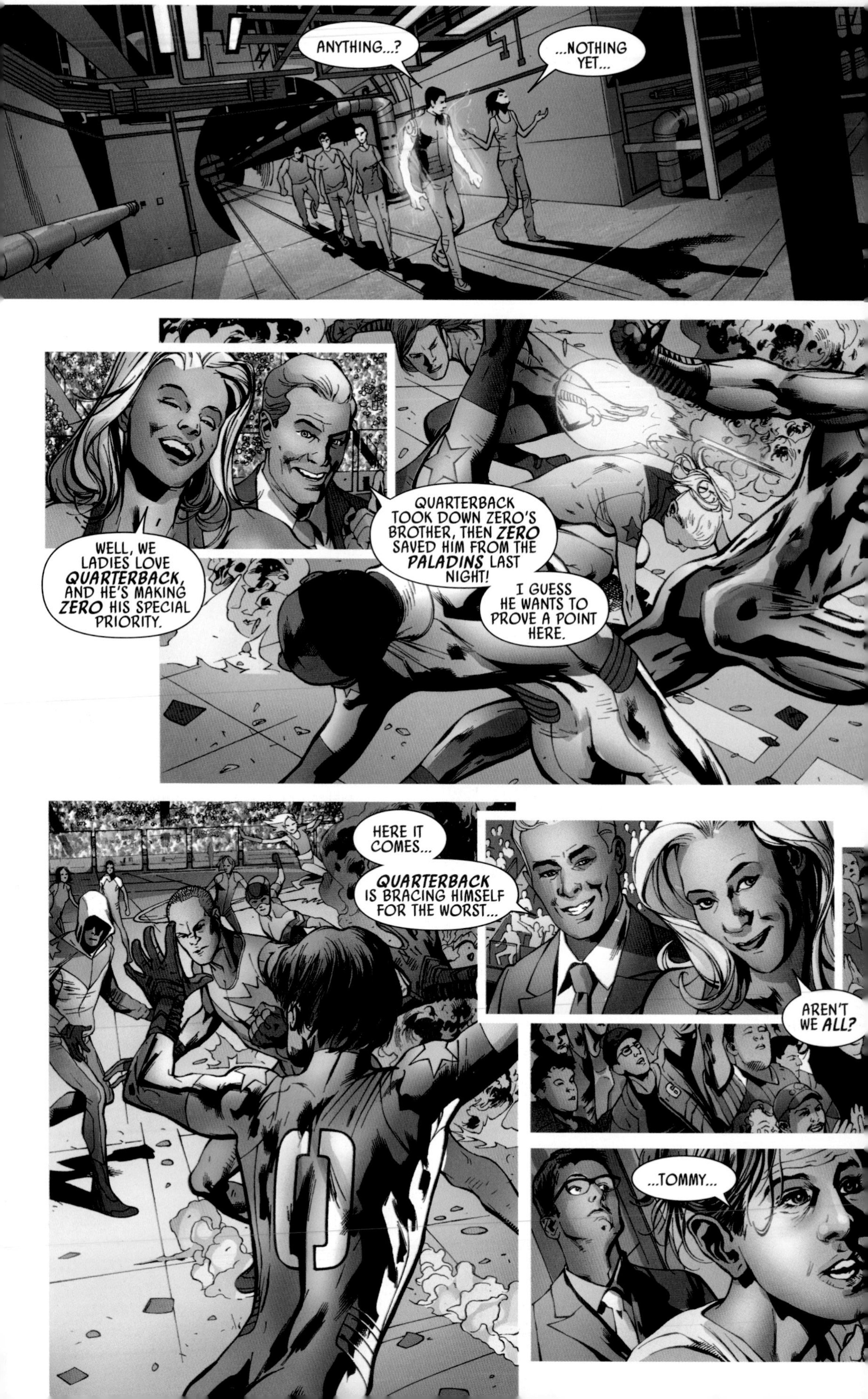
ANYTHING...?
...NOTHING YET...
QUARTERBACK TOOK DOWN ZERO'S BROTHER, THEN ZERO SAVED HIM FROM THE PALADINS LAST NIGHT!
WELL, WE LADIES LOVE QUARTERBACK, AND HE'S MAKING ZERO HIS SPECIAL PRIORITY.
I GUESS HE WANTS TO PROVE A POINT HERE.
HERE IT COMES...
QUARTERBACK IS BRACING HIMSELF FOR THE WORST...
AREN'T WE ALL?
...TOMMY...

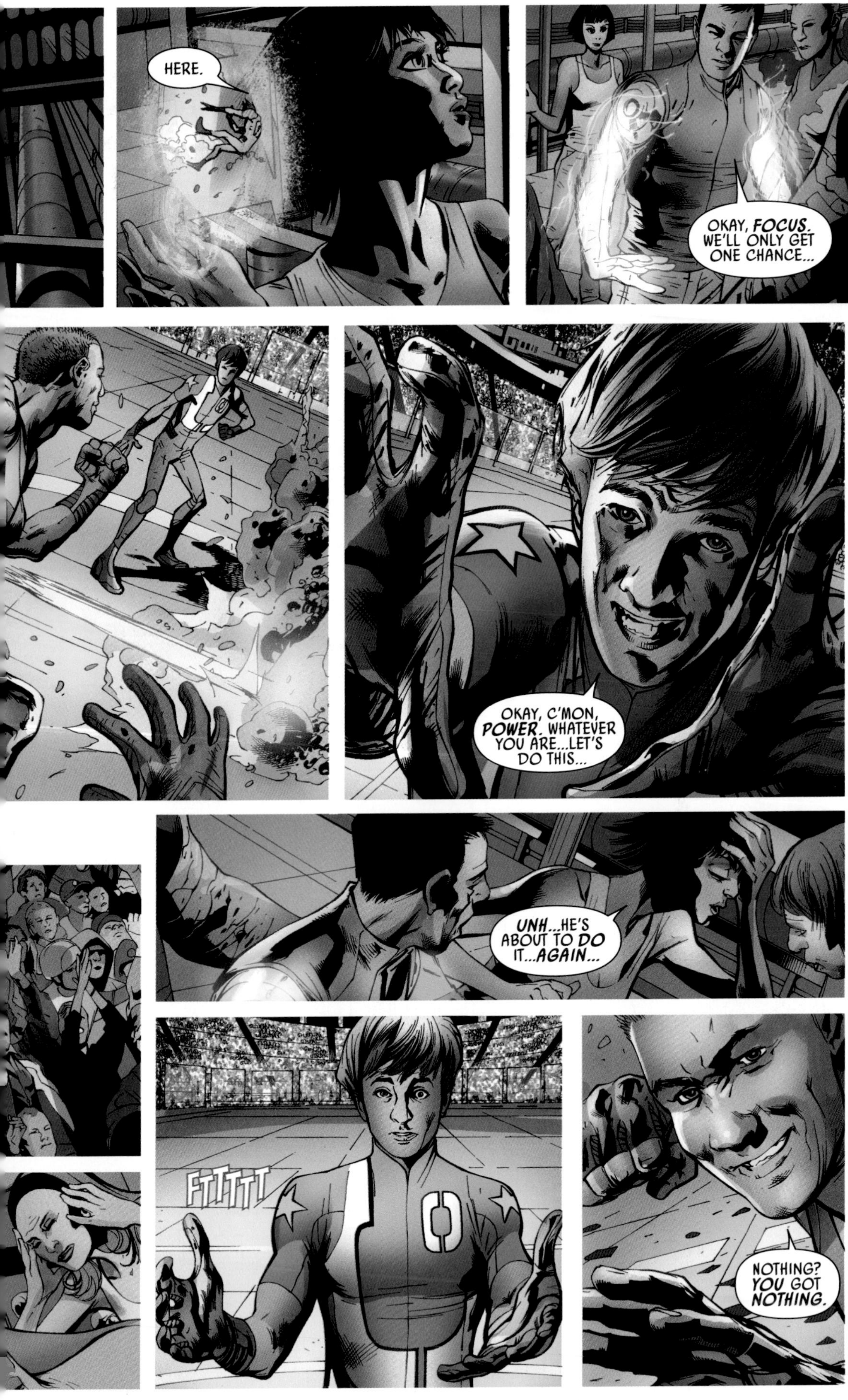
HERE.
OKAY, FOCUS. WE'LL ONLY GET ONE CHANCE...
OKAY, C'MON, POWER. WHATEVER YOU ARE...LET'S DO THIS...
UNH...HE'S ABOUT TO DO IT...AGAIN...
FTTTTT
NOTHING? YOU GOT NOTHING.

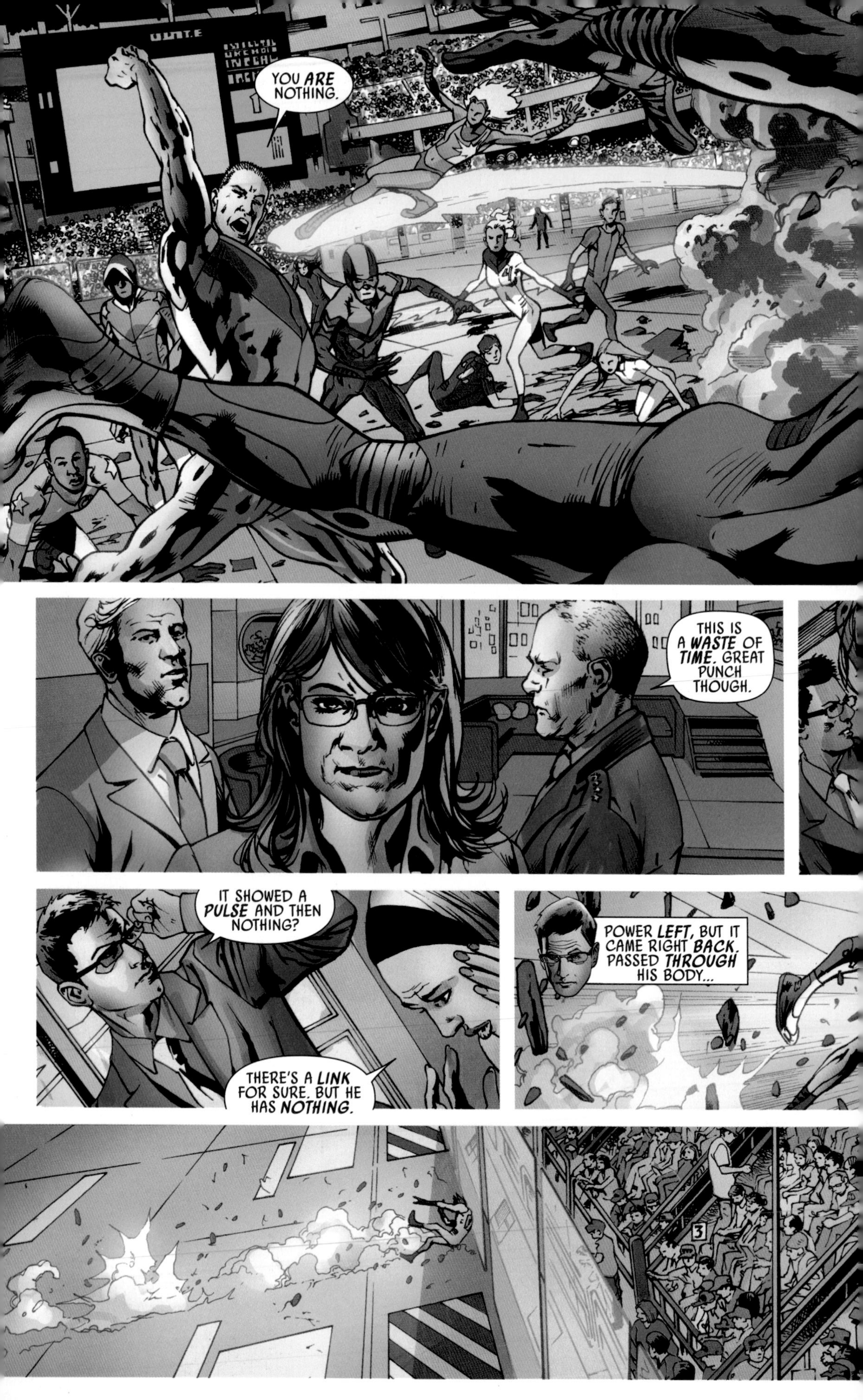
YOU ARE NOTHING.
THIS IS A WASTE OF TIME. GREAT PUNCH THOUGH.
IT SHOWED A PULSE AND THEN NOTHING?
THERE'S A LINK FOR SURE. BUT HE HAS NOTHING.
POWER LEFT, BUT IT CAME RIGHT BACK. PASSED THROUGH HIS BODY...

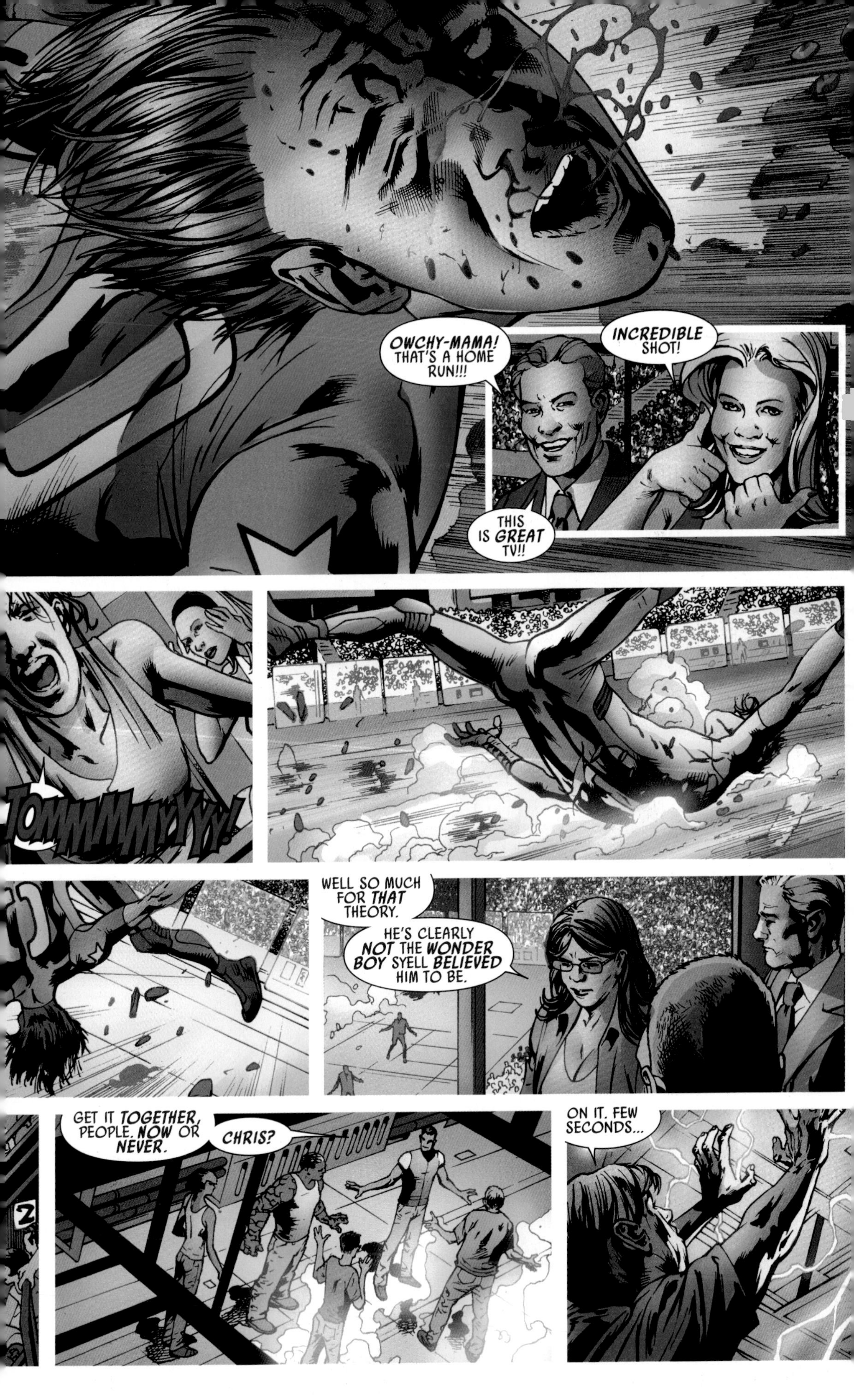
OWCHY-MAMA! THAT'S A HOME RUN!!!
INCREDIBLE SHOT!
THIS IS GREAT TV!!
TOMMMMMYYYY!
WELL SO MUCH FOR THAT THEORY.
HE'S CLEARLY NOT THE WONDER BOY SYELL BELIEVED HIM TO BE.
GET IT TOGETHER, PEOPLE. NOW OR NEVER.
CHRIS?
ON IT. FEW SECONDS...

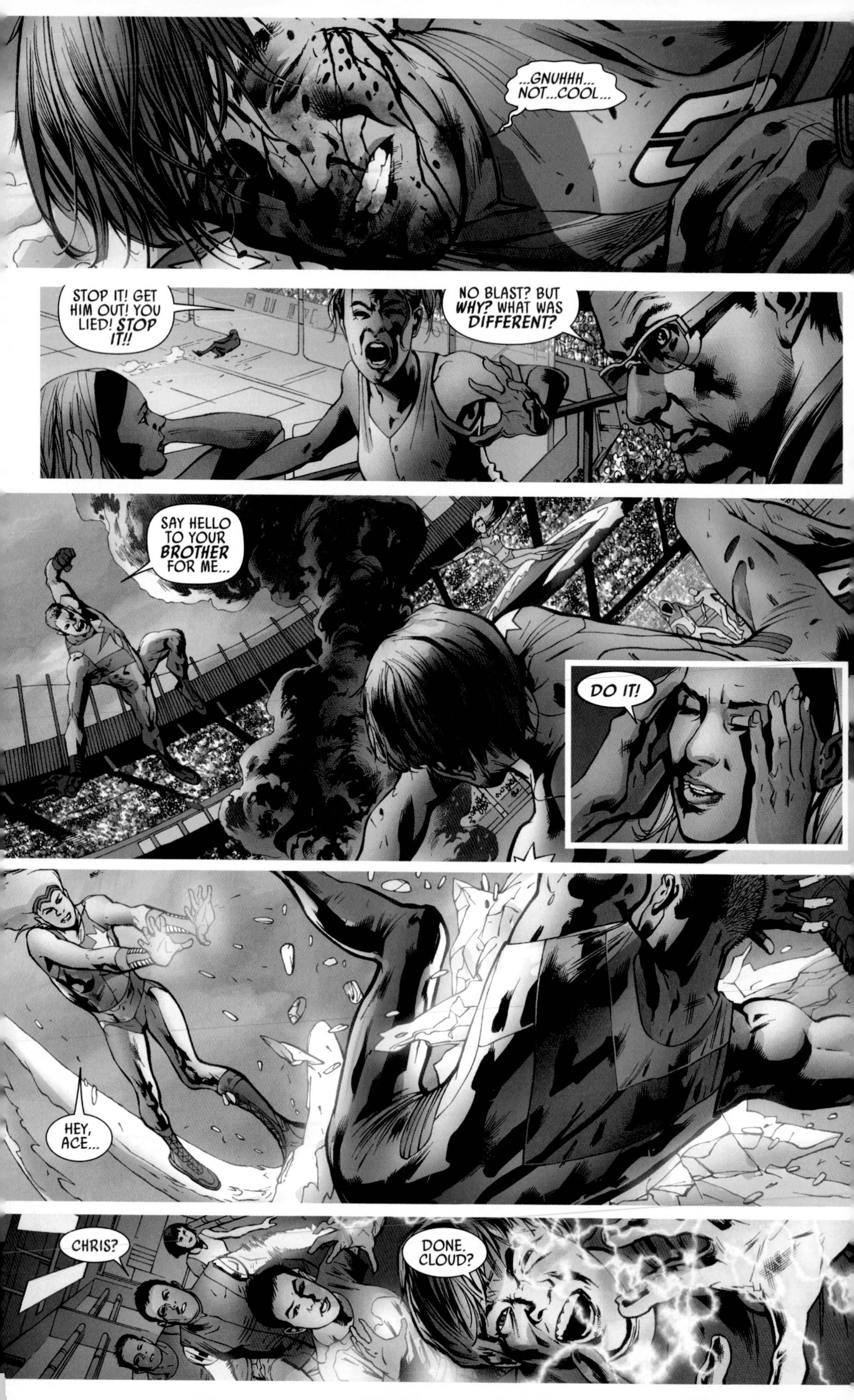
...GNUHHH... NOT...COOL...
STOP IT! GET HIM OUT! YOU LIED! STOP IT!!
NO BLAST? BUT WHY? WHAT WAS DIFFERENT?
SAY HELLO TO YOUR BROTHER FOR ME...
DO IT!
HEY, ACE...
CHRIS?
DONE, CLOUD?

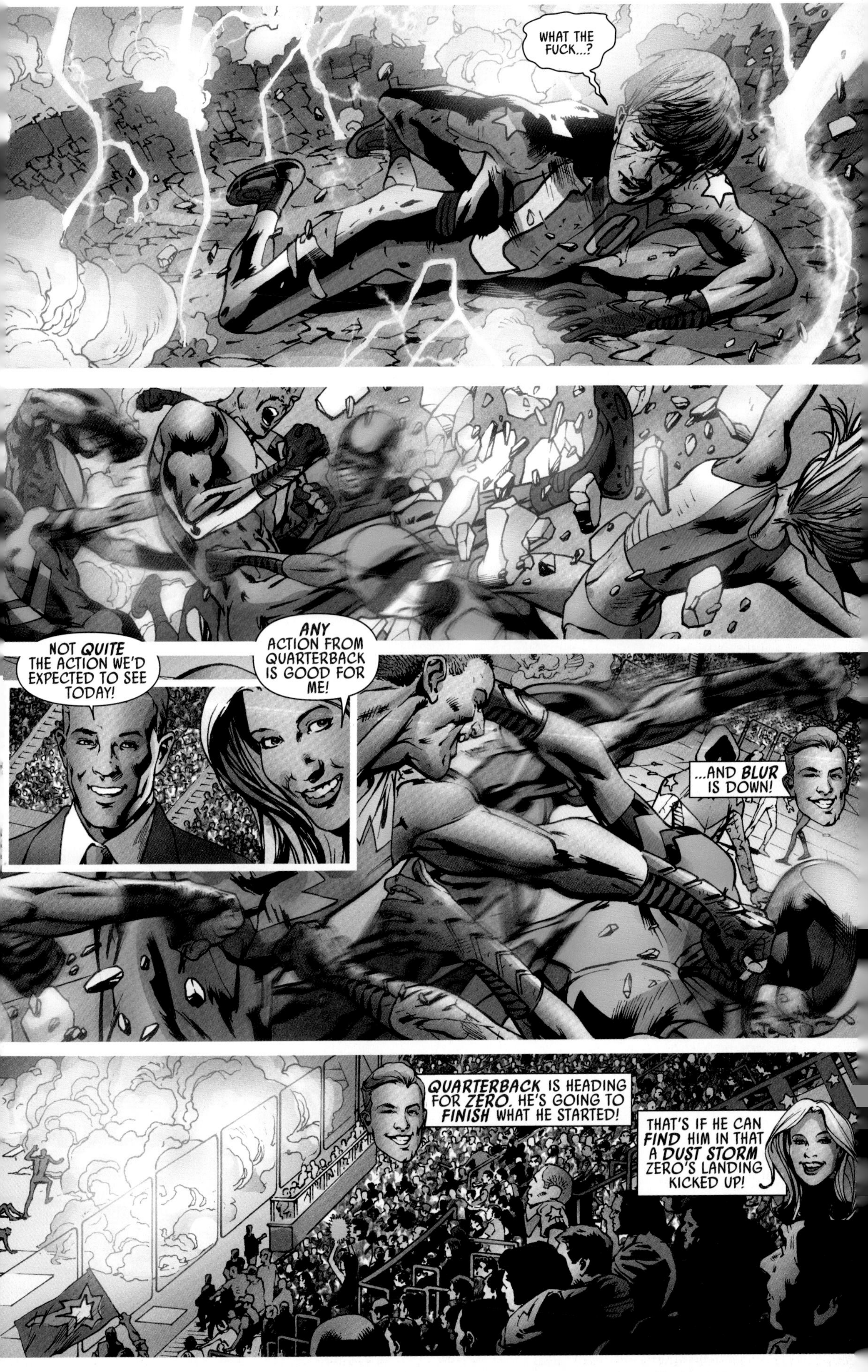
WHAT THE FUCK...?
NOT QUITE THE ACTION WE'D EXPECTED TO SEE TODAY!
ANY ACTION FROM QUARTERBACK IS GOOD FOR ME!
...AND BLUR IS DOWN!
QUARTERBACK IS HEADING FOR ZERO. HE'S GOING TO FINISH WHAT HE STARTED!
THAT'S IF HE CAN FIND HIM IN THAT A DUST STORM ZERO'S LANDING KICKED UP!

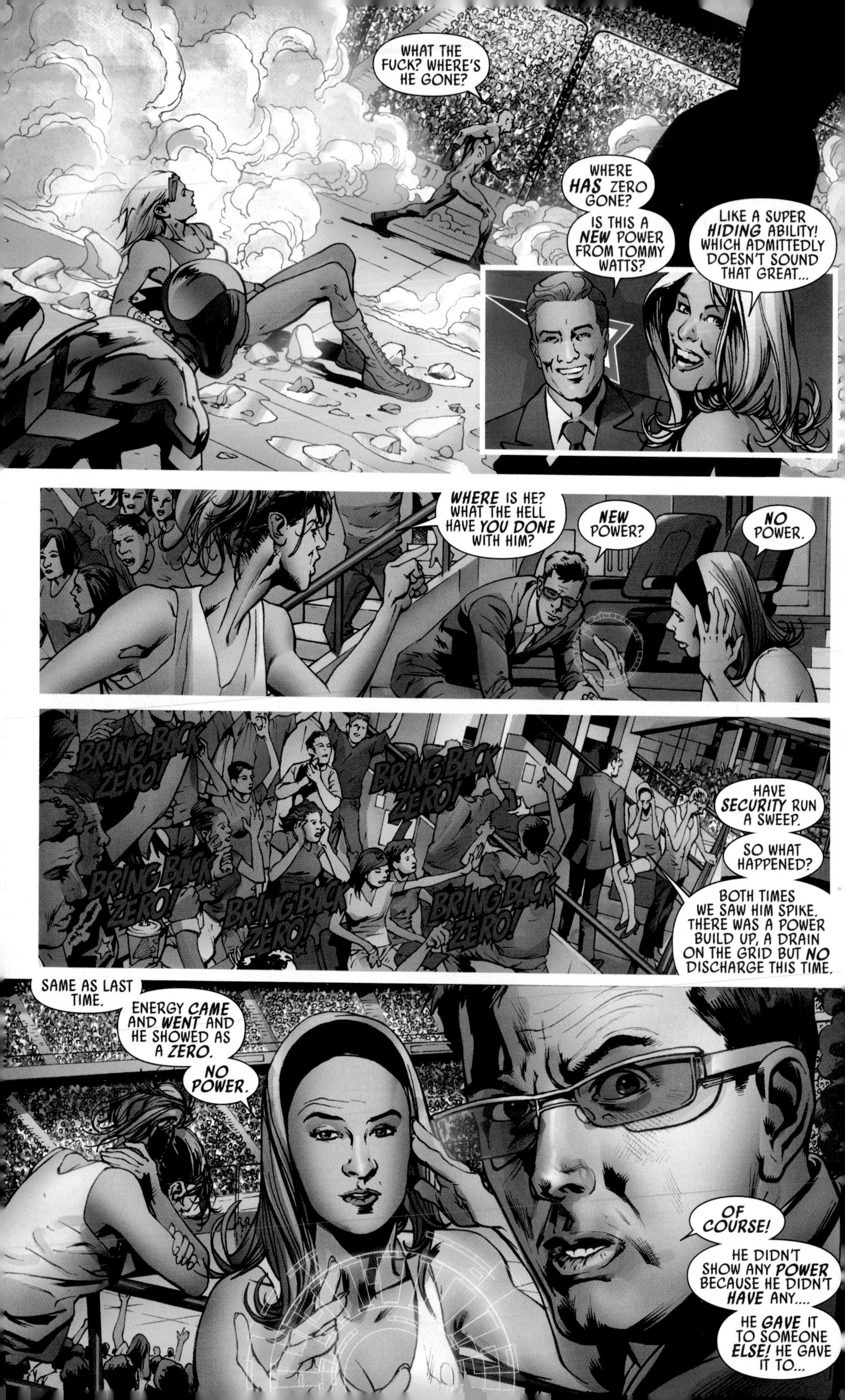
WHAT THE FUCK? WHERE'S HE GONE?
WHERE HAS ZERO GONE?
IS THIS A NEW POWER FROM TOMMY WATTS?
LIKE A SUPER HIDING ABILITY! WHICH ADMITTEDLY DOESN'T SOUND THAT GREAT...
WHERE IS HE? WHAT THE HELL HAVE YOU DONE WITH HIM?
NEW POWER?
NO POWER.
BRING BACK ZERO!
BRING BACK ZERO!
BRING BACK ZERO!
BRING BACK ZERO!
BRING BACK ZERO!
HAVE SECURITY RUN A SWEEP.
SO WHAT HAPPENED?
BOTH TIMES WE SAW HIM SPIKE. THERE WAS A POWER BUILD UP, A DRAIN ON THE GRID BUT NO DISCHARGE THIS TIME.
SAME AS LAST TIME.
ENERGY CAME AND WENT AND HE SHOWED AS A ZERO.
NO POWER.
OF COURSE!
HE DIDN'T SHOW ANY POWER BECAUSE HE DIDN'T HAVE ANY....
HE GAVE IT TO SOMEONE ELSE! HE GAVE IT TO...

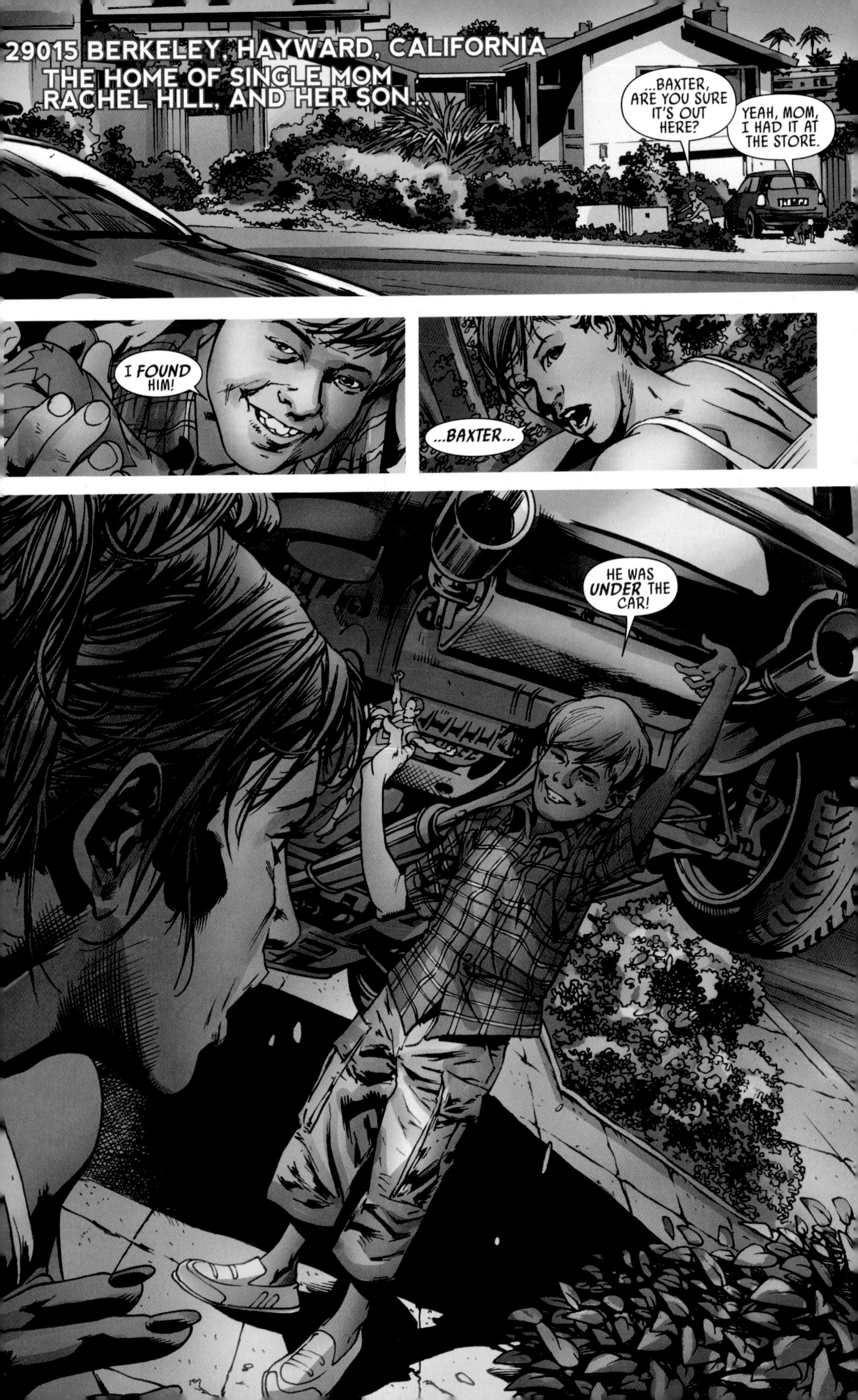
29015 BERKELEY, HAYWARD, CALIFORNIA
THE HOME OF SINGLE MOM RACHEL HILL, AND HER SON...
...BAXTER, ARE YOU SURE IT'S OUT HERE?
YEAH, MOM, I HAD IT AT THE STORE.
I FOUND HIM!
...BAXTER...
HE WAS UNDER THE CAR!

UNITED STATES GOVERNMENT INTERAGENCY DOMESTIC TERRORISM INVOLVING POWERED INDIVIDUALS CONCEPT OF OPER ~~~ONS PLAN

January 20

TABLE OF CC

~reword
~etter of Agreement
~ignatories to the Plan
~ist of Figures
~igure 1: Incident Command System / Unified Cc
Figure 2: FBI Command Post
Figure 3: Coordinating Relationships
Figure 4: Joint Operations Center
Figure 5: On-Scene Coordination
I. Introduction and Background
A. Introduction
B. Primary Agency Responsibilities
1. Department of Justice (DOJ)/ Federal Burea
2. Federal Emergency Management Agency (~
3. Department of Defense (DOD)
4. Department of Health and Super Human S
II. Policies
A. Authorities
B. Other Plans and Directives
C. Federal Agency Authorities
D. Federal Response to a Powered Individ
E. Training and Exercises
III. Situation
A. Introduction
B. Differences between WMD Incidents
C. Threat Levels
1. Level #4 - Minimal Threat
2. Level #3 - Potential Threat
3. Level #2 - Credible Threat
4. Level #1 - WMD Incident
5. Level #0 - Powered Individuals Th
D. Lead Federal Agency Responsibil
IV. Concept of Operations
A. Mission
B. Command and Control

- The FBI manages a PI Terrorist Threat Warning System to ens~ regarding PI terrorism reaches those in the U.S. counterterroris~ community responsible for countering such threats. This infor~ secure teletype. Each message transmitted under this system is~ assessment of alert if the terrorist threat is credible and specifi~ credible but general in both timing and target; or an assessmen~ threats.

- **B. Activation and Deployment** Upon determination that the ~ terrorism has occurred, FBIHQ will initiate appropriate liaiso~ to activate their operations centers and provide liaison officers FBIHQ will initiate communications with the SAC of the resp~ him/her of possible courses of action and discussing deployme~ SAC will establish initial operational priorities based upon the threat or incident. This information will then be forwarded to identification and deployment of appropriate resources.

  Based upon a credible threat assessment and a request by the S~ consultation with the Attorney General, may request authoriza~ Council groups to deploy the DEST to assist the SAC in mitig~ MOAB is the most powerful non nuclear bomb produced in th~

Figure 5. MOAB

APPENDIX A: ACRONYMS

CONPLAN	Concept of Operations Plan
DEST	Domestic Emergency Support Team
DOD	Department of Defense
DOE	Department of Energy
DOJ	Department of Justice
EM	Emergency Management
EMS	Emergency Medical Services
EOC	Emergency Operations Center
EPA	Environmental Protection Agency
ERT	Evidence Response Team (FBI)
FBI	Federal Bureau of Investigation
FCO	Federal Coordinating Officer
FEMA	Federal Emergency Management Agency
FRP	Federal Response Plan

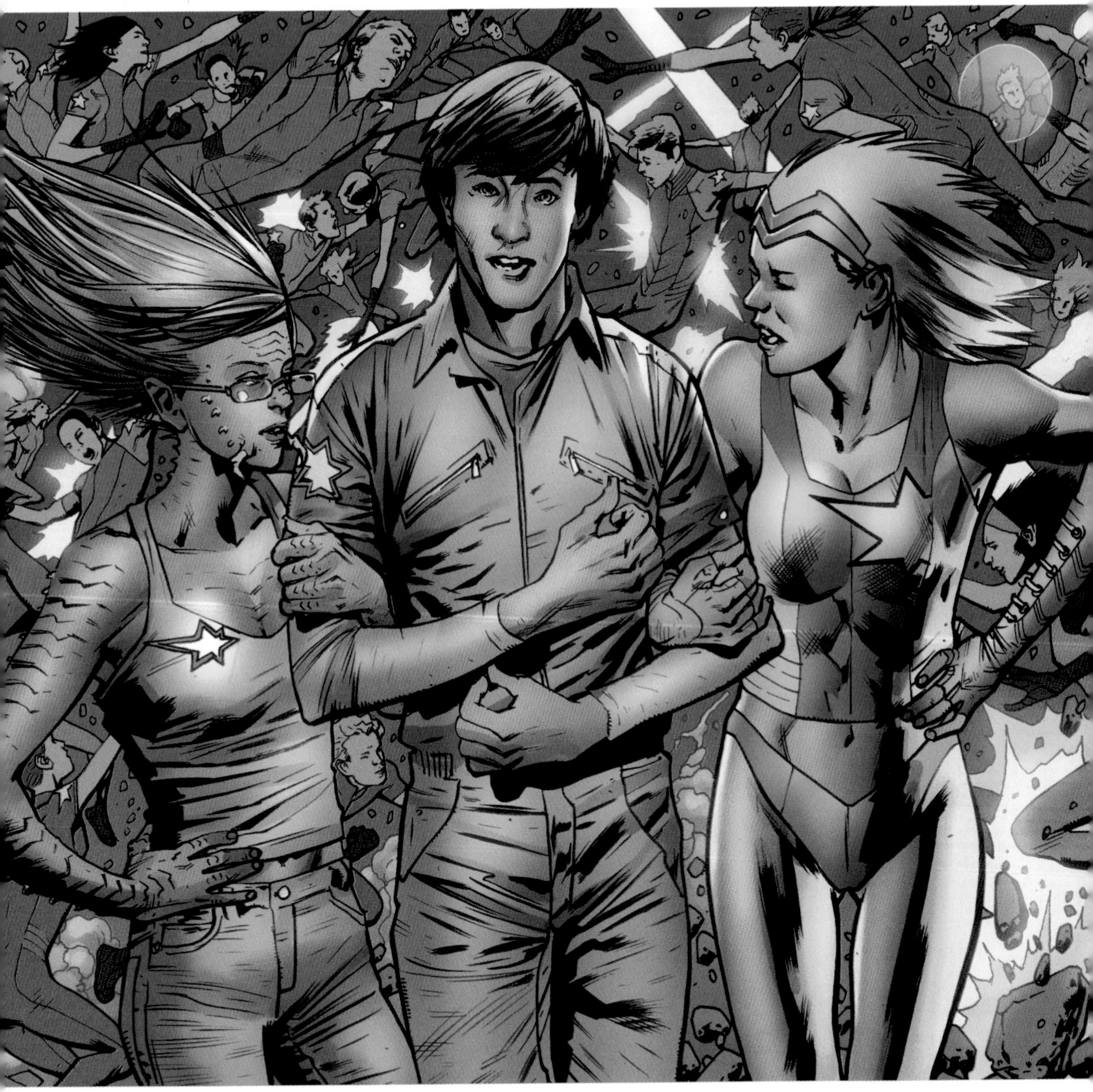

CHAPTER **FOUR**

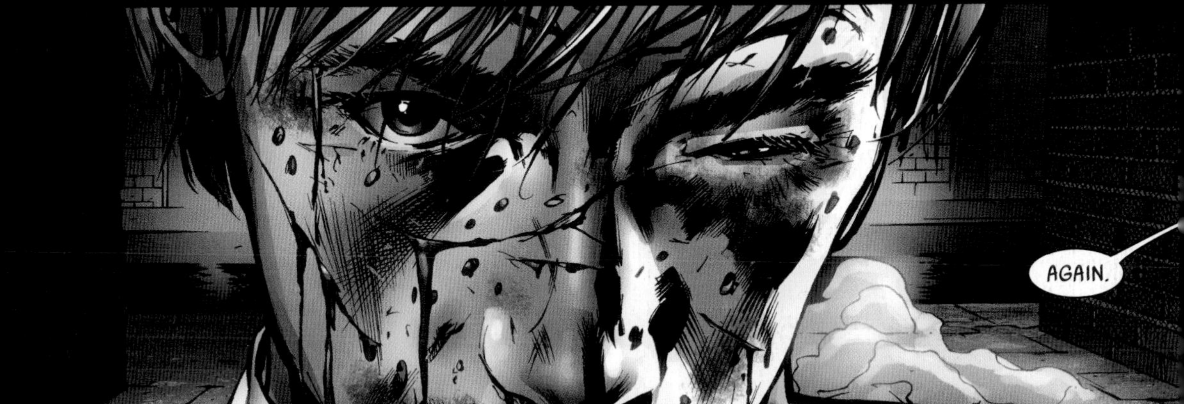
AGAIN.

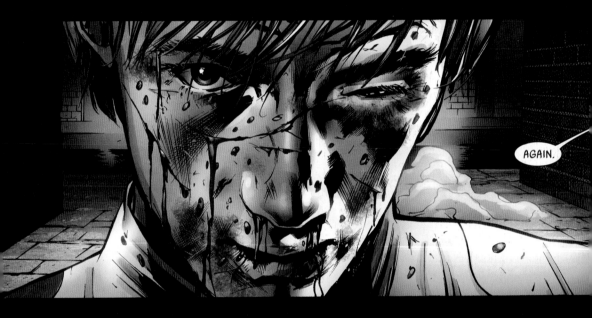

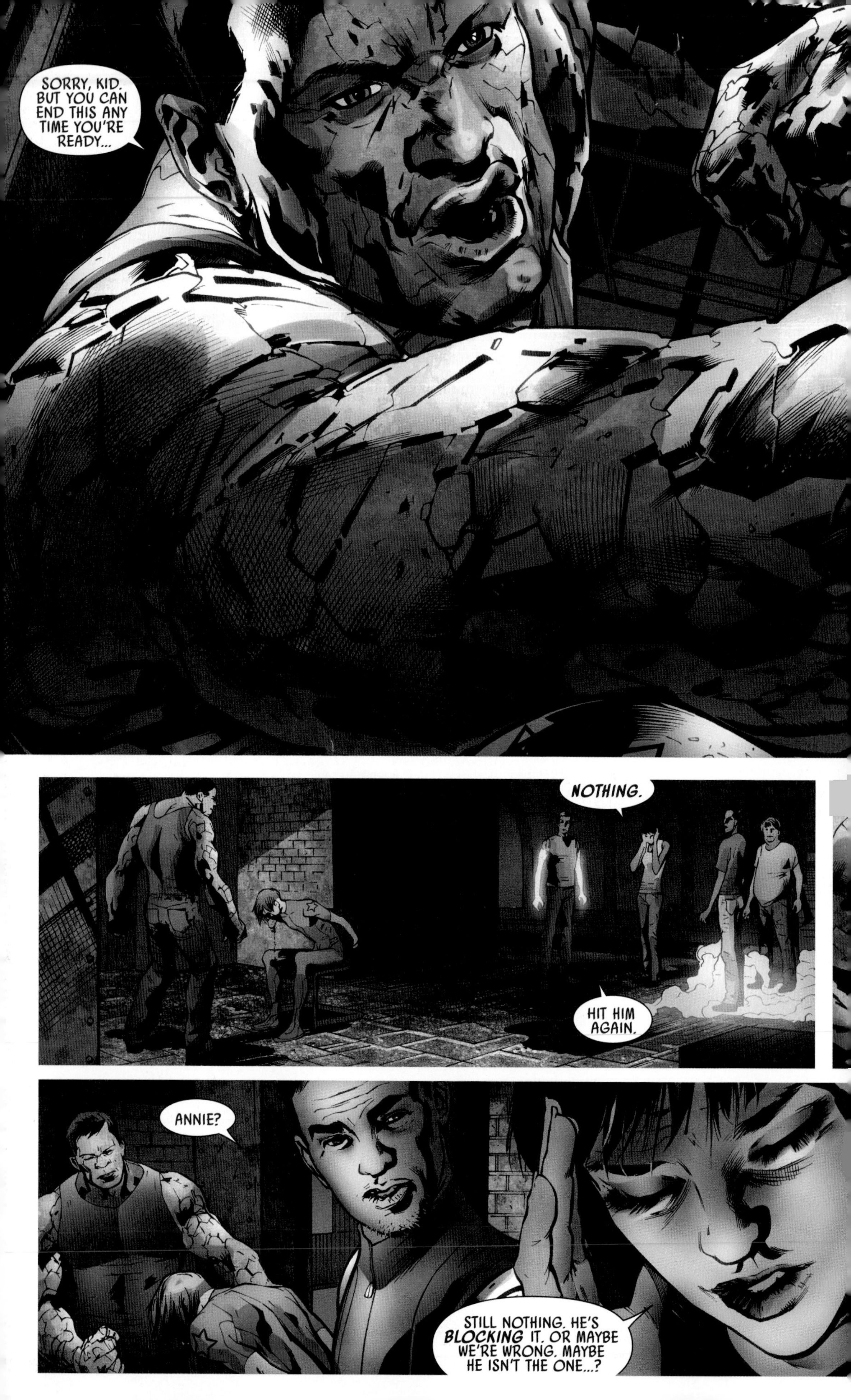
SORRY, KID. BUT YOU CAN END THIS ANY TIME YOU'RE READY...
NOTHING.
HIT HIM AGAIN.
ANNIE?
STILL NOTHING. HE'S BLOCKING IT. OR MAYBE WE'RE WRONG. MAYBE HE ISN'T THE ONE...?

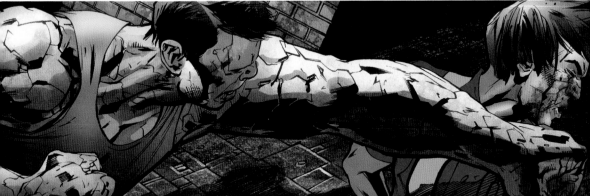

NO. HE'S THE ONE. AND HE'S A STUPID, SELFISH, *ASSHOLE!* HIT HIM AGAIN. AND MAKE IT *COUNT!*

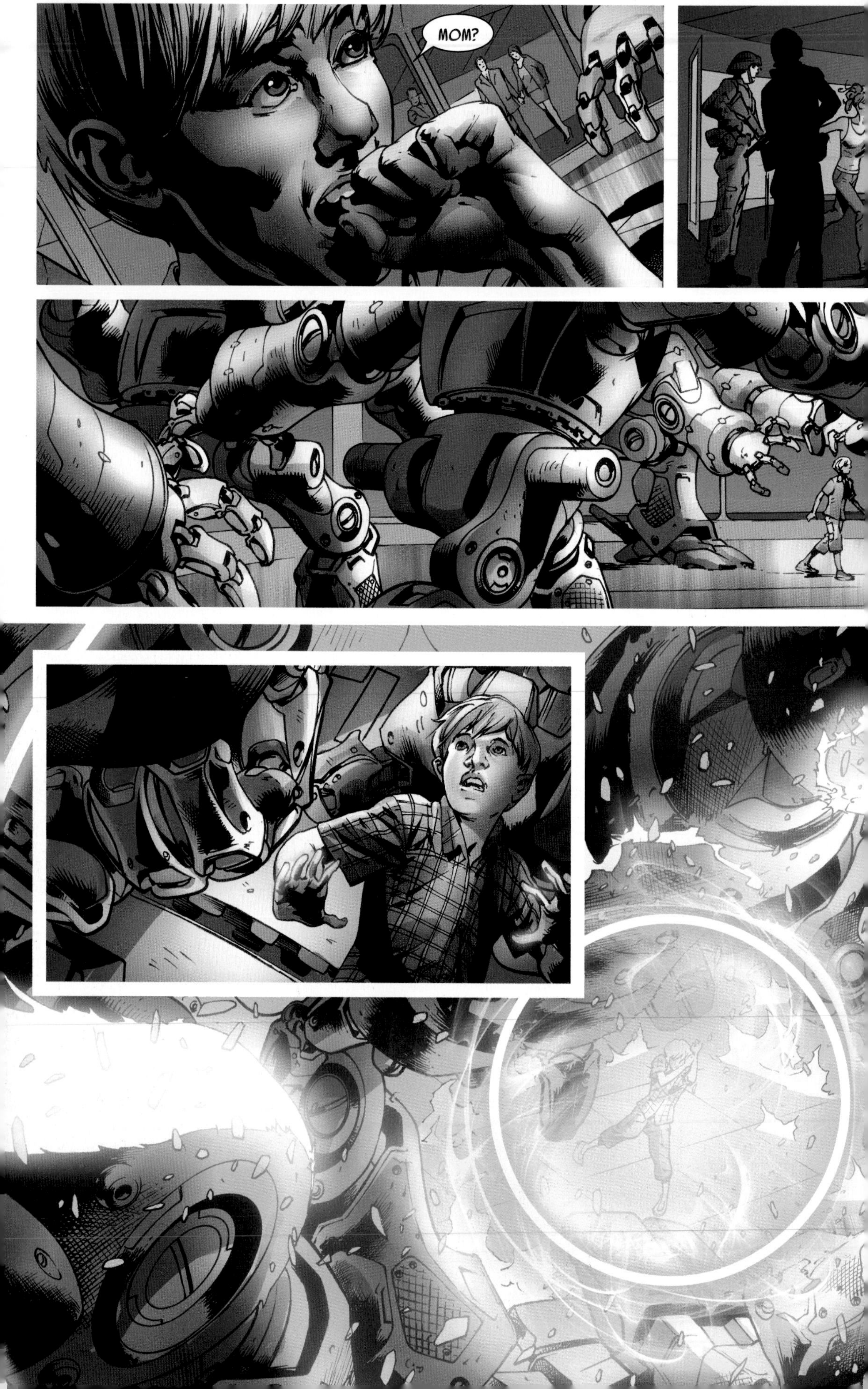
MOM?

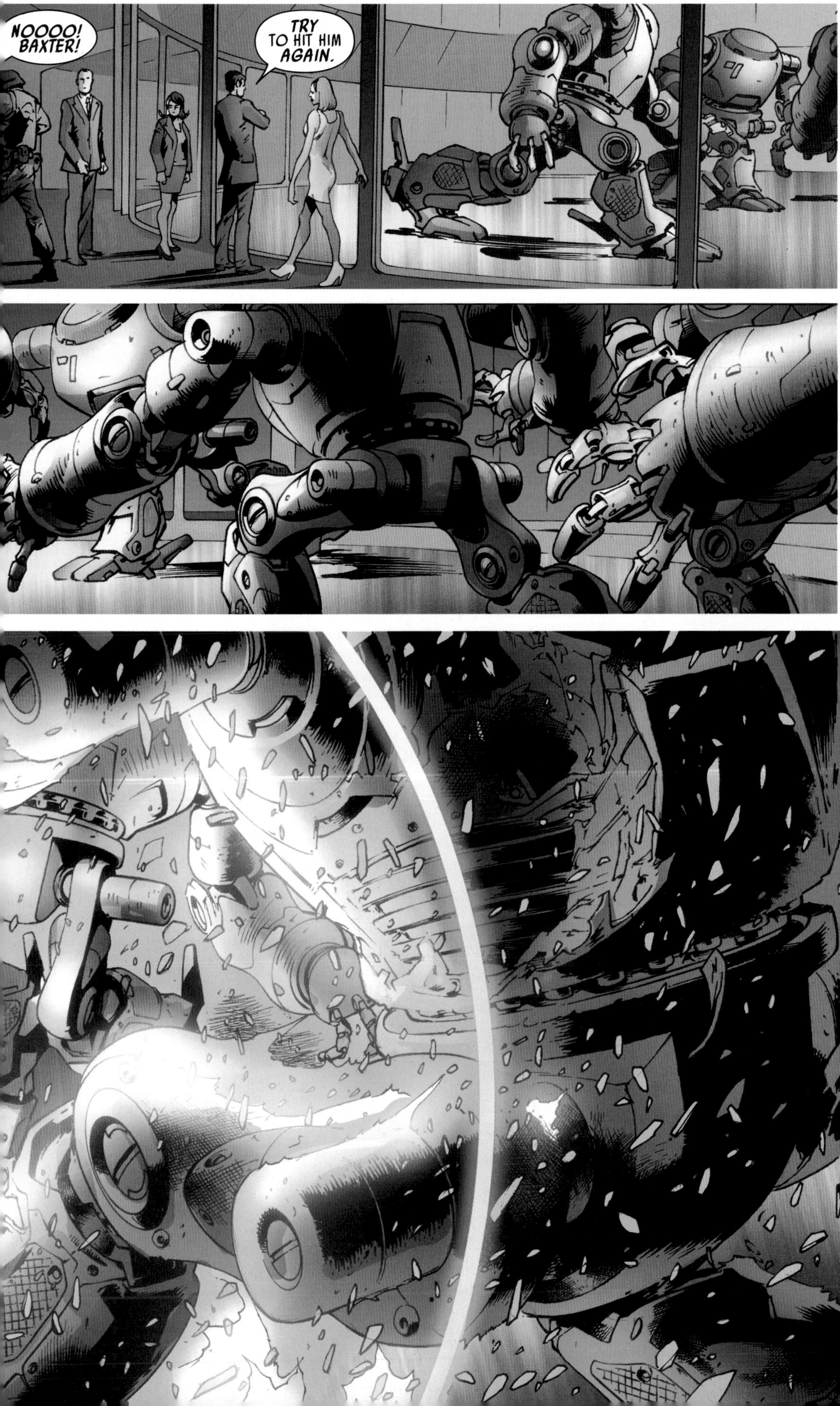
NOOOO! BAXTER!
TRY TO HIT HIM AGAIN.

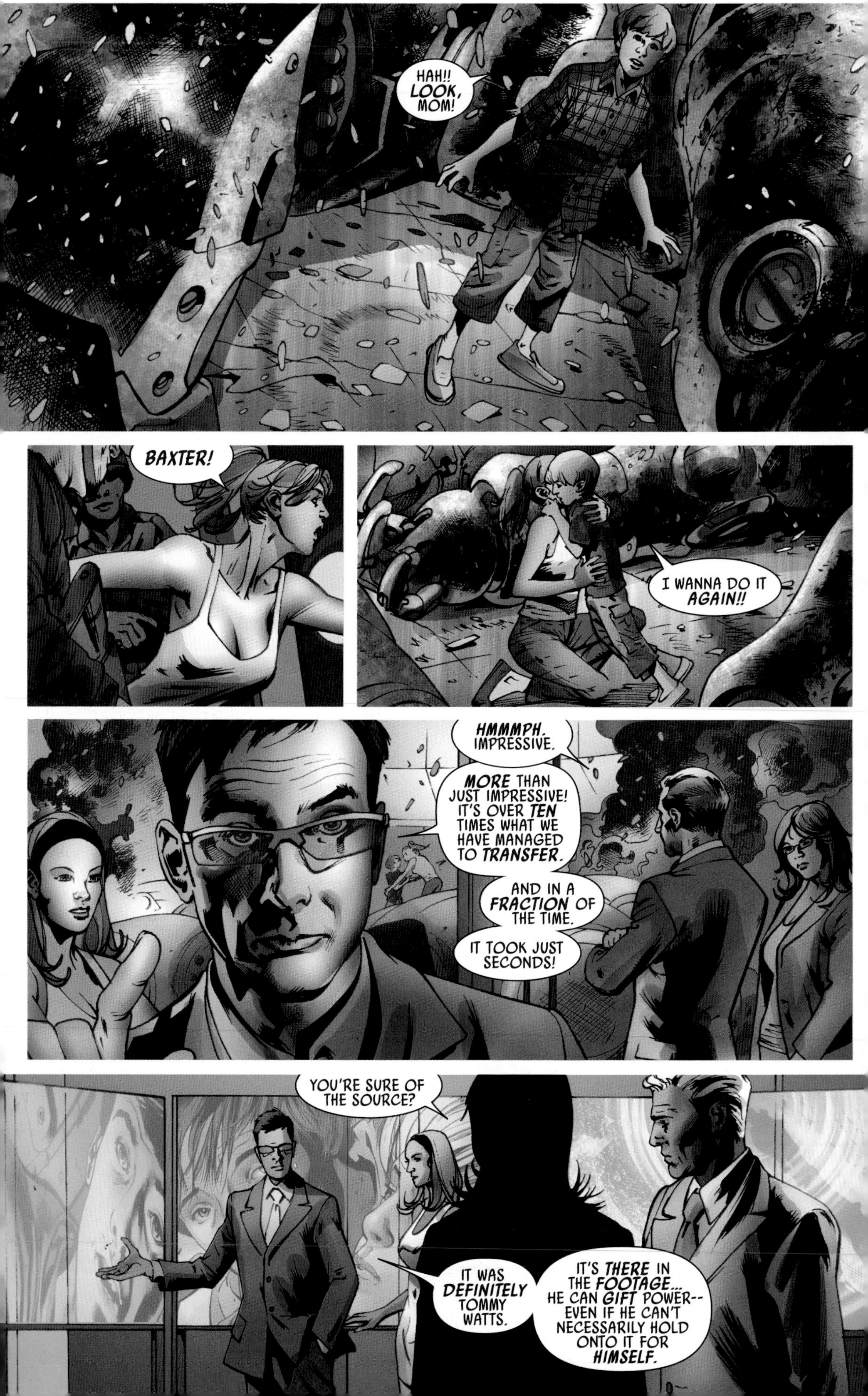
HAH!! LOOK, MOM!
BAXTER!
I WANNA DO IT AGAIN!!
HMMMPH. IMPRESSIVE.
MORE THAN JUST IMPRESSIVE! IT'S OVER TEN TIMES WHAT WE HAVE MANAGED TO TRANSFER.
AND IN A FRACTION OF THE TIME.
IT TOOK JUST SECONDS!
YOU'RE SURE OF THE SOURCE?
IT WAS DEFINITELY TOMMY WATTS.
IT'S THERE IN THE FOOTAGE... HE CAN GIFT POWER-- EVEN IF HE CAN'T NECESSARILY HOLD ONTO IT FOR HIMSELF.

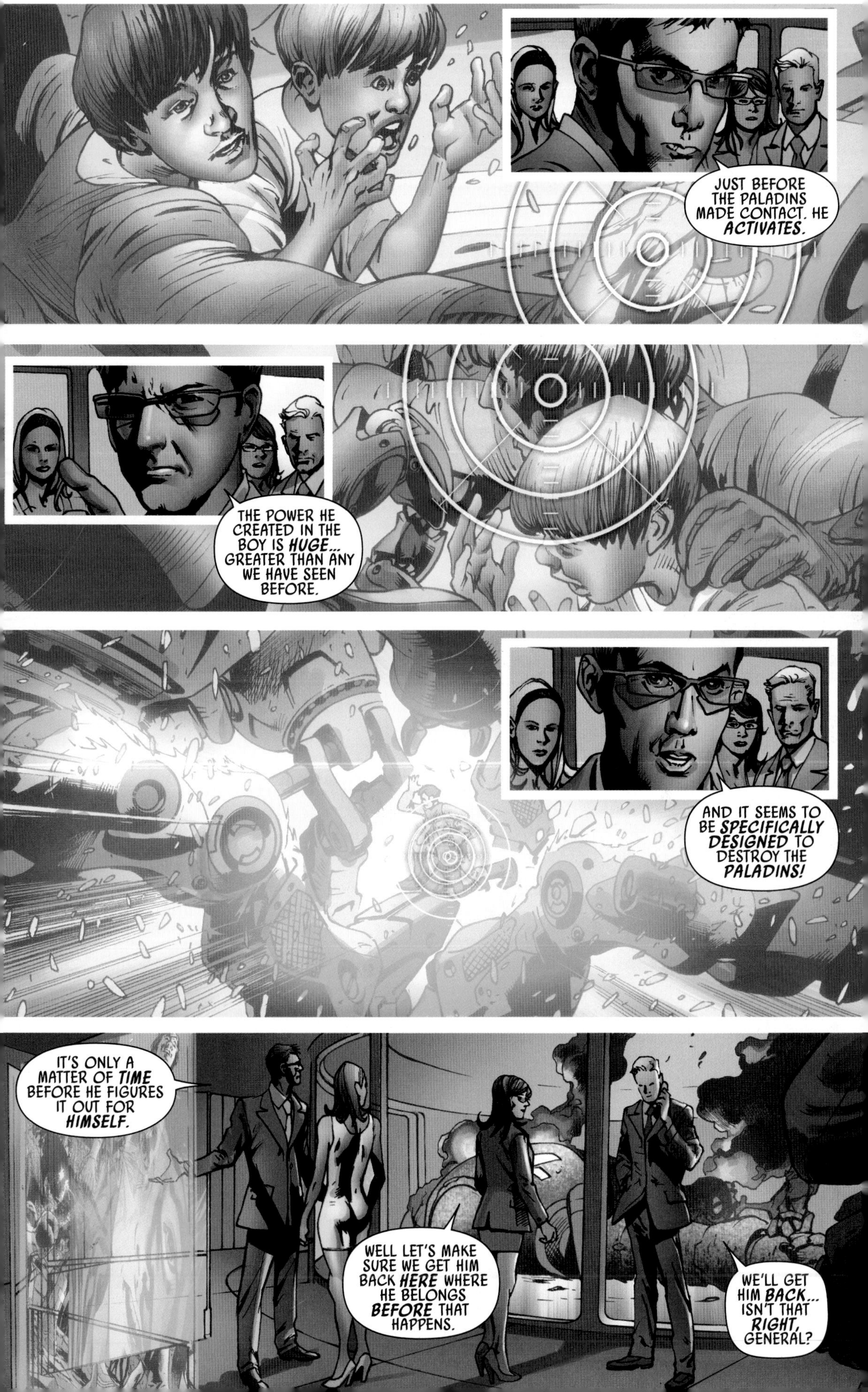
JUST BEFORE THE PALADINS MADE CONTACT. HE ACTIVATES.
THE POWER HE CREATED IN THE BOY IS HUGE... GREATER THAN ANY WE HAVE SEEN BEFORE.
AND IT SEEMS TO BE SPECIFICALLY DESIGNED TO DESTROY THE PALADINS!
IT'S ONLY A MATTER OF TIME BEFORE HE FIGURES IT OUT FOR HIMSELF.
WELL LET'S MAKE SURE WE GET HIM BACK HERE WHERE HE BELONGS BEFORE THAT HAPPENS.
WE'LL GET HIM BACK... ISN'T THAT RIGHT, GENERAL?

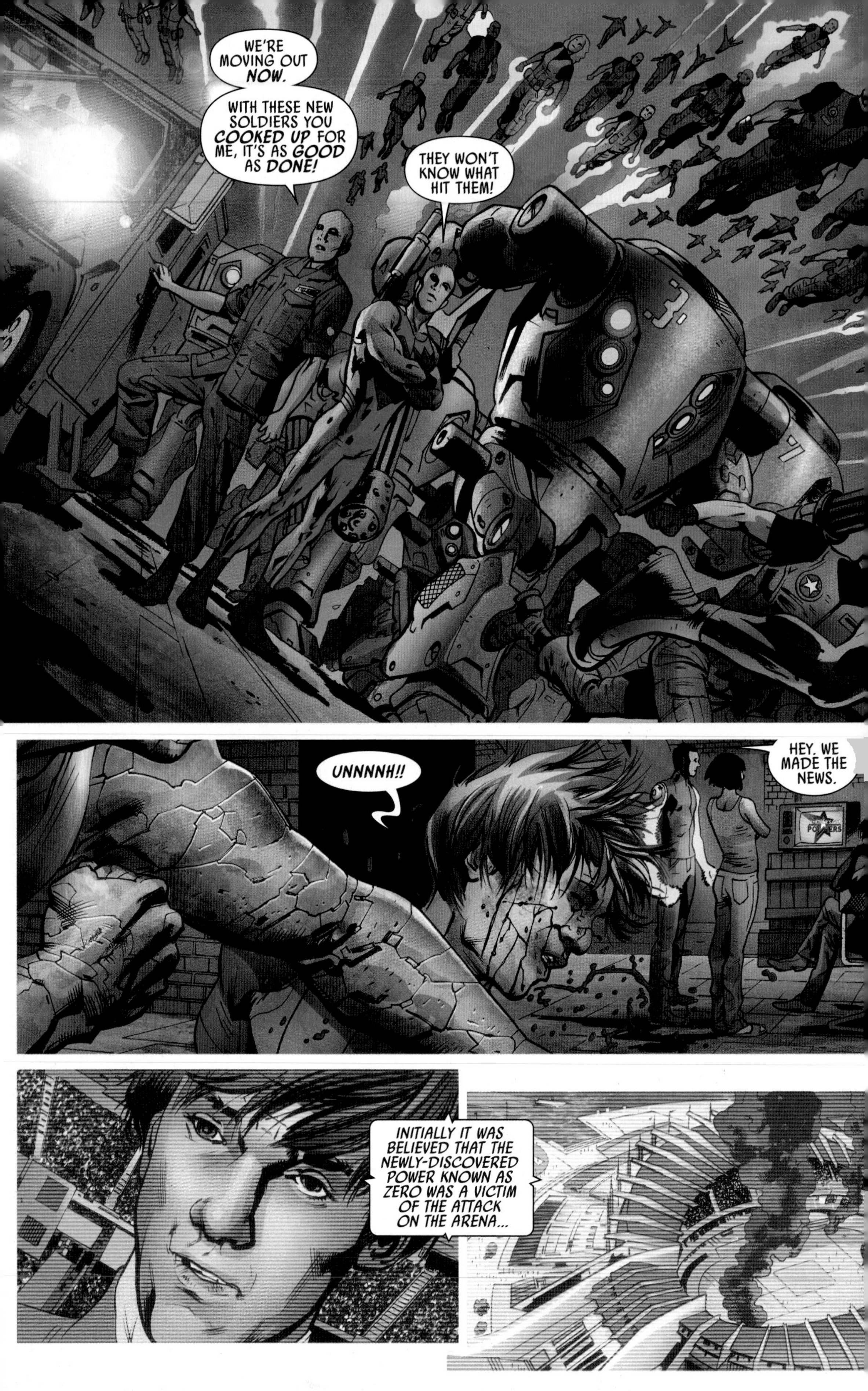
WE'RE MOVING OUT NOW.
WITH THESE NEW SOLDIERS YOU COOKED UP FOR ME, IT'S AS GOOD AS DONE!
THEY WON'T KNOW WHAT HIT THEM!
UNNNNH!!
HEY. WE MADE THE NEWS.
INITIALLY IT WAS BELIEVED THAT THE NEWLY-DISCOVERED POWER KNOWN AS ZERO WAS A VICTIM OF THE ATTACK ON THE ARENA...

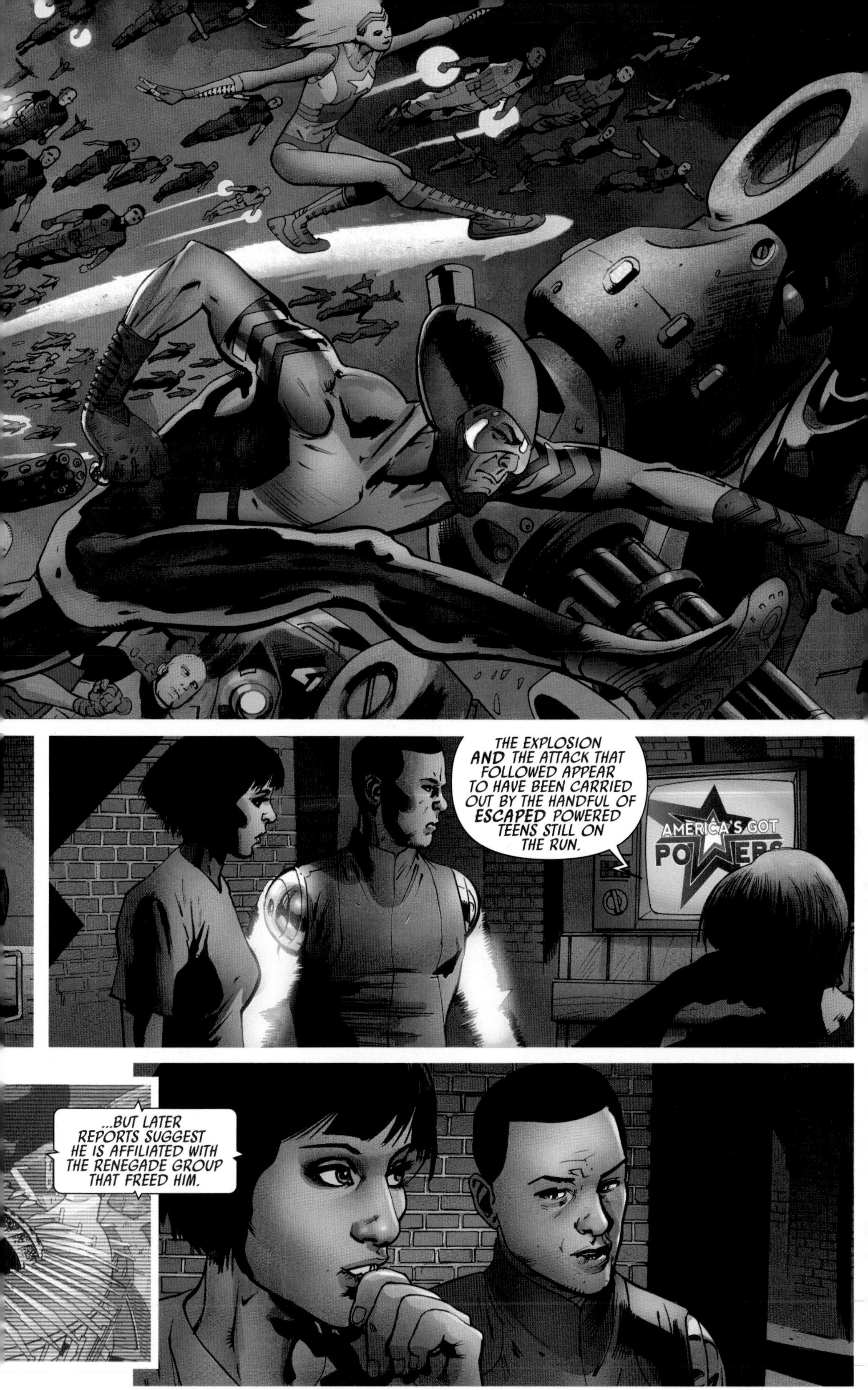
THE EXPLOSION AND THE ATTACK THAT FOLLOWED APPEAR TO HAVE BEEN CARRIED OUT BY THE HANDFUL OF ESCAPED POWERED TEENS STILL ON THE RUN.
AMERICA'S GOT POWERS
...BUT LATER REPORTS SUGGEST HE IS AFFILIATED WITH THE RENEGADE GROUP THAT FREED HIM.

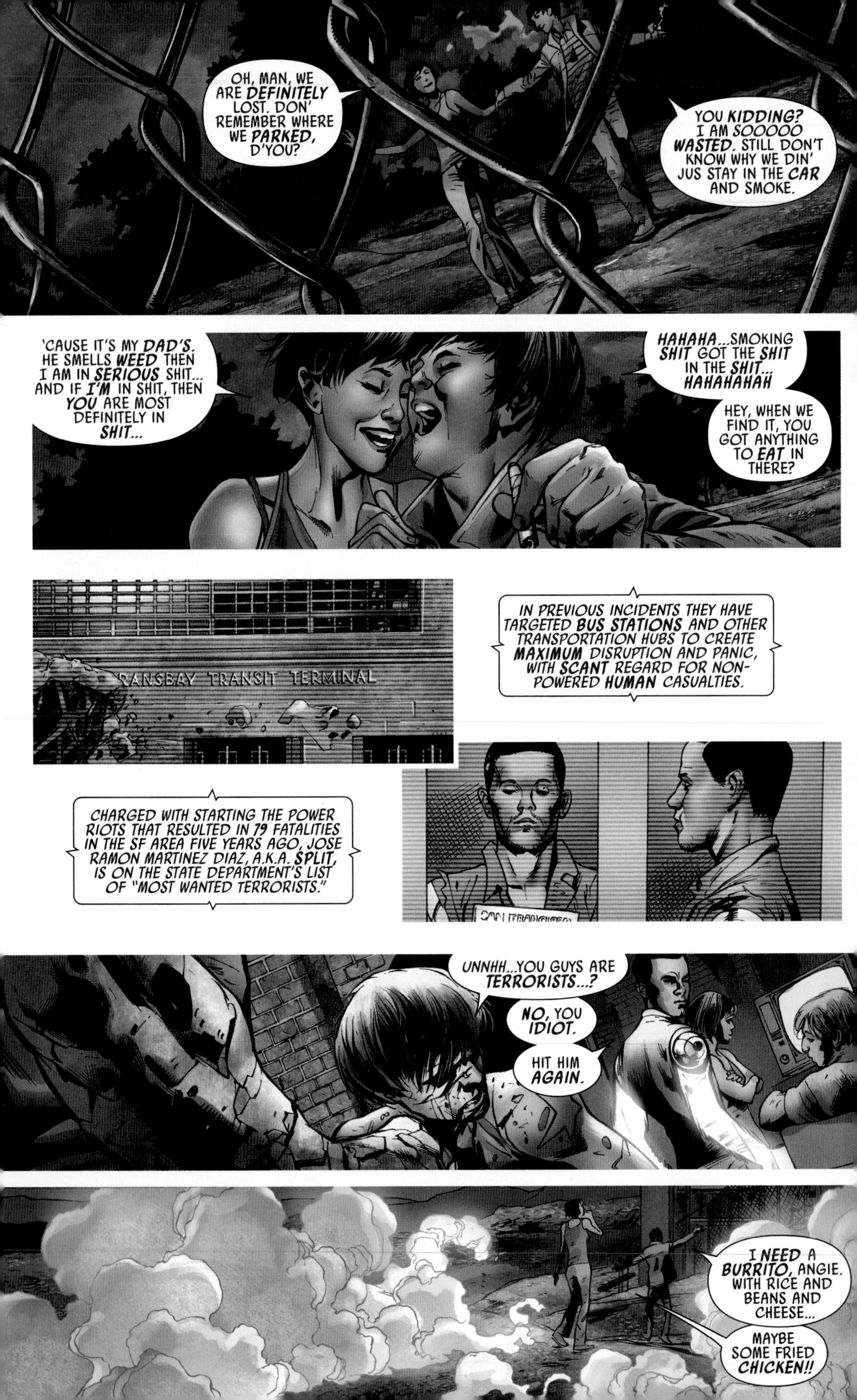

OH, MAN, WE ARE DEFINITELY LOST. DON' REMEMBER WHERE WE PARKED, D'YOU?
YOU KIDDING? I AM SOOOOO WASTED. STILL DON'T KNOW WHY WE DIN' JUS STAY IN THE CAR AND SMOKE.
'CAUSE IT'S MY DAD'S. HE SMELLS WEED THEN I AM IN SERIOUS SHIT... AND IF I'M IN SHIT, THEN YOU ARE MOST DEFINITELY IN SHIT...
HAHAHA...SMOKING SHIT GOT THE SHIT IN THE SHIT... HAHAHAHAH
HEY, WHEN WE FIND IT, YOU GOT ANYTHING TO EAT IN THERE?
RANSBAY TRANSIT TERMINAL
IN PREVIOUS INCIDENTS THEY HAVE TARGETED BUS STATIONS AND OTHER TRANSPORTATION HUBS TO CREATE MAXIMUM DISRUPTION AND PANIC, WITH SCANT REGARD FOR NON-POWERED HUMAN CASUALTIES.
CHARGED WITH STARTING THE POWER RIOTS THAT RESULTED IN 79 FATALITIES IN THE SF AREA FIVE YEARS AGO, JOSE RAMON MARTINEZ DIAZ, A.K.A. SPLIT, IS ON THE STATE DEPARTMENT'S LIST OF "MOST WANTED TERRORISTS."
UNNHH...YOU GUYS ARE TERRORISTS...?
NO, YOU IDIOT.
HIT HIM AGAIN.
I NEED A BURRITO, ANGIE. WITH RICE AND BEANS AND CHEESE...
MAYBE SOME FRIED CHICKEN!!

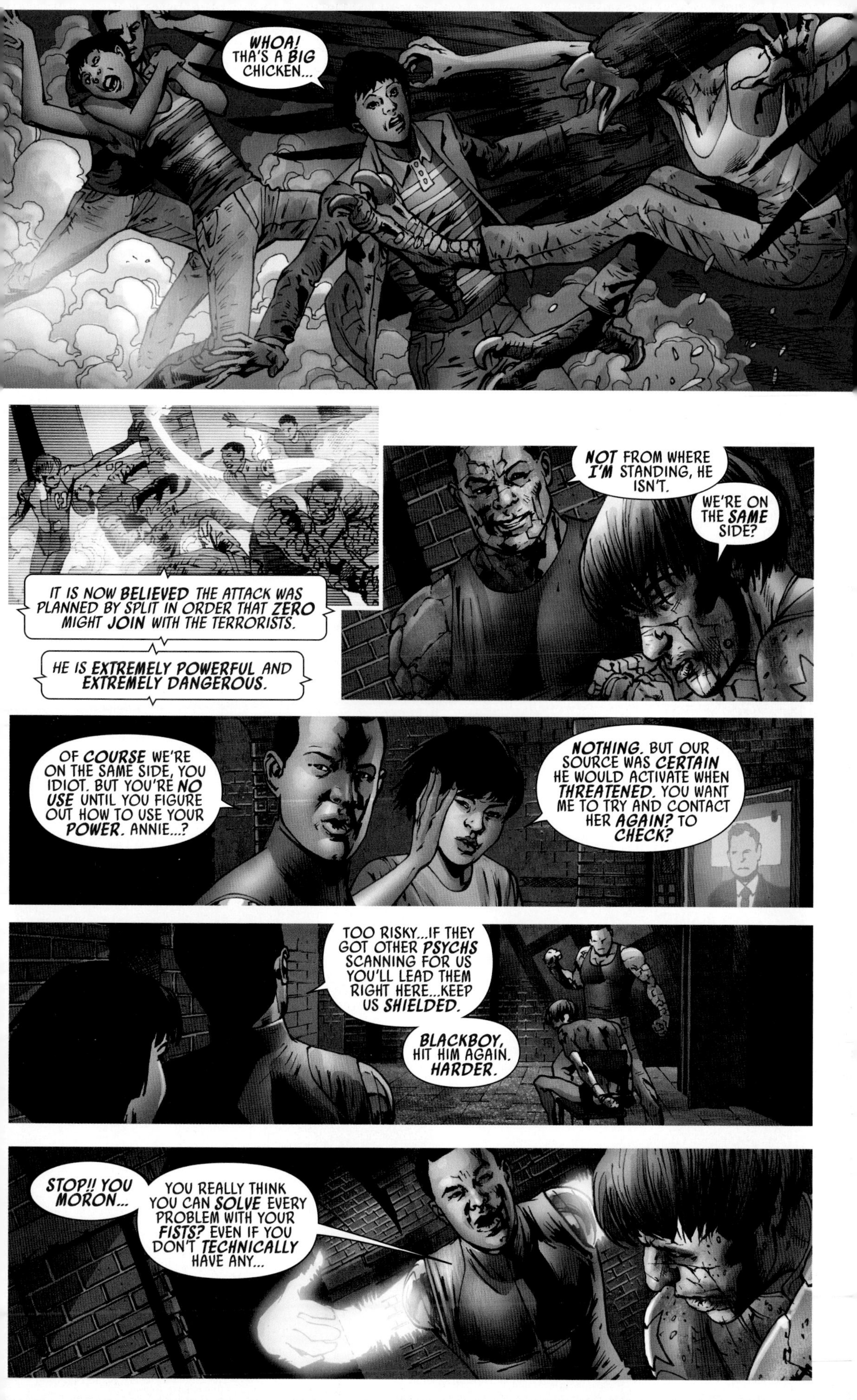
WHOA! THA'S A BIG CHICKEN...
IT IS NOW BELIEVED THE ATTACK WAS PLANNED BY SPLIT IN ORDER THAT ZERO MIGHT JOIN WITH THE TERRORISTS.
HE IS EXTREMELY POWERFUL AND EXTREMELY DANGEROUS.
NOT FROM WHERE I'M STANDING, HE ISN'T.
WE'RE ON THE SAME SIDE?
OF COURSE WE'RE ON THE SAME SIDE, YOU IDIOT. BUT YOU'RE NO USE UNTIL YOU FIGURE OUT HOW TO USE YOUR POWER. ANNIE...?
NOTHING. BUT OUR SOURCE WAS CERTAIN HE WOULD ACTIVATE WHEN THREATENED. YOU WANT ME TO TRY AND CONTACT HER AGAIN? TO CHECK?
TOO RISKY...IF THEY GOT OTHER PSYCHS SCANNING FOR US YOU'LL LEAD THEM RIGHT HERE...KEEP US SHIELDED.
BLACKBOY, HIT HIM AGAIN. HARDER.
STOP!! YOU MORON...
YOU REALLY THINK YOU CAN SOLVE EVERY PROBLEM WITH YOUR FISTS? EVEN IF YOU DON'T TECHNICALLY HAVE ANY...

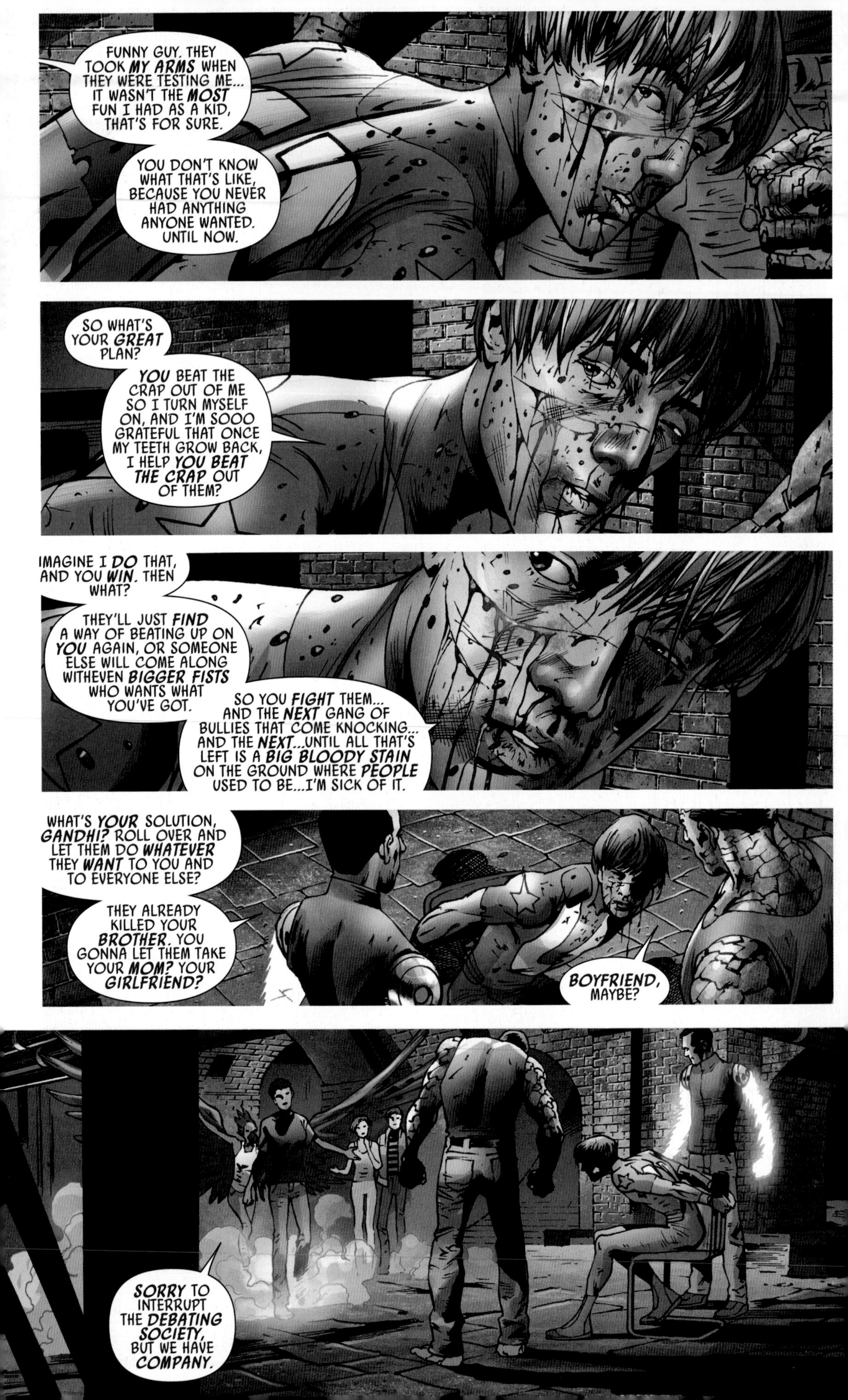

FUNNY GUY. THEY TOOK MY ARMS WHEN THEY WERE TESTING ME... IT WASN'T THE MOST FUN I HAD AS A KID, THAT'S FOR SURE.
YOU DON'T KNOW WHAT THAT'S LIKE, BECAUSE YOU NEVER HAD ANYTHING ANYONE WANTED. UNTIL NOW.
SO WHAT'S YOUR GREAT PLAN?
YOU BEAT THE CRAP OUT OF ME SO I TURN MYSELF ON, AND I'M SOOO GRATEFUL THAT ONCE MY TEETH GROW BACK, I HELP YOU BEAT THE CRAP OUT OF THEM?
IMAGINE I DO THAT, AND YOU WIN. THEN WHAT?
THEY'LL JUST FIND A WAY OF BEATING UP ON YOU AGAIN, OR SOMEONE ELSE WILL COME ALONG WITHEVEN BIGGER FISTS WHO WANTS WHAT YOU'VE GOT.
SO YOU FIGHT THEM... AND THE NEXT GANG OF BULLIES THAT COME KNOCKING... AND THE NEXT...UNTIL ALL THAT'S LEFT IS A BIG BLOODY STAIN ON THE GROUND WHERE PEOPLE USED TO BE...I'M SICK OF IT.
WHAT'S YOUR SOLUTION, GANDHI? ROLL OVER AND LET THEM DO WHATEVER THEY WANT TO YOU AND TO EVERYONE ELSE?
THEY ALREADY KILLED YOUR BROTHER. YOU GONNA LET THEM TAKE YOUR MOM? YOUR GIRLFRIEND?
BOYFRIEND, MAYBE?
SORRY TO INTERRUPT THE DEBATING SOCIETY, BUT WE HAVE COMPANY.

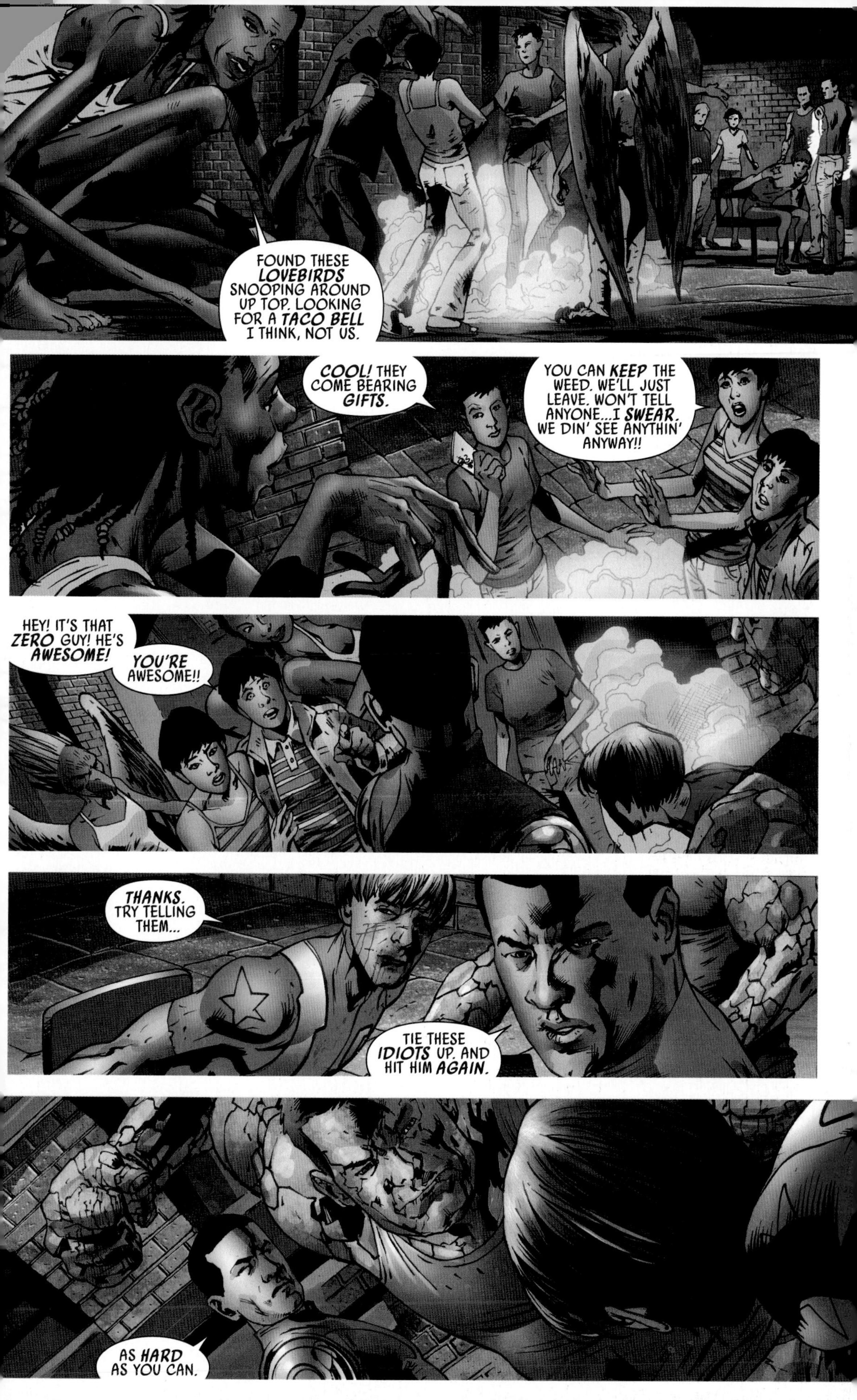
FOUND THESE LOVEBIRDS SNOOPING AROUND UP TOP. LOOKING FOR A TACO BELL I THINK, NOT US.
COOL! THEY COME BEARING GIFTS.
YOU CAN KEEP THE WEED. WE'LL JUST LEAVE. WON'T TELL ANYONE...I SWEAR. WE DIN' SEE ANYTHIN' ANYWAY!!
HEY! IT'S THAT ZERO GUY! HE'S AWESOME!
YOU'RE AWESOME!!
THANKS. TRY TELLING THEM...
TIE THESE IDIOTS UP. AND HIT HIM AGAIN.
AS HARD AS YOU CAN.

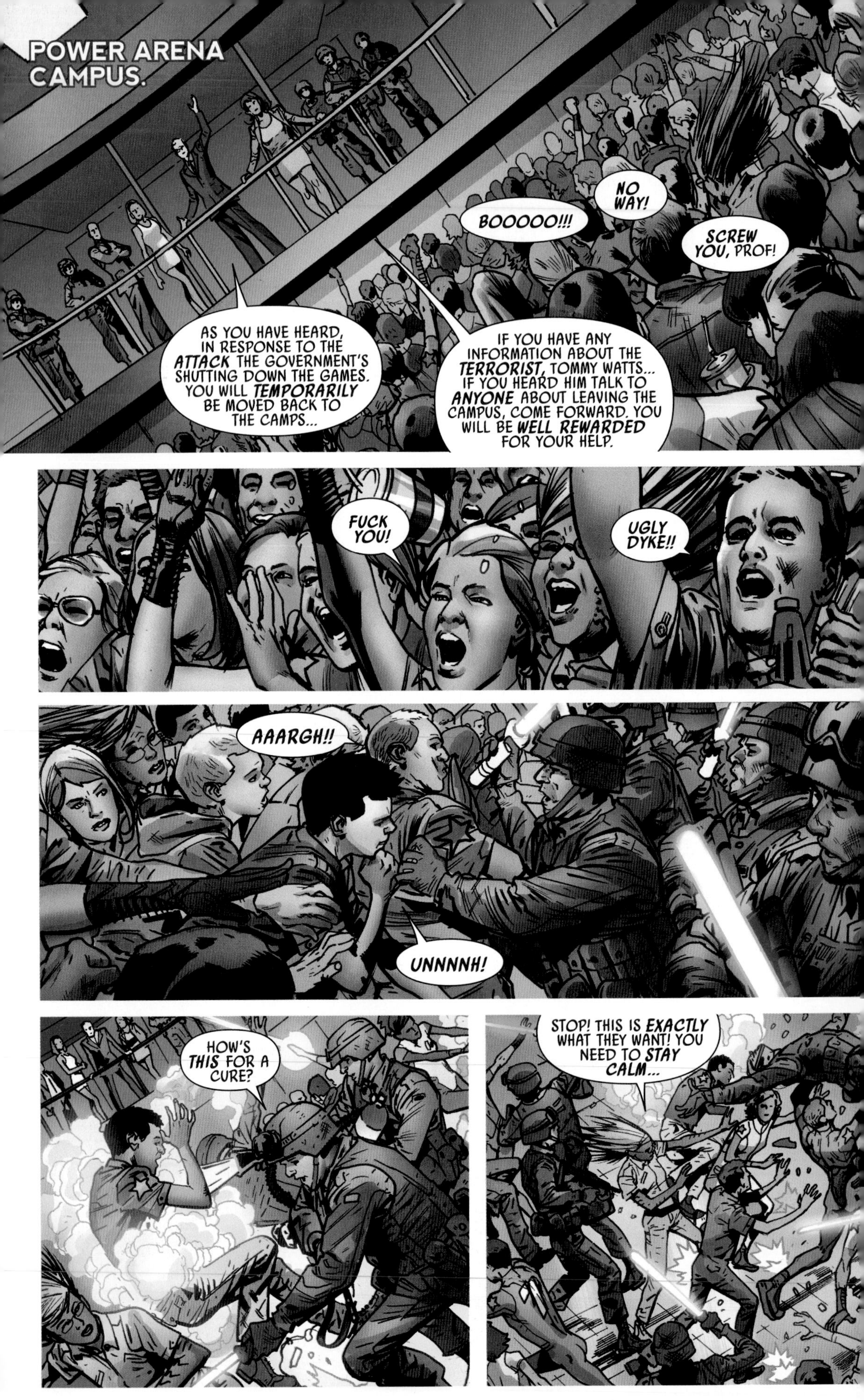
POWER ARENA CAMPUS.
AS YOU HAVE HEARD, IN RESPONSE TO THE ATTACK THE GOVERNMENT'S SHUTTING DOWN THE GAMES. YOU WILL TEMPORARILY BE MOVED BACK TO THE CAMPS...
IF YOU HAVE ANY INFORMATION ABOUT THE TERRORIST, TOMMY WATTS... IF YOU HEARD HIM TALK TO ANYONE ABOUT LEAVING THE CAMPUS, COME FORWARD. YOU WILL BE WELL REWARDED FOR YOUR HELP.
BOOOOO!!!
NO WAY!
SCREW YOU, PROF!
FUCK YOU!
UGLY DYKE!!
AAARGH!!
UNNNNH!
HOW'S THIS FOR A CURE?
STOP! THIS IS EXACTLY WHAT THEY WANT! YOU NEED TO STAY CALM...

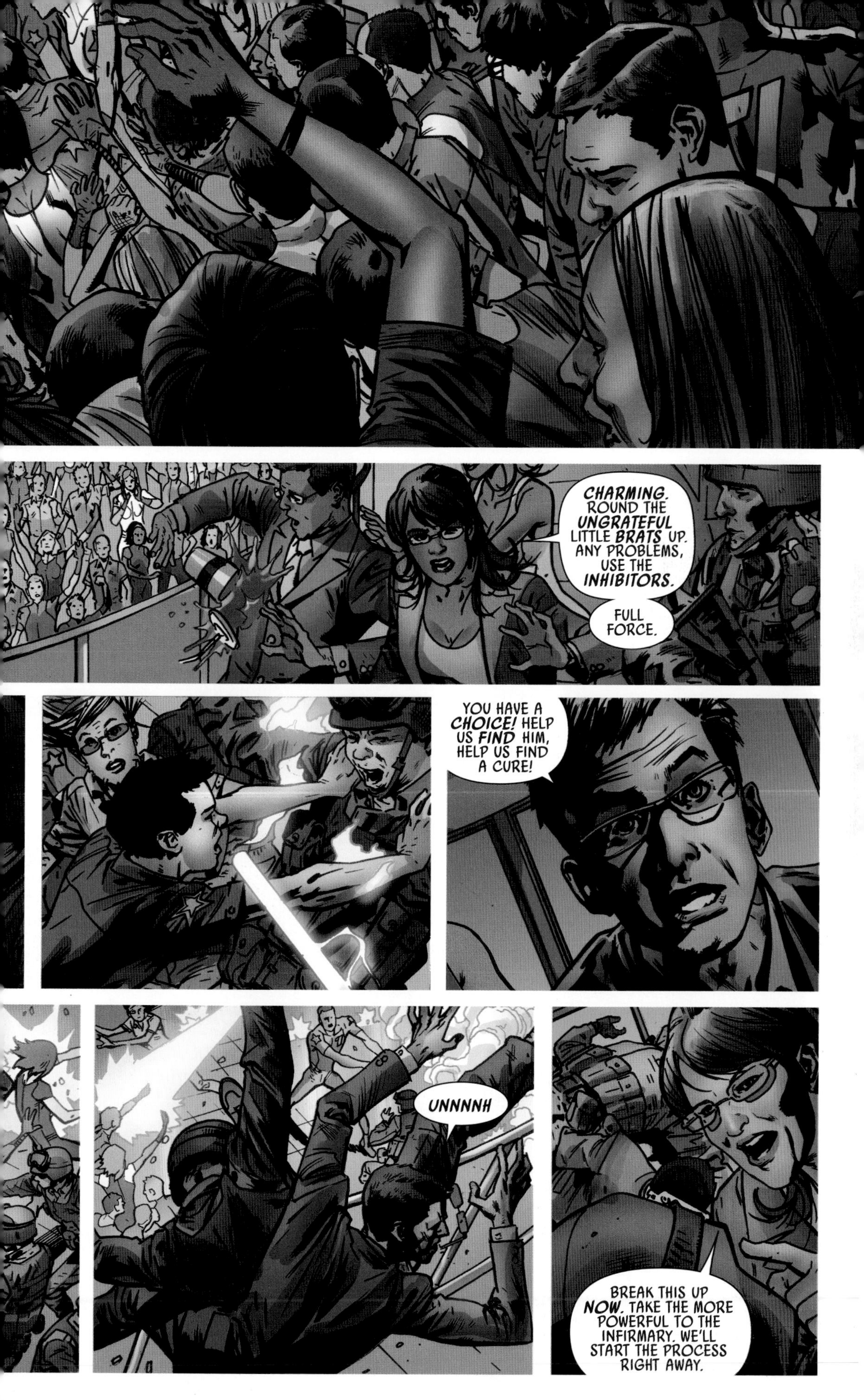
CHARMING. ROUND THE UNGRATEFUL LITTLE BRATS UP. ANY PROBLEMS, USE THE INHIBITORS.
FULL FORCE.
YOU HAVE A CHOICE! HELP US FIND HIM, HELP US FIND A CURE!
UNNNNH
BREAK THIS UP NOW. TAKE THE MORE POWERFUL TO THE INFIRMARY. WE'LL START THE PROCESS RIGHT AWAY.

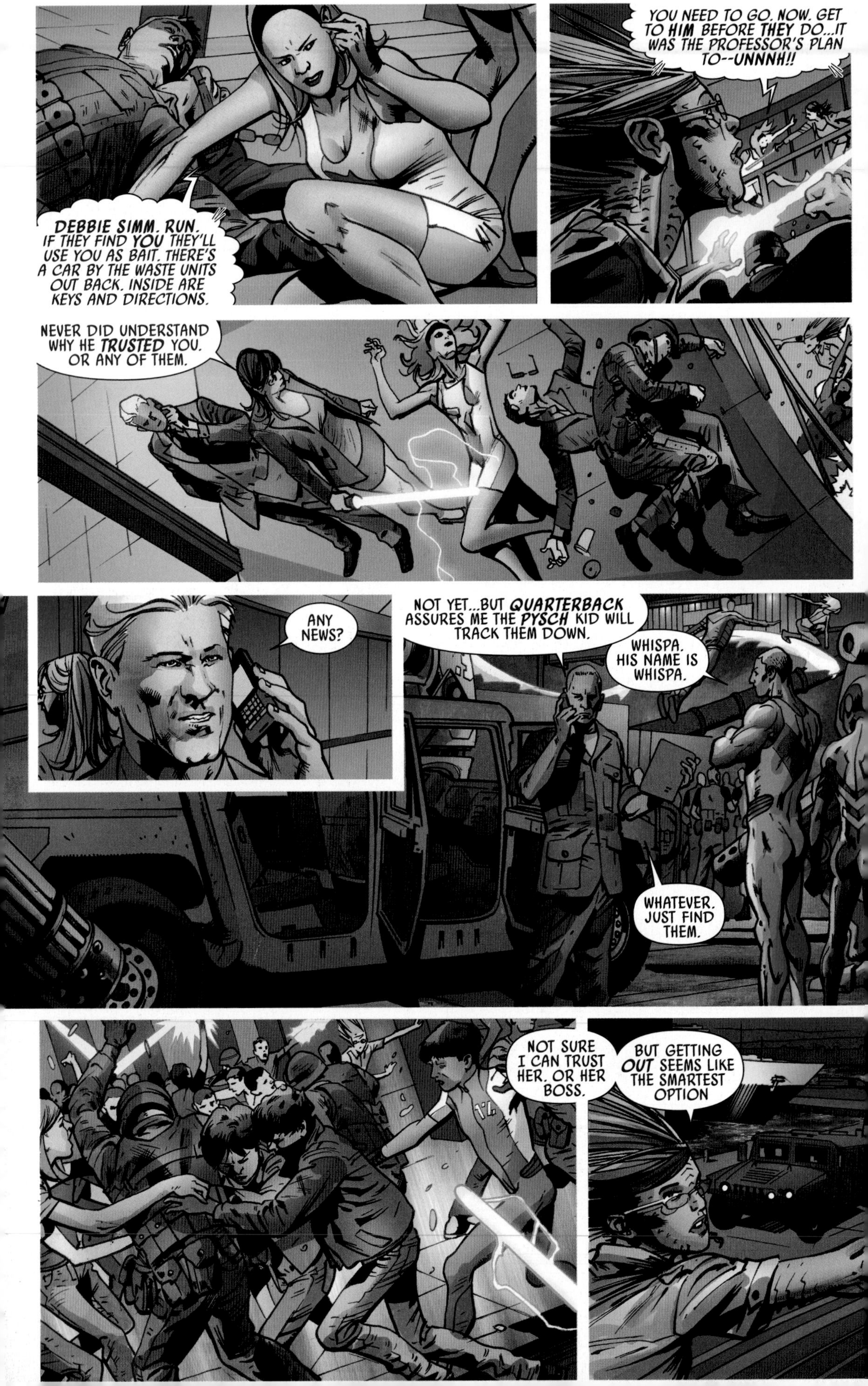
DEBBIE SIMM. RUN. IF THEY FIND YOU THEY'LL USE YOU AS BAIT. THERE'S A CAR BY THE WASTE UNITS OUT BACK. INSIDE ARE KEYS AND DIRECTIONS.
YOU NEED TO GO. NOW. GET TO HIM BEFORE THEY DO...IT WAS THE PROFESSOR'S PLAN TO--UNNNH!!
NEVER DID UNDERSTAND WHY HE TRUSTED YOU. OR ANY OF THEM.
ANY NEWS?
NOT YET...BUT QUARTERBACK ASSURES ME THE PYSCH KID WILL TRACK THEM DOWN.
WHISPA. HIS NAME IS WHISPA.
WHATEVER. JUST FIND THEM.
NOT SURE I CAN TRUST HER. OR HER BOSS.
BUT GETTING OUT SEEMS LIKE THE SMARTEST OPTION

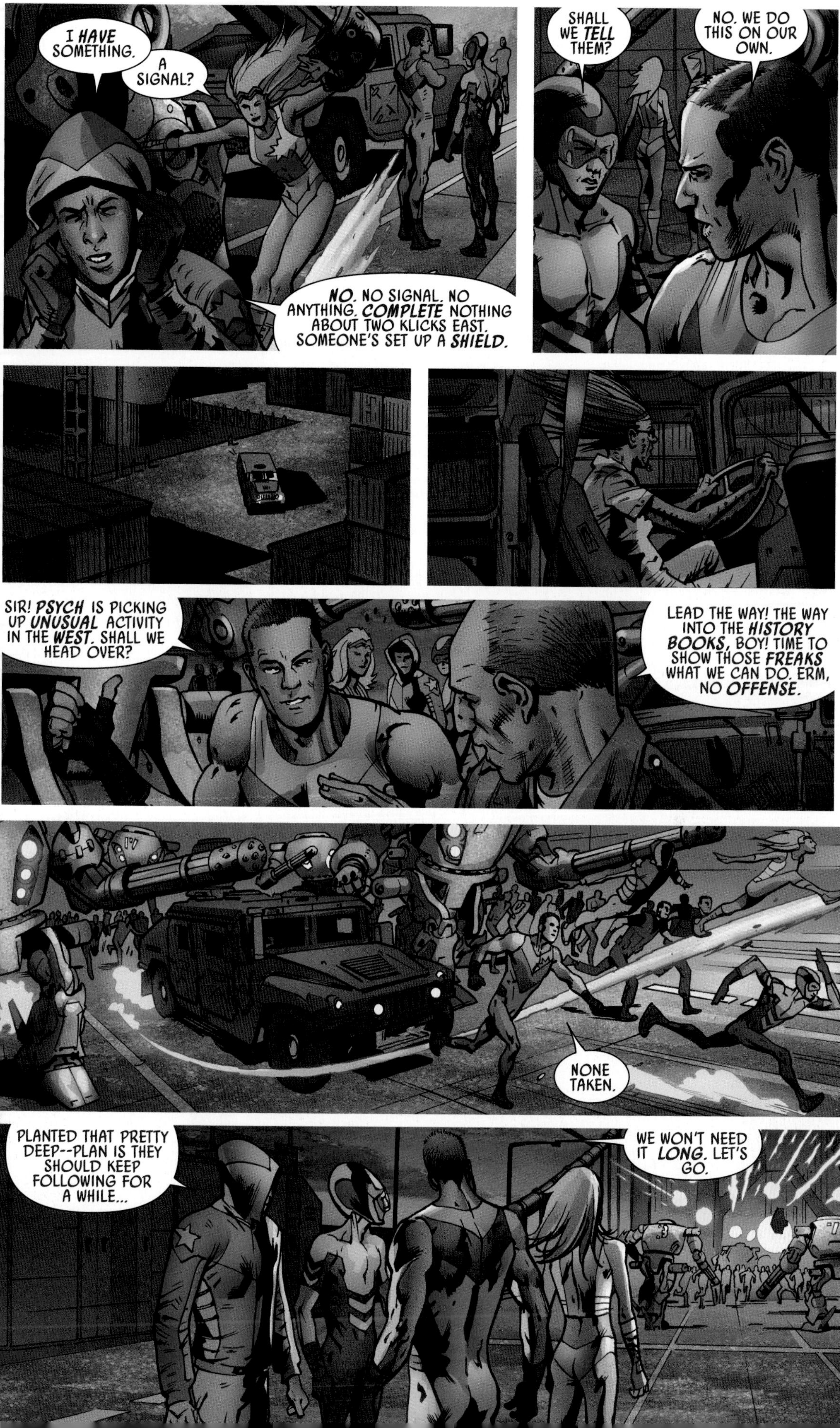
I HAVE SOMETHING.
A SIGNAL?
NO. NO SIGNAL. NO ANYTHING. COMPLETE NOTHING ABOUT TWO KLICKS EAST. SOMEONE'S SET UP A SHIELD.
SHALL WE TELL THEM?
NO. WE DO THIS ON OUR OWN.
SIR! PSYCH IS PICKING UP UNUSUAL ACTIVITY IN THE WEST. SHALL WE HEAD OVER?
LEAD THE WAY! THE WAY INTO THE HISTORY BOOKS, BOY! TIME TO SHOW THOSE FREAKS WHAT WE CAN DO. ERM, NO OFFENSE.
NONE TAKEN.
PLANTED THAT PRETTY DEEP--PLAN IS THEY SHOULD KEEP FOLLOWING FOR A WHILE...
WE WON'T NEED IT LONG. LET'S GO.

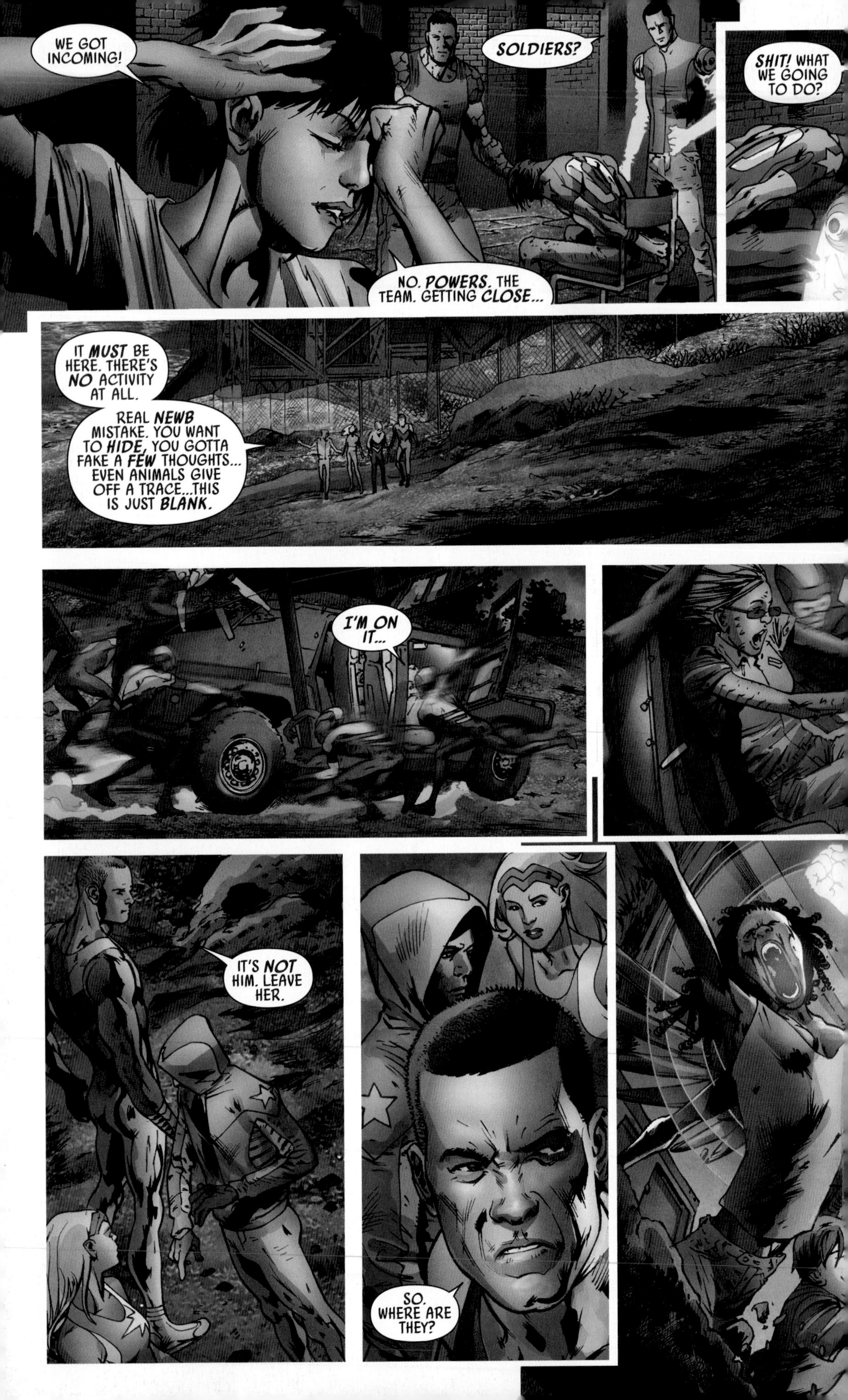
WE GOT INCOMING!
SOLDIERS?
NO. POWERS. THE TEAM. GETTING CLOSE...
SHIT! WHAT WE GOING TO DO?
IT MUST BE HERE. THERE'S NO ACTIVITY AT ALL.
REAL NEWB MISTAKE. YOU WANT TO HIDE, YOU GOTTA FAKE A FEW THOUGHTS... EVEN ANIMALS GIVE OFF A TRACE...THIS IS JUST BLANK.
I'M ON IT...
IT'S NOT HIM. LEAVE HER.
SO. WHERE ARE THEY?

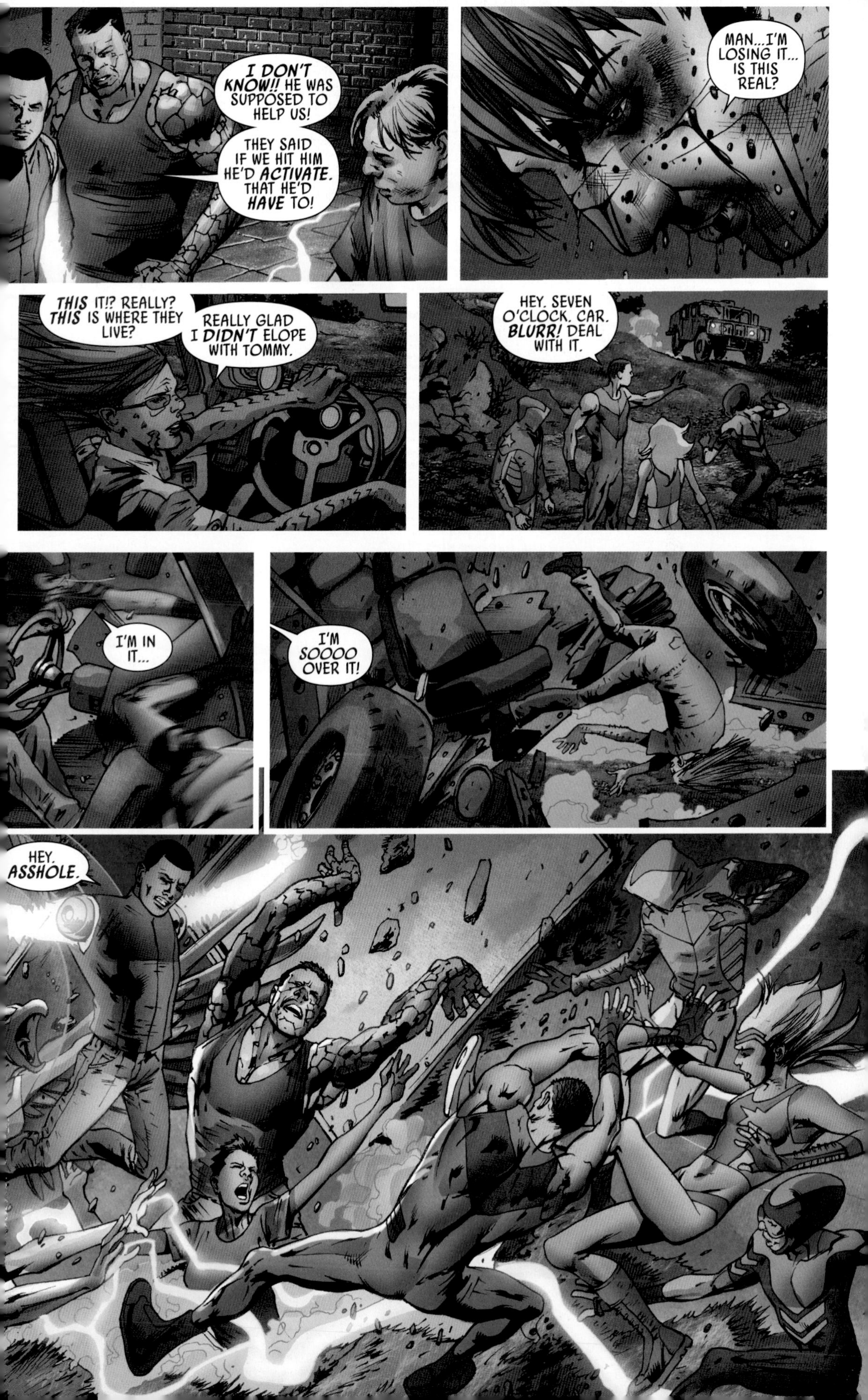
I DON'T KNOW!! HE WAS SUPPOSED TO HELP US!
THEY SAID IF WE HIT HIM HE'D ACTIVATE. THAT HE'D HAVE TO!
MAN...I'M LOSING IT... IS THIS REAL?
THIS IT!? REALLY? THIS IS WHERE THEY LIVE?
REALLY GLAD I DIDN'T ELOPE WITH TOMMY.
HEY. SEVEN O'CLOCK. CAR. BLURR! DEAL WITH IT.
I'M IN IT...
I'M SOOOO OVER IT!
HEY. ASSHOLE.

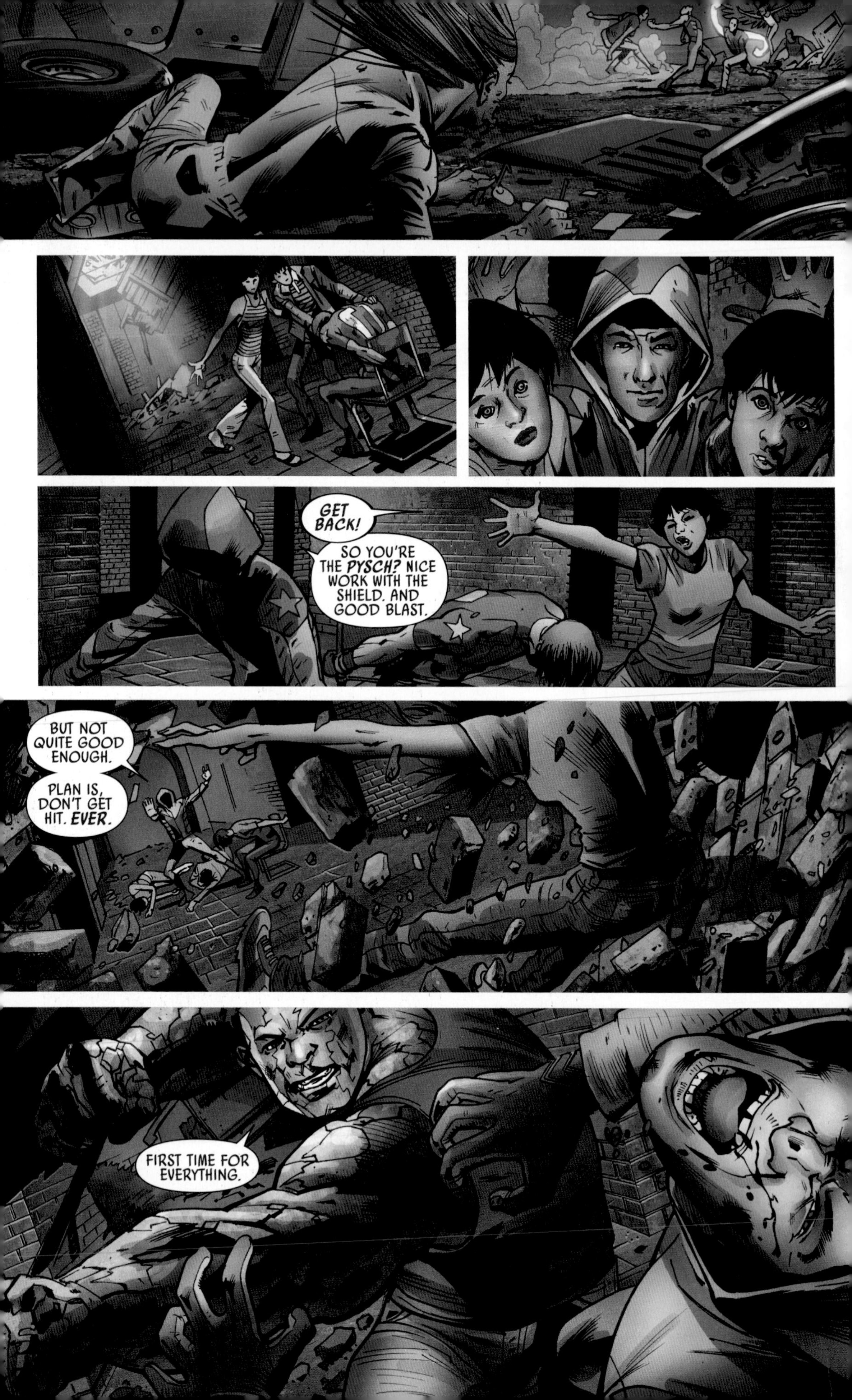
GET BACK!
SO YOU'RE THE PYSCH? NICE WORK WITH THE SHIELD. AND GOOD BLAST.
BUT NOT QUITE GOOD ENOUGH.
PLAN IS, DON'T GET HIT. EVER.
FIRST TIME FOR EVERYTHING.

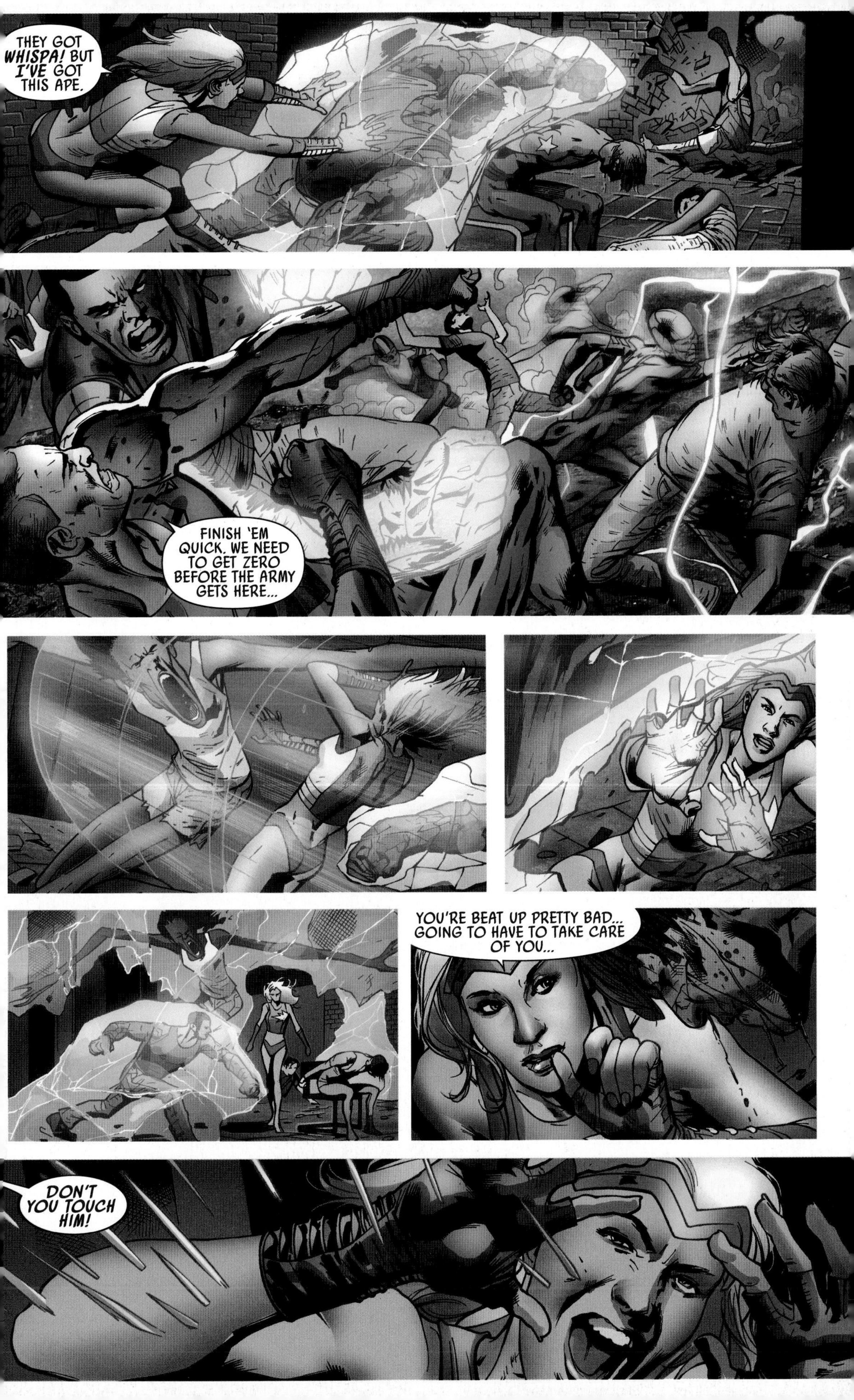
THEY GOT WHISPA! BUT I'VE GOT THIS APE.
FINISH 'EM QUICK. WE NEED TO GET ZERO BEFORE THE ARMY GETS HERE...
YOU'RE BEAT UP PRETTY BAD... GOING TO HAVE TO TAKE CARE OF YOU...
DON'T YOU TOUCH HIM!

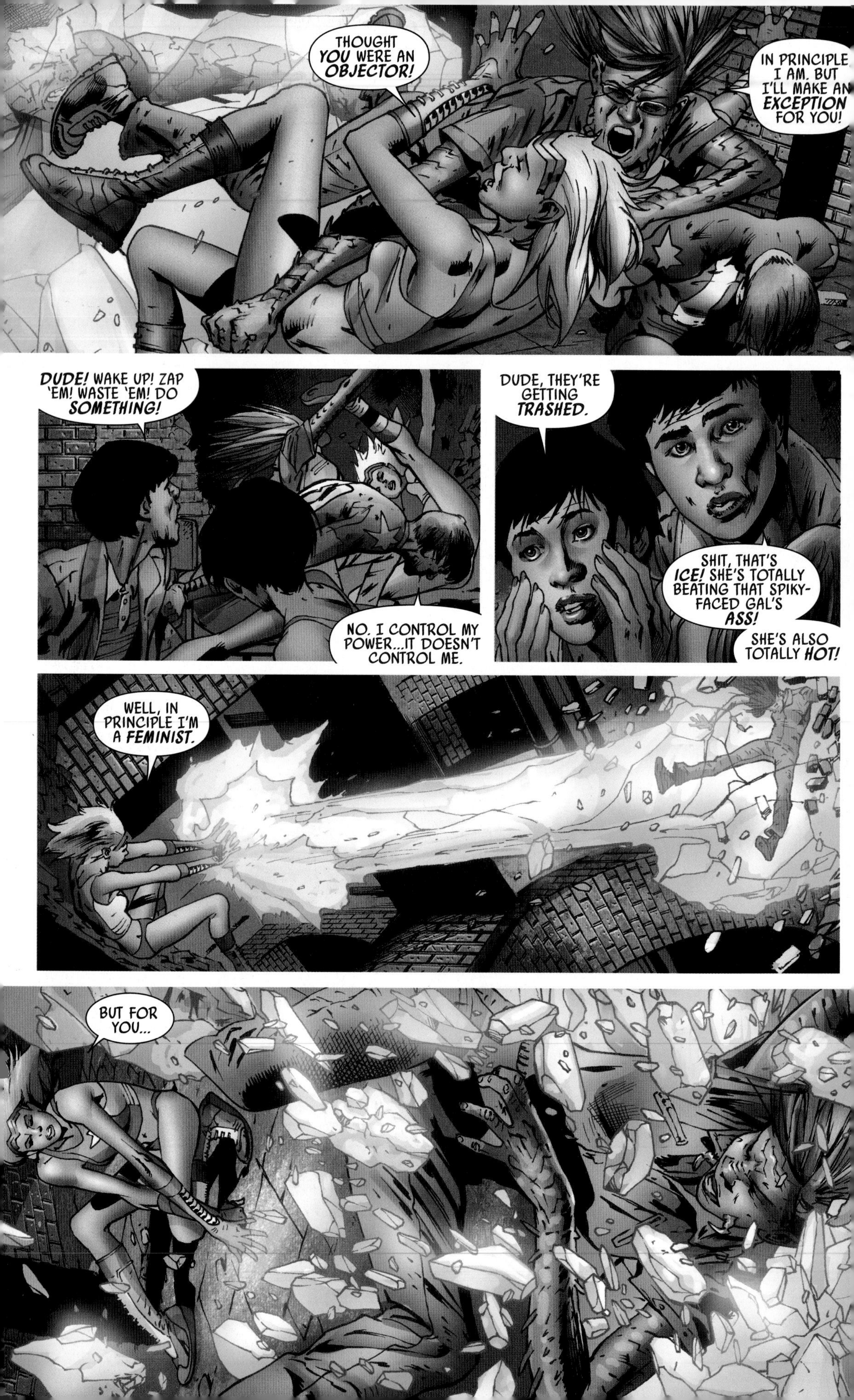
THOUGHT YOU WERE AN OBJECTOR!
IN PRINCIPLE I AM. BUT I'LL MAKE AN EXCEPTION FOR YOU!
DUDE! WAKE UP! ZAP 'EM! WASTE 'EM! DO SOMETHING!
NO. I CONTROL MY POWER...IT DOESN'T CONTROL ME.
DUDE, THEY'RE GETTING TRASHED.
SHIT, THAT'S ICE! SHE'S TOTALLY BEATING THAT SPIKY-FACED GAL'S ASS!
SHE'S ALSO TOTALLY HOT!
WELL, IN PRINCIPLE I'M A FEMINIST.
BUT FOR YOU...

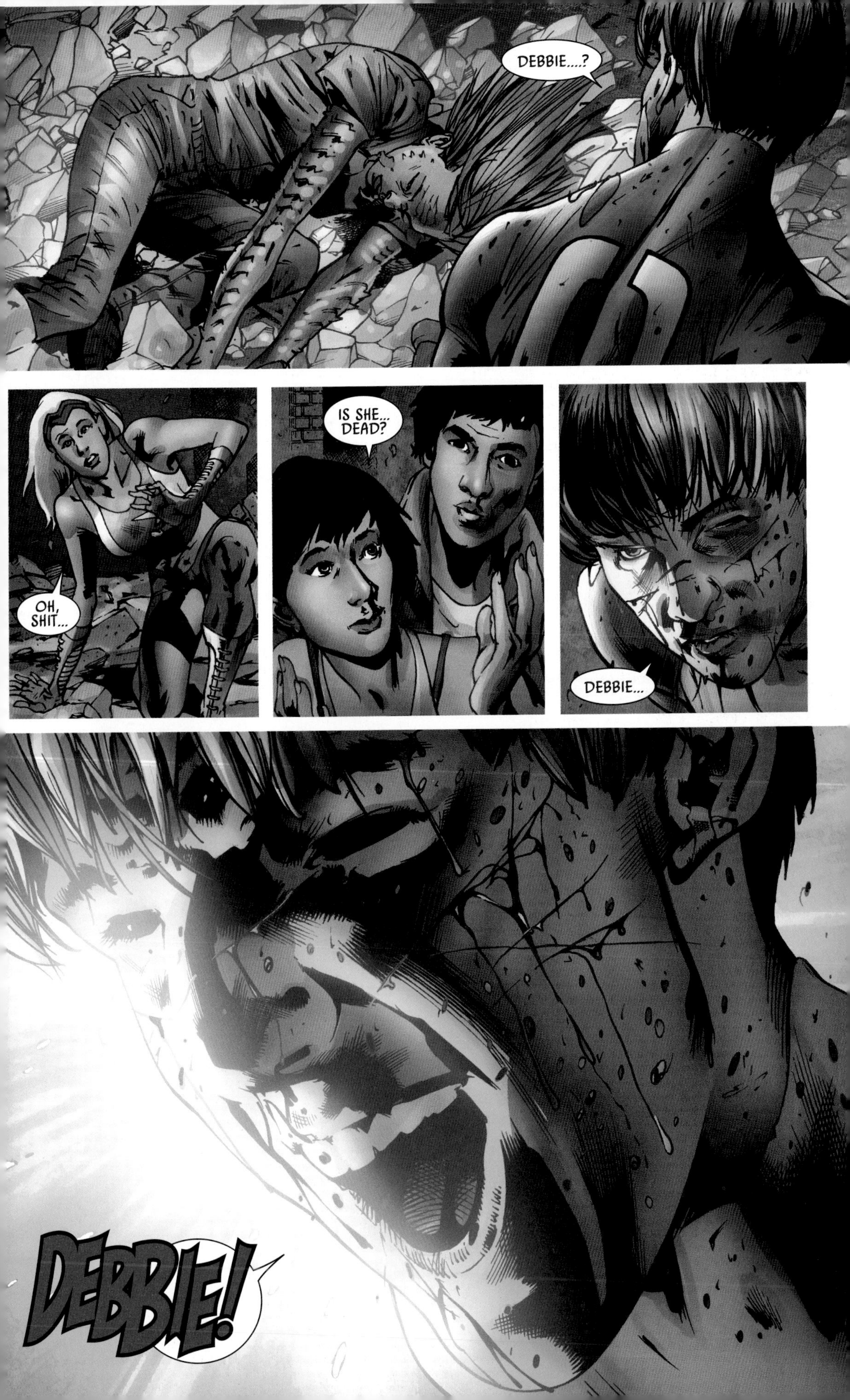
DEBBIE....?
OH, SHIT...
IS SHE... DEAD?
DEBBIE...
DEBBIE!

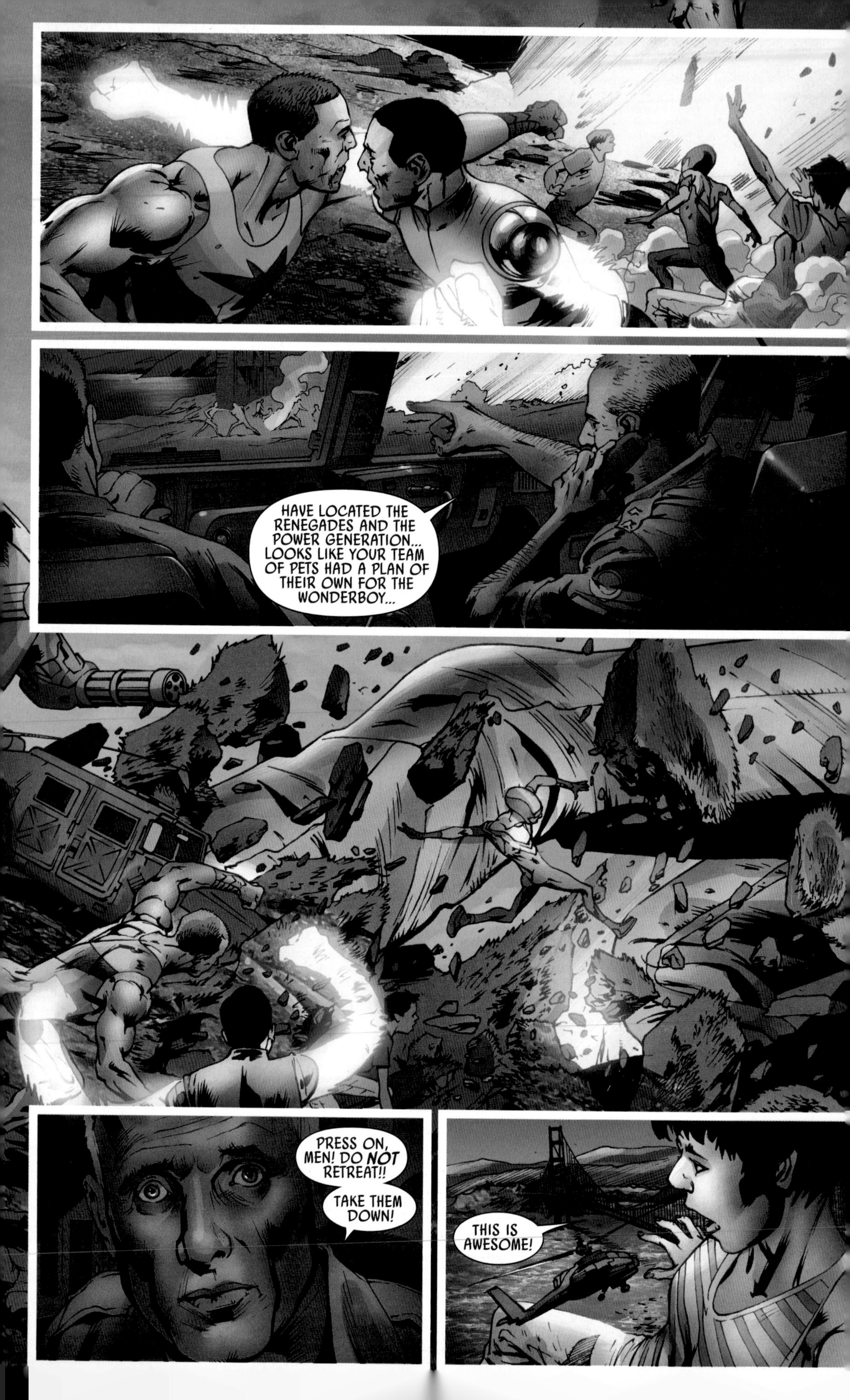
HAVE LOCATED THE RENEGADES AND THE POWER GENERATION... LOOKS LIKE YOUR TEAM OF PETS HAD A PLAN OF THEIR OWN FOR THE WONDERBOY...
PRESS ON, MEN! DO NOT RETREAT!!
TAKE THEM DOWN!
THIS IS AWESOME!

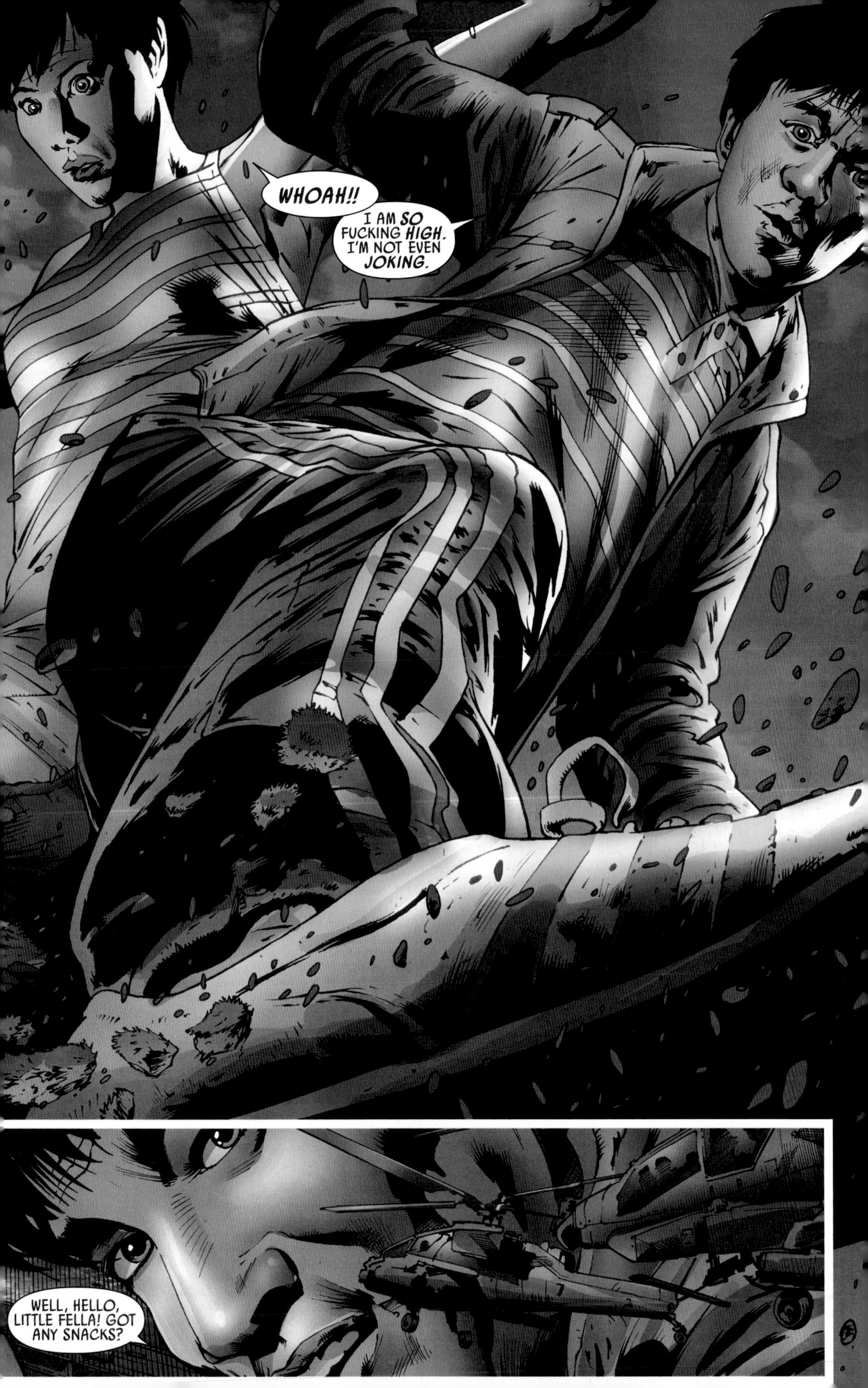
WHOAH!!
I AM SO FUCKING HIGH. I'M NOT EVEN JOKING.
WELL, HELLO, LITTLE FELLA! GOT ANY SNACKS?

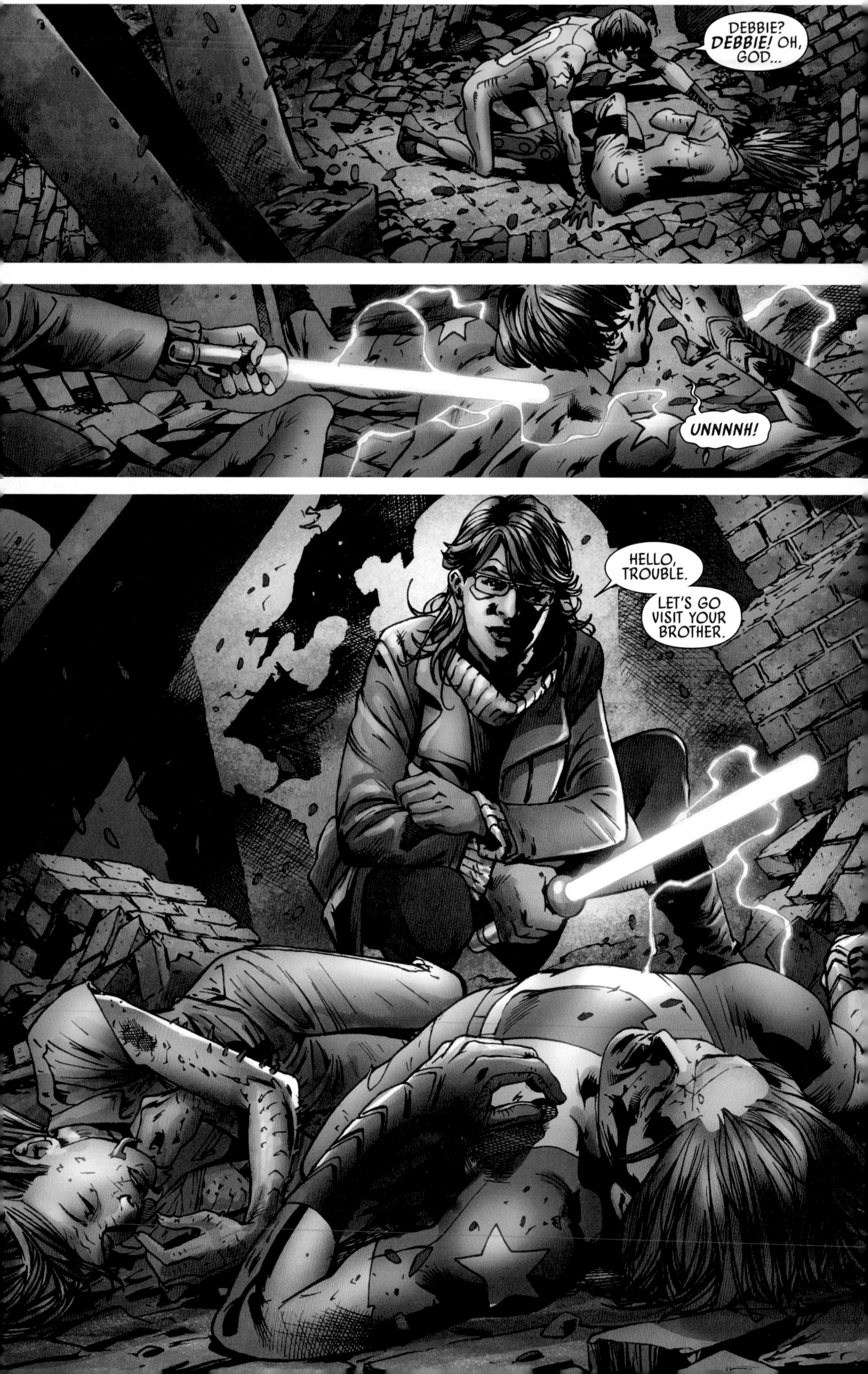
DEBBIE? **DEBBIE!** OH, GOD...
UNNNNH!
HELLO, TROUBLE.
LET'S GO VISIT YOUR BROTHER.

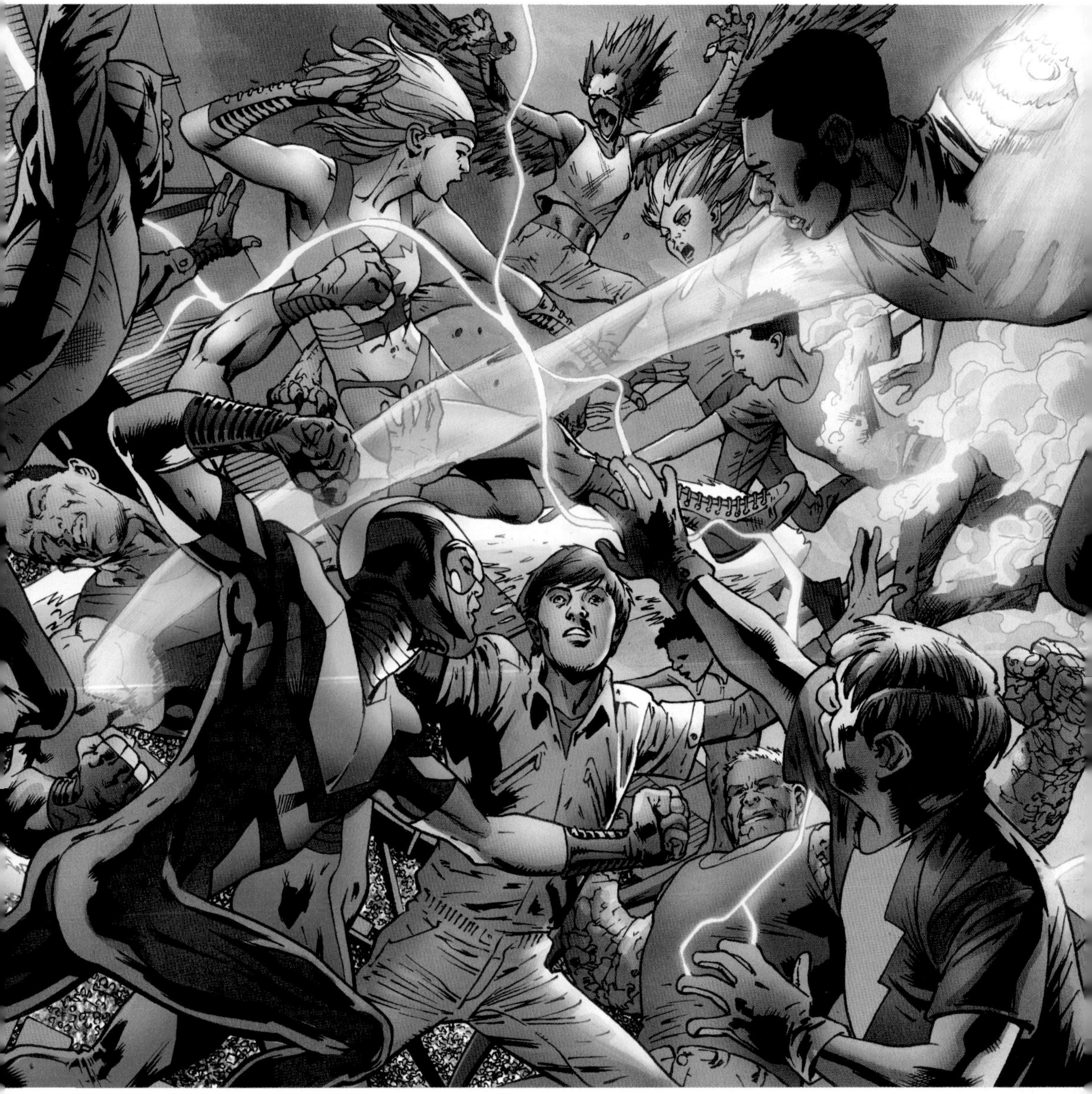

CHAPTER **FIVE**

The Massive Ordnance Air Blast (MOAB) bomb produced in the United States is the second most powerful conventional bomb in the world.

The most powerful is said to be the **Aviation Thermobaric Bomb of Increased Power (ATBIP)** *[Russian: Авиационная вакуумная бомба повышенной мощности (АВБПМ)]*, nicknamed **"Father of All Bombs" (FOAB)** *(Отец всех бомб)*, a Russian-made, air-delivered/ land-activated thermobaric weapon. In describing the bomb's destructive power, Russian deputy armed forces chief of staff Alexander Rukshin was quoted as saying, "All that is alive merely evaporates." [1] The bomb is reportedly four times more powerful than the U.S. military's GBU-43/B Massive Ordnance Air Blast bomb (whose official military acronym "MOAB" is often colloquially said as the "Mother of All Bombs"). This would make it the most powerful conventional (non-nuclear) weapon in the world. [2] although the veracity of Russia's claims of the weapon's size and power has been called into question by some U.S defense analysts.

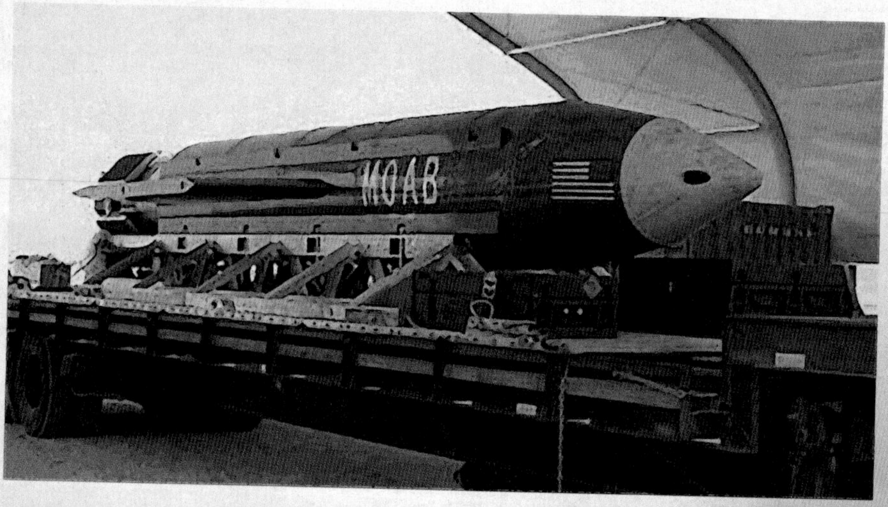
MOAB

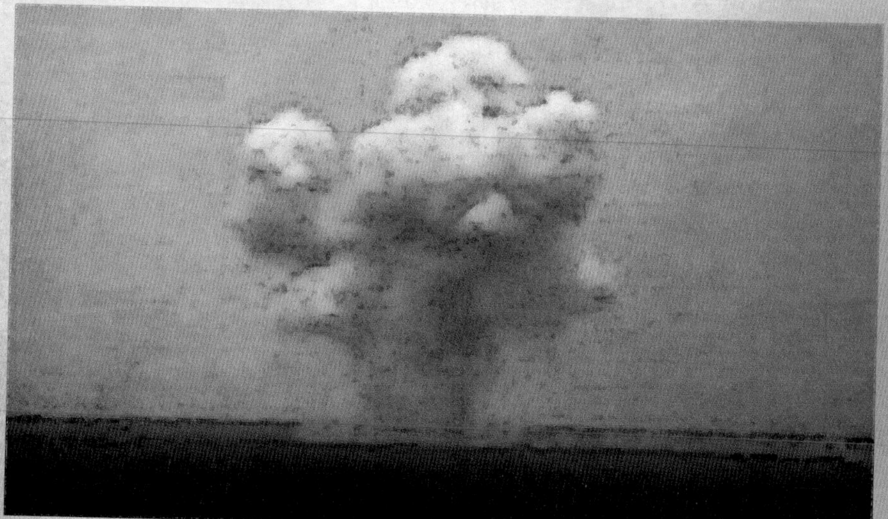

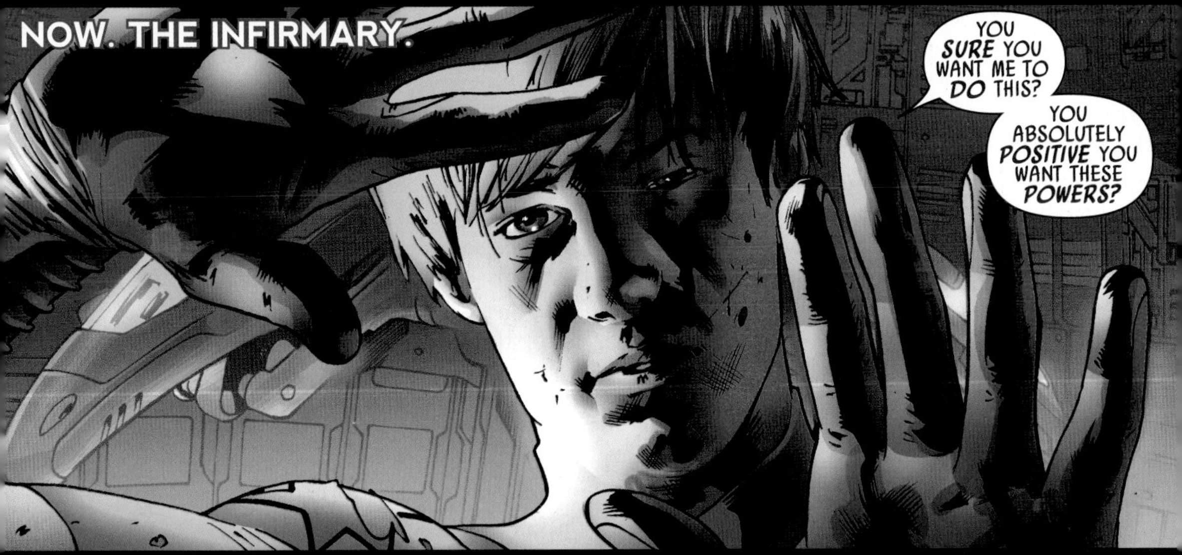
NOW. THE INFIRMARY.
YOU SURE YOU WANT ME TO DO THIS?
YOU ABSOLUTELY POSITIVE YOU WANT THESE POWERS?

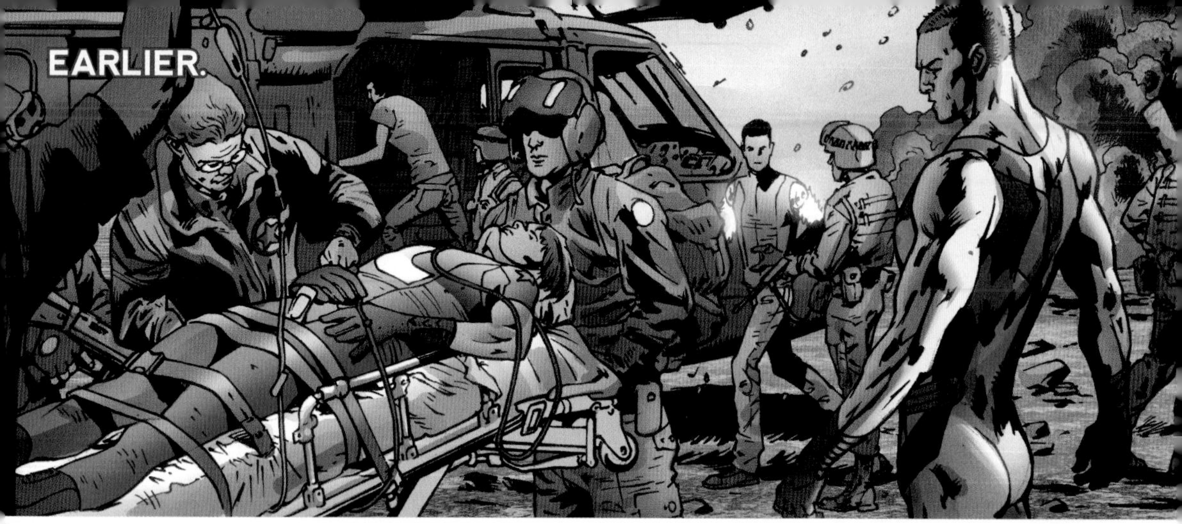
EARLIER.

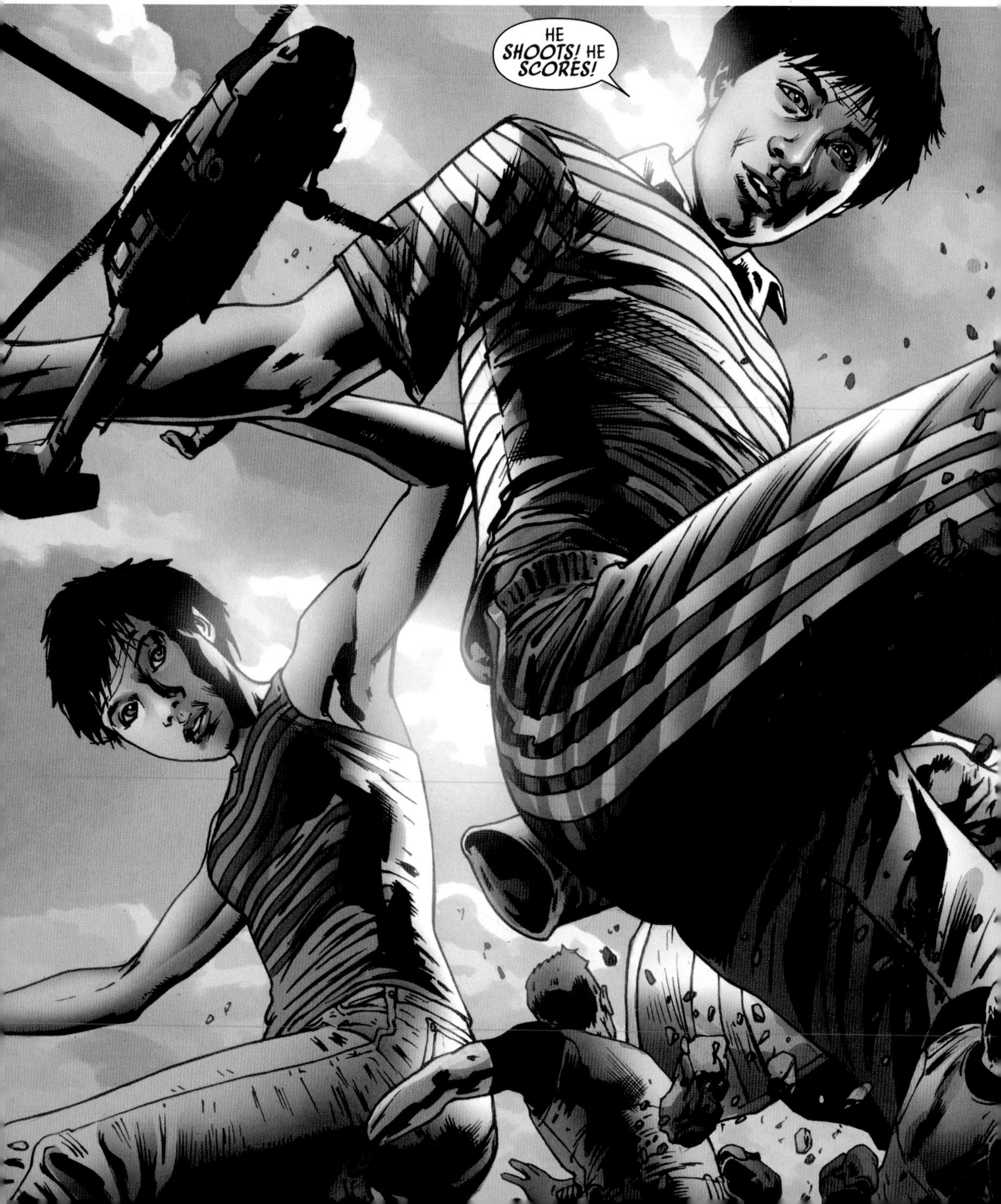
HE SHOOTS! HE SCORES!

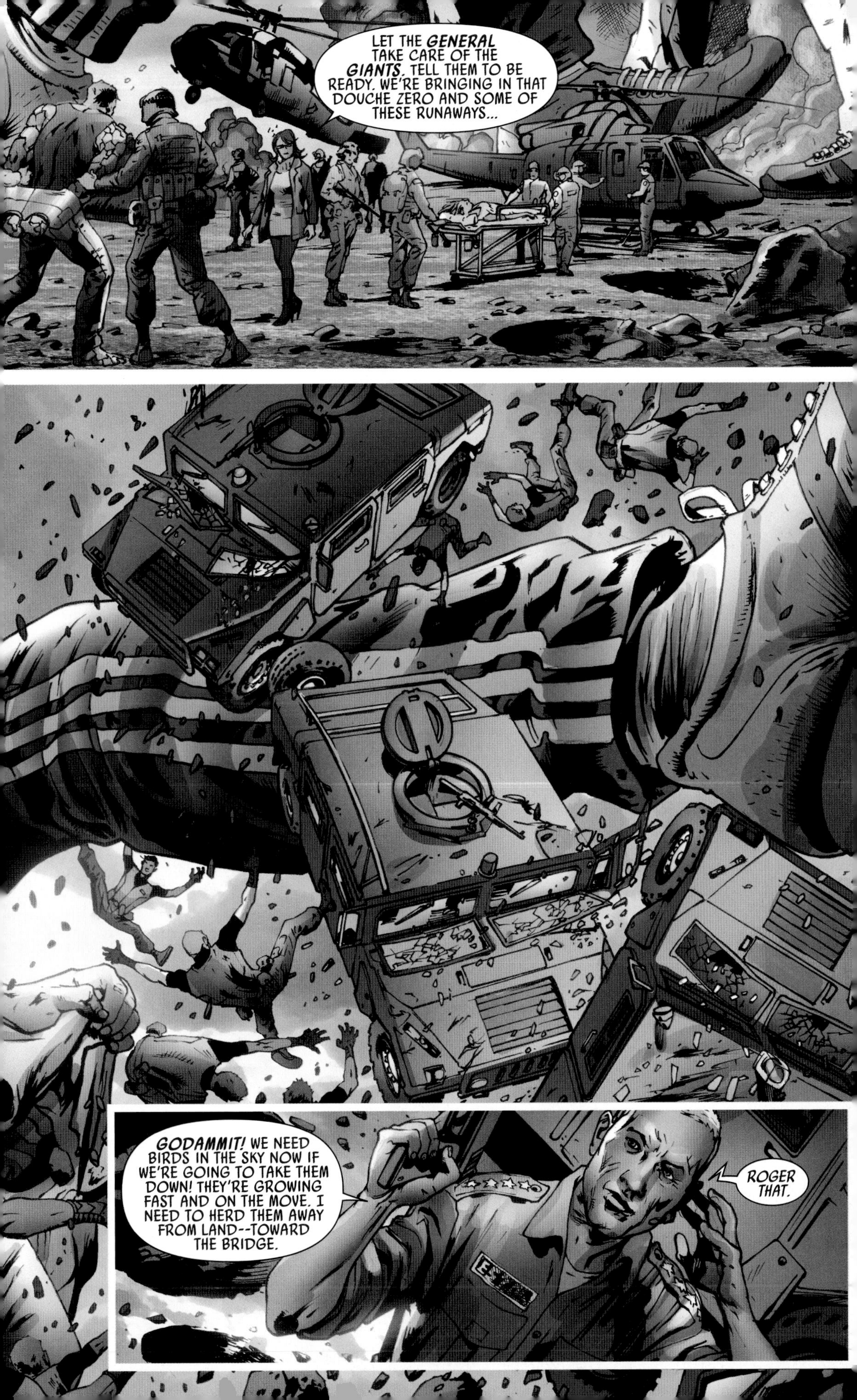
LET THE GENERAL TAKE CARE OF THE GIANTS. TELL THEM TO BE READY. WE'RE BRINGING IN THAT DOUCHE ZERO AND SOME OF THESE RUNAWAYS...
GODAMMIT! WE NEED BIRDS IN THE SKY NOW IF WE'RE GOING TO TAKE THEM DOWN! THEY'RE GROWING FAST AND ON THE MOVE. I NEED TO HERD THEM AWAY FROM LAND--TOWARD THE BRIDGE.
ROGER THAT.

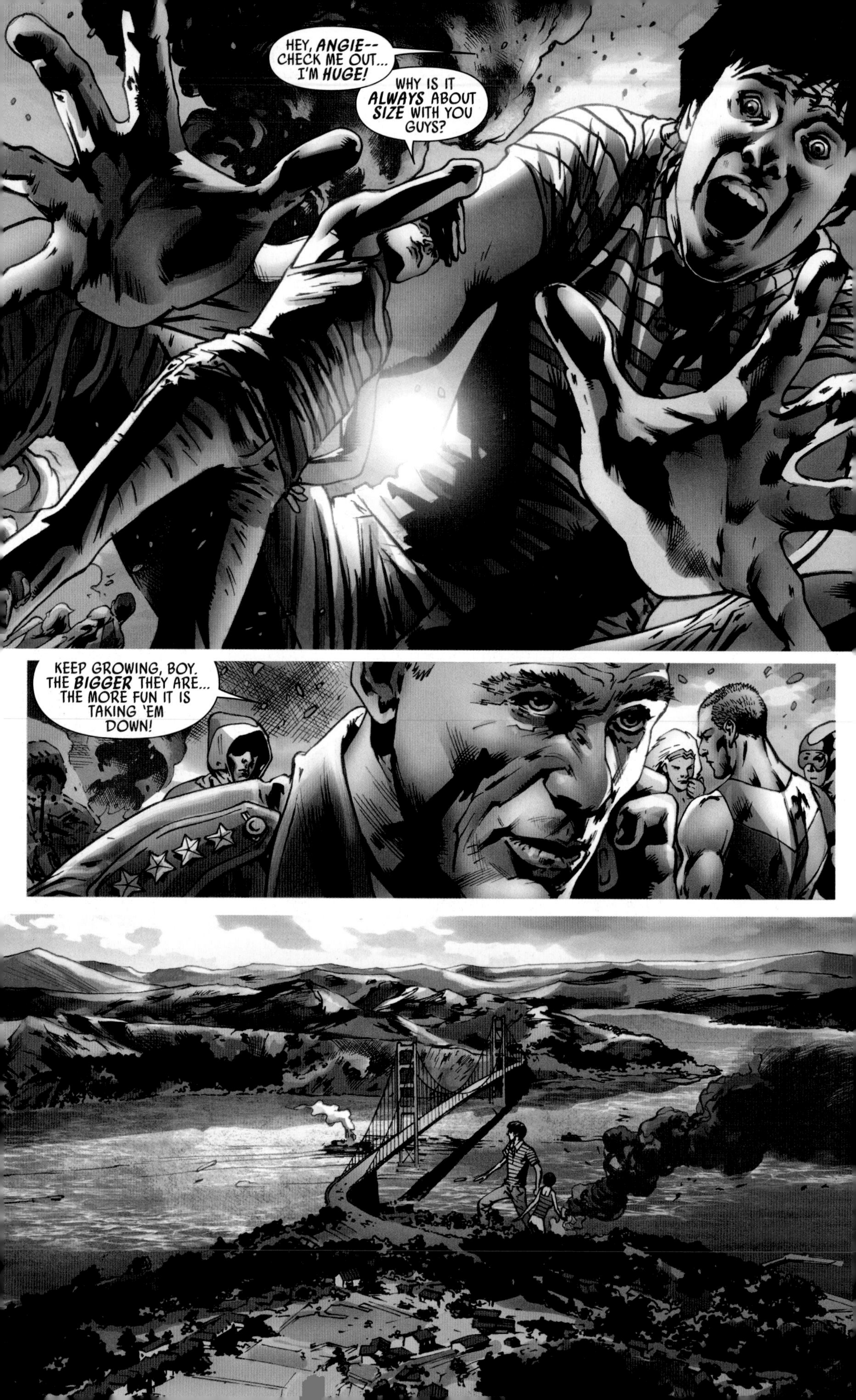
HEY, ANGIE-- CHECK ME OUT... I'M HUGE!
WHY IS IT ALWAYS ABOUT SIZE WITH YOU GUYS?
KEEP GROWING, BOY. THE BIGGER THEY ARE... THE MORE FUN IT IS TAKING 'EM DOWN!

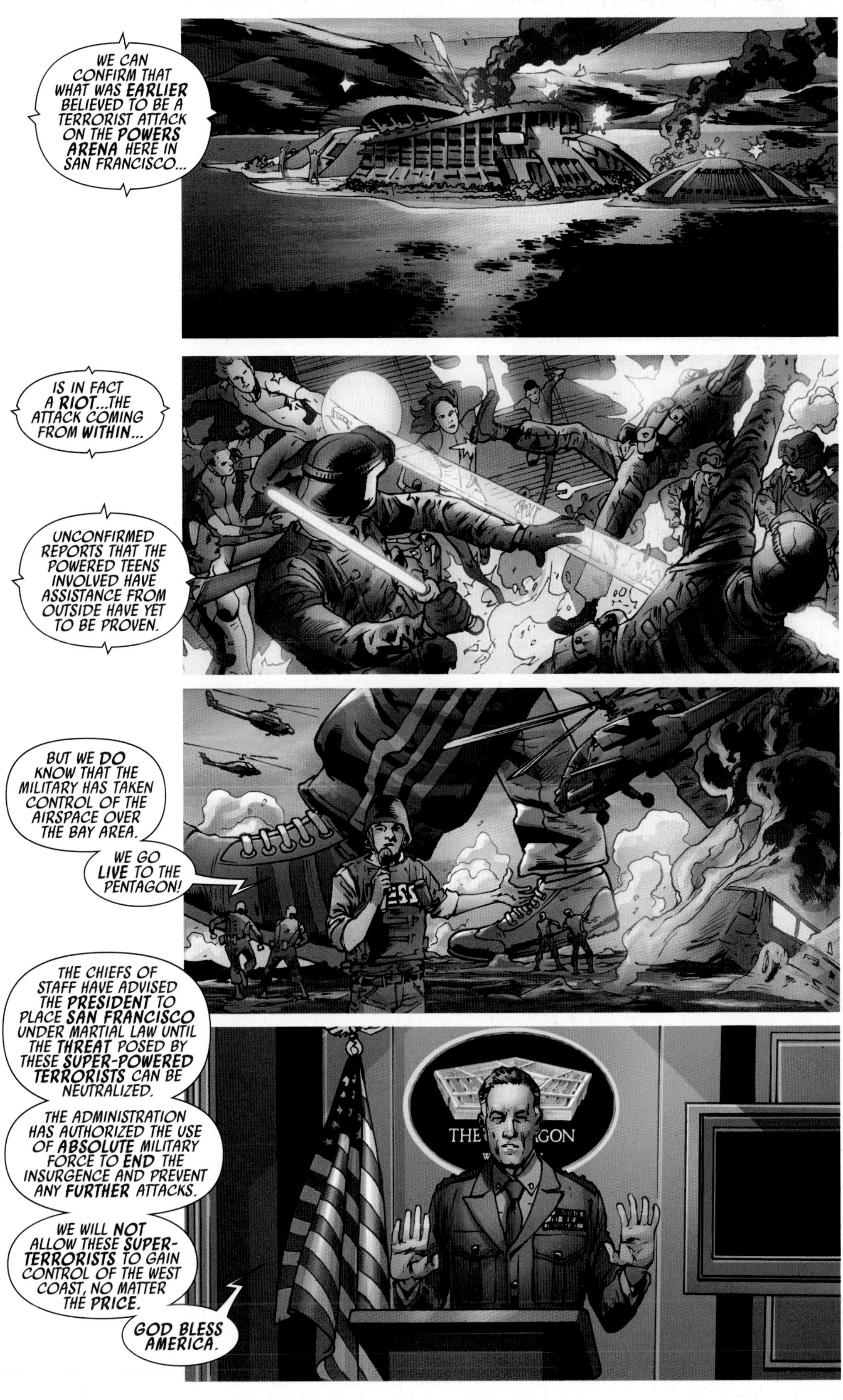
WE CAN CONFIRM THAT WHAT WAS EARLIER BELIEVED TO BE A TERRORIST ATTACK ON THE POWERS ARENA HERE IN SAN FRANCISCO...
IS IN FACT A RIOT...THE ATTACK COMING FROM WITHIN...
UNCONFIRMED REPORTS THAT THE POWERED TEENS INVOLVED HAVE ASSISTANCE FROM OUTSIDE HAVE YET TO BE PROVEN.
BUT WE DO KNOW THAT THE MILITARY HAS TAKEN CONTROL OF THE AIRSPACE OVER THE BAY AREA.
WE GO LIVE TO THE PENTAGON!
THE CHIEFS OF STAFF HAVE ADVISED THE PRESIDENT TO PLACE SAN FRANCISCO UNDER MARTIAL LAW UNTIL THE THREAT POSED BY THESE SUPER-POWERED TERRORISTS CAN BE NEUTRALIZED.
THE ADMINISTRATION HAS AUTHORIZED THE USE OF ABSOLUTE MILITARY FORCE TO END THE INSURGENCE AND PREVENT ANY FURTHER ATTACKS.
WE WILL NOT ALLOW THESE SUPER-TERRORISTS TO GAIN CONTROL OF THE WEST COAST, NO MATTER THE PRICE.
GOD BLESS AMERICA.

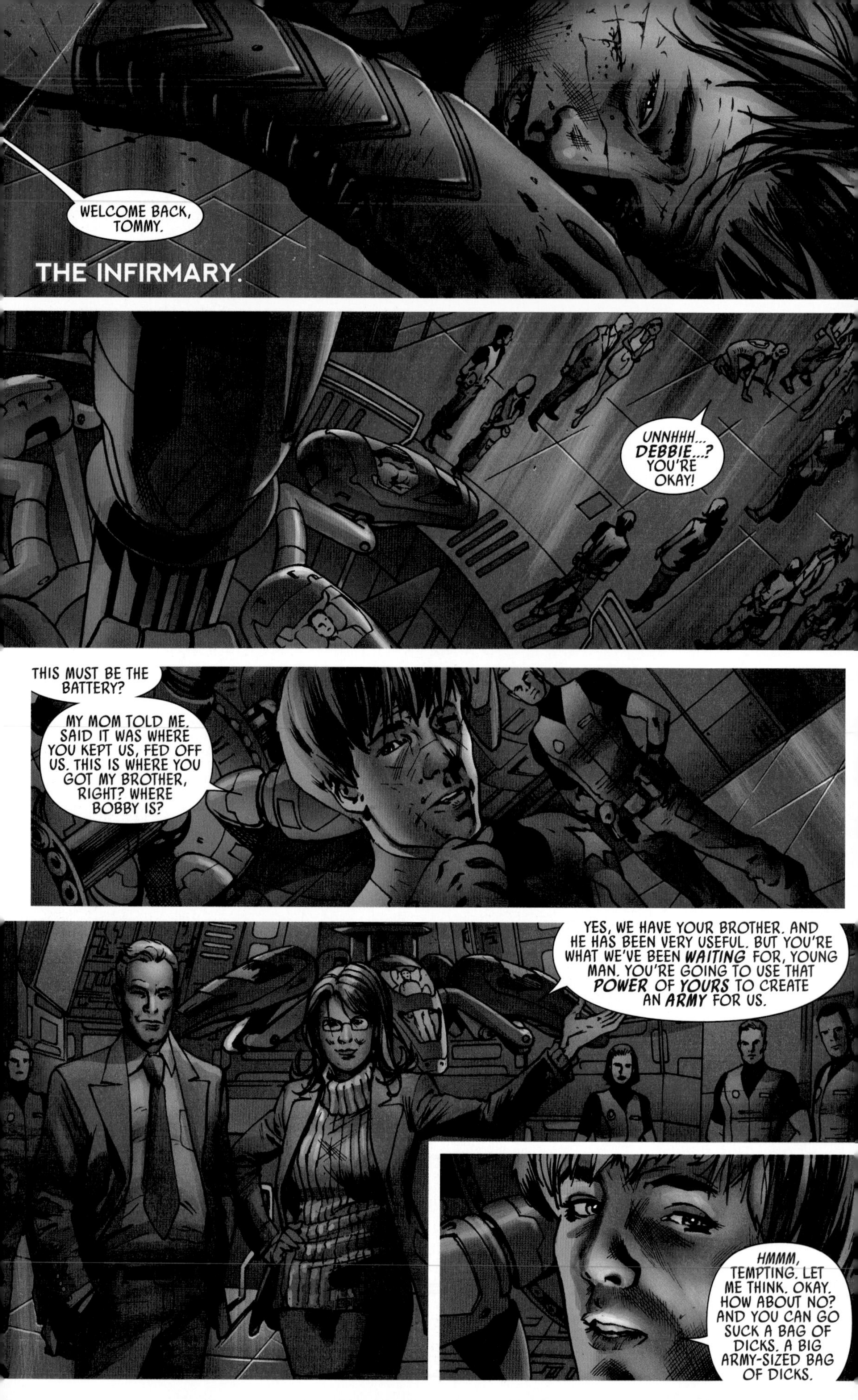
WELCOME BACK, TOMMY.
THE INFIRMARY.
UNNHHH... DEBBIE...? YOU'RE OKAY!
THIS MUST BE THE BATTERY?
MY MOM TOLD ME. SAID IT WAS WHERE YOU KEPT US, FED OFF US. THIS IS WHERE YOU GOT MY BROTHER, RIGHT? WHERE BOBBY IS?
YES, WE HAVE YOUR BROTHER. AND HE HAS BEEN VERY USEFUL. BUT YOU'RE WHAT WE'VE BEEN WAITING FOR, YOUNG MAN. YOU'RE GOING TO USE THAT POWER OF YOURS TO CREATE AN ARMY FOR US.
HMMM, TEMPTING. LET ME THINK. OKAY. HOW ABOUT NO? AND YOU CAN GO SUCK A BAG OF DICKS. A BIG ARMY-SIZED BAG OF DICKS.

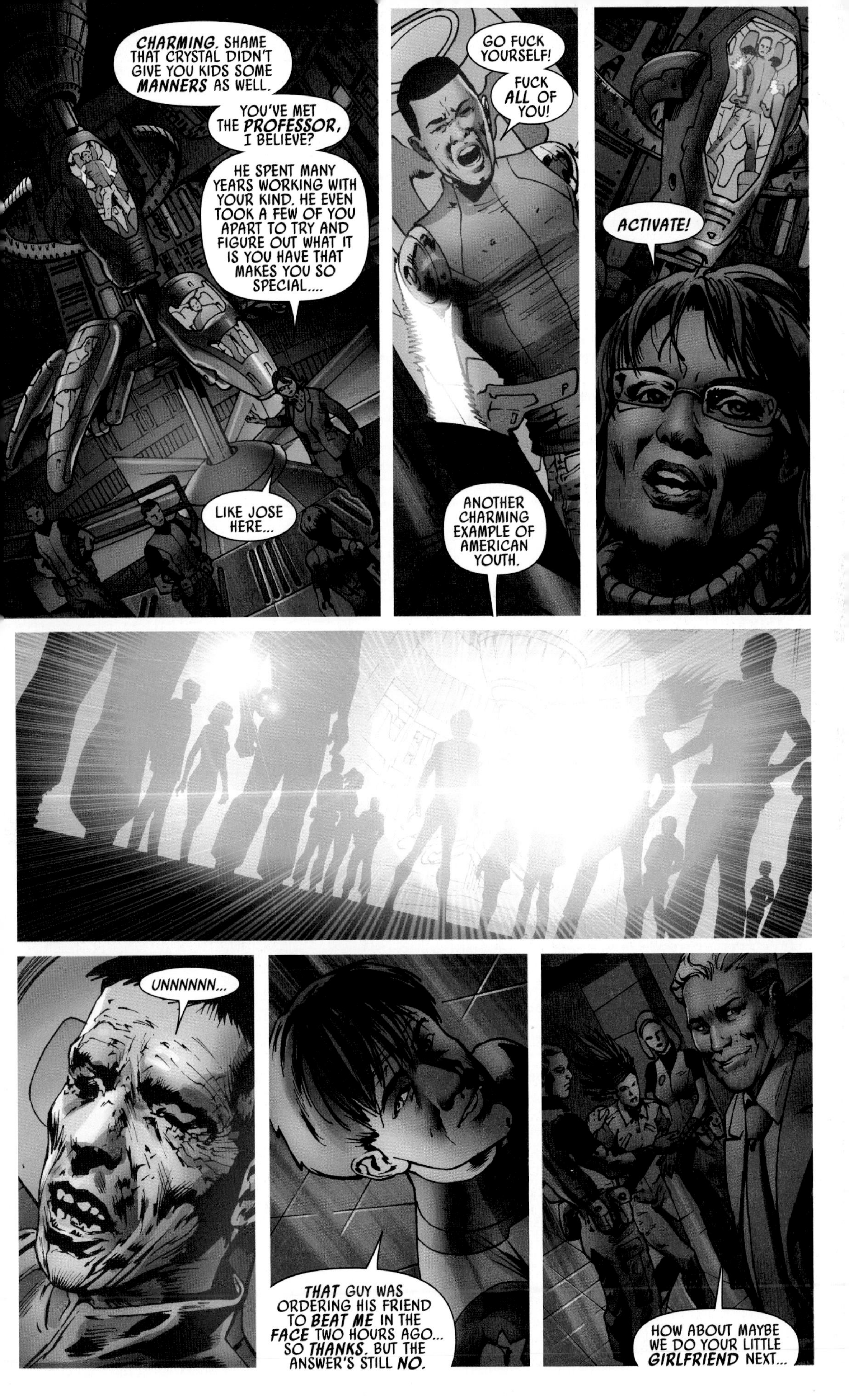

CHARMING. SHAME THAT CRYSTAL DIDN'T GIVE YOU KIDS SOME MANNERS AS WELL.
YOU'VE MET THE PROFESSOR, I BELIEVE?
HE SPENT MANY YEARS WORKING WITH YOUR KIND. HE EVEN TOOK A FEW OF YOU APART TO TRY AND FIGURE OUT WHAT IT IS YOU HAVE THAT MAKES YOU SO SPECIAL....
LIKE JOSE HERE...
GO FUCK YOURSELF!
FUCK ALL OF YOU!
ANOTHER CHARMING EXAMPLE OF AMERICAN YOUTH.
ACTIVATE!
UNNNNNN...
THAT GUY WAS ORDERING HIS FRIEND TO BEAT ME IN THE FACE TWO HOURS AGO... SO THANKS, BUT THE ANSWER'S STILL NO.
HOW ABOUT MAYBE WE DO YOUR LITTLE GIRLFRIEND NEXT...

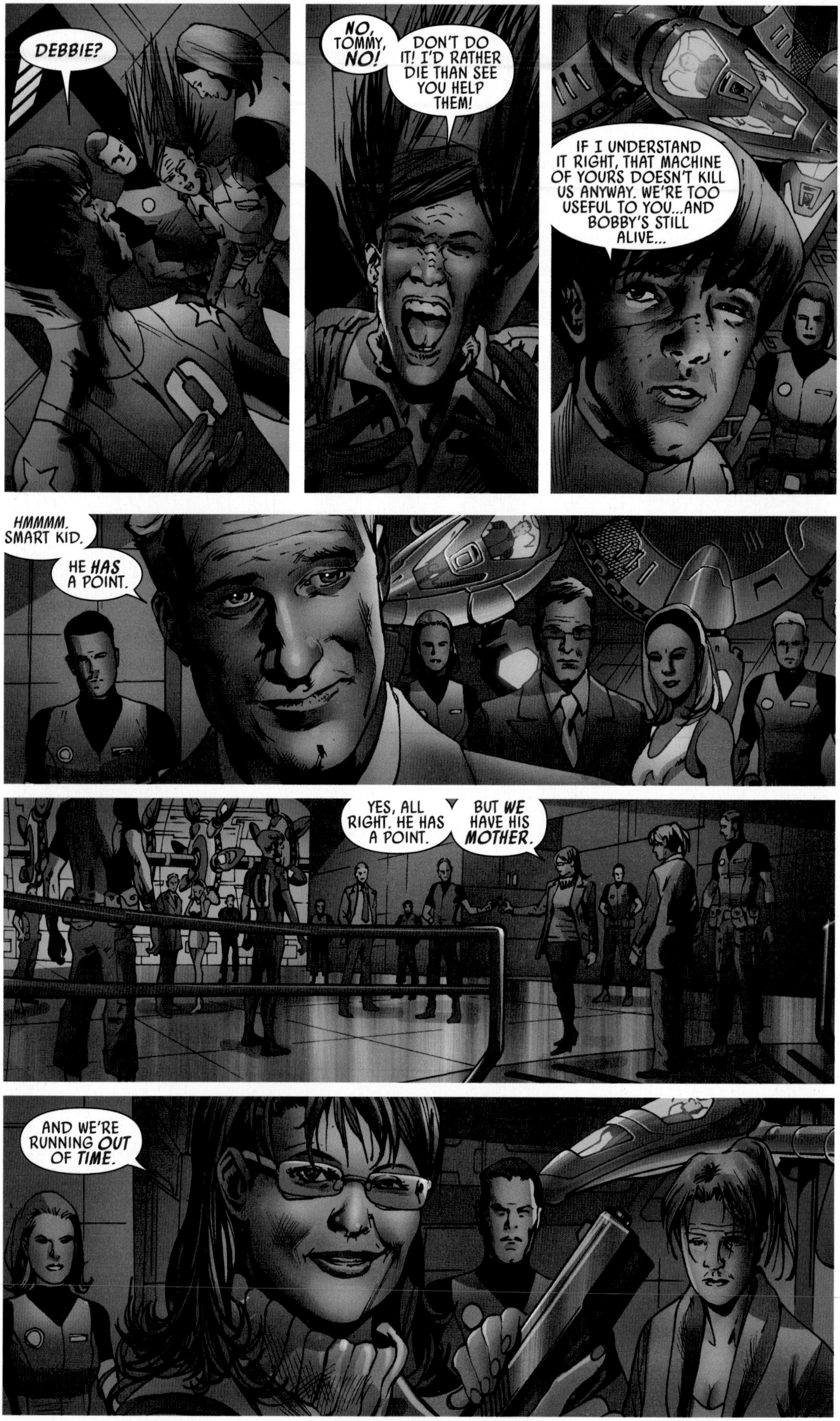
DEBBIE?
NO, TOMMY, NO!
DON'T DO IT! I'D RATHER DIE THAN SEE YOU HELP THEM!
IF I UNDERSTAND IT RIGHT, THAT MACHINE OF YOURS DOESN'T KILL US ANYWAY. WE'RE TOO USEFUL TO YOU...AND BOBBY'S STILL ALIVE...
HMMMM. SMART KID.
HE HAS A POINT.
YES, ALL RIGHT. HE HAS A POINT.
BUT WE HAVE HIS MOTHER.
AND WE'RE RUNNING OUT OF TIME.

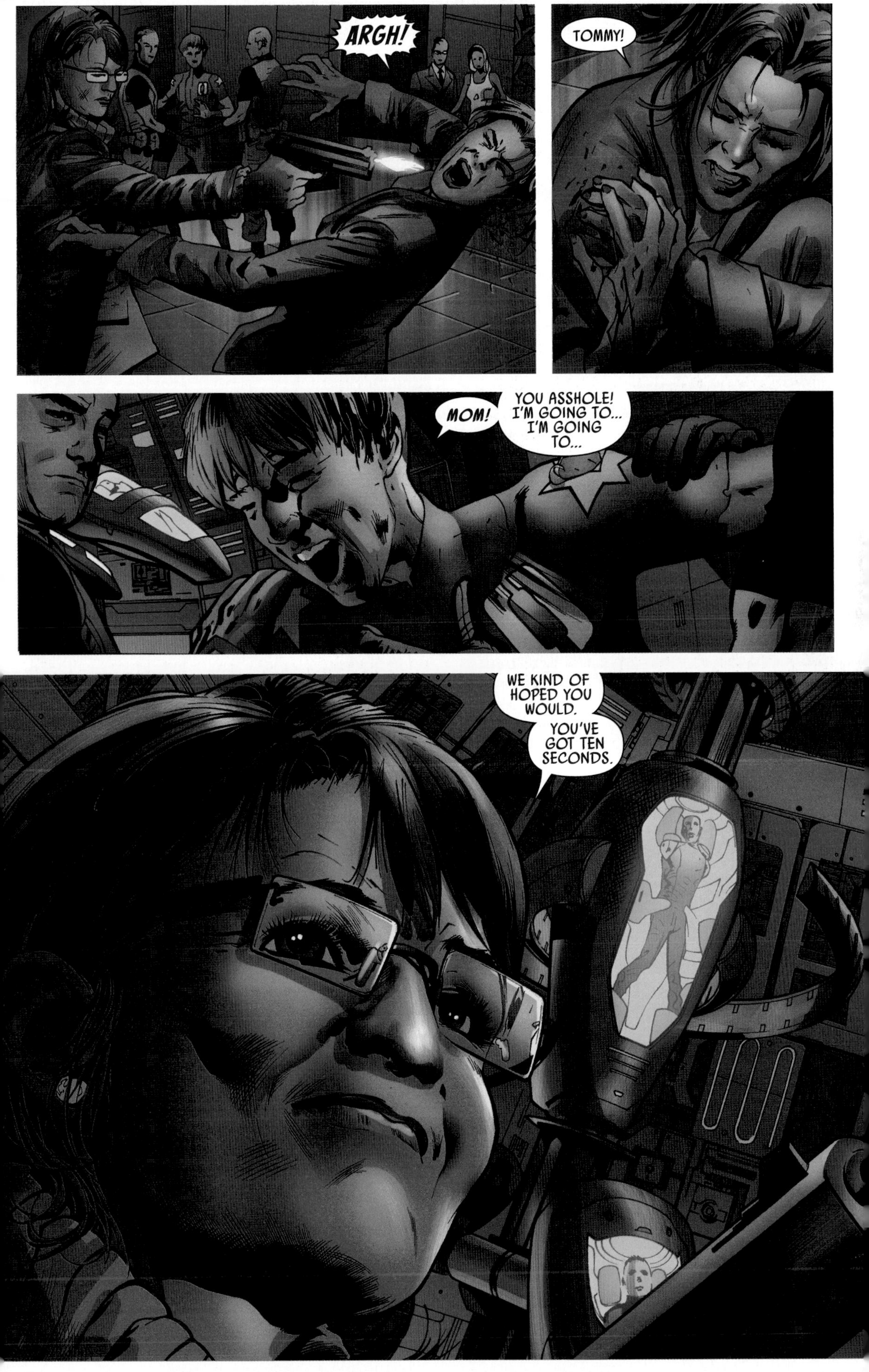
ARGH!
TOMMY!
MOM!
YOU ASSHOLE! I'M GOING TO... I'M GOING TO...
WE KIND OF HOPED YOU WOULD.
YOU'VE GOT TEN SECONDS.

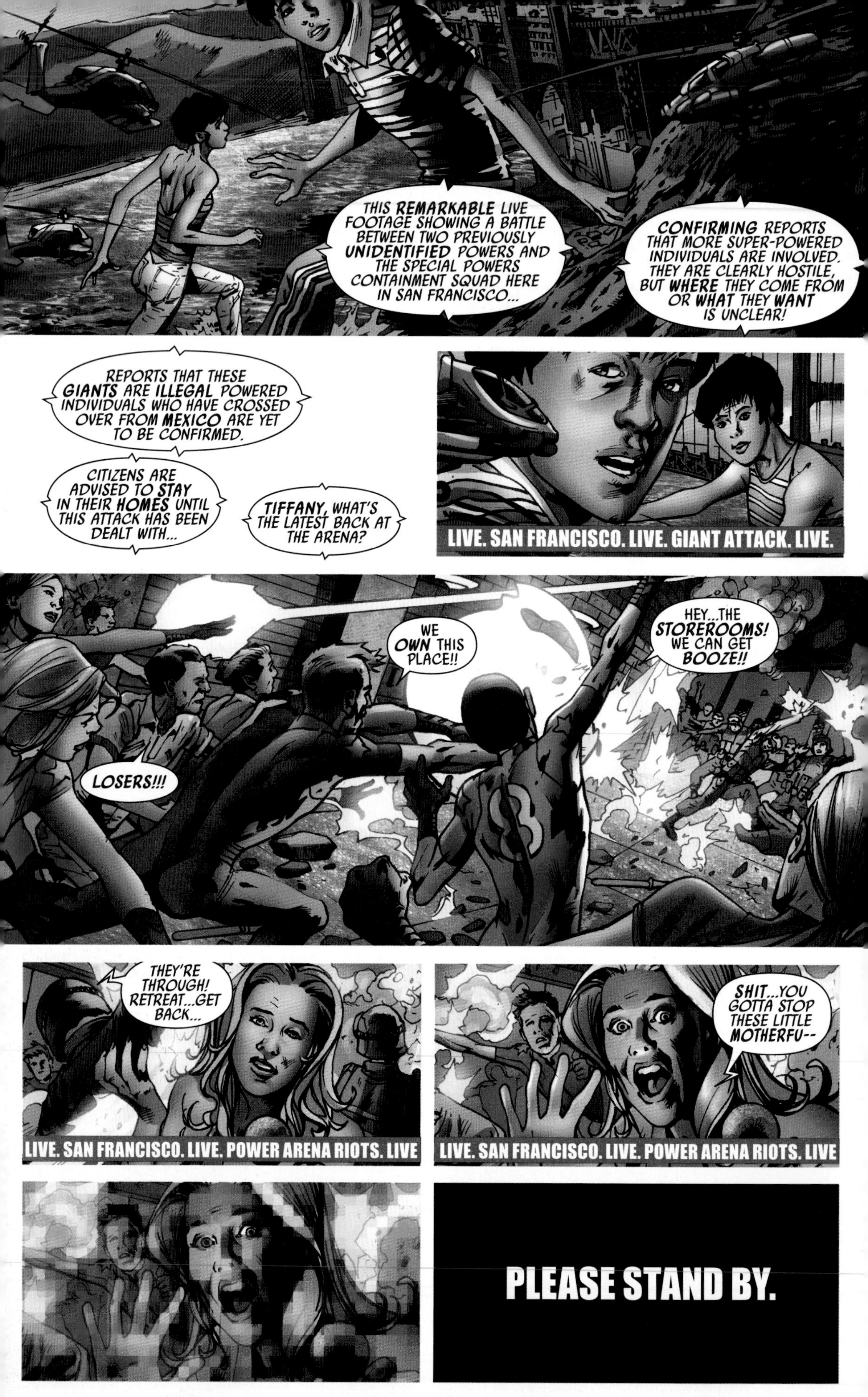
THIS REMARKABLE LIVE FOOTAGE SHOWING A BATTLE BETWEEN TWO PREVIOUSLY UNIDENTIFIED POWERS AND THE SPECIAL POWERS CONTAINMENT SQUAD HERE IN SAN FRANCISCO...
CONFIRMING REPORTS THAT MORE SUPER-POWERED INDIVIDUALS ARE INVOLVED. THEY ARE CLEARLY HOSTILE, BUT WHERE THEY COME FROM OR WHAT THEY WANT IS UNCLEAR!
REPORTS THAT THESE GIANTS ARE ILLEGAL POWERED INDIVIDUALS WHO HAVE CROSSED OVER FROM MEXICO ARE YET TO BE CONFIRMED.
CITIZENS ARE ADVISED TO STAY IN THEIR HOMES UNTIL THIS ATTACK HAS BEEN DEALT WITH...
TIFFANY, WHAT'S THE LATEST BACK AT THE ARENA?
LIVE. SAN FRANCISCO. LIVE. GIANT ATTACK. LIVE.
WE OWN THIS PLACE!!
HEY...THE STOREROOMS! WE CAN GET BOOZE!!
LOSERS!!!
THEY'RE THROUGH! RETREAT...GET BACK...
LIVE. SAN FRANCISCO. LIVE. POWER ARENA RIOTS. LIVE
SHIT...YOU GOTTA STOP THESE LITTLE MOTHERFU--
LIVE. SAN FRANCISCO. LIVE. POWER ARENA RIOTS. LIVE
PLEASE STAND BY.

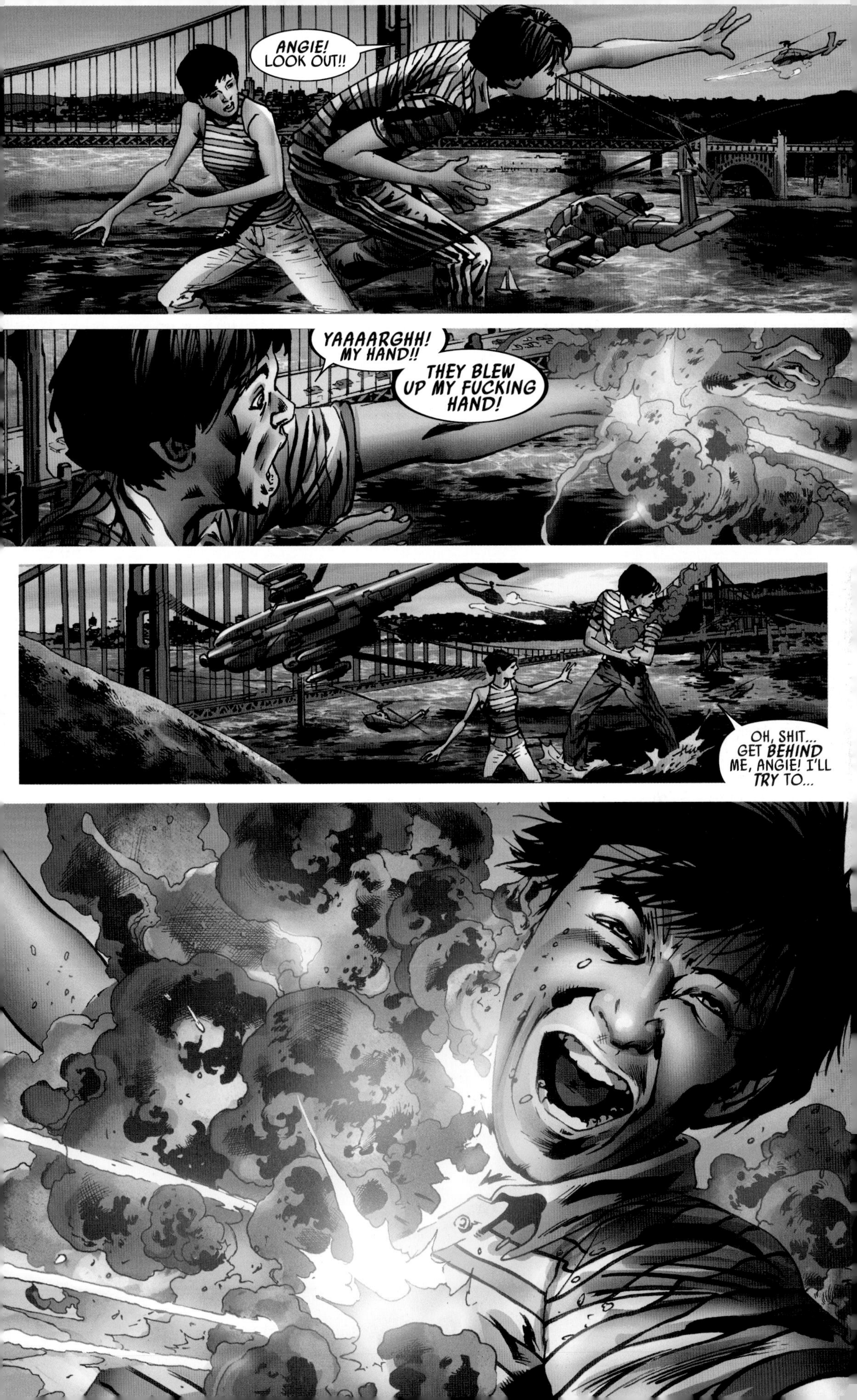
ANGIE! LOOK OUT!!
YAAAARGHH! MY HAND!!
THEY BLEW UP MY FUCKING HAND!
OH, SHIT... GET BEHIND ME, ANGIE! I'LL TRY TO...

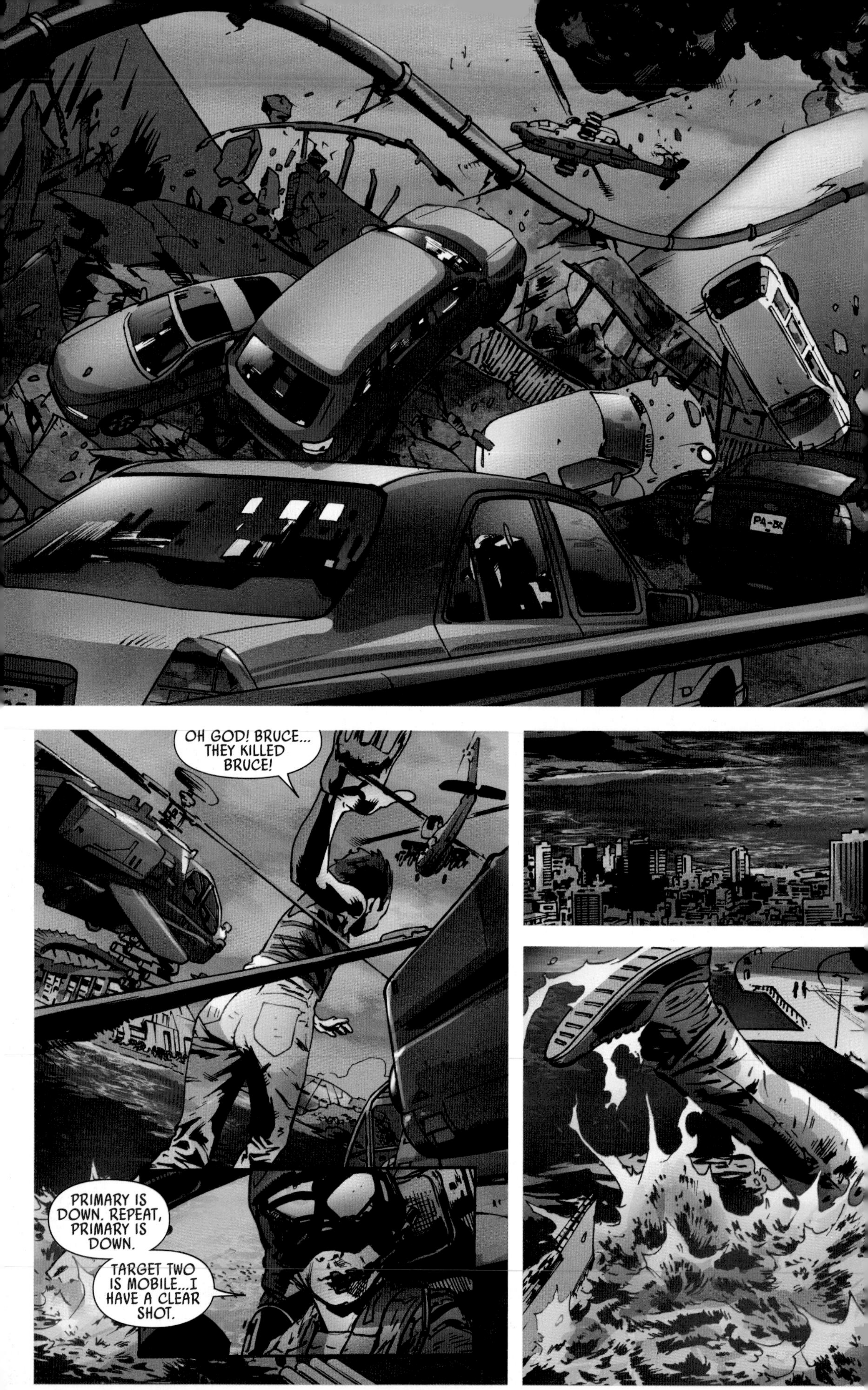
PA-BR
OH GOD! BRUCE... THEY KILLED BRUCE!
PRIMARY IS DOWN. REPEAT, PRIMARY IS DOWN.
TARGET TWO IS MOBILE...I HAVE A CLEAR SHOT.

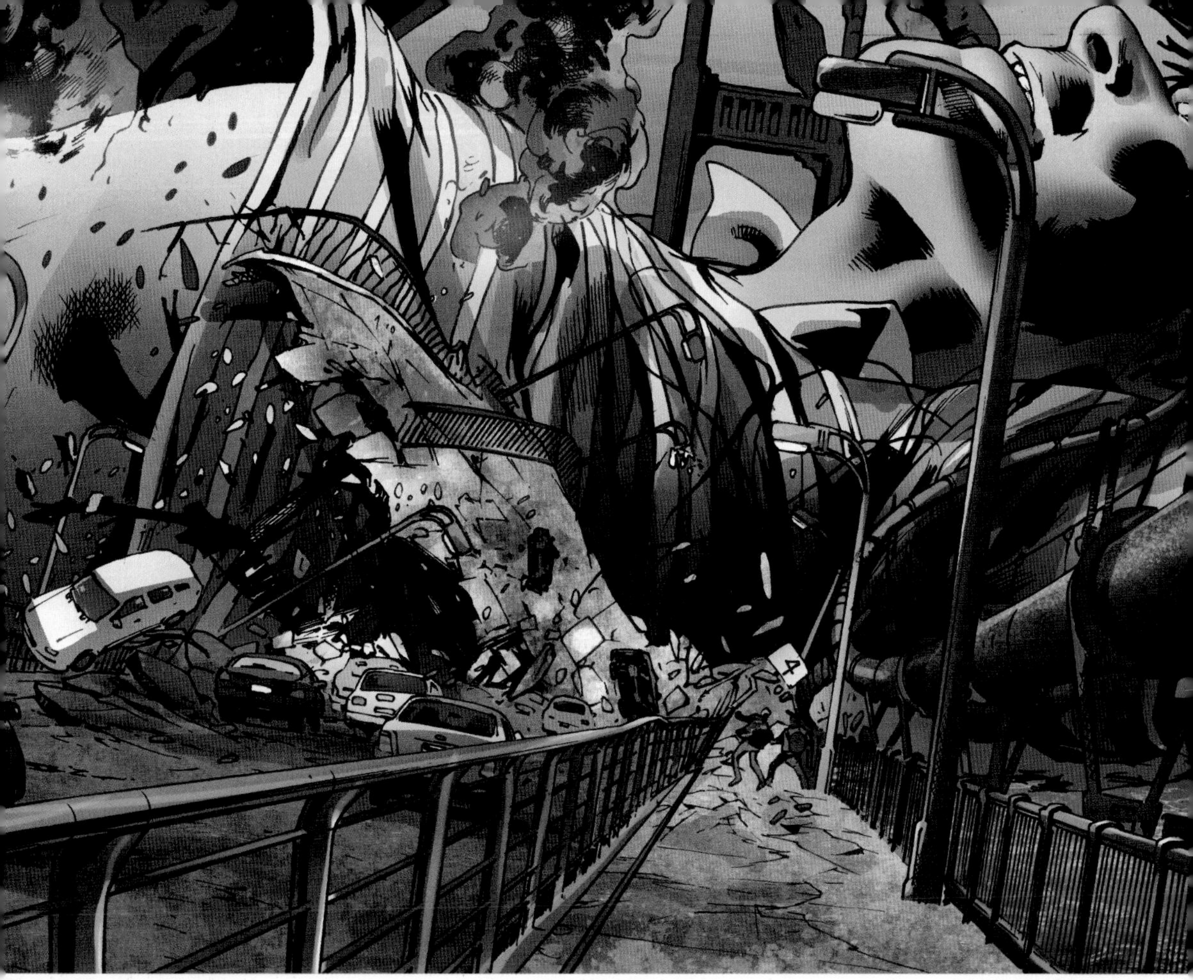

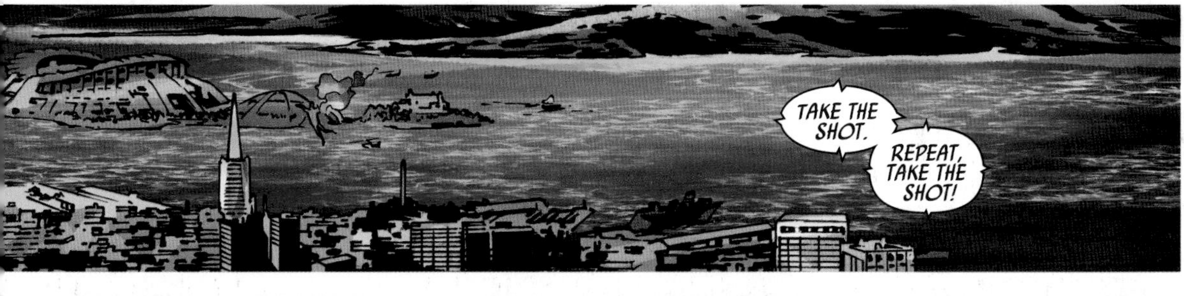
TAKE THE SHOT.
REPEAT, TAKE THE SHOT!

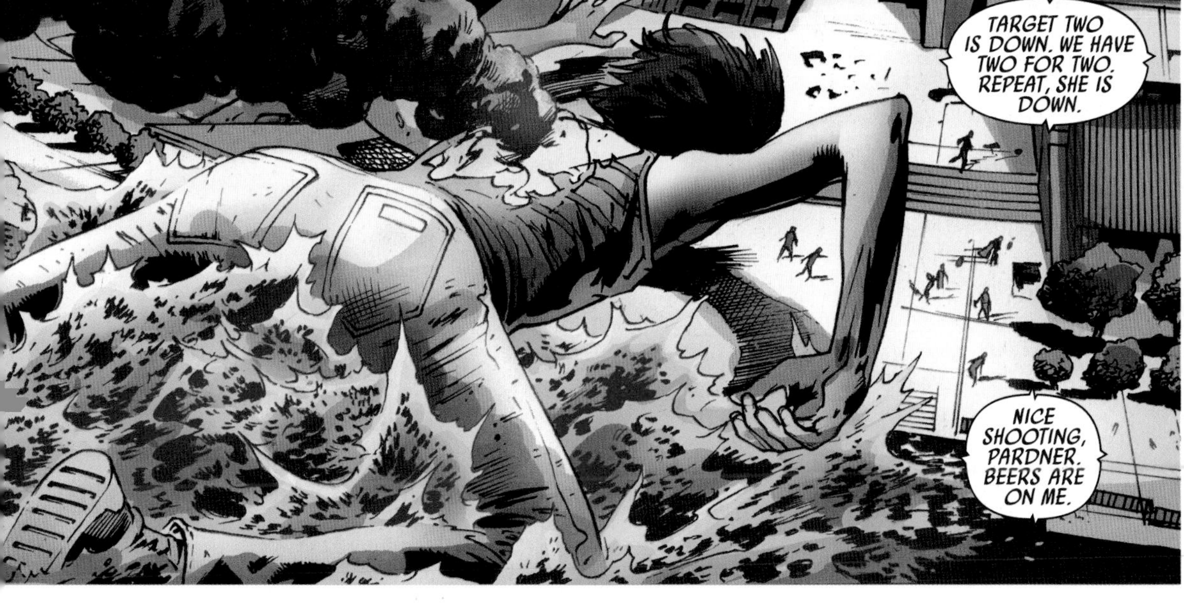
TARGET TWO IS DOWN. WE HAVE TWO FOR TWO. REPEAT, SHE IS DOWN.
NICE SHOOTING, PARDNER. BEERS ARE ON ME.

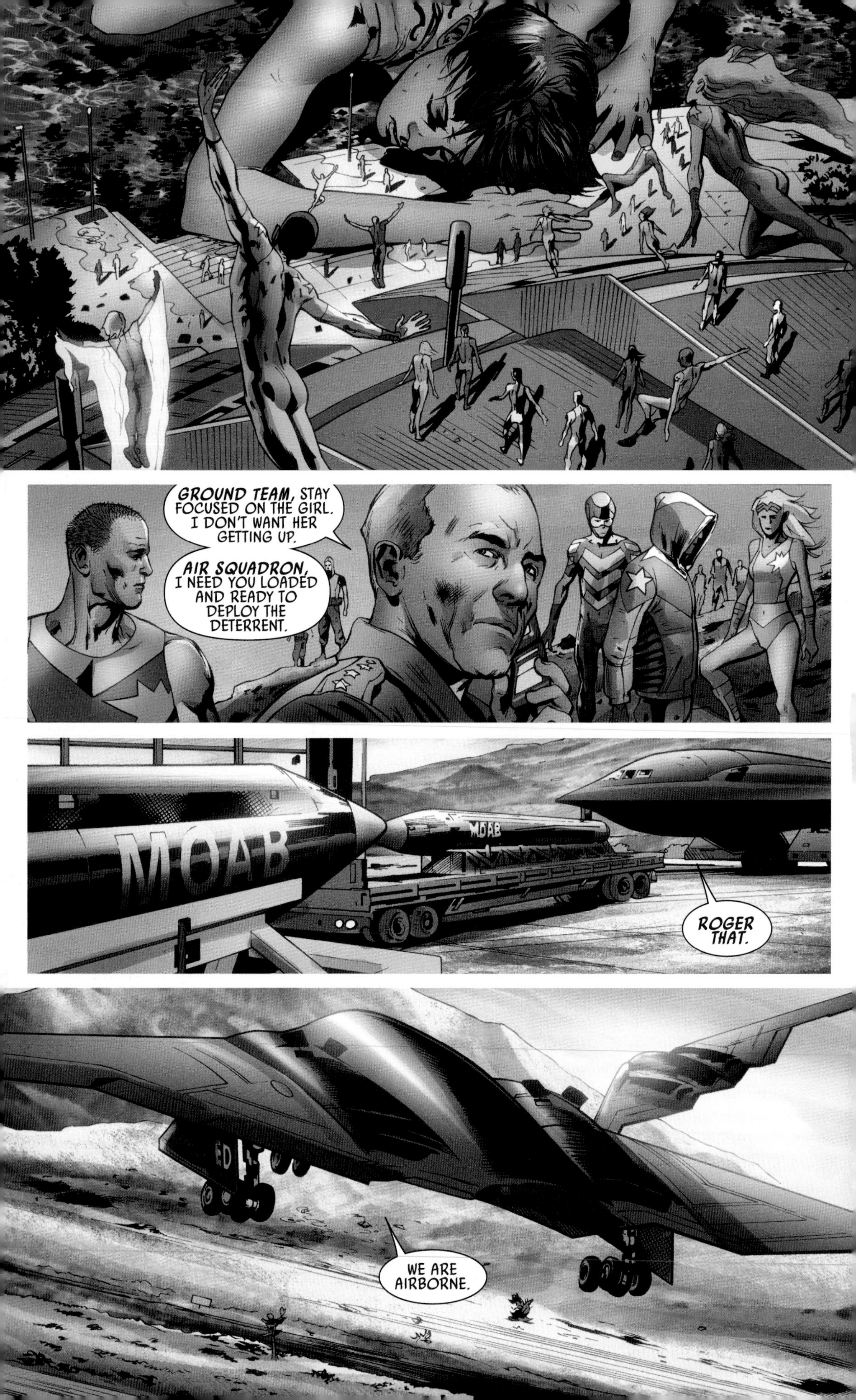
GROUND TEAM, STAY FOCUSED ON THE GIRL. I DON'T WANT HER GETTING UP.
AIR SQUADRON, I NEED YOU LOADED AND READY TO DEPLOY THE DETERRENT.
MOAB
MOAB
ROGER THAT.
WE ARE AIRBORNE.

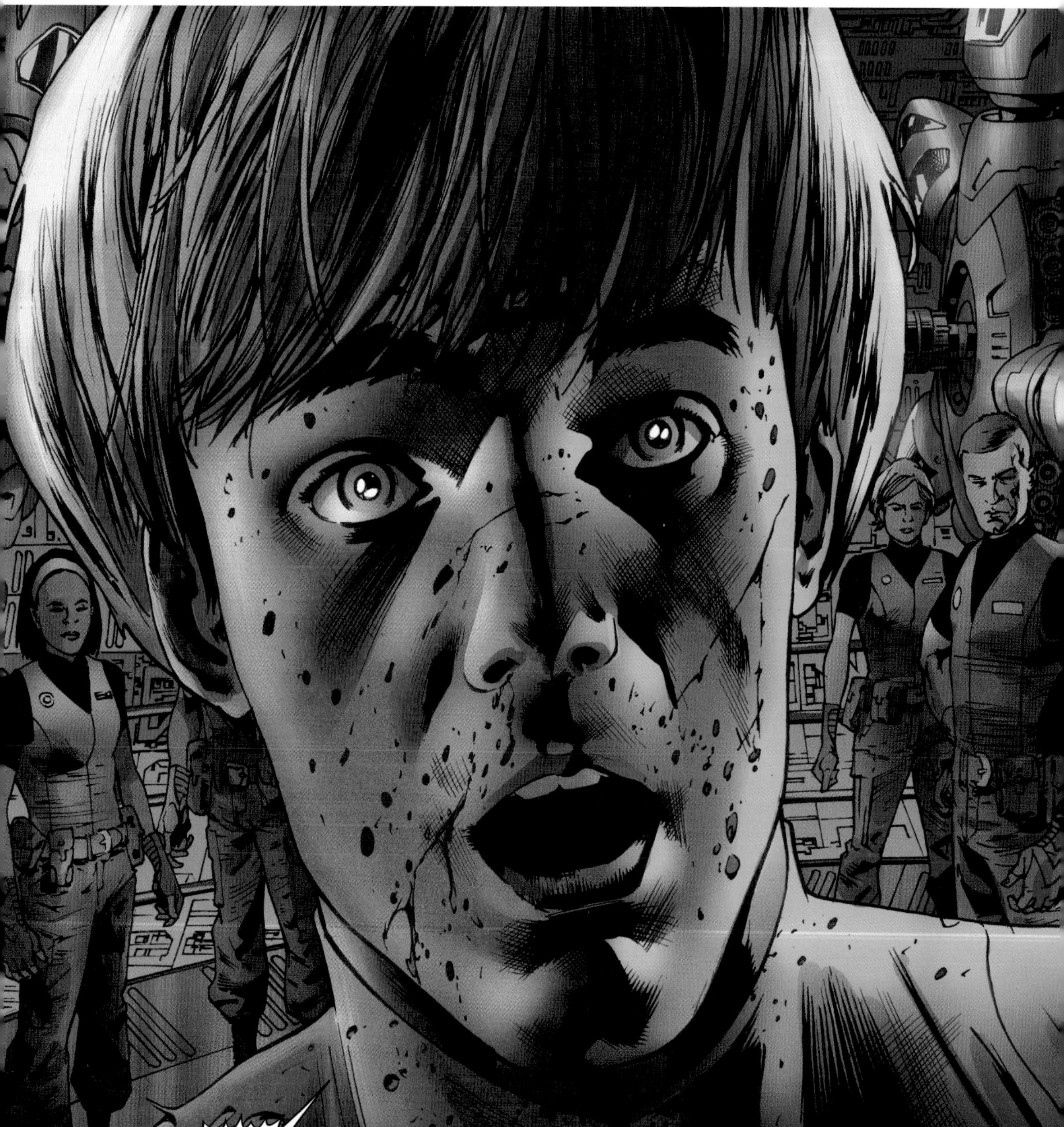
STOP!! ARE YOU FUCKING INSANE?

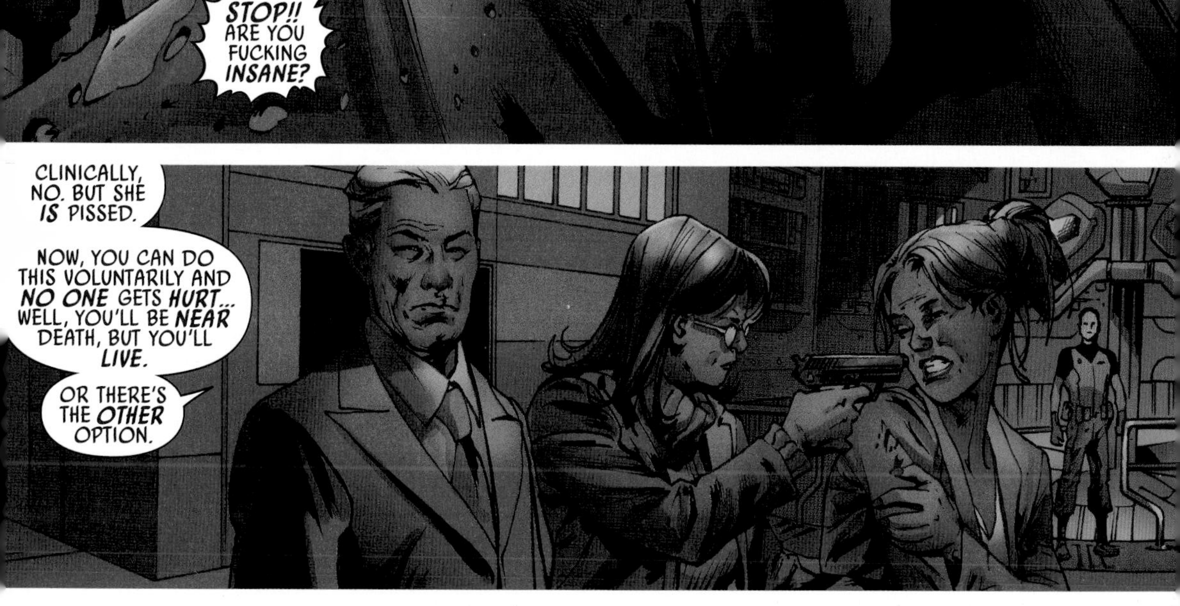
CLINICALLY, NO. BUT SHE IS PISSED.
NOW, YOU CAN DO THIS VOLUNTARILY AND NO ONE GETS HURT... WELL, YOU'LL BE NEAR DEATH, BUT YOU'LL LIVE.
OR THERE'S THE OTHER OPTION.

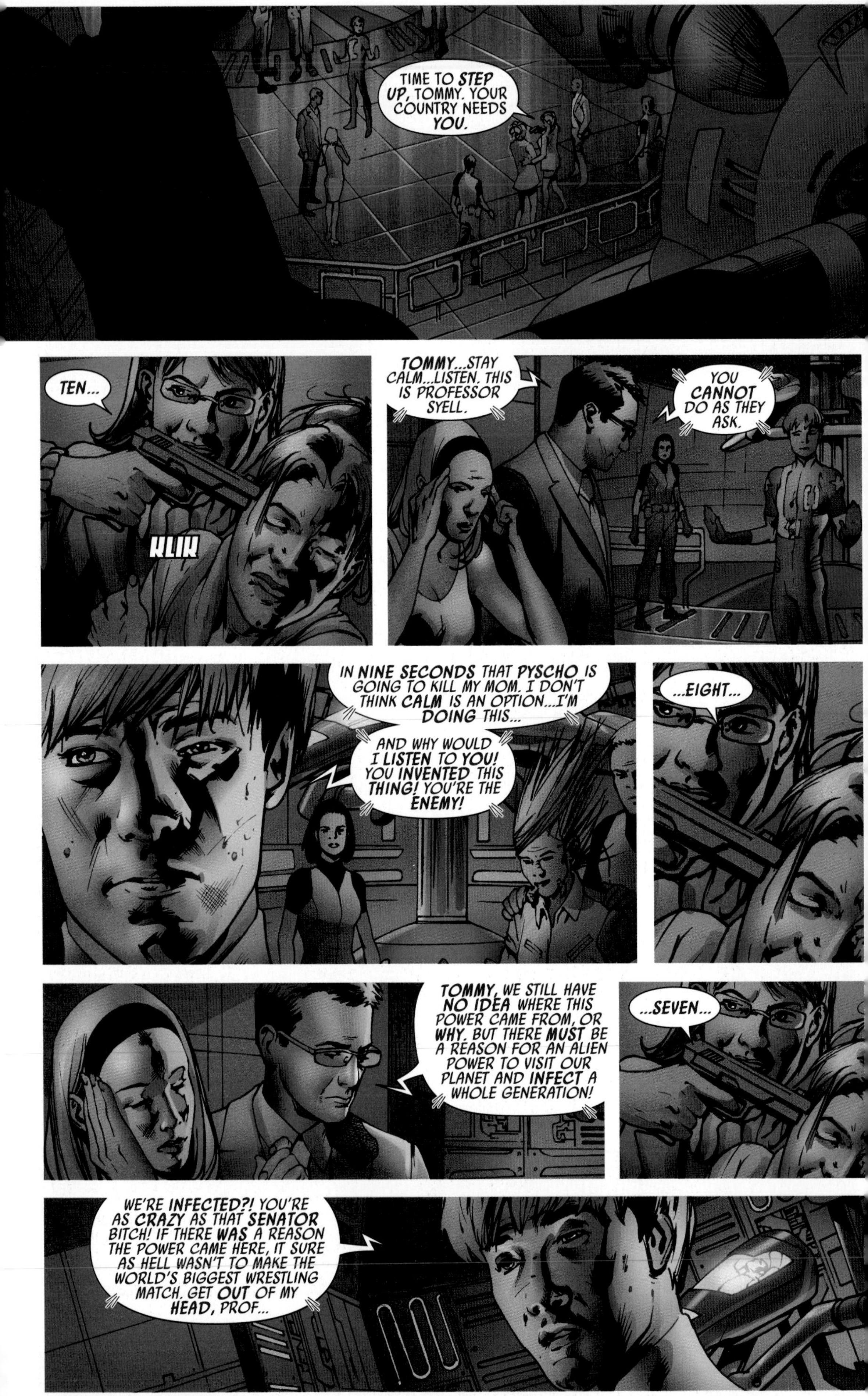

TIME TO STEP UP, TOMMY. YOUR COUNTRY NEEDS YOU.
TEN...
KLIK
TOMMY...STAY CALM...LISTEN. THIS IS PROFESSOR SYELL.
YOU CANNOT DO AS THEY ASK.
IN NINE SECONDS THAT PYSCHO IS GOING TO KILL MY MOM. I DON'T THINK CALM IS AN OPTION...I'M DOING THIS...
AND WHY WOULD I LISTEN TO YOU! YOU INVENTED THIS THING! YOU'RE THE ENEMY!
...EIGHT...
TOMMY, WE STILL HAVE NO IDEA WHERE THIS POWER CAME FROM, OR WHY. BUT THERE MUST BE A REASON FOR AN ALIEN POWER TO VISIT OUR PLANET AND INFECT A WHOLE GENERATION!
...SEVEN...
WE'RE INFECTED?! YOU'RE AS CRAZY AS THAT SENATOR BITCH! IF THERE WAS A REASON THE POWER CAME HERE, IT SURE AS HELL WASN'T TO MAKE THE WORLD'S BIGGEST WRESTLING MATCH. GET OUT OF MY HEAD, PROF...

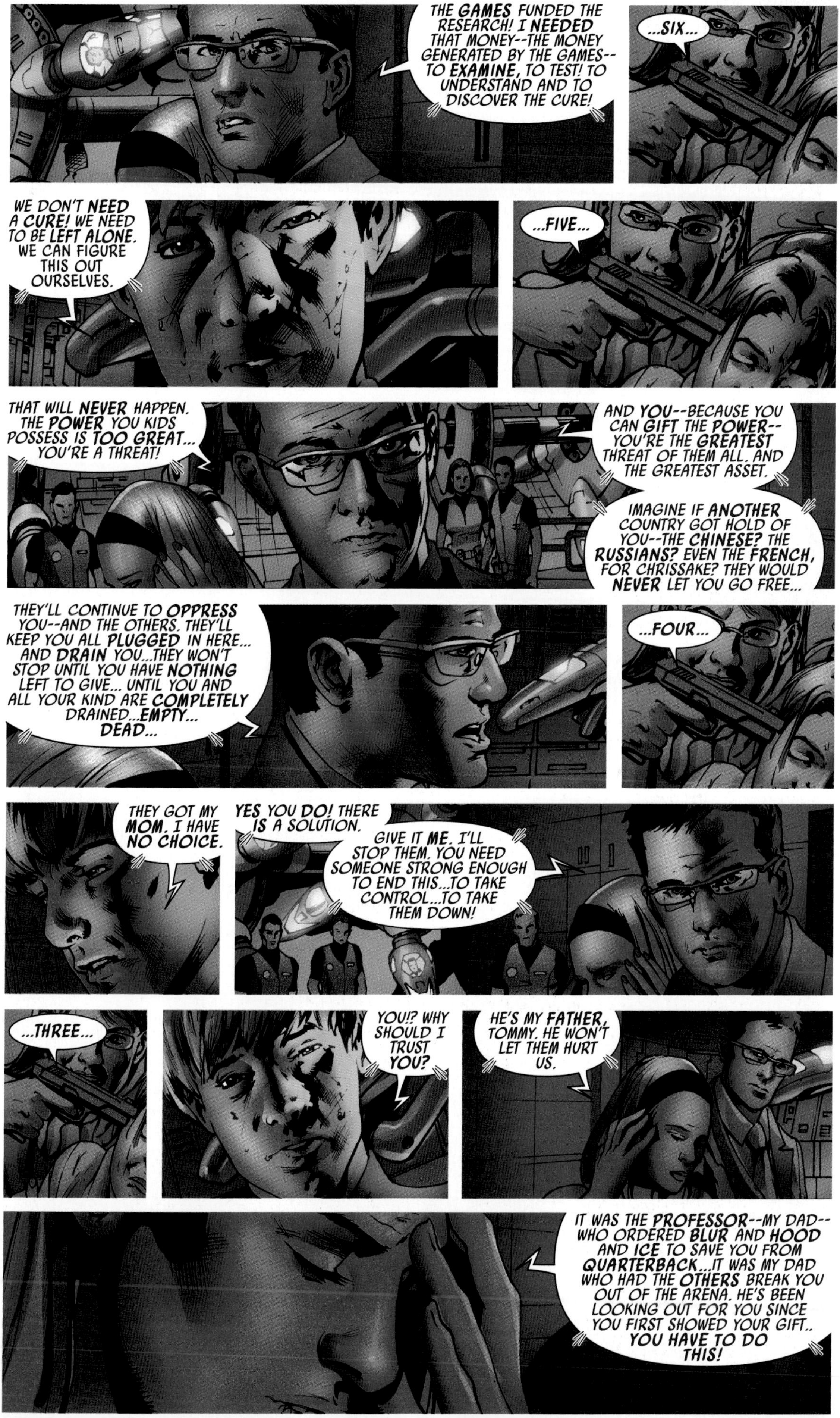
THE GAMES FUNDED THE RESEARCH! I NEEDED THAT MONEY--THE MONEY GENERATED BY THE GAMES--TO EXAMINE, TO TEST! TO UNDERSTAND AND TO DISCOVER THE CURE!
...SIX...
WE DON'T NEED A CURE! WE NEED TO BE LEFT ALONE. WE CAN FIGURE THIS OUT OURSELVES.
...FIVE...
THAT WILL NEVER HAPPEN. THE POWER YOU KIDS POSSESS IS TOO GREAT... YOU'RE A THREAT!
AND YOU--BECAUSE YOU CAN GIFT THE POWER--YOU'RE THE GREATEST THREAT OF THEM ALL. AND THE GREATEST ASSET.
IMAGINE IF ANOTHER COUNTRY GOT HOLD OF YOU--THE CHINESE? THE RUSSIANS? EVEN THE FRENCH, FOR CHRISSAKE? THEY WOULD NEVER LET YOU GO FREE...
THEY'LL CONTINUE TO OPPRESS YOU--AND THE OTHERS. THEY'LL KEEP YOU ALL PLUGGED IN HERE... AND DRAIN YOU...THEY WON'T STOP UNTIL YOU HAVE NOTHING LEFT TO GIVE... UNTIL YOU AND ALL YOUR KIND ARE COMPLETELY DRAINED...EMPTY... DEAD...
...FOUR...
THEY GOT MY MOM. I HAVE NO CHOICE.
YES YOU DO! THERE IS A SOLUTION.
GIVE IT ME. I'LL STOP THEM. YOU NEED SOMEONE STRONG ENOUGH TO END THIS...TO TAKE CONTROL...TO TAKE THEM DOWN!
...THREE...
YOU!? WHY SHOULD I TRUST YOU?
HE'S MY FATHER, TOMMY. HE WON'T LET THEM HURT US.
IT WAS THE PROFESSOR--MY DAD--WHO ORDERED BLUR AND HOOD AND ICE TO SAVE YOU FROM QUARTERBACK...IT WAS MY DAD WHO HAD THE OTHERS BREAK YOU OUT OF THE ARENA. HE'S BEEN LOOKING OUT FOR YOU SINCE YOU FIRST SHOWED YOUR GIFT.. YOU HAVE TO DO THIS!

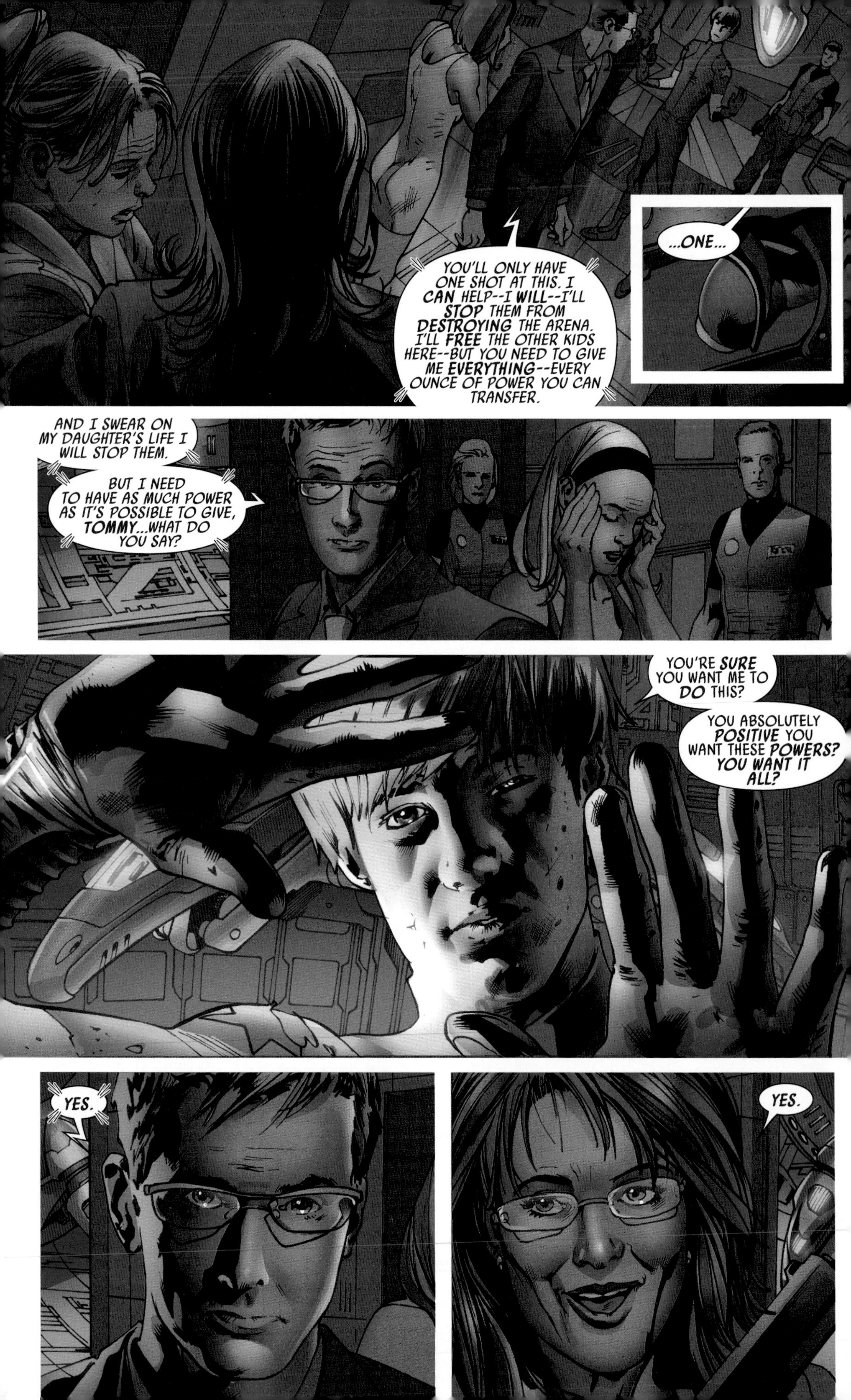
...ONE...
YOU'LL ONLY HAVE ONE SHOT AT THIS. I CAN HELP--I WILL--I'LL STOP THEM FROM DESTROYING THE ARENA. I'LL FREE THE OTHER KIDS HERE--BUT YOU NEED TO GIVE ME EVERYTHING--EVERY OUNCE OF POWER YOU CAN TRANSFER.
AND I SWEAR ON MY DAUGHTER'S LIFE I WILL STOP THEM.
BUT I NEED TO HAVE AS MUCH POWER AS IT'S POSSIBLE TO GIVE, TOMMY...WHAT DO YOU SAY?
YOU'RE SURE YOU WANT ME TO DO THIS?
YOU ABSOLUTELY POSITIVE YOU WANT THESE POWERS? YOU WANT IT ALL?
YES.
YES.

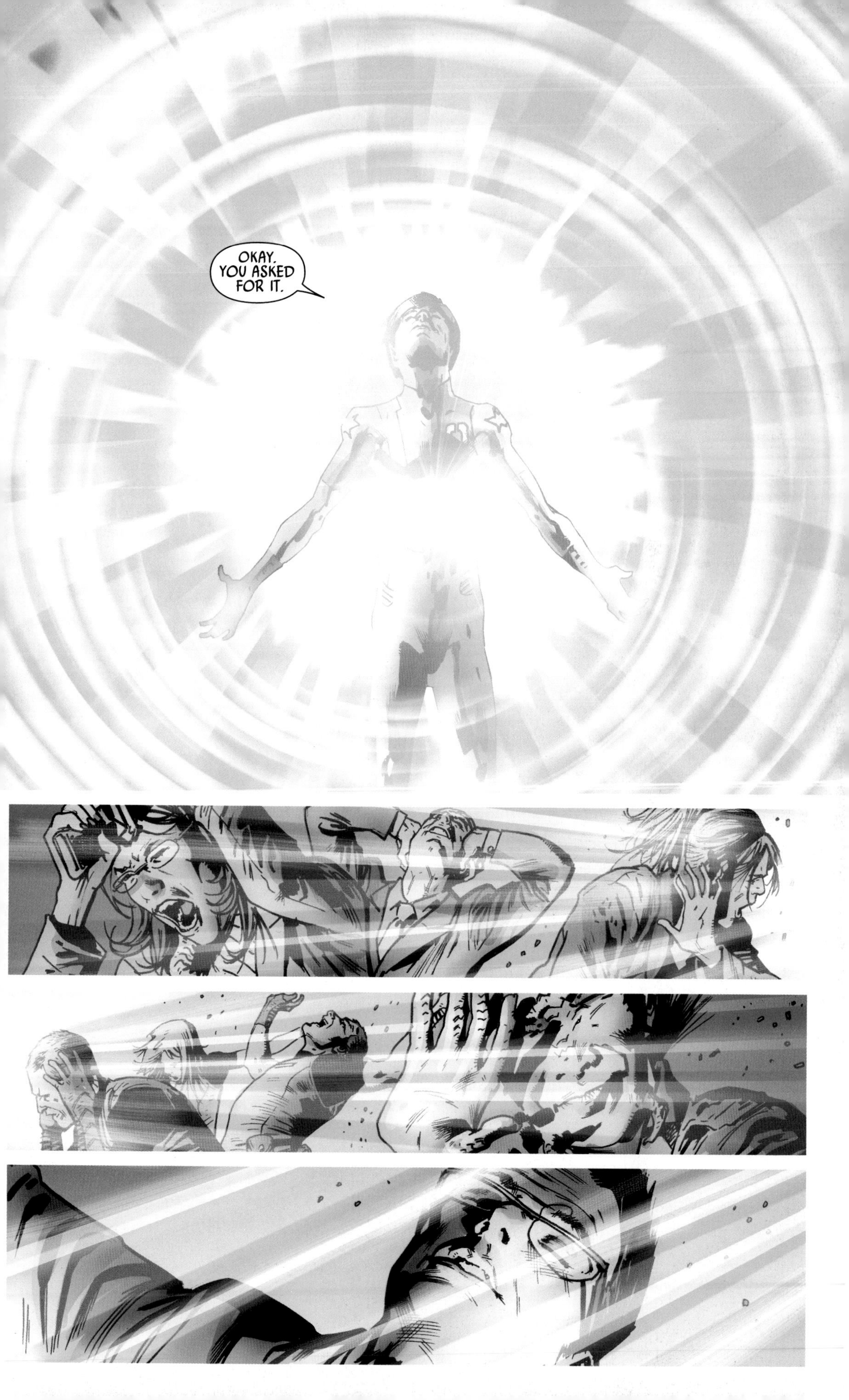
OKAY. YOU ASKED FOR IT.

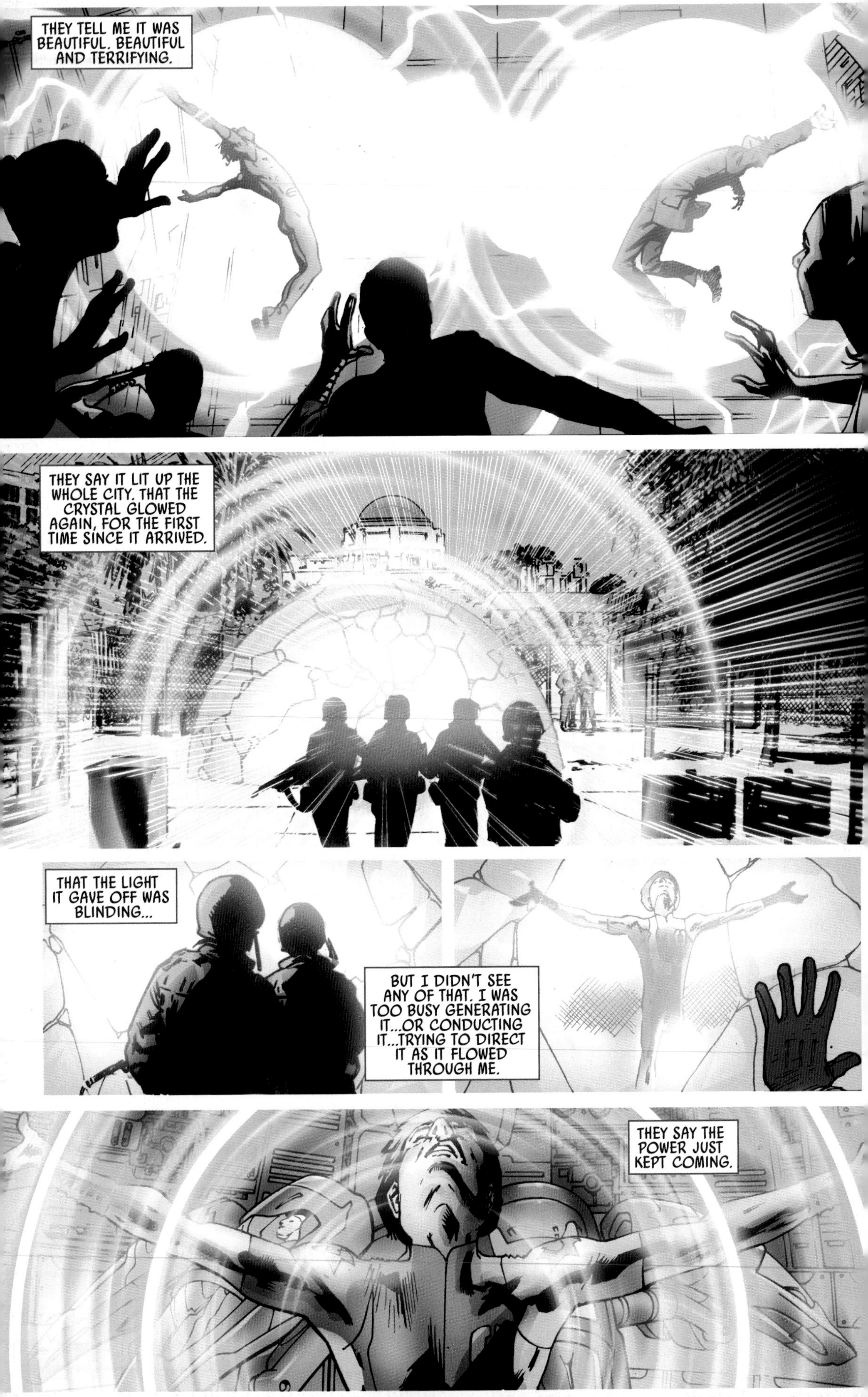
THEY TELL ME IT WAS BEAUTIFUL. BEAUTIFUL AND TERRIFYING.
THEY SAY IT LIT UP THE WHOLE CITY. THAT THE CRYSTAL GLOWED AGAIN, FOR THE FIRST TIME SINCE IT ARRIVED.
THAT THE LIGHT IT GAVE OFF WAS BLINDING...
BUT I DIDN'T SEE ANY OF THAT. I WAS TOO BUSY GENERATING IT...OR CONDUCTING IT...TRYING TO DIRECT IT AS IT FLOWED THROUGH ME.
THEY SAY THE POWER JUST KEPT COMING.

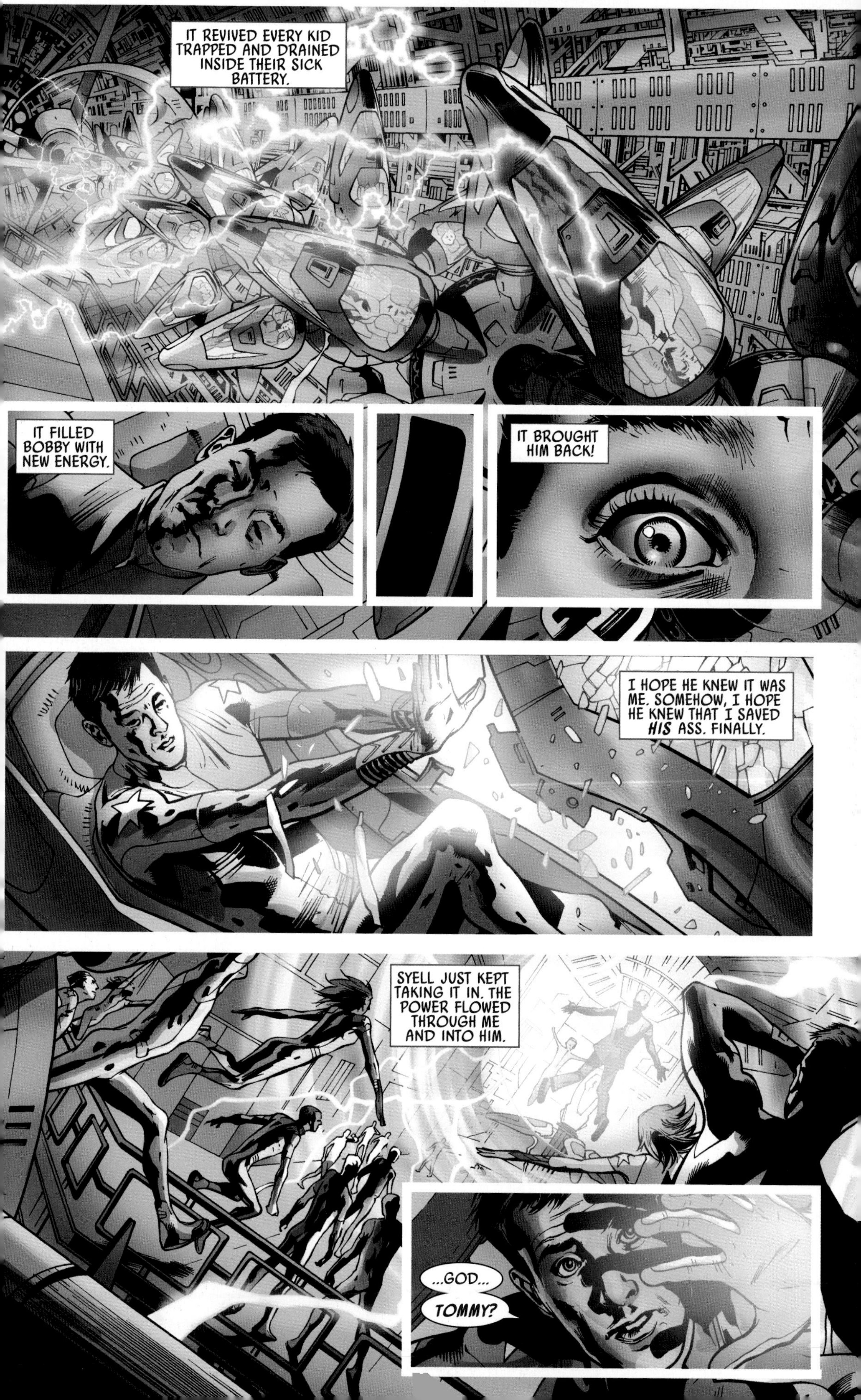
IT REVIVED EVERY KID TRAPPED AND DRAINED INSIDE THEIR SICK BATTERY.
IT FILLED BOBBY WITH NEW ENERGY.
IT BROUGHT HIM BACK!
I HOPE HE KNEW IT WAS ME. SOMEHOW, I HOPE HE KNEW THAT I SAVED HIS ASS. FINALLY.
SYELL JUST KEPT TAKING IT IN. THE POWER FLOWED THROUGH ME AND INTO HIM.
...GOD...
TOMMY?

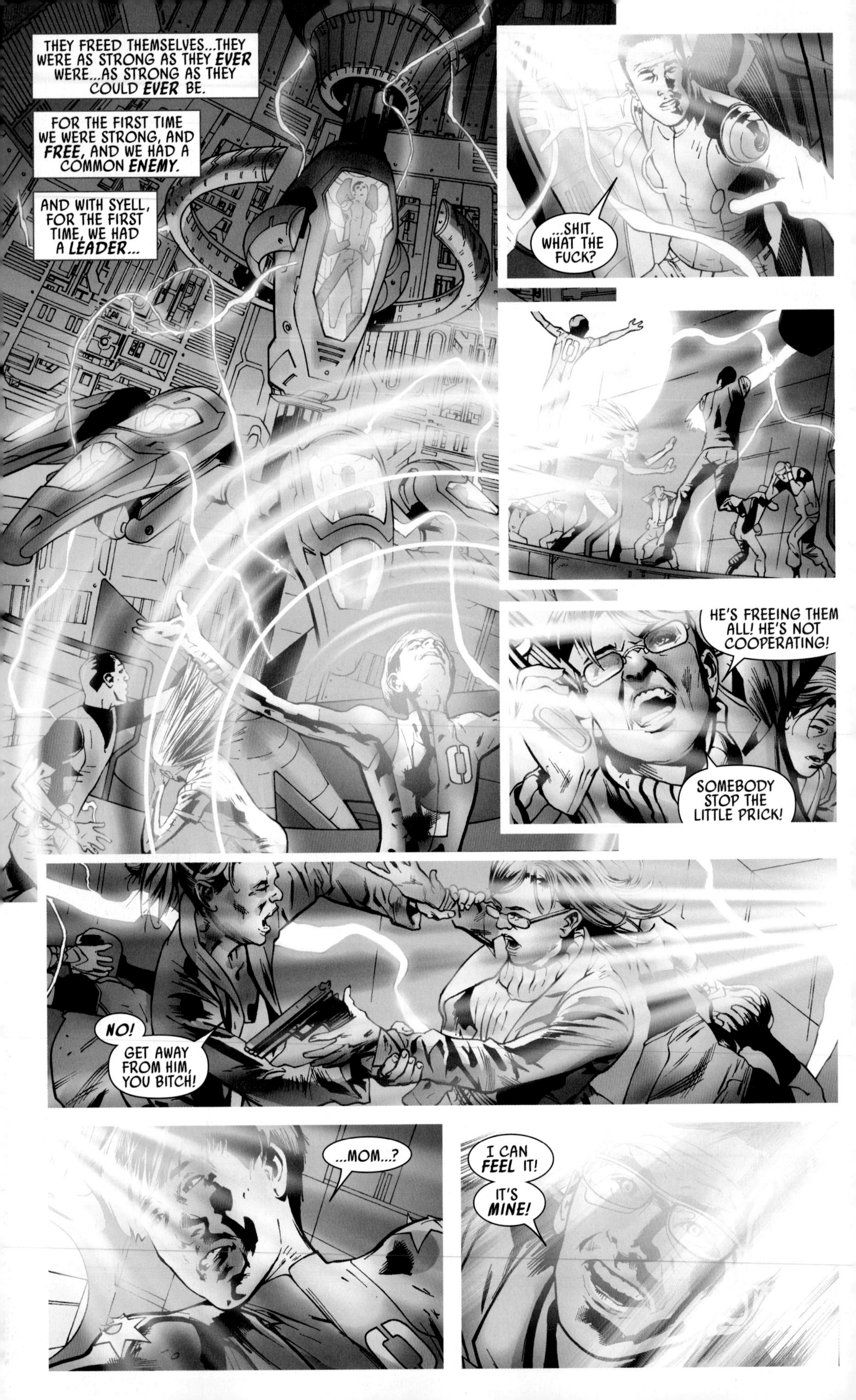
THEY FREED THEMSELVES...THEY WERE AS STRONG AS THEY EVER WERE...AS STRONG AS THEY COULD EVER BE.
FOR THE FIRST TIME WE WERE STRONG, AND FREE, AND WE HAD A COMMON ENEMY.
AND WITH SYELL, FOR THE FIRST TIME, WE HAD A LEADER...
...SHIT. WHAT THE FUCK?
HE'S FREEING THEM ALL! HE'S NOT COOPERATING!
SOMEBODY STOP THE LITTLE PRICK!
NO!
GET AWAY FROM HIM, YOU BITCH!
...MOM...?
I CAN FEEL IT!
IT'S MINE!

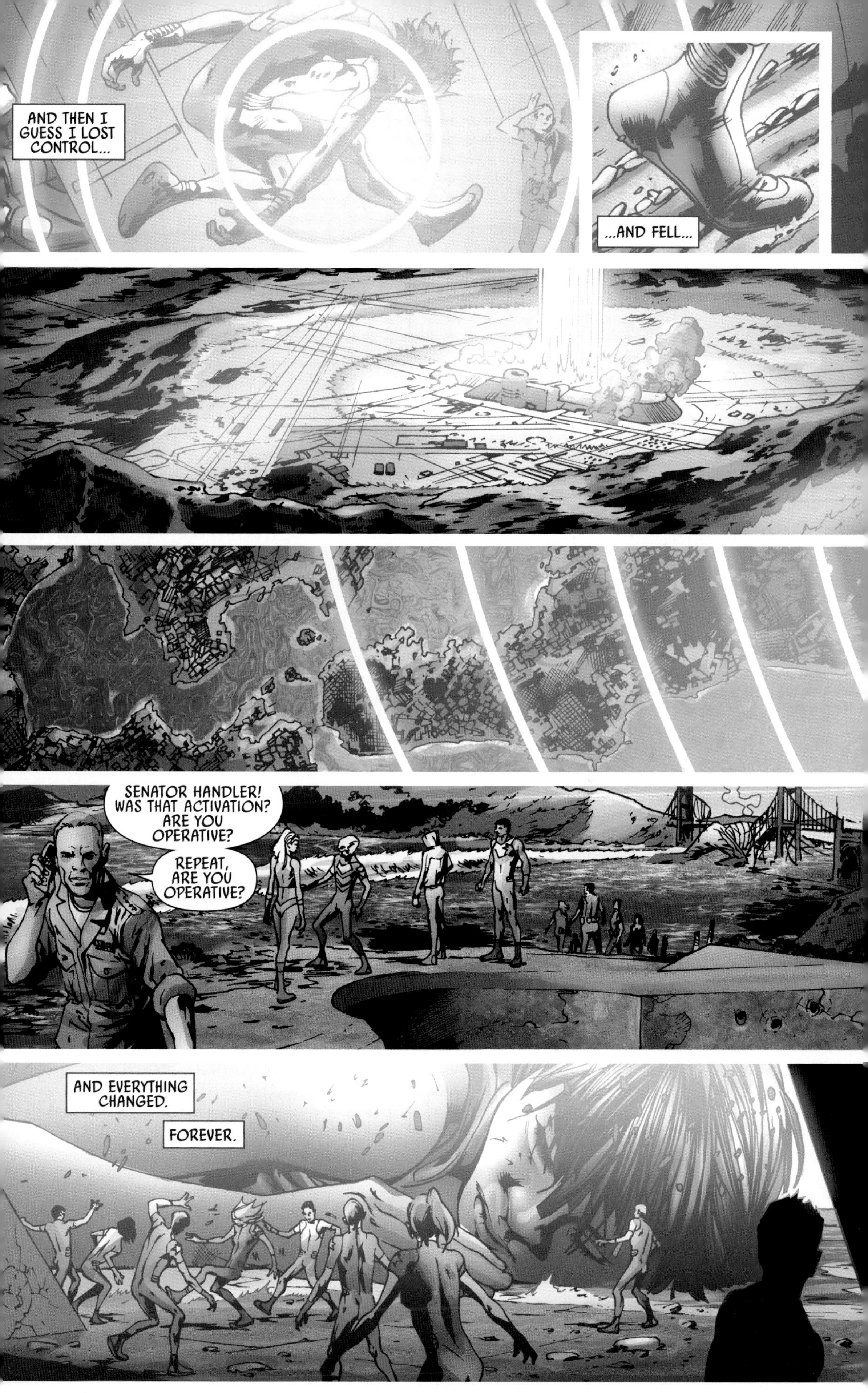
AND THEN I GUESS I LOST CONTROL...
...AND FELL...
SENATOR HANDLER! WAS THAT ACTIVATION? ARE YOU OPERATIVE?
REPEAT, ARE YOU OPERATIVE?
AND EVERYTHING CHANGED.
FOREVER.

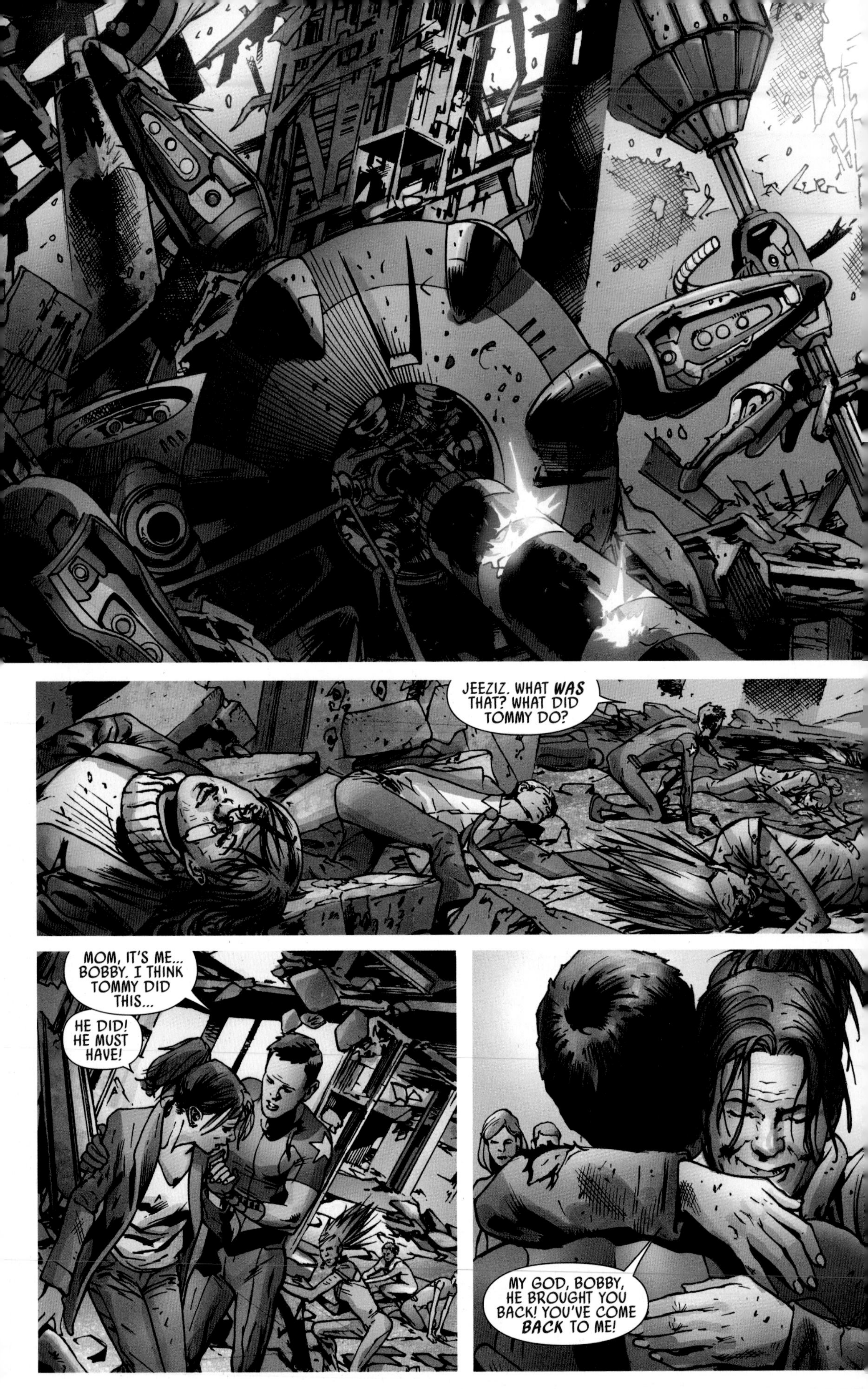
JEEZIZ. WHAT WAS THAT? WHAT DID TOMMY DO?
MOM, IT'S ME... BOBBY. I THINK TOMMY DID THIS...
HE DID! HE MUST HAVE!
MY GOD, BOBBY, HE BROUGHT YOU BACK! YOU'VE COME BACK TO ME!

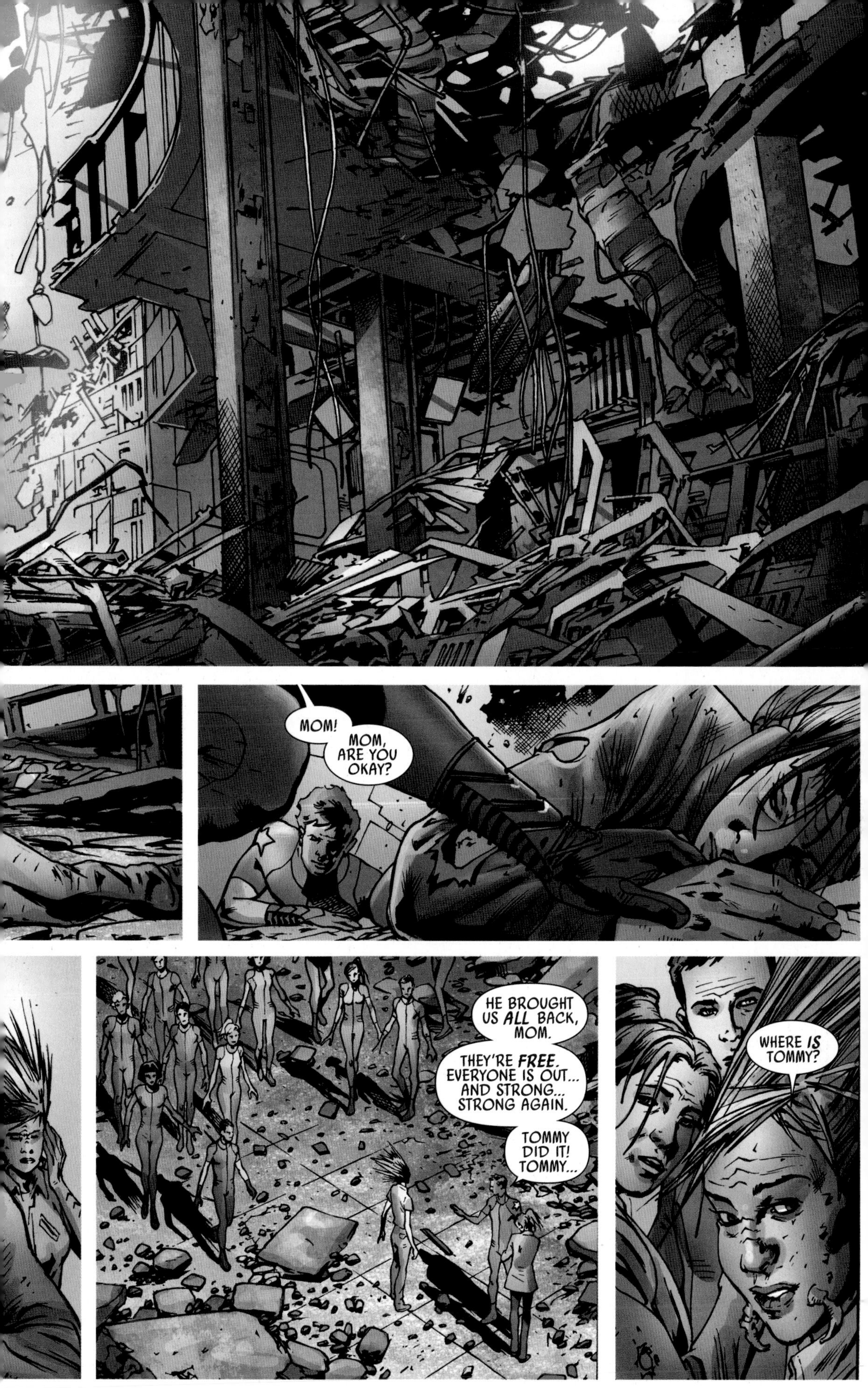
MOM!
MOM, ARE YOU OKAY?
HE BROUGHT US ALL BACK, MOM.
THEY'RE FREE. EVERYONE IS OUT... AND STRONG... STRONG AGAIN.
TOMMY DID IT! TOMMY...
WHERE IS TOMMY?

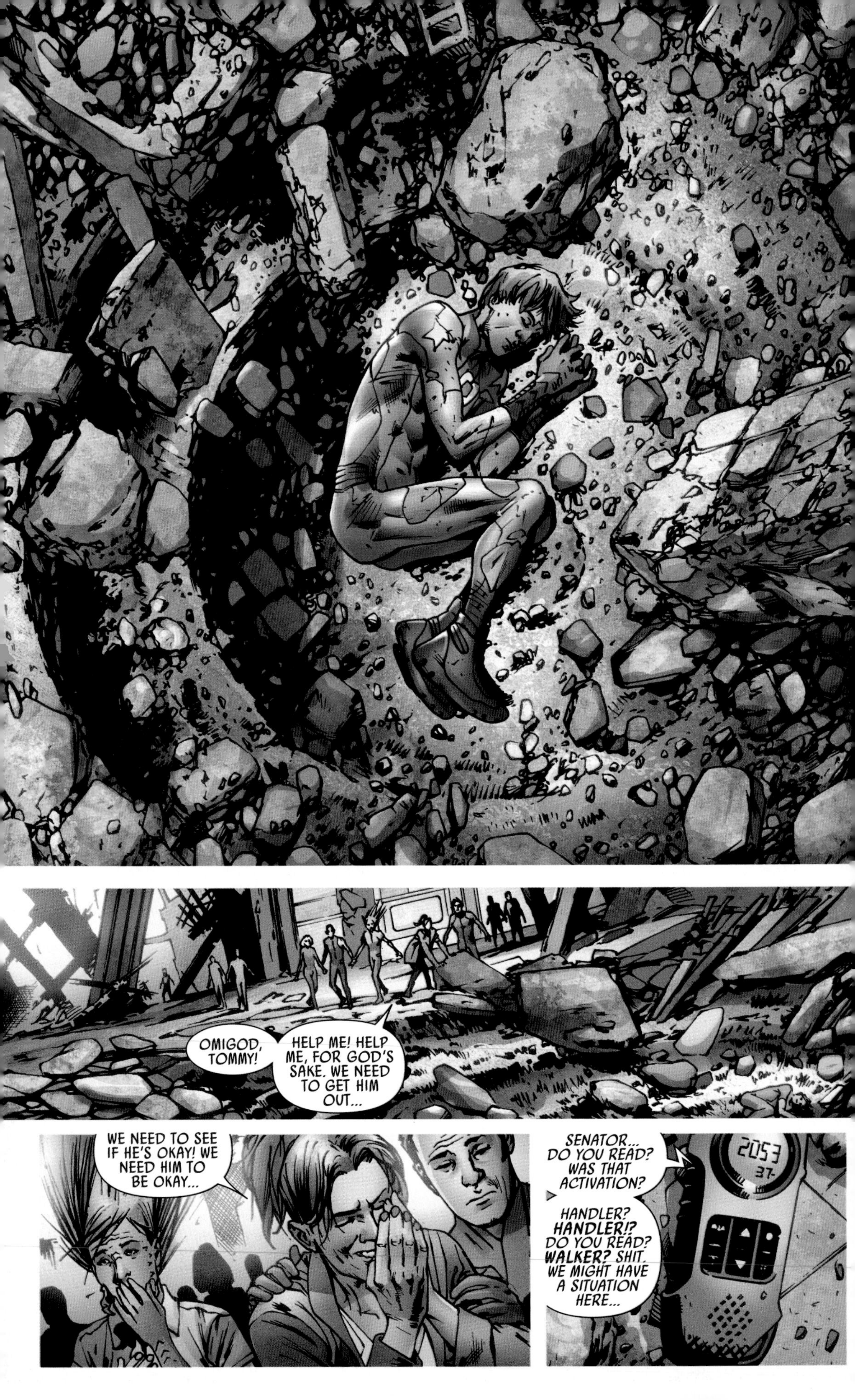
OMIGOD, TOMMY!
HELP ME! HELP ME, FOR GOD'S SAKE. WE NEED TO GET HIM OUT...
WE NEED TO SEE IF HE'S OKAY! WE NEED HIM TO BE OKAY...
SENATOR... DO YOU READ? WAS THAT ACTIVATION?
HANDLER? HANDLER!? DO YOU READ? WALKER? SHIT. WE MIGHT HAVE A SITUATION HERE...
2053
37-

THIS IS GENERAL BURR. IT'S ALPHA MIKE FOXTROT TO THE ARENA, SON. LOOKS LIKE IT'S TIME TO CLOSE DOWN THE SHOP.

JUST WAITING FOR THE ALL-CLEAR, AND THEN YOU CAN LIGHT UP THE BAY.

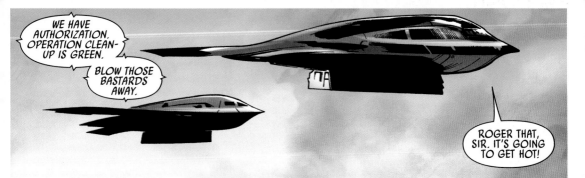

THIS IS COBRA-FOUR-SEVEN. WE ARE PRIMED AND GOOD TO GO, SIR.

REQUEST PERMISSION TO DELIVER THE PAYLOAD, SIR.

WE HAVE AUTHORIZATION. OPERATION CLEAN-UP IS GREEN.

BLOW THOSE BASTARDS AWAY.

ROGER THAT, SIR. IT'S GOING TO GET HOT!

HOLY SHIT!

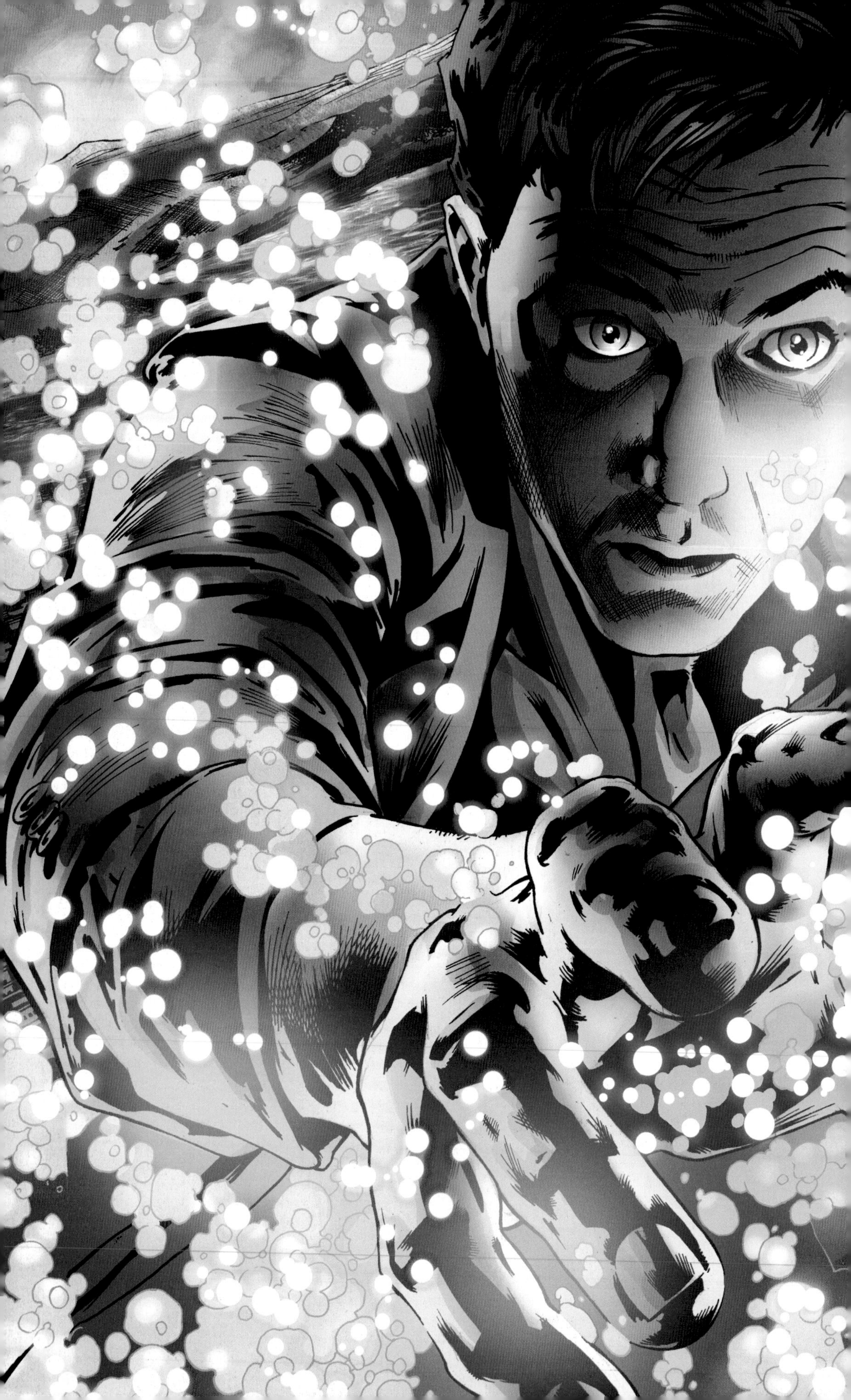

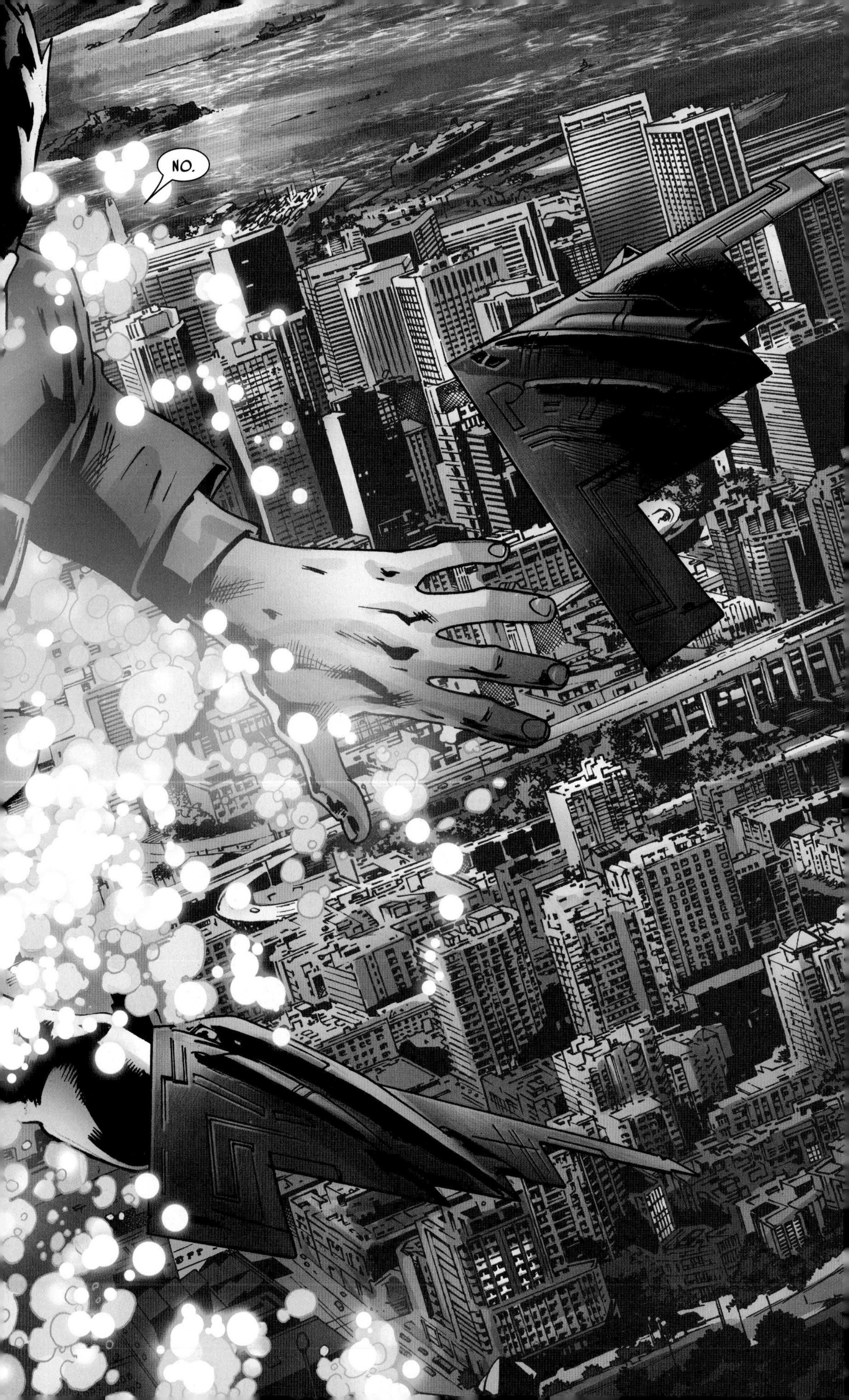
NO.

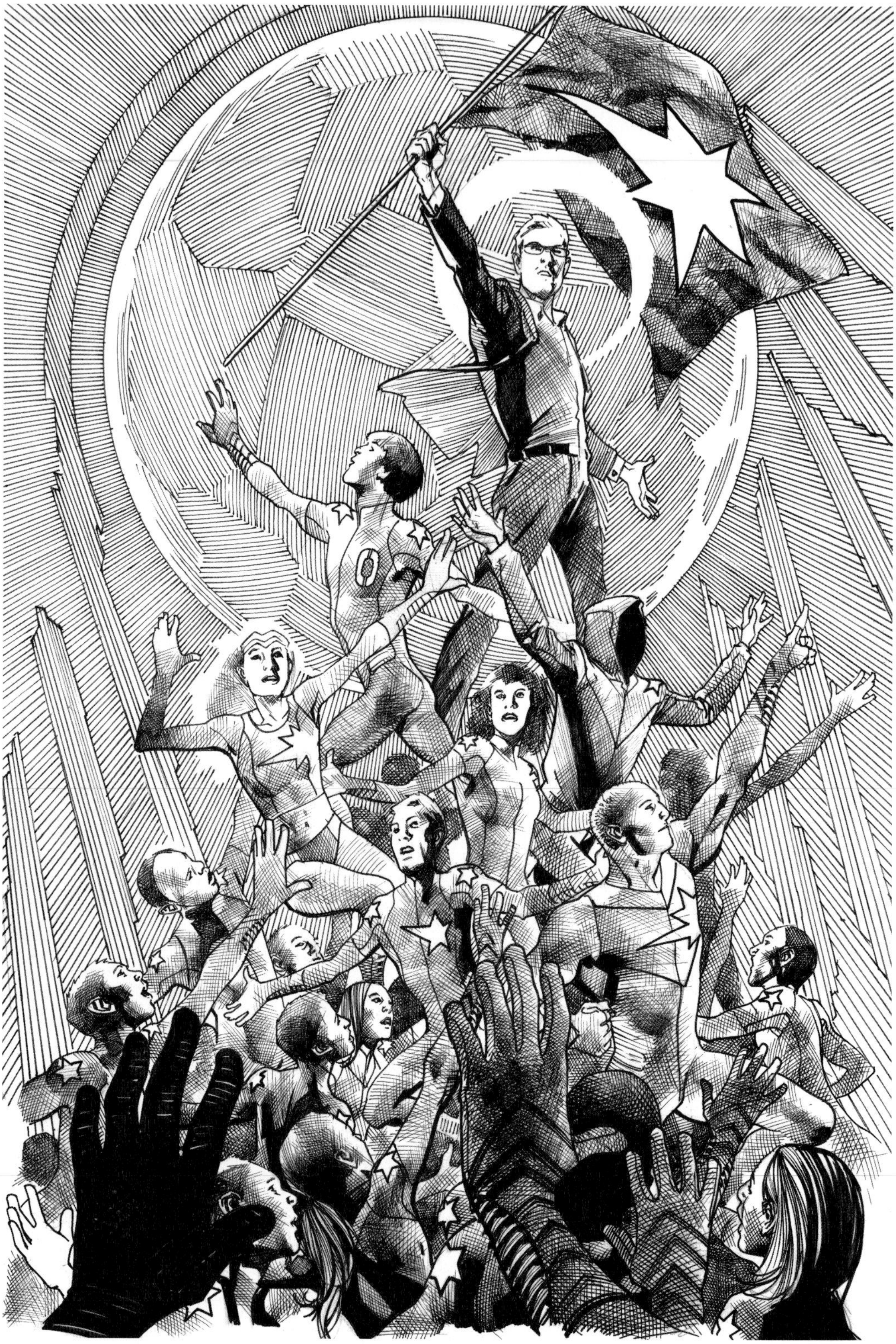

"Bliss was it in that dawn to be alive,
But to be young was very heaven!"

William Wordsworth

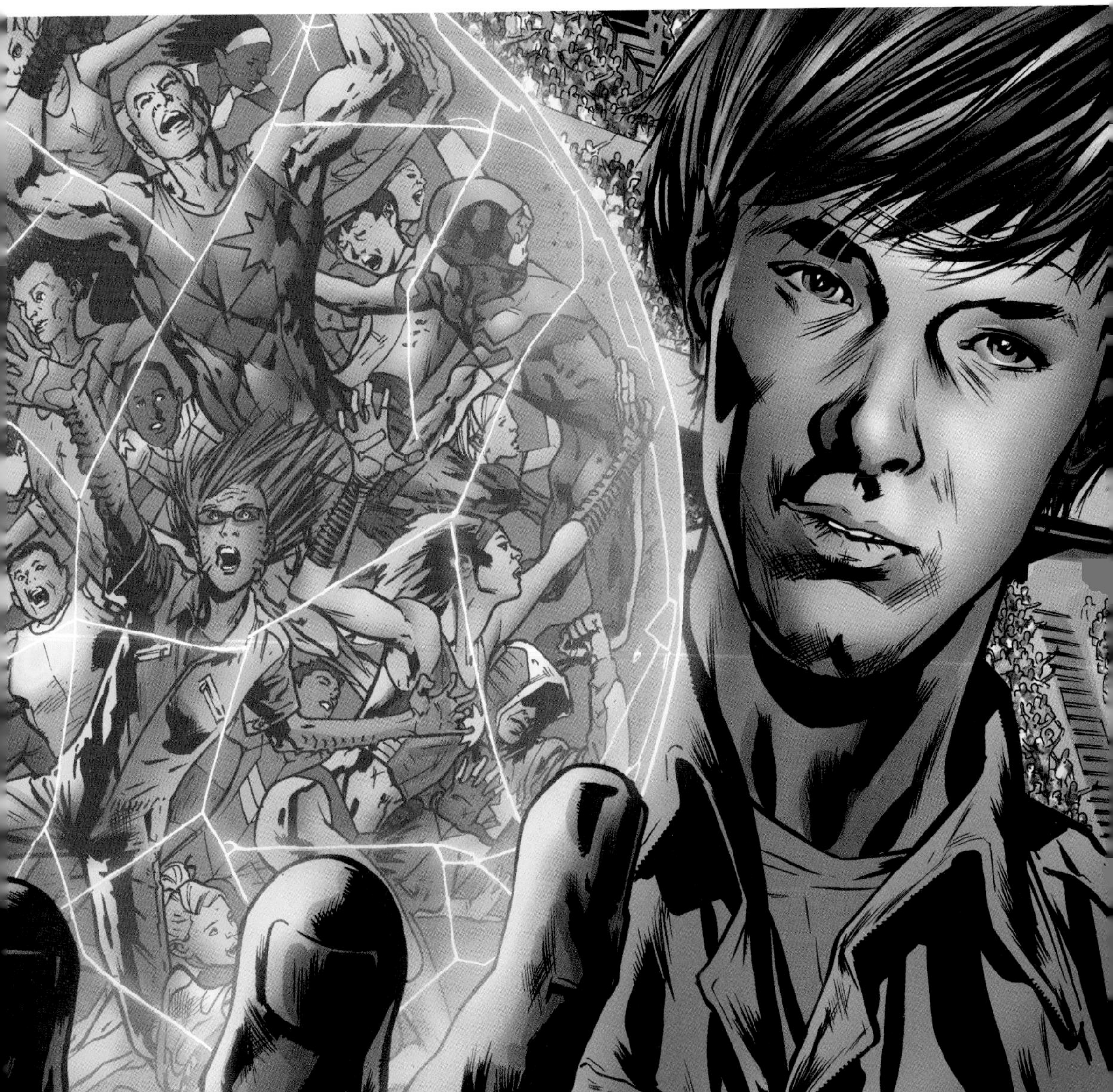

CHAPTER **SIX**

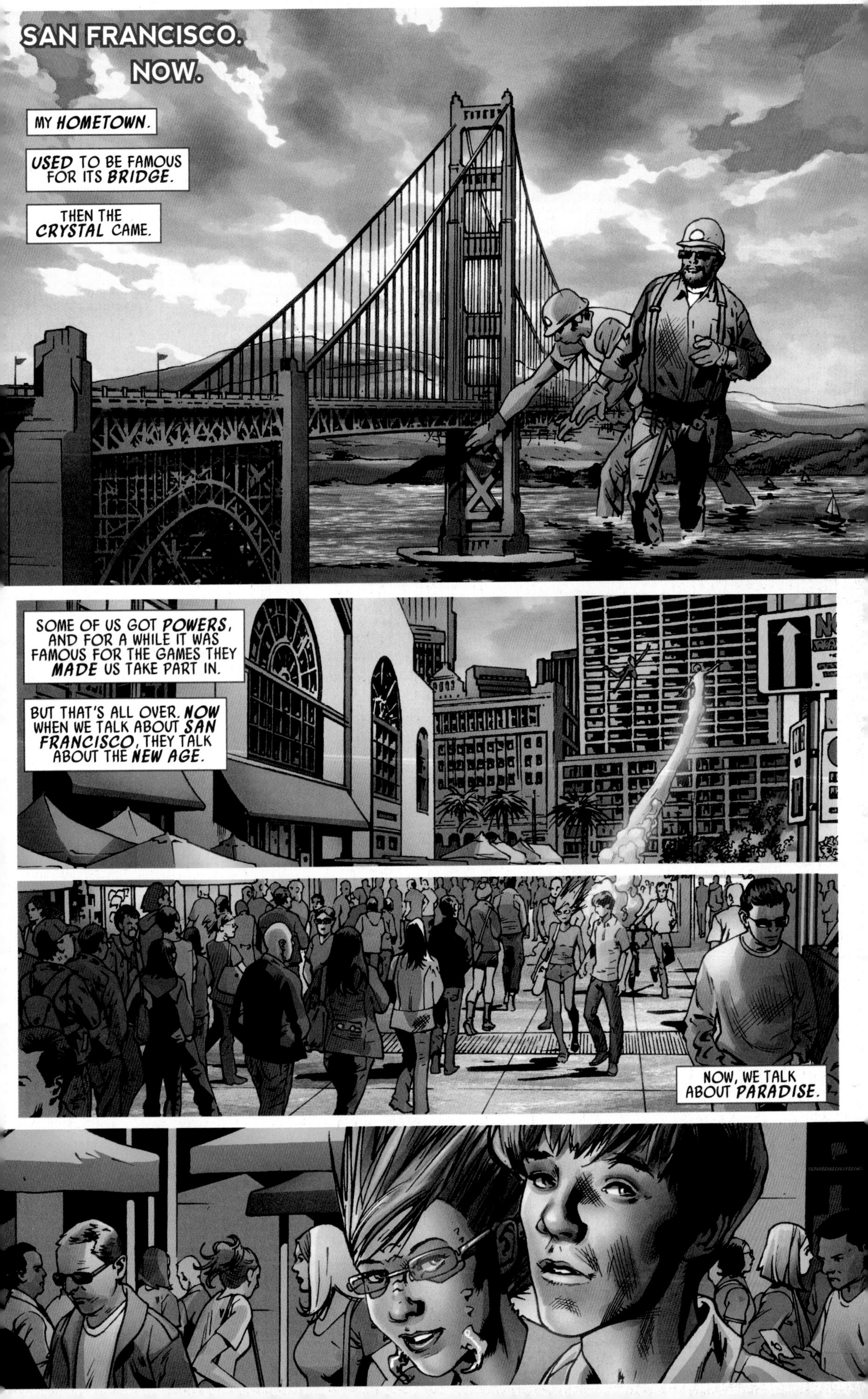
SAN FRANCISCO. NOW.
MY HOMETOWN.
USED TO BE FAMOUS FOR ITS BRIDGE.
THEN THE CRYSTAL CAME.
SOME OF US GOT POWERS, AND FOR A WHILE IT WAS FAMOUS FOR THE GAMES THEY MADE US TAKE PART IN.
BUT THAT'S ALL OVER. NOW WHEN WE TALK ABOUT SAN FRANCISCO, THEY TALK ABOUT THE NEW AGE.
NOW, WE TALK ABOUT PARADISE.

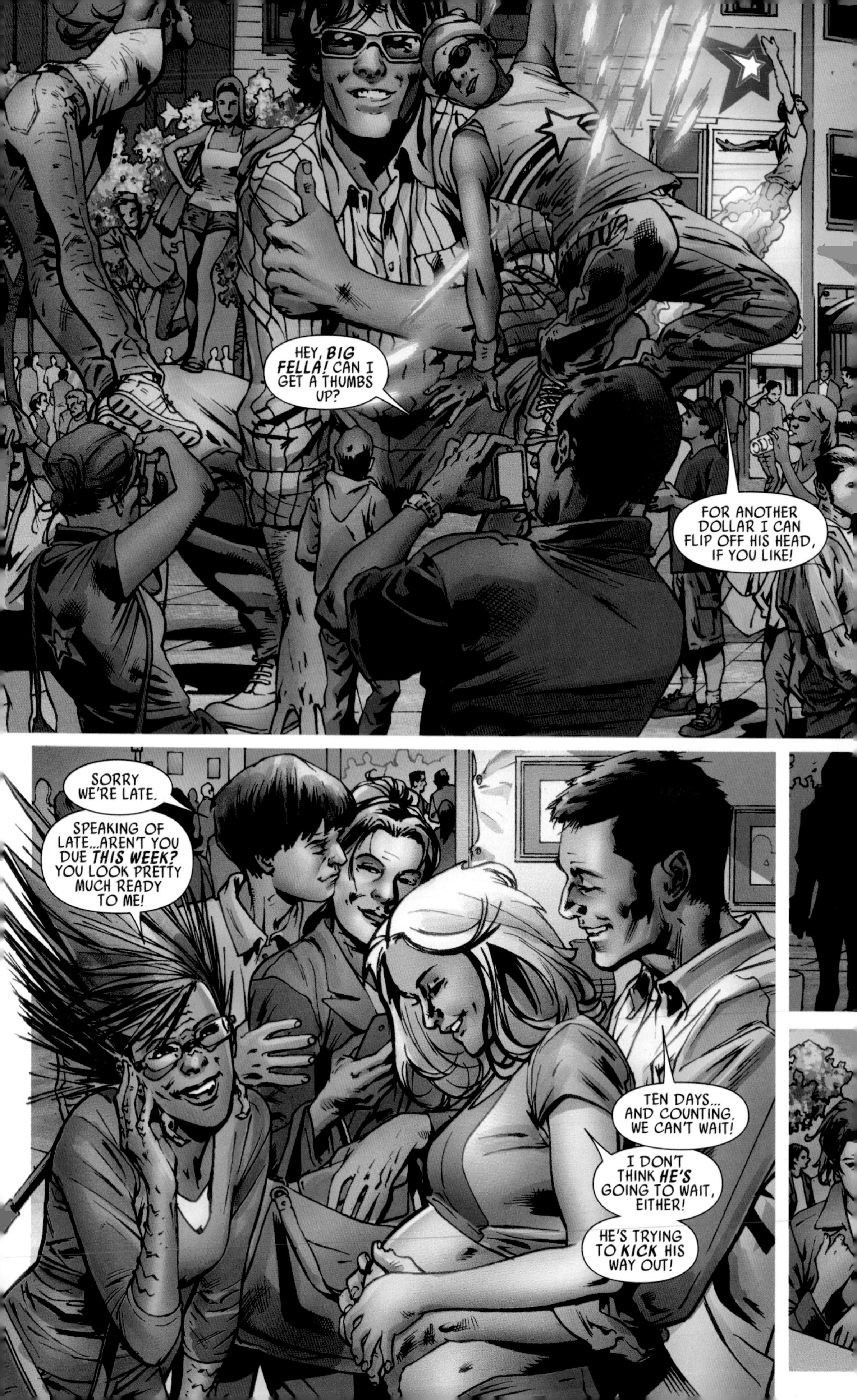
HEY, BIG FELLA! CAN I GET A THUMBS UP?
FOR ANOTHER DOLLAR I CAN FLIP OFF HIS HEAD, IF YOU LIKE!
SORRY WE'RE LATE.
SPEAKING OF LATE...AREN'T YOU DUE THIS WEEK? YOU LOOK PRETTY MUCH READY TO ME!
TEN DAYS... AND COUNTING. WE CAN'T WAIT!
I DON'T THINK HE'S GOING TO WAIT, EITHER!
HE'S TRYING TO KICK HIS WAY OUT!

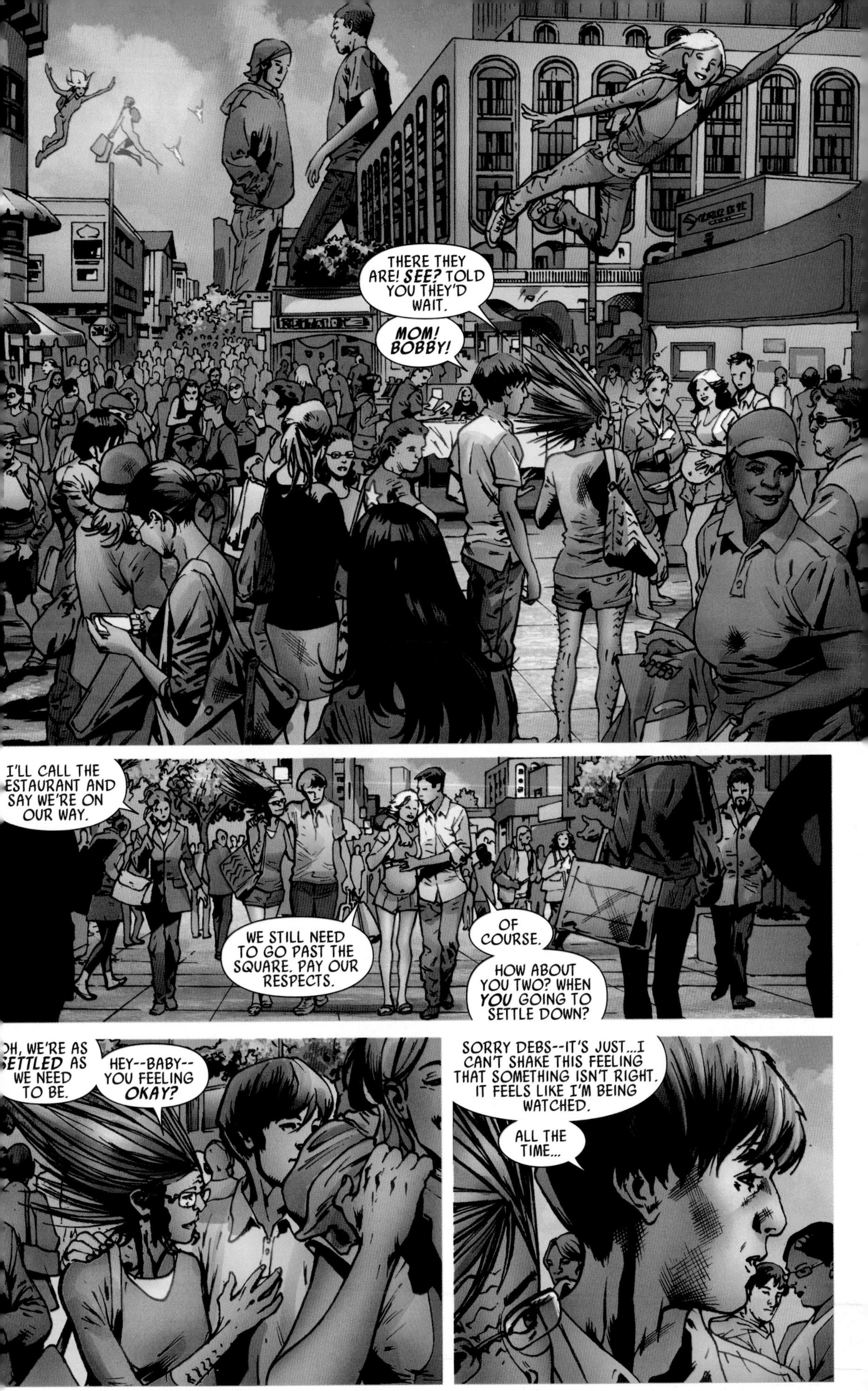
THERE THEY ARE! SEE? TOLD YOU THEY'D WAIT.
MOM! BOBBY!
I'LL CALL THE ESTAURANT AND SAY WE'RE ON OUR WAY.
WE STILL NEED TO GO PAST THE SQUARE. PAY OUR RESPECTS.
OF COURSE.
HOW ABOUT YOU TWO? WHEN YOU GOING TO SETTLE DOWN?
OH, WE'RE AS SETTLED AS WE NEED TO BE.
HEY--BABY--YOU FEELING OKAY?
SORRY DEBS--IT'S JUST...I CAN'T SHAKE THIS FEELING THAT SOMETHING ISN'T RIGHT. IT FEELS LIKE I'M BEING WATCHED.
ALL THE TIME...

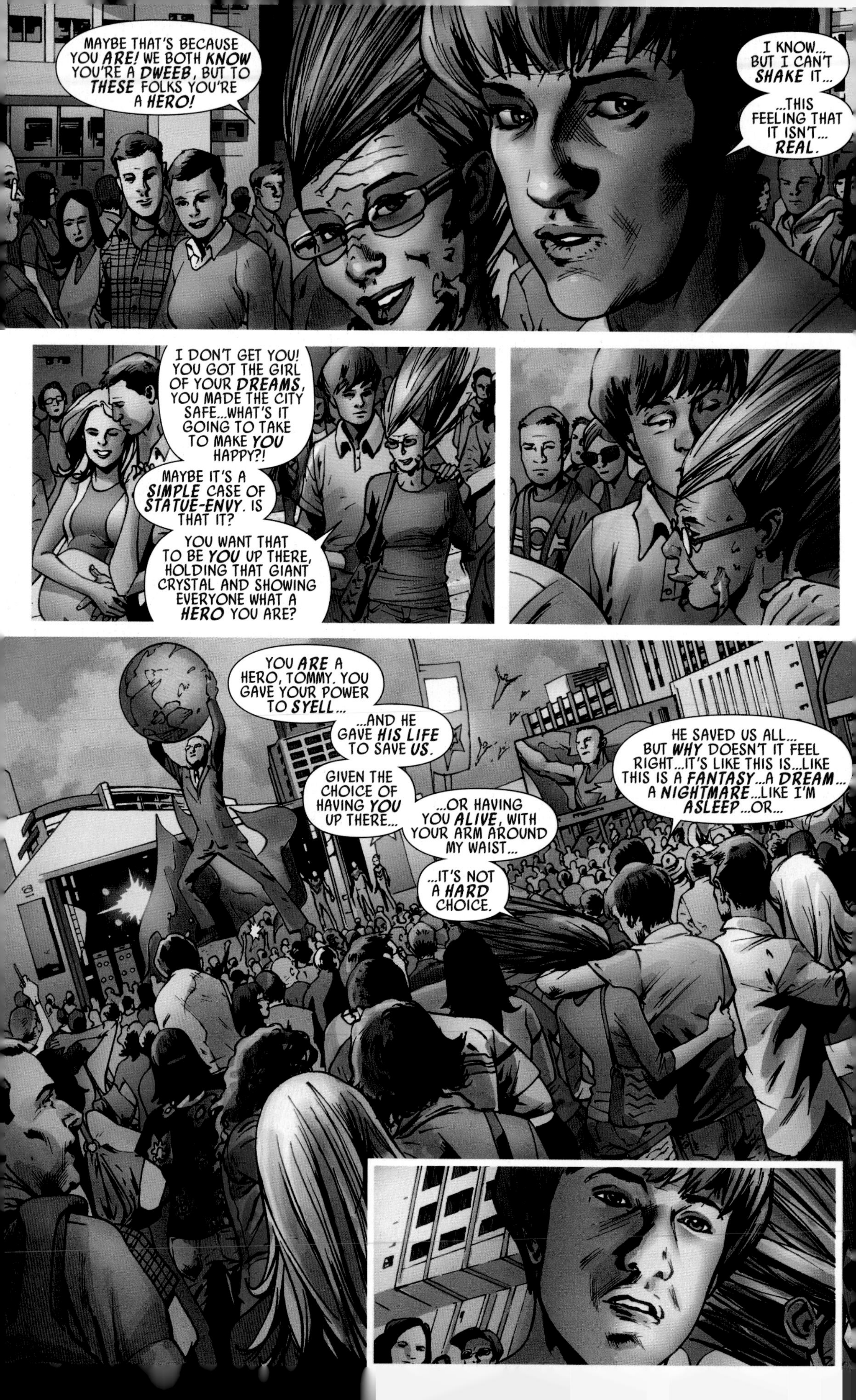
MAYBE THAT'S BECAUSE YOU ARE! WE BOTH KNOW YOU'RE A DWEEB, BUT TO THESE FOLKS YOU'RE A HERO!
I KNOW... BUT I CAN'T SHAKE IT...
...THIS FEELING THAT IT ISN'T... REAL.
I DON'T GET YOU! YOU GOT THE GIRL OF YOUR DREAMS, YOU MADE THE CITY SAFE...WHAT'S IT GOING TO TAKE TO MAKE YOU HAPPY?!
MAYBE IT'S A SIMPLE CASE OF STATUE-ENVY. IS THAT IT?
YOU WANT THAT TO BE YOU UP THERE, HOLDING THAT GIANT CRYSTAL AND SHOWING EVERYONE WHAT A HERO YOU ARE?
YOU ARE A HERO, TOMMY. YOU GAVE YOUR POWER TO SYELL...
...AND HE GAVE HIS LIFE TO SAVE US.
GIVEN THE CHOICE OF HAVING YOU UP THERE...
...OR HAVING YOU ALIVE, WITH YOUR ARM AROUND MY WAIST...
...IT'S NOT A HARD CHOICE.
HE SAVED US ALL... BUT WHY DOESN'T IT FEEL RIGHT...IT'S LIKE THIS IS...LIKE THIS IS A FANTASY...A DREAM... A NIGHTMARE...LIKE I'M ASLEEP...OR...

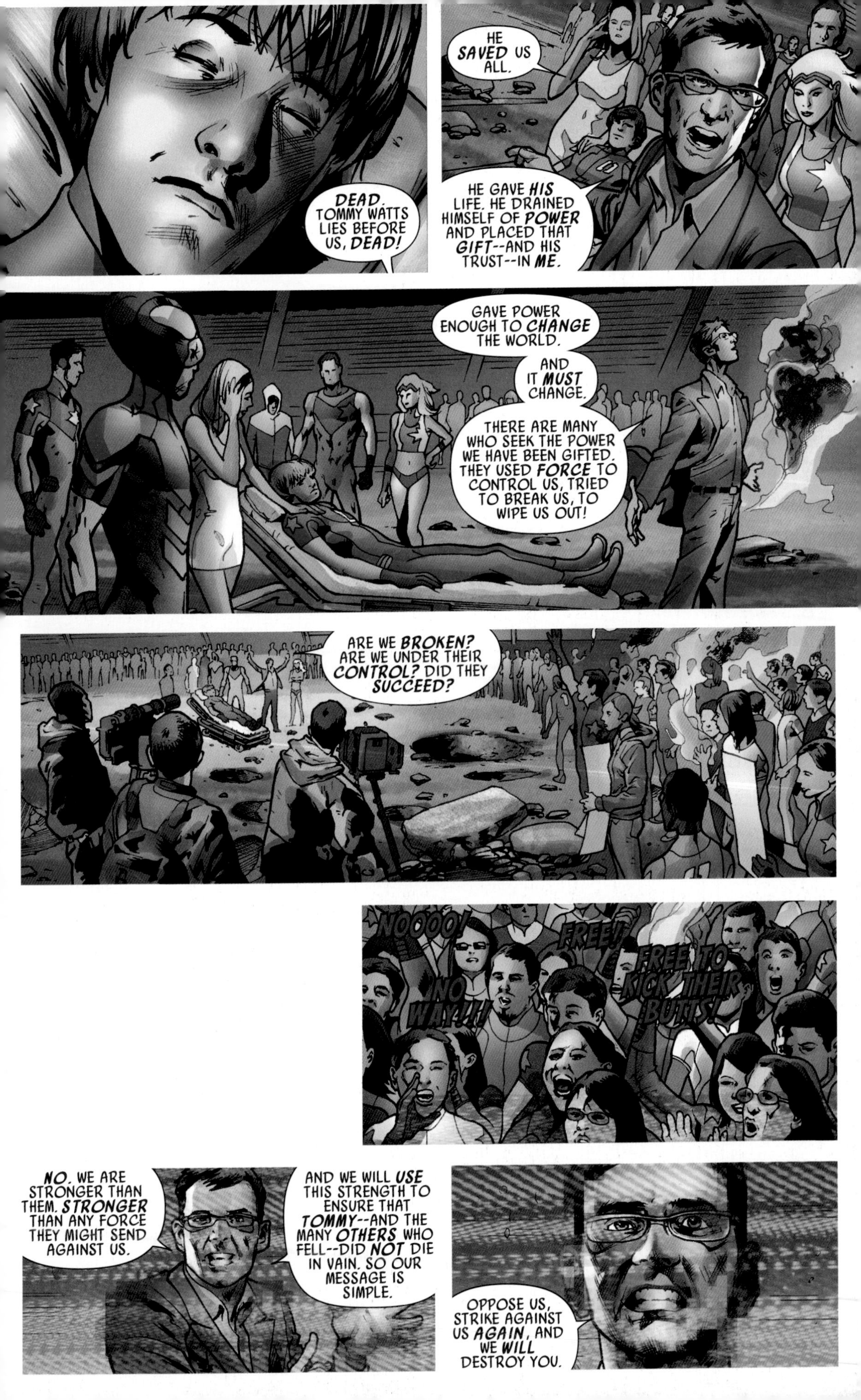
DEAD. TOMMY WATTS LIES BEFORE US, DEAD!
HE SAVED US ALL.
HE GAVE HIS LIFE. HE DRAINED HIMSELF OF POWER AND PLACED THAT GIFT--AND HIS TRUST--IN ME.
GAVE POWER ENOUGH TO CHANGE THE WORLD.
AND IT MUST CHANGE.
THERE ARE MANY WHO SEEK THE POWER WE HAVE BEEN GIFTED. THEY USED FORCE TO CONTROL US, TRIED TO BREAK US, TO WIPE US OUT!
ARE WE BROKEN? ARE WE UNDER THEIR CONTROL? DID THEY SUCCEED?
NOOOO!
NO WAY!!!
FREE!
FREE TO KICK THEIR BUTTS!
NO. WE ARE STRONGER THAN THEM. STRONGER THAN ANY FORCE THEY MIGHT SEND AGAINST US.
AND WE WILL USE THIS STRENGTH TO ENSURE THAT TOMMY--AND THE MANY OTHERS WHO FELL--DID NOT DIE IN VAIN. SO OUR MESSAGE IS SIMPLE.
OPPOSE US, STRIKE AGAINST US AGAIN, AND WE WILL DESTROY YOU.

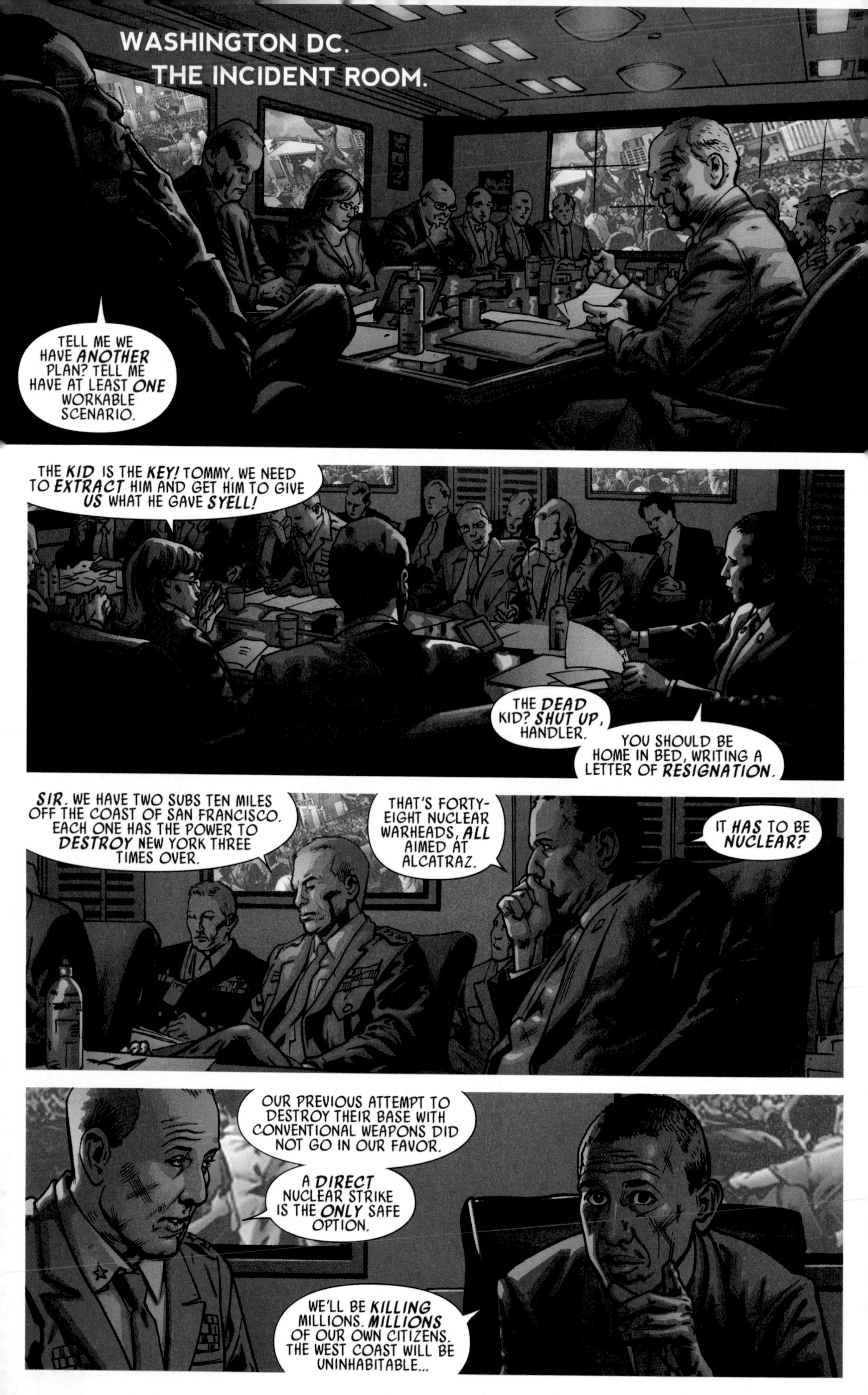
WASHINGTON DC.
THE INCIDENT ROOM.
TELL ME WE HAVE ANOTHER PLAN? TELL ME HAVE AT LEAST ONE WORKABLE SCENARIO.
THE KID IS THE KEY! TOMMY. WE NEED TO EXTRACT HIM AND GET HIM TO GIVE US WHAT HE GAVE SYELL!
THE DEAD KID? SHUT UP, HANDLER.
YOU SHOULD BE HOME IN BED, WRITING A LETTER OF RESIGNATION.
SIR. WE HAVE TWO SUBS TEN MILES OFF THE COAST OF SAN FRANCISCO. EACH ONE HAS THE POWER TO DESTROY NEW YORK THREE TIMES OVER.
THAT'S FORTY-EIGHT NUCLEAR WARHEADS, ALL AIMED AT ALCATRAZ.
IT HAS TO BE NUCLEAR?
OUR PREVIOUS ATTEMPT TO DESTROY THEIR BASE WITH CONVENTIONAL WEAPONS DID NOT GO IN OUR FAVOR.
A DIRECT NUCLEAR STRIKE IS THE ONLY SAFE OPTION.
WE'LL BE KILLING MILLIONS. MILLIONS OF OUR OWN CITIZENS. THE WEST COAST WILL BE UNINHABITABLE...

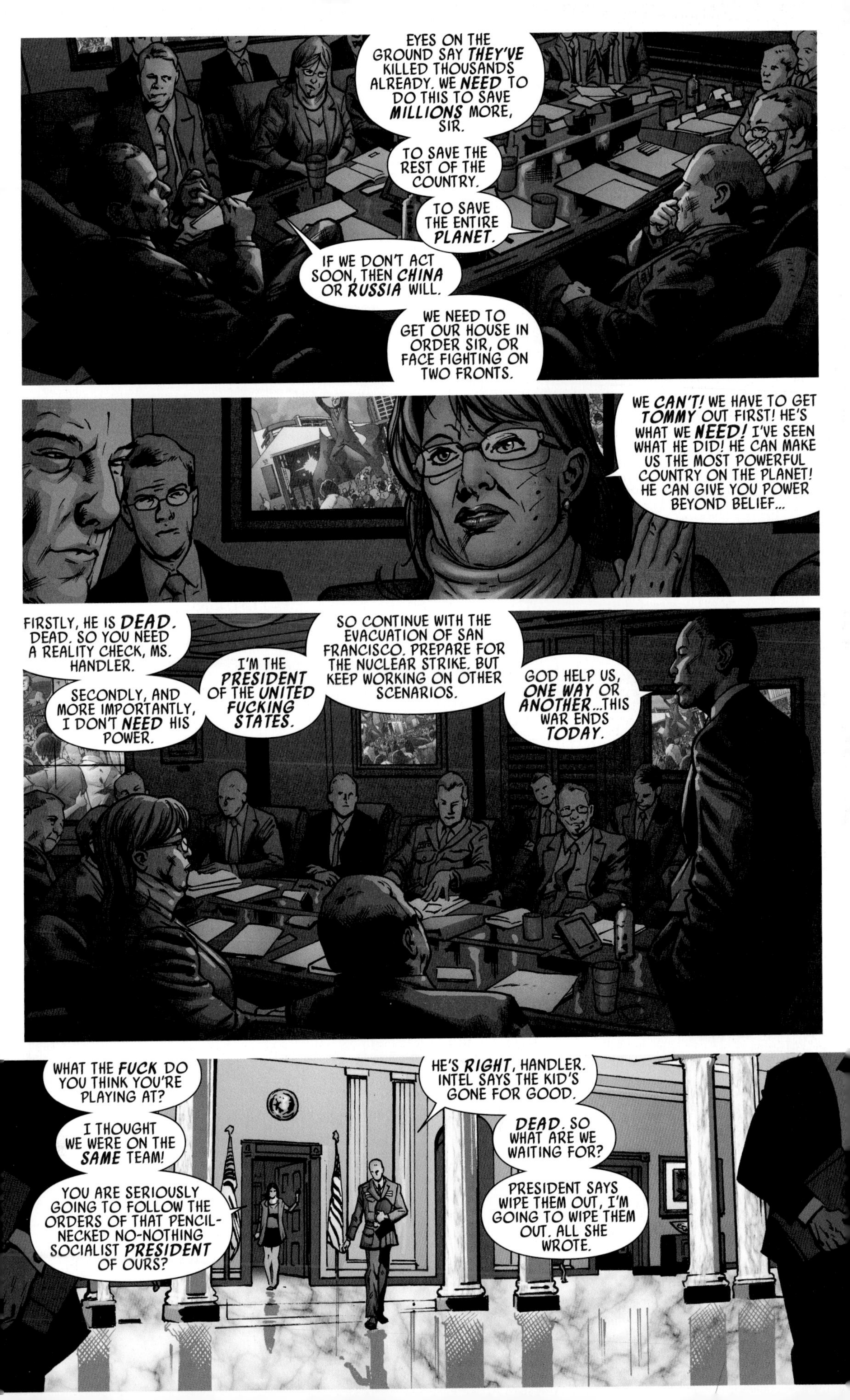

EYES ON THE GROUND SAY THEY'VE KILLED THOUSANDS ALREADY. WE NEED TO DO THIS TO SAVE MILLIONS MORE, SIR.
TO SAVE THE REST OF THE COUNTRY.
TO SAVE THE ENTIRE PLANET.
IF WE DON'T ACT SOON, THEN CHINA OR RUSSIA WILL.
WE NEED TO GET OUR HOUSE IN ORDER SIR, OR FACE FIGHTING ON TWO FRONTS.
WE CAN'T! WE HAVE TO GET TOMMY OUT FIRST! HE'S WHAT WE NEED! I'VE SEEN WHAT HE DID! HE CAN MAKE US THE MOST POWERFUL COUNTRY ON THE PLANET! HE CAN GIVE YOU POWER BEYOND BELIEF...
FIRSTLY, HE IS DEAD. DEAD. SO YOU NEED A REALITY CHECK, MS. HANDLER.
SECONDLY, AND MORE IMPORTANTLY, I DON'T NEED HIS POWER.
I'M THE PRESIDENT OF THE UNITED FUCKING STATES.
SO CONTINUE WITH THE EVACUATION OF SAN FRANCISCO. PREPARE FOR THE NUCLEAR STRIKE. BUT KEEP WORKING ON OTHER SCENARIOS.
GOD HELP US, ONE WAY OR ANOTHER...THIS WAR ENDS TODAY.
WHAT THE FUCK DO YOU THINK YOU'RE PLAYING AT?
I THOUGHT WE WERE ON THE SAME TEAM!
YOU ARE SERIOUSLY GOING TO FOLLOW THE ORDERS OF THAT PENCIL-NECKED NO-NOTHING SOCIALIST PRESIDENT OF OURS?
HE'S RIGHT, HANDLER. INTEL SAYS THE KID'S GONE FOR GOOD.
DEAD. SO WHAT ARE WE WAITING FOR?
PRESIDENT SAYS WIPE THEM OUT, I'M GOING TO WIPE THEM OUT. ALL SHE WROTE.

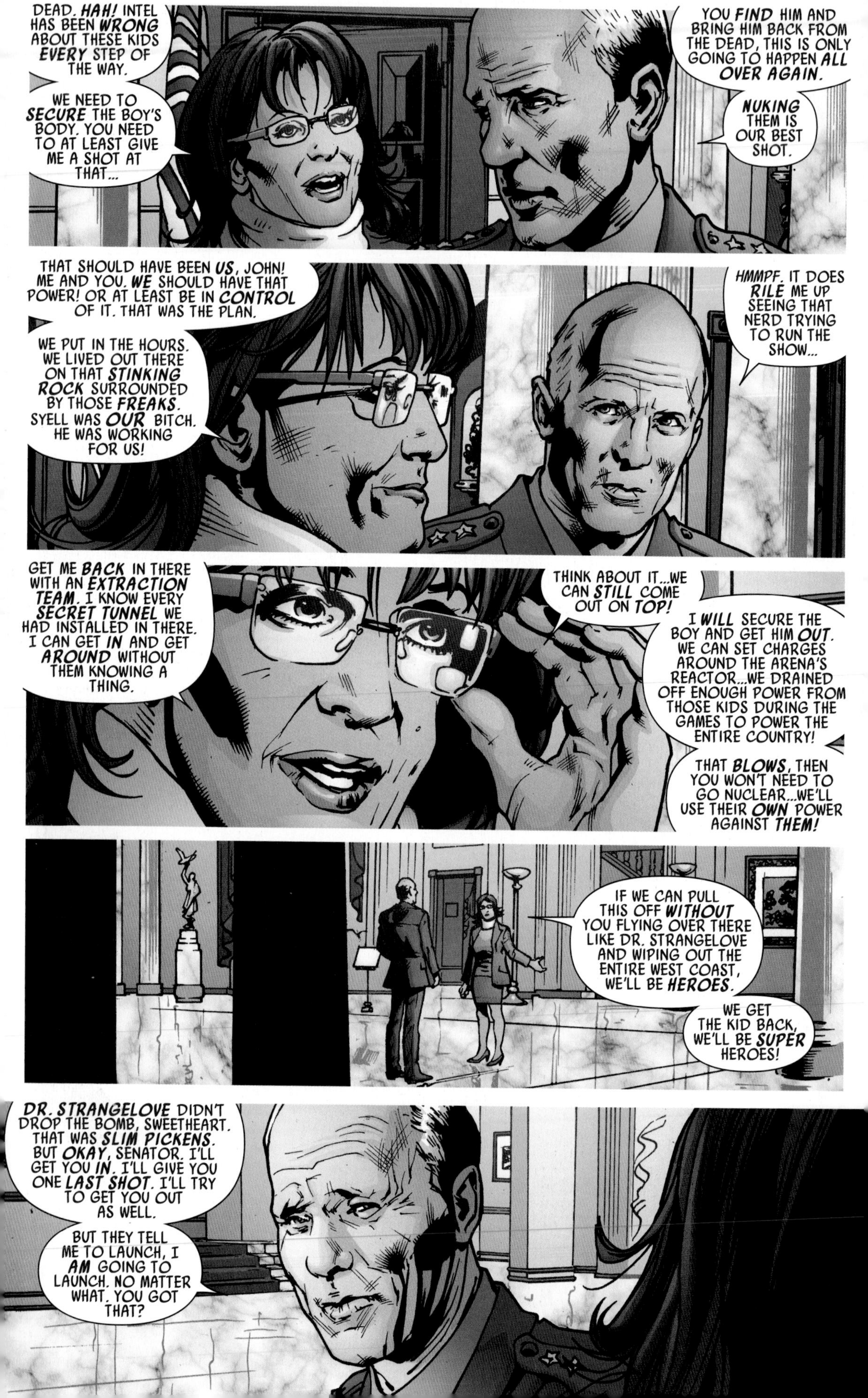
DEAD. HAH! INTEL HAS BEEN WRONG ABOUT THESE KIDS EVERY STEP OF THE WAY.
WE NEED TO SECURE THE BOY'S BODY. YOU NEED TO AT LEAST GIVE ME A SHOT AT THAT...
YOU FIND HIM AND BRING HIM BACK FROM THE DEAD, THIS IS ONLY GOING TO HAPPEN ALL OVER AGAIN.
NUKING THEM IS OUR BEST SHOT.
THAT SHOULD HAVE BEEN US, JOHN! ME AND YOU. WE SHOULD HAVE THAT POWER! OR AT LEAST BE IN CONTROL OF IT. THAT WAS THE PLAN.
WE PUT IN THE HOURS. WE LIVED OUT THERE ON THAT STINKING ROCK SURROUNDED BY THOSE FREAKS. SYELL WAS OUR BITCH. HE WAS WORKING FOR US!
HMMPF. IT DOES RILE ME UP SEEING THAT NERD TRYING TO RUN THE SHOW...
GET ME BACK IN THERE WITH AN EXTRACTION TEAM. I KNOW EVERY SECRET TUNNEL WE HAD INSTALLED IN THERE. I CAN GET IN AND GET AROUND WITHOUT THEM KNOWING A THING.
THINK ABOUT IT...WE CAN STILL COME OUT ON TOP!
I WILL SECURE THE BOY AND GET HIM OUT. WE CAN SET CHARGES AROUND THE ARENA'S REACTOR...WE DRAINED OFF ENOUGH POWER FROM THOSE KIDS DURING THE GAMES TO POWER THE ENTIRE COUNTRY!
THAT BLOWS, THEN YOU WON'T NEED TO GO NUCLEAR...WE'LL USE THEIR OWN POWER AGAINST THEM!
IF WE CAN PULL THIS OFF WITHOUT YOU FLYING OVER THERE LIKE DR. STRANGELOVE AND WIPING OUT THE ENTIRE WEST COAST, WE'LL BE HEROES.
WE GET THE KID BACK, WE'LL BE SUPER HEROES!
DR. STRANGELOVE DIDN'T DROP THE BOMB, SWEETHEART. THAT WAS SLIM PICKENS. BUT OKAY, SENATOR. I'LL GET YOU IN. I'LL GIVE YOU ONE LAST SHOT. I'LL TRY TO GET YOU OUT AS WELL.
BUT THEY TELL ME TO LAUNCH, I AM GOING TO LAUNCH. NO MATTER WHAT. YOU GOT THAT?

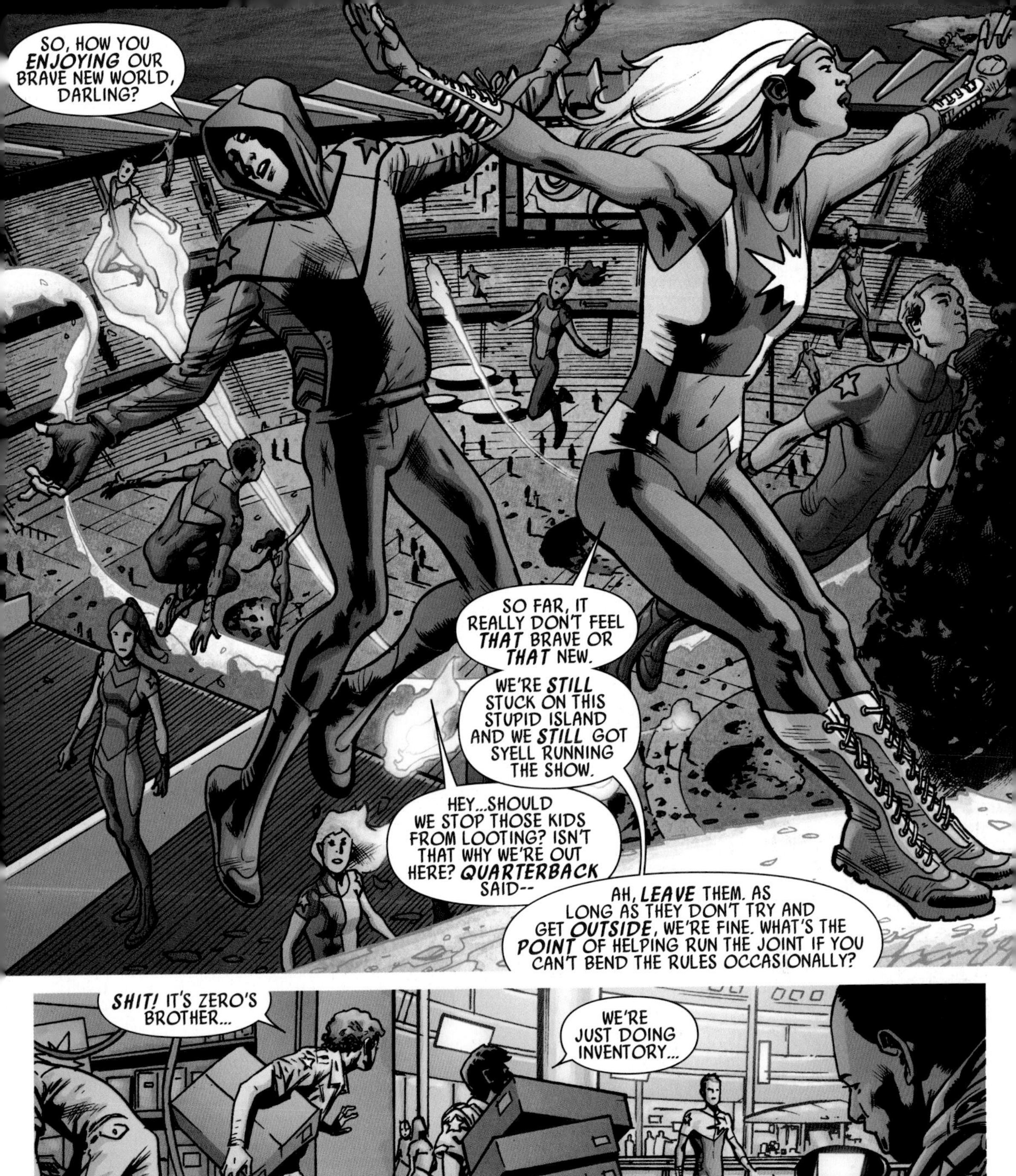
SO, HOW YOU ENJOYING OUR BRAVE NEW WORLD, DARLING?
SO FAR, IT REALLY DON'T FEEL THAT BRAVE OR THAT NEW.
WE'RE STILL STUCK ON THIS STUPID ISLAND AND WE STILL GOT SYELL RUNNING THE SHOW.
HEY...SHOULD WE STOP THOSE KIDS FROM LOOTING? ISN'T THAT WHY WE'RE OUT HERE? QUARTERBACK SAID--
AH, LEAVE THEM. AS LONG AS THEY DON'T TRY AND GET OUTSIDE, WE'RE FINE. WHAT'S THE POINT OF HELPING RUN THE JOINT IF YOU CAN'T BEND THE RULES OCCASIONALLY?
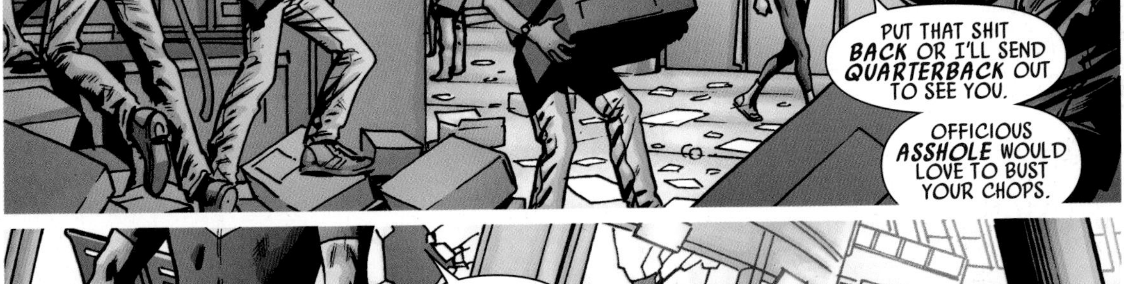
SHIT! IT'S ZERO'S BROTHER...
WE'RE JUST DOING INVENTORY...
PUT THAT SHIT BACK OR I'LL SEND QUARTERBACK OUT TO SEE YOU.
OFFICIOUS ASSHOLE WOULD LOVE TO BUST YOUR CHOPS.
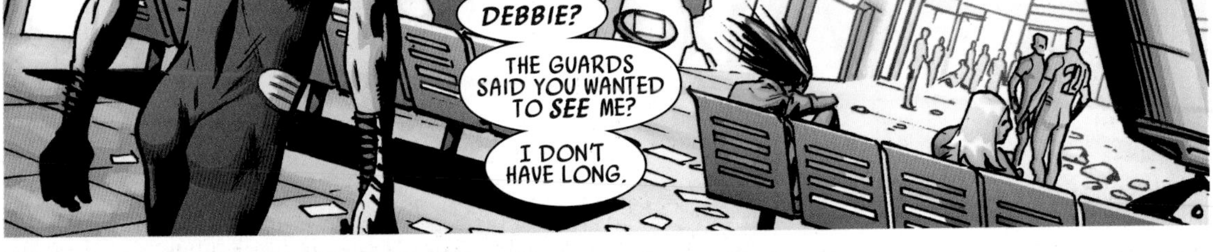
DEBBIE?
THE GUARDS SAID YOU WANTED TO SEE ME?
I DON'T HAVE LONG.

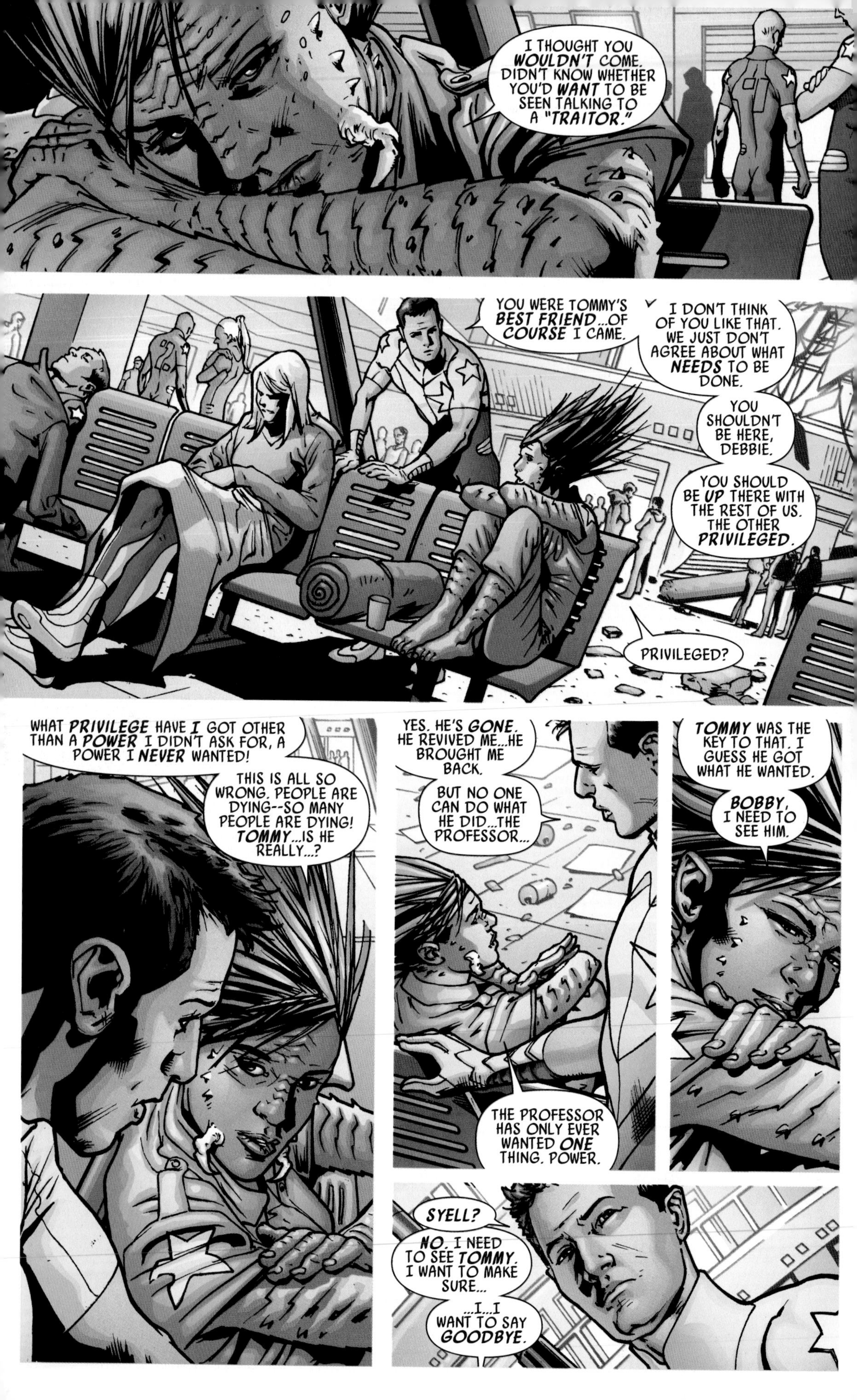
I THOUGHT YOU WOULDN'T COME. DIDN'T KNOW WHETHER YOU'D WANT TO BE SEEN TALKING TO A "TRAITOR."
YOU WERE TOMMY'S BEST FRIEND...OF COURSE I CAME.
I DON'T THINK OF YOU LIKE THAT. WE JUST DON'T AGREE ABOUT WHAT NEEDS TO BE DONE.
YOU SHOULDN'T BE HERE, DEBBIE.
YOU SHOULD BE UP THERE WITH THE REST OF US. THE OTHER PRIVILEGED.
PRIVILEGED?
WHAT PRIVILEGE HAVE I GOT OTHER THAN A POWER I DIDN'T ASK FOR, A POWER I NEVER WANTED!
THIS IS ALL SO WRONG. PEOPLE ARE DYING--SO MANY PEOPLE ARE DYING! TOMMY...IS HE REALLY...?
YES. HE'S GONE. HE REVIVED ME...HE BROUGHT ME BACK.
BUT NO ONE CAN DO WHAT HE DID...THE PROFESSOR...
THE PROFESSOR HAS ONLY EVER WANTED ONE THING. POWER.
TOMMY WAS THE KEY TO THAT. I GUESS HE GOT WHAT HE WANTED.
BOBBY, I NEED TO SEE HIM.
SYELL?
NO. I NEED TO SEE TOMMY. I WANT TO MAKE SURE...
...I...I WANT TO SAY GOODBYE.

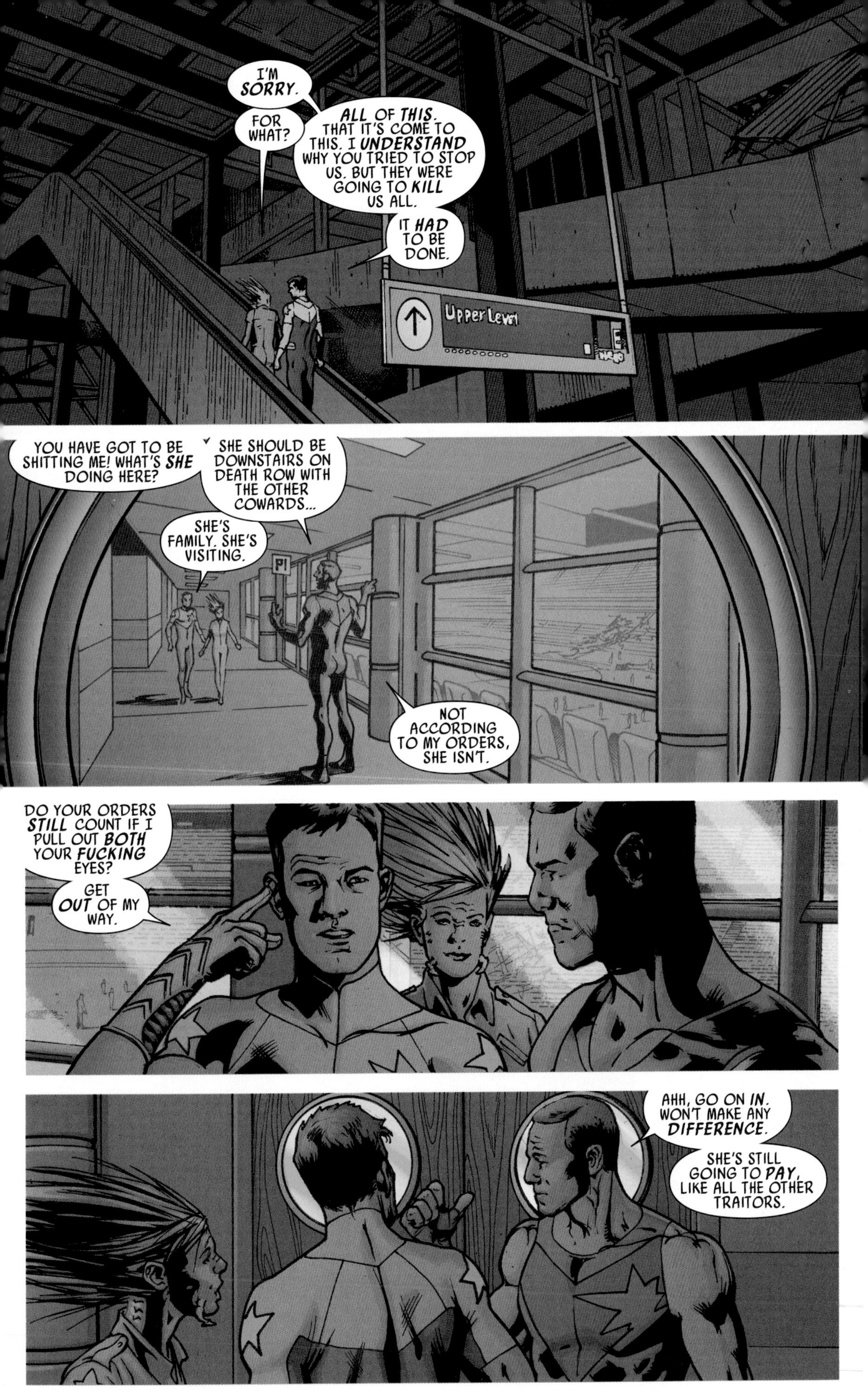
I'M SORRY.
FOR WHAT?
ALL OF THIS. THAT IT'S COME TO THIS. I UNDERSTAND WHY YOU TRIED TO STOP US. BUT THEY WERE GOING TO KILL US ALL.
IT HAD TO BE DONE.
Upper Level
YOU HAVE GOT TO BE SHITTING ME! WHAT'S SHE DOING HERE?
SHE SHOULD BE DOWNSTAIRS ON DEATH ROW WITH THE OTHER COWARDS...
SHE'S FAMILY. SHE'S VISITING.
NOT ACCORDING TO MY ORDERS, SHE ISN'T.
DO YOUR ORDERS STILL COUNT IF I PULL OUT BOTH YOUR FUCKING EYES?
GET OUT OF MY WAY.
AHH, GO ON IN. WON'T MAKE ANY DIFFERENCE.
SHE'S STILL GOING TO PAY, LIKE ALL THE OTHER TRAITORS.

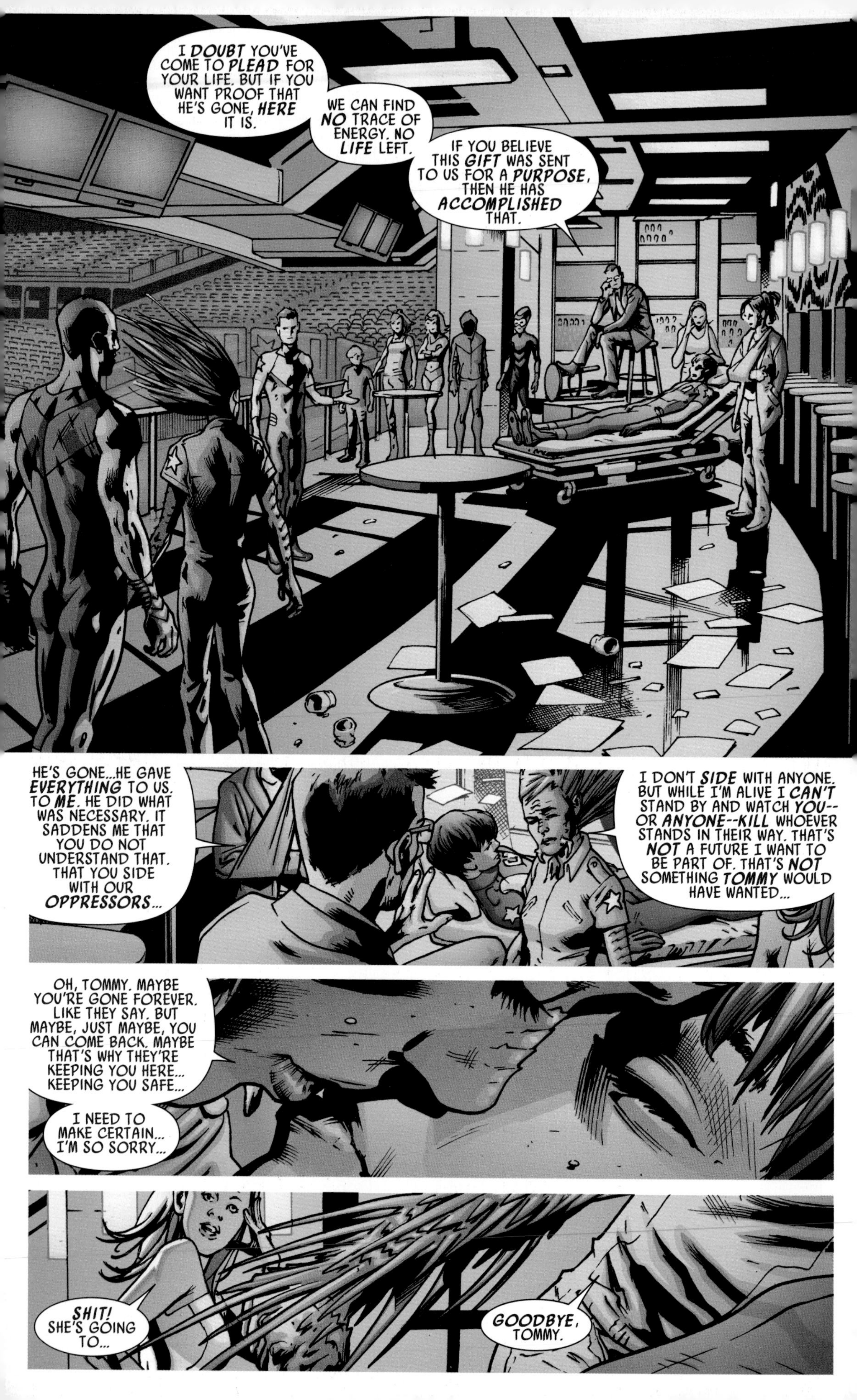
I DOUBT YOU'VE COME TO PLEAD FOR YOUR LIFE. BUT IF YOU WANT PROOF THAT HE'S GONE, HERE IT IS.
WE CAN FIND NO TRACE OF ENERGY. NO LIFE LEFT.
IF YOU BELIEVE THIS GIFT WAS SENT TO US FOR A PURPOSE, THEN HE HAS ACCOMPLISHED THAT.
HE'S GONE...HE GAVE EVERYTHING TO US. TO ME. HE DID WHAT WAS NECESSARY. IT SADDENS ME THAT YOU DO NOT UNDERSTAND THAT. THAT YOU SIDE WITH OUR OPPRESSORS...
I DON'T SIDE WITH ANYONE. BUT WHILE I'M ALIVE I CAN'T STAND BY AND WATCH YOU--OR ANYONE--KILL WHOEVER STANDS IN THEIR WAY. THAT'S NOT A FUTURE I WANT TO BE PART OF. THAT'S NOT SOMETHING TOMMY WOULD HAVE WANTED...
OH, TOMMY. MAYBE YOU'RE GONE FOREVER. LIKE THEY SAY. BUT MAYBE, JUST MAYBE, YOU CAN COME BACK. MAYBE THAT'S WHY THEY'RE KEEPING YOU HERE... KEEPING YOU SAFE...
I NEED TO MAKE CERTAIN... I'M SO SORRY...
SHIT! SHE'S GOING TO...
GOODBYE, TOMMY.

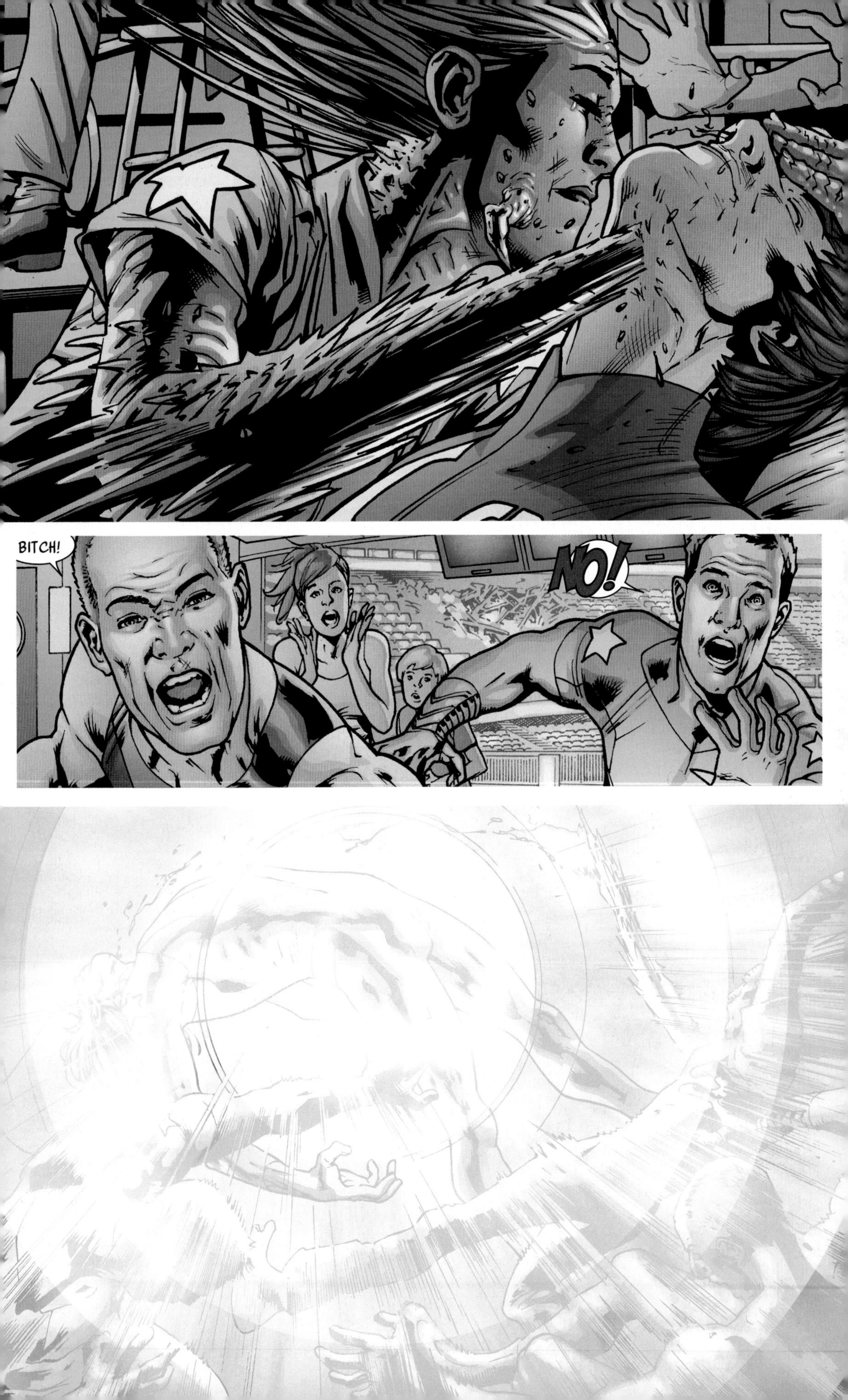
BITCH!
NO!

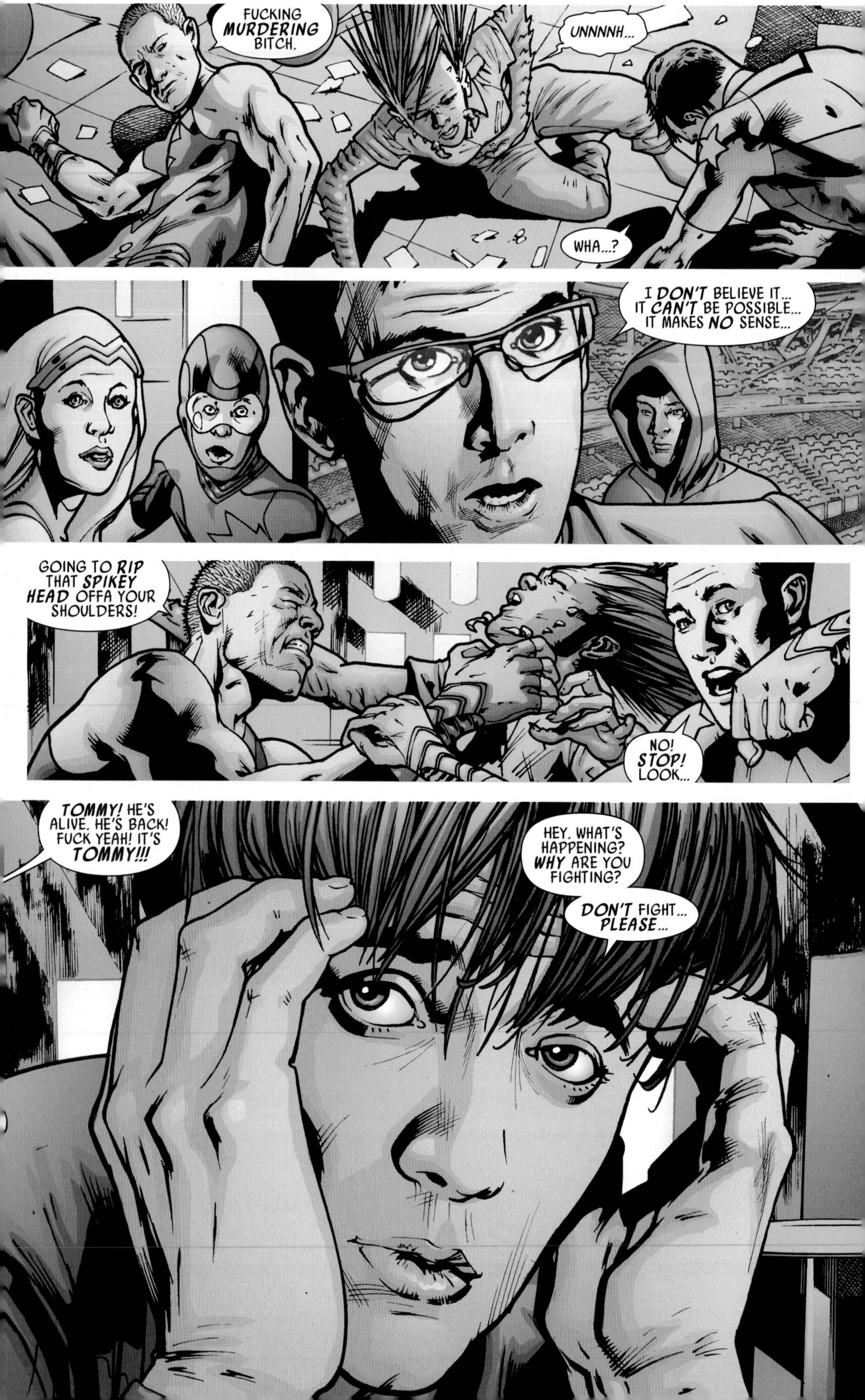
FUCKING MURDERING BITCH.
UNNNNH...
WHA...?
I DON'T BELIEVE IT... IT CAN'T BE POSSIBLE... IT MAKES NO SENSE...
GOING TO RIP THAT SPIKEY HEAD OFFA YOUR SHOULDERS!
NO! STOP! LOOK...
TOMMY! HE'S ALIVE. HE'S BACK! FUCK YEAH! IT'S TOMMY!!!
HEY. WHAT'S HAPPENING? WHY ARE YOU FIGHTING?
DON'T FIGHT... PLEASE...

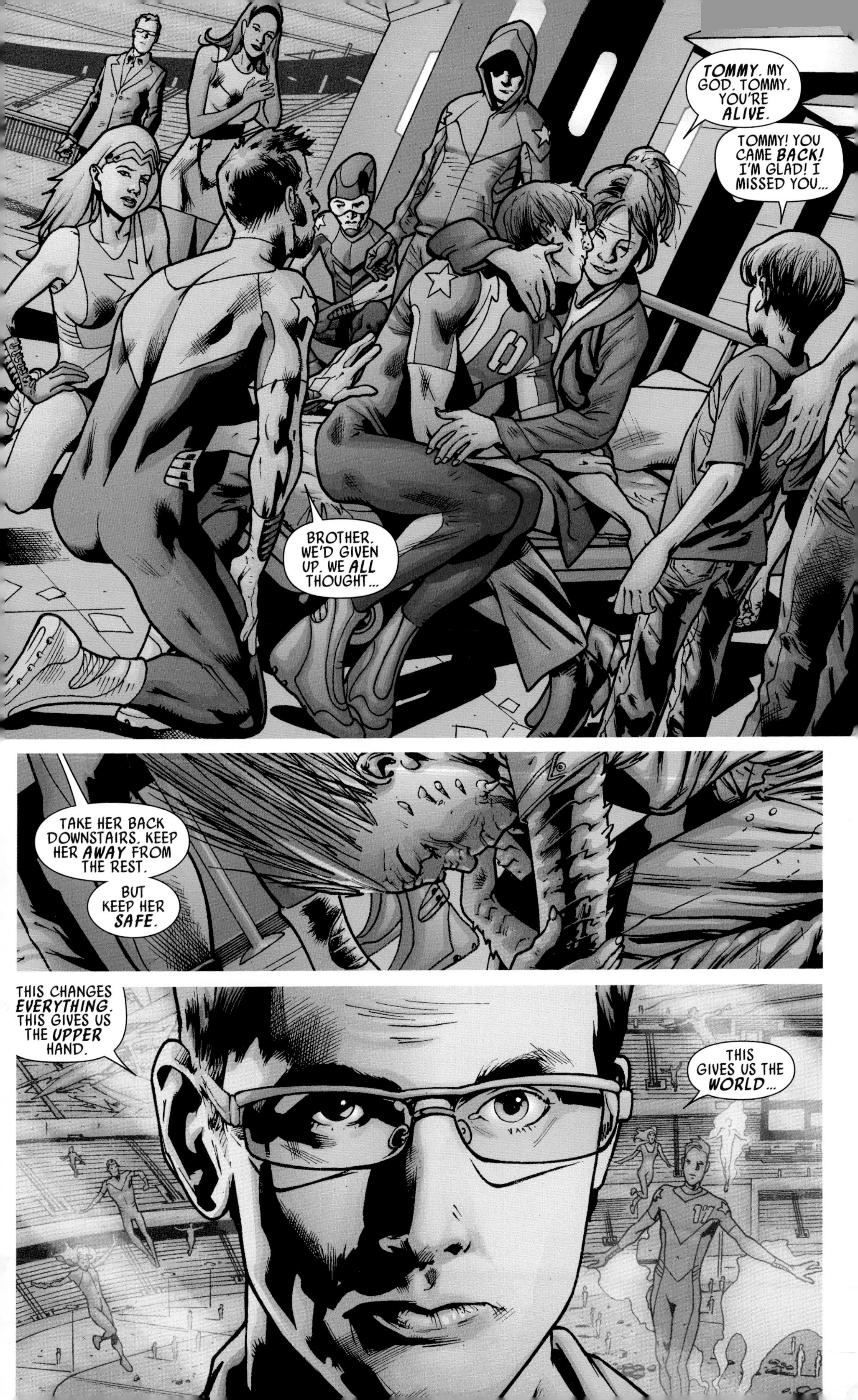
TOMMY. MY GOD. TOMMY. YOU'RE ALIVE.
TOMMY! YOU CAME BACK! I'M GLAD! I MISSED YOU...
BROTHER. WE'D GIVEN UP. WE ALL THOUGHT...
TAKE HER BACK DOWNSTAIRS. KEEP HER AWAY FROM THE REST.
BUT KEEP HER SAFE.
THIS CHANGES EVERYTHING. THIS GIVES US THE UPPER HAND.
THIS GIVES US THE WORLD...

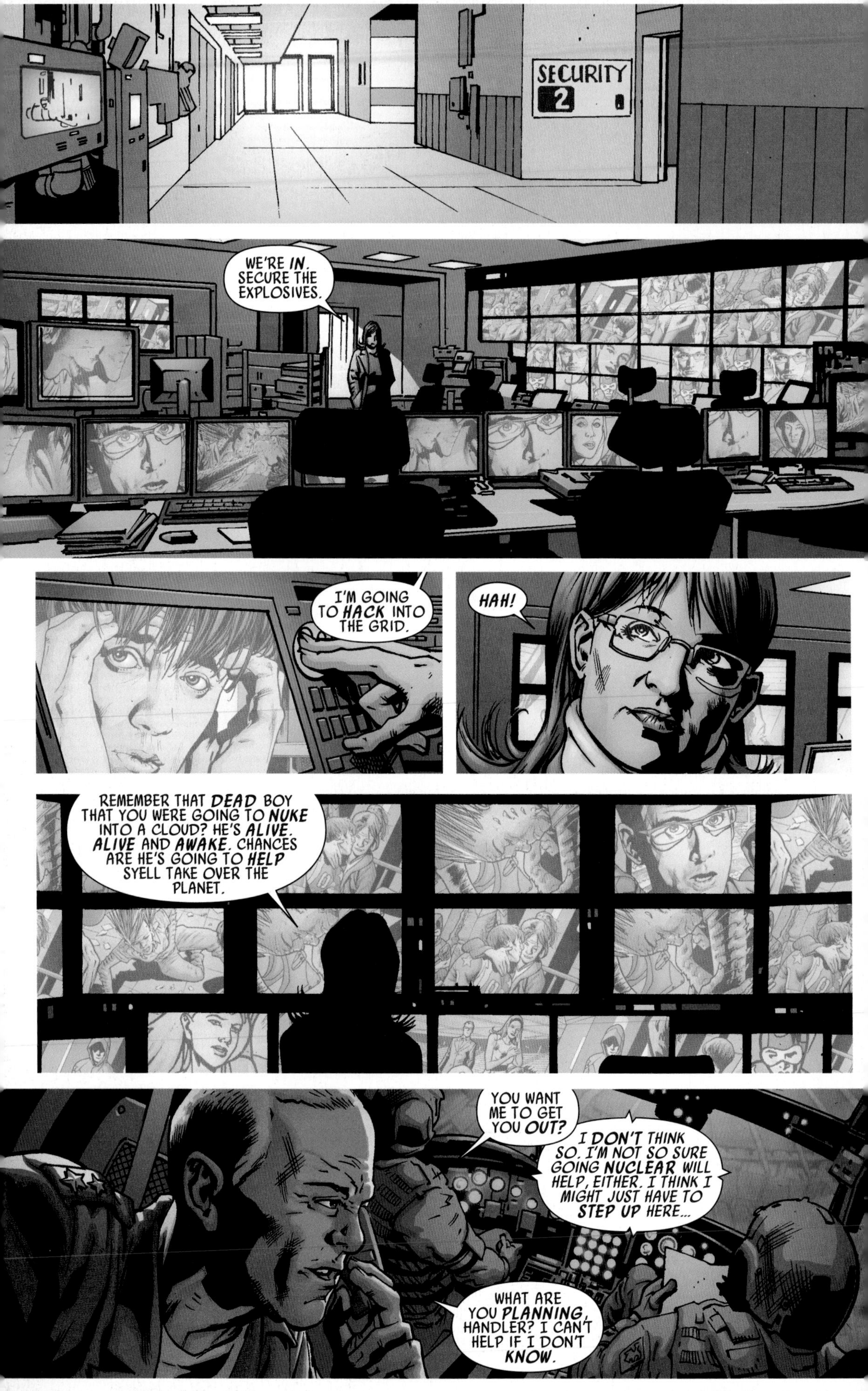
SECURITY
2
WE'RE IN. SECURE THE EXPLOSIVES.
I'M GOING TO HACK INTO THE GRID.
HAH!
REMEMBER THAT DEAD BOY THAT YOU WERE GOING TO NUKE INTO A CLOUD? HE'S ALIVE. ALIVE AND AWAKE. CHANCES ARE HE'S GOING TO HELP SYELL TAKE OVER THE PLANET.
YOU WANT ME TO GET YOU OUT?
I DON'T THINK SO. I'M NOT SO SURE GOING NUCLEAR WILL HELP, EITHER. I THINK I MIGHT JUST HAVE TO STEP UP HERE...
WHAT ARE YOU PLANNING, HANDLER? I CAN'T HELP IF I DON'T KNOW.

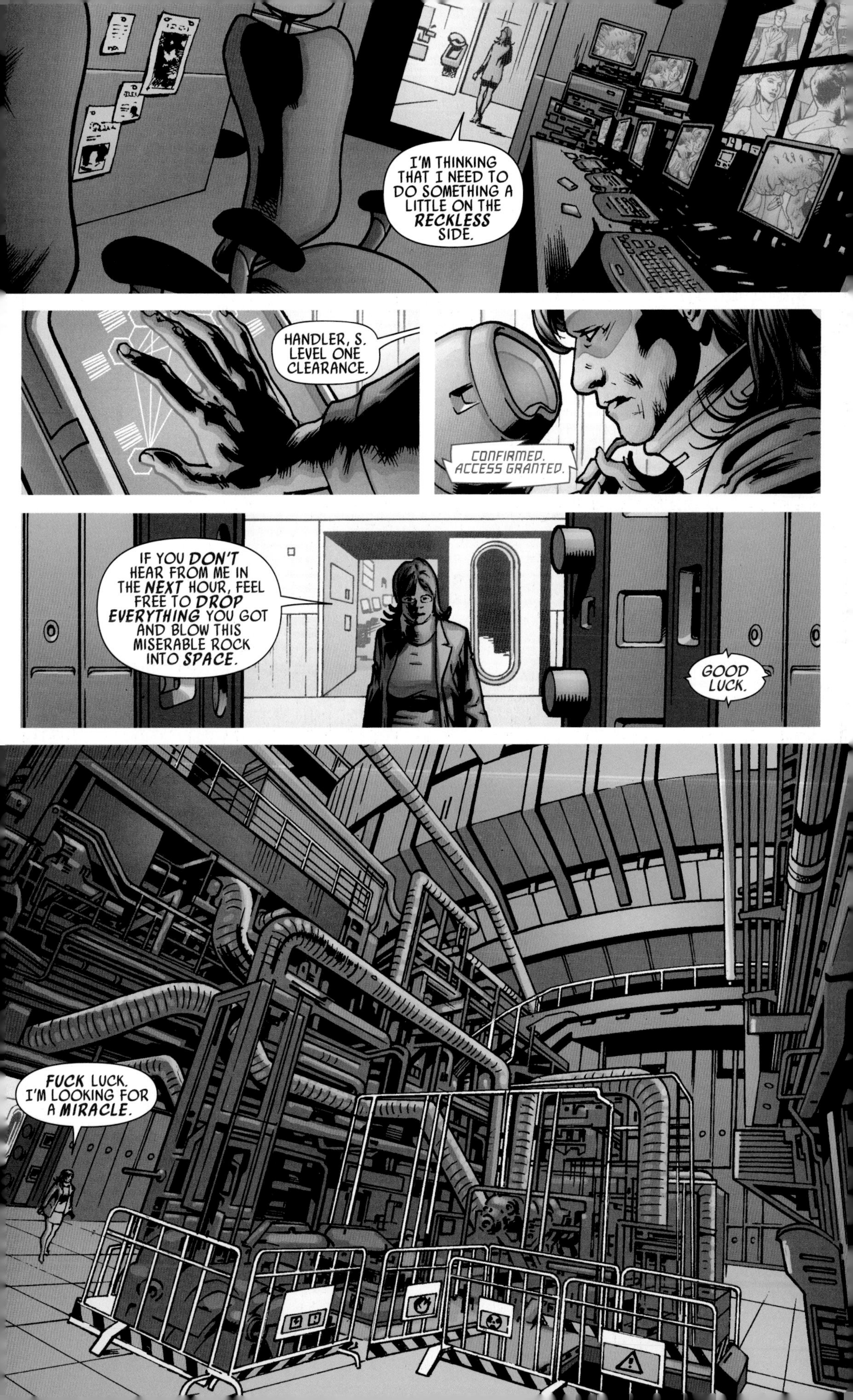
I'M THINKING THAT I NEED TO DO SOMETHING A LITTLE ON THE RECKLESS SIDE.
HANDLER, S. LEVEL ONE CLEARANCE.
CONFIRMED. ACCESS GRANTED.
IF YOU DON'T HEAR FROM ME IN THE NEXT HOUR, FEEL FREE TO DROP EVERYTHING YOU GOT AND BLOW THIS MISERABLE ROCK INTO SPACE.
GOOD LUCK.
FUCK LUCK. I'M LOOKING FOR A MIRACLE.

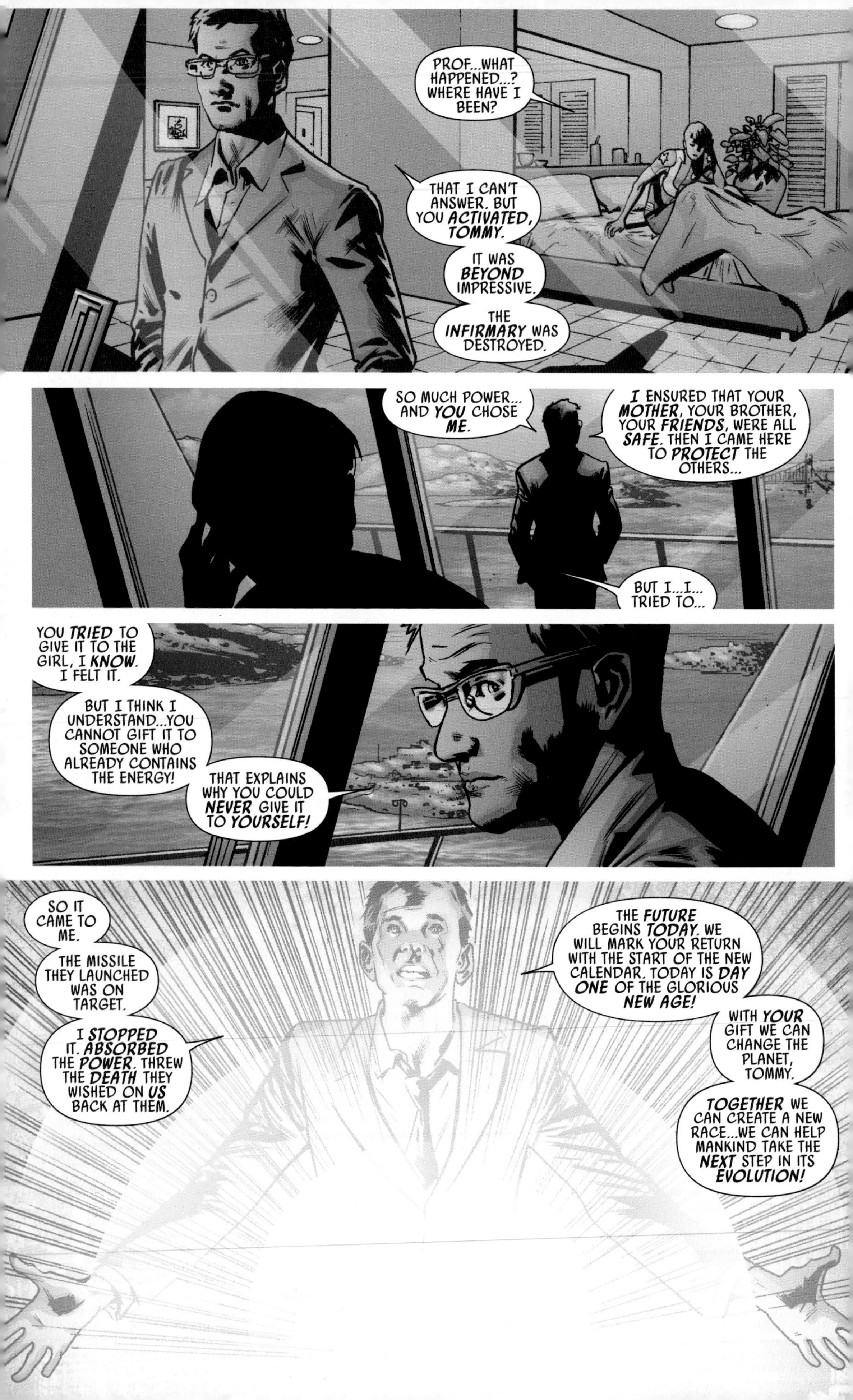
PROF...WHAT HAPPENED...? WHERE HAVE I BEEN?
THAT I CAN'T ANSWER. BUT YOU ACTIVATED, TOMMY.
IT WAS BEYOND IMPRESSIVE.
THE INFIRMARY WAS DESTROYED.
SO MUCH POWER... AND YOU CHOSE ME.
I ENSURED THAT YOUR MOTHER, YOUR BROTHER, YOUR FRIENDS, WERE ALL SAFE. THEN I CAME HERE TO PROTECT THE OTHERS...
BUT I...I... TRIED TO...
YOU TRIED TO GIVE IT TO THE GIRL, I KNOW. I FELT IT.
BUT I THINK I UNDERSTAND...YOU CANNOT GIFT IT TO SOMEONE WHO ALREADY CONTAINS THE ENERGY!
THAT EXPLAINS WHY YOU COULD NEVER GIVE IT TO YOURSELF!
SO IT CAME TO ME.
THE MISSILE THEY LAUNCHED WAS ON TARGET.
I STOPPED IT. ABSORBED THE POWER. THREW THE DEATH THEY WISHED ON US BACK AT THEM.
THE FUTURE BEGINS TODAY. WE WILL MARK YOUR RETURN WITH THE START OF THE NEW CALENDAR. TODAY IS DAY ONE OF THE GLORIOUS NEW AGE!
WITH YOUR GIFT WE CAN CHANGE THE PLANET, TOMMY.
TOGETHER WE CAN CREATE A NEW RACE...WE CAN HELP MANKIND TAKE THE NEXT STEP IN ITS EVOLUTION!

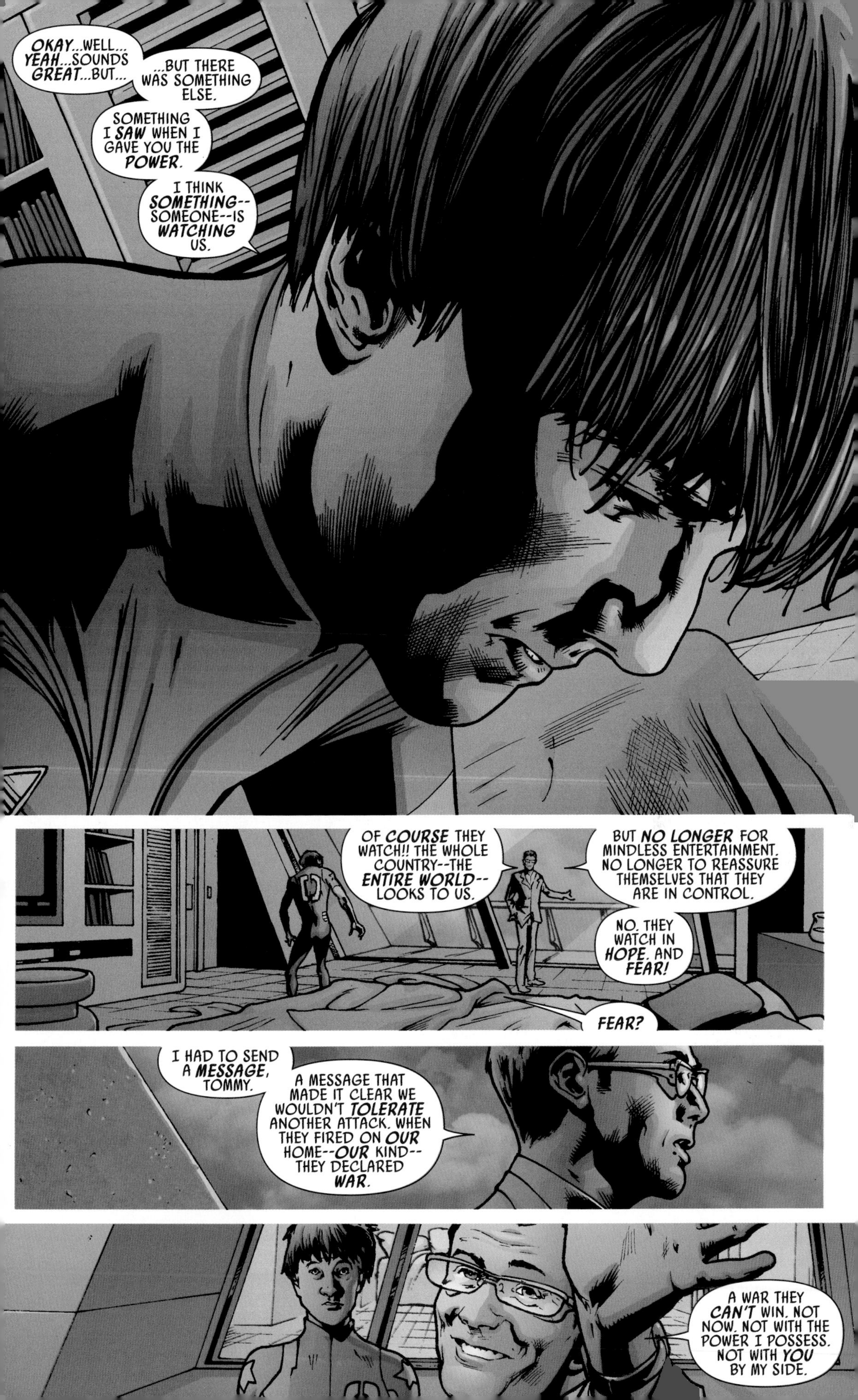
OKAY...WELL... YEAH...SOUNDS GREAT...BUT...
...BUT THERE WAS SOMETHING ELSE.
SOMETHING I SAW WHEN I GAVE YOU THE POWER.
I THINK SOMETHING--SOMEONE--IS WATCHING US.
OF COURSE THEY WATCH!! THE WHOLE COUNTRY--THE ENTIRE WORLD--LOOKS TO US.
BUT NO LONGER FOR MINDLESS ENTERTAINMENT. NO LONGER TO REASSURE THEMSELVES THAT THEY ARE IN CONTROL.
NO. THEY WATCH IN HOPE. AND FEAR!
FEAR?
I HAD TO SEND A MESSAGE, TOMMY.
A MESSAGE THAT MADE IT CLEAR WE WOULDN'T TOLERATE ANOTHER ATTACK. WHEN THEY FIRED ON OUR HOME--OUR KIND--THEY DECLARED WAR.
A WAR THEY CAN'T WIN. NOT NOW. NOT WITH THE POWER I POSSESS. NOT WITH YOU BY MY SIDE.

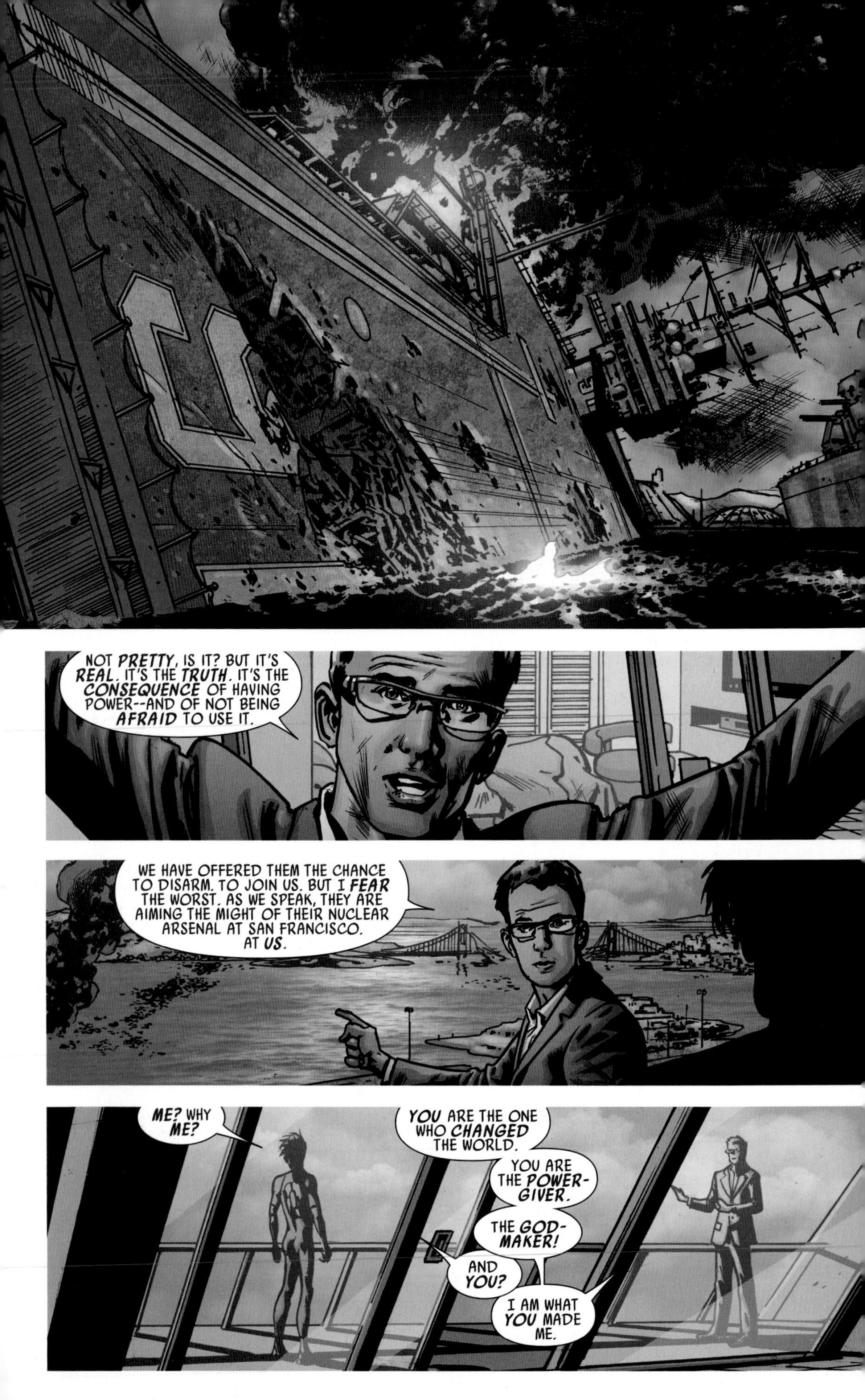
NOT PRETTY, IS IT? BUT IT'S REAL. IT'S THE TRUTH. IT'S THE CONSEQUENCE OF HAVING POWER--AND OF NOT BEING AFRAID TO USE IT.
WE HAVE OFFERED THEM THE CHANCE TO DISARM. TO JOIN US. BUT I FEAR THE WORST. AS WE SPEAK, THEY ARE AIMING THE MIGHT OF THEIR NUCLEAR ARSENAL AT SAN FRANCISCO. AT US.
ME? WHY ME?
YOU ARE THE ONE WHO CHANGED THE WORLD.
YOU ARE THE POWER-GIVER.
THE GOD-MAKER!
AND YOU?
I AM WHAT YOU MADE ME.

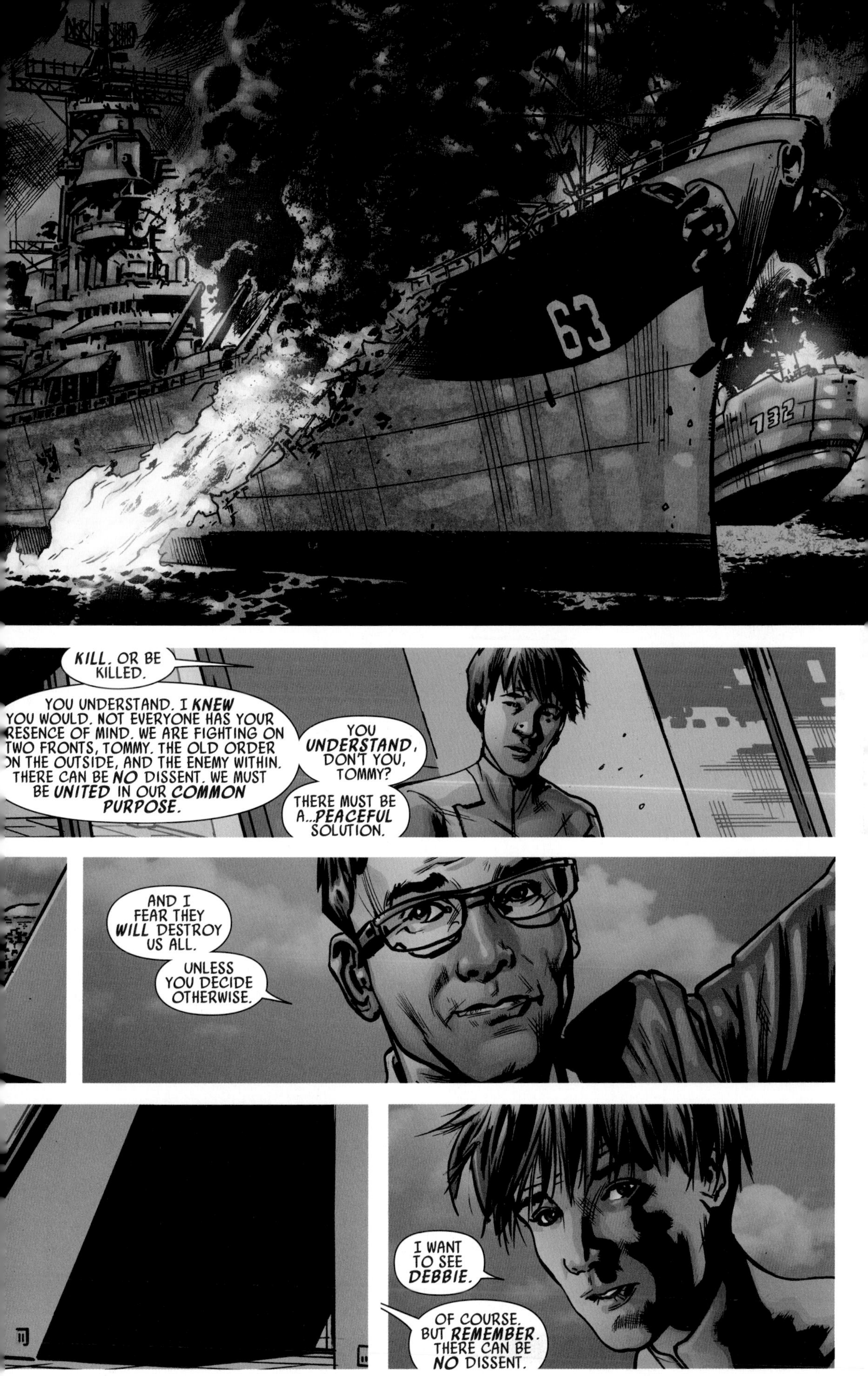
63
732
KILL. OR BE KILLED.
YOU UNDERSTAND. I KNEW YOU WOULD. NOT EVERYONE HAS YOUR PRESENCE OF MIND. WE ARE FIGHTING ON TWO FRONTS, TOMMY. THE OLD ORDER ON THE OUTSIDE, AND THE ENEMY WITHIN. THERE CAN BE NO DISSENT. WE MUST BE UNITED IN OUR COMMON PURPOSE.
YOU UNDERSTAND, DON'T YOU, TOMMY?
THERE MUST BE A...PEACEFUL SOLUTION.
AND I FEAR THEY WILL DESTROY US ALL.
UNLESS YOU DECIDE OTHERWISE.
I WANT TO SEE DEBBIE.
OF COURSE. BUT REMEMBER. THERE CAN BE NO DISSENT.

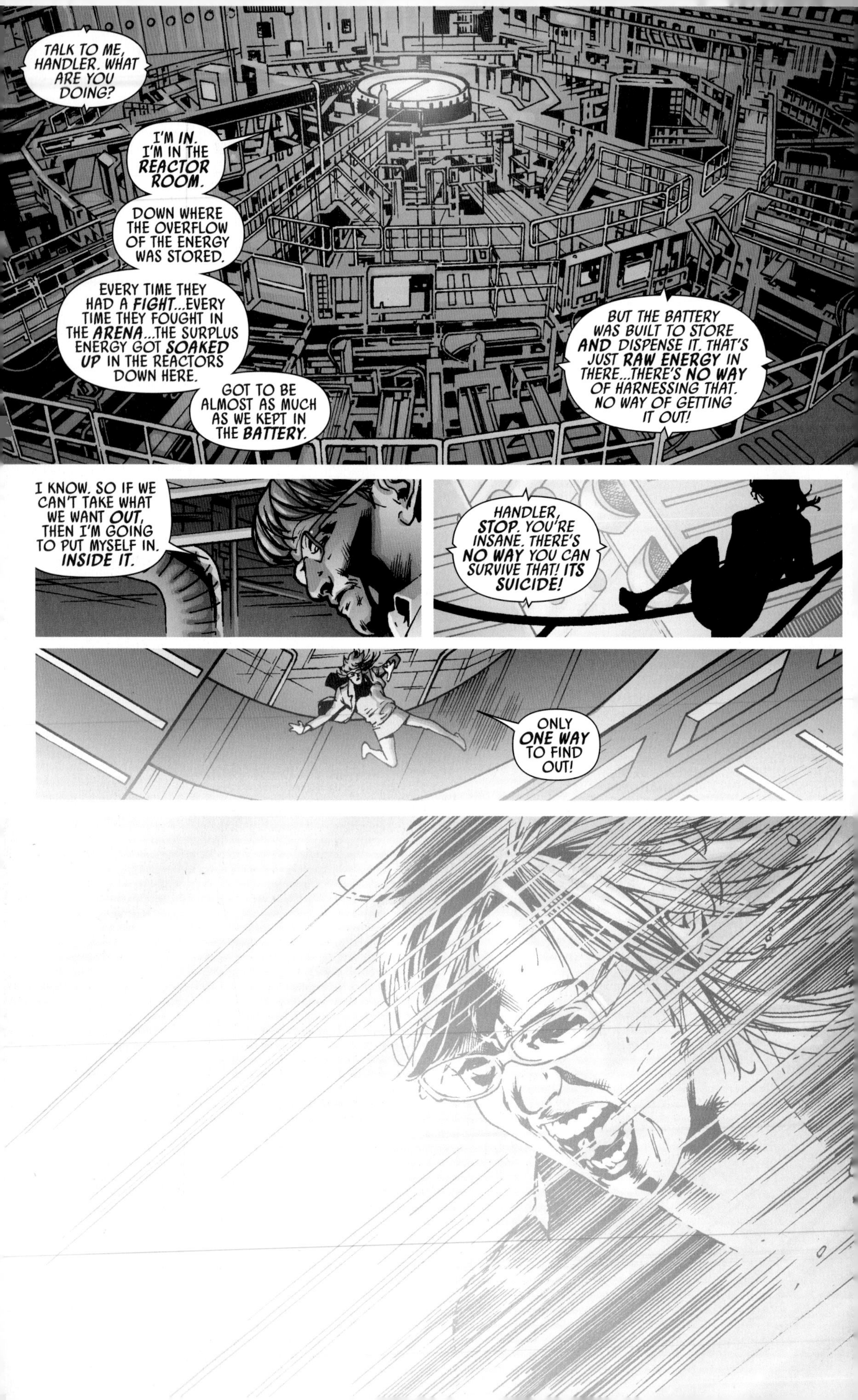
TALK TO ME, HANDLER. WHAT ARE YOU DOING?
I'M IN. I'M IN THE REACTOR ROOM.
DOWN WHERE THE OVERFLOW OF THE ENERGY WAS STORED.
EVERY TIME THEY HAD A FIGHT...EVERY TIME THEY FOUGHT IN THE ARENA...THE SURPLUS ENERGY GOT SOAKED UP IN THE REACTORS DOWN HERE.
GOT TO BE ALMOST AS MUCH AS WE KEPT IN THE BATTERY.
BUT THE BATTERY WAS BUILT TO STORE AND DISPENSE IT. THAT'S JUST RAW ENERGY IN THERE...THERE'S NO WAY OF HARNESSING THAT. NO WAY OF GETTING IT OUT!
I KNOW. SO IF WE CAN'T TAKE WHAT WE WANT OUT, THEN I'M GOING TO PUT MYSELF IN. INSIDE IT.
HANDLER, STOP. YOU'RE INSANE. THERE'S NO WAY YOU CAN SURVIVE THAT! ITS SUICIDE!
ONLY ONE WAY TO FIND OUT!

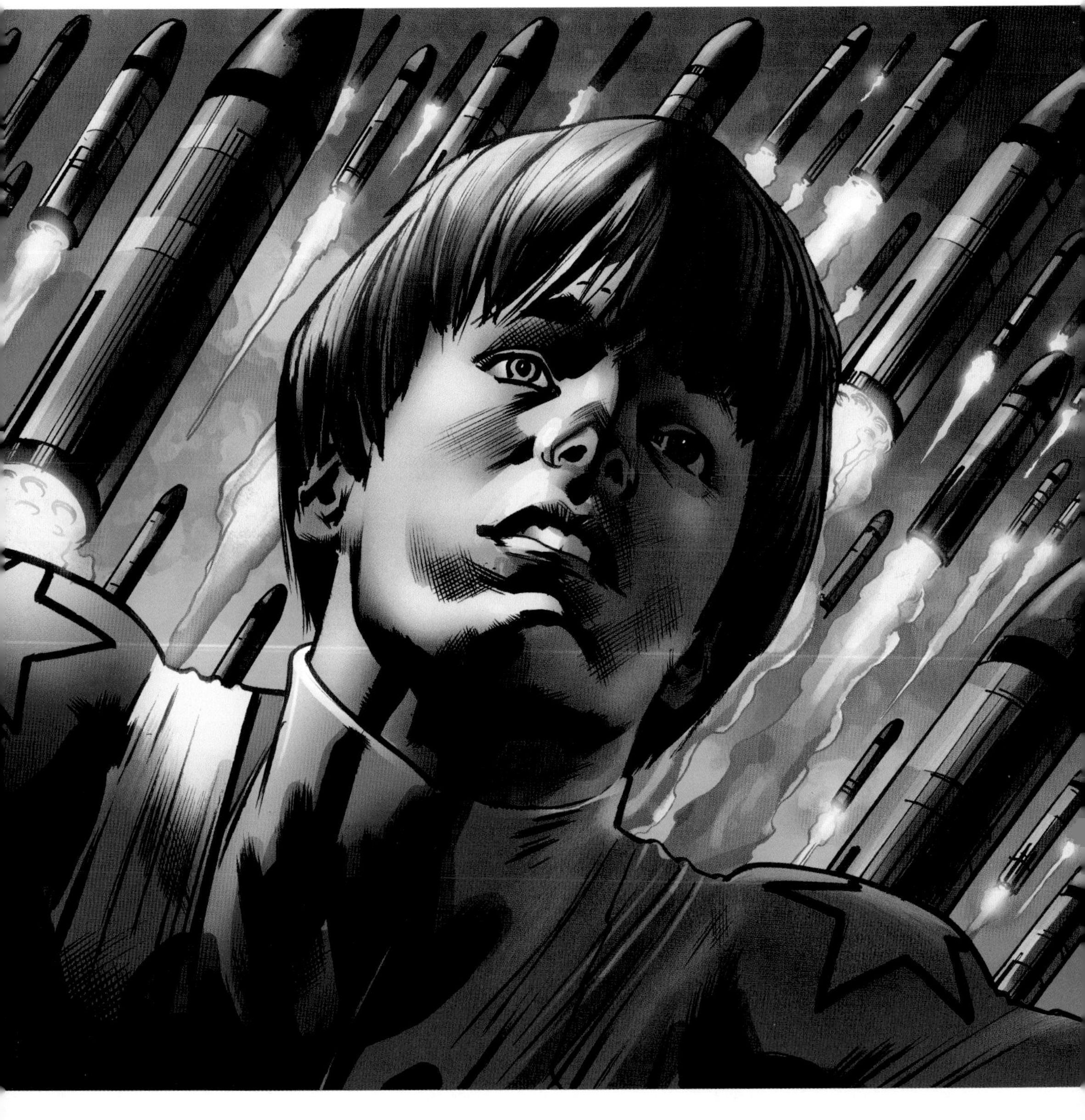

CHAPTER **SEVEN**

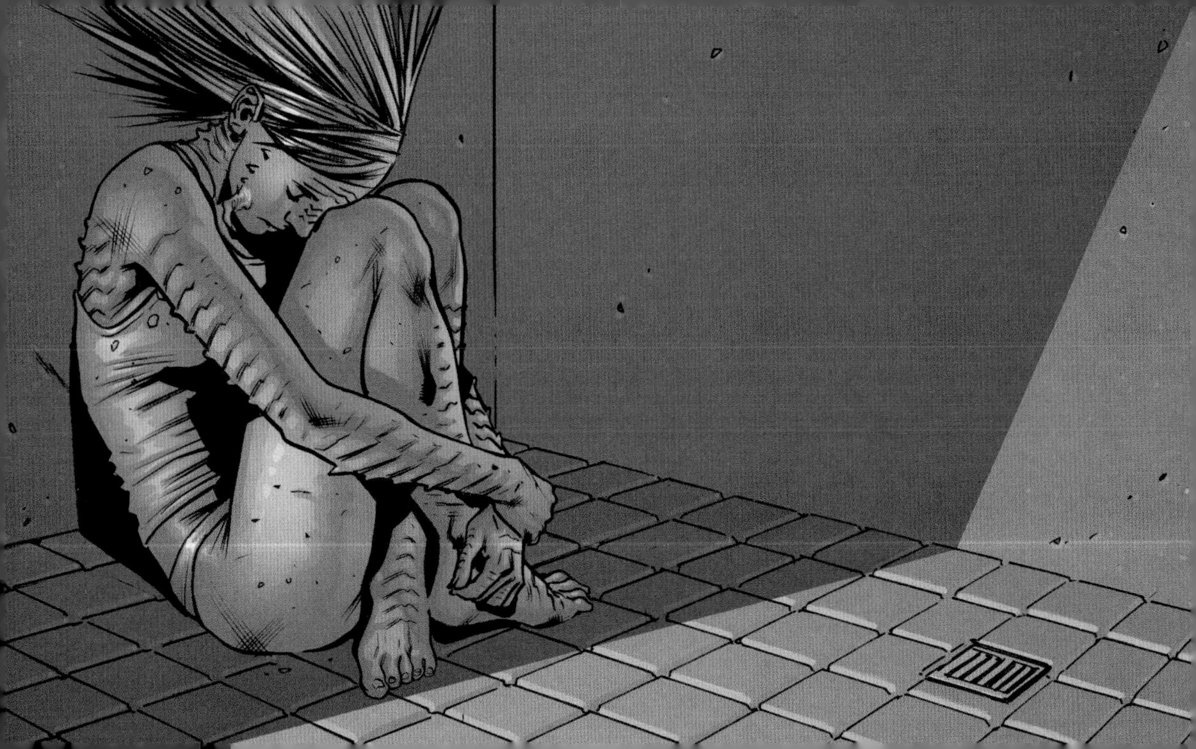

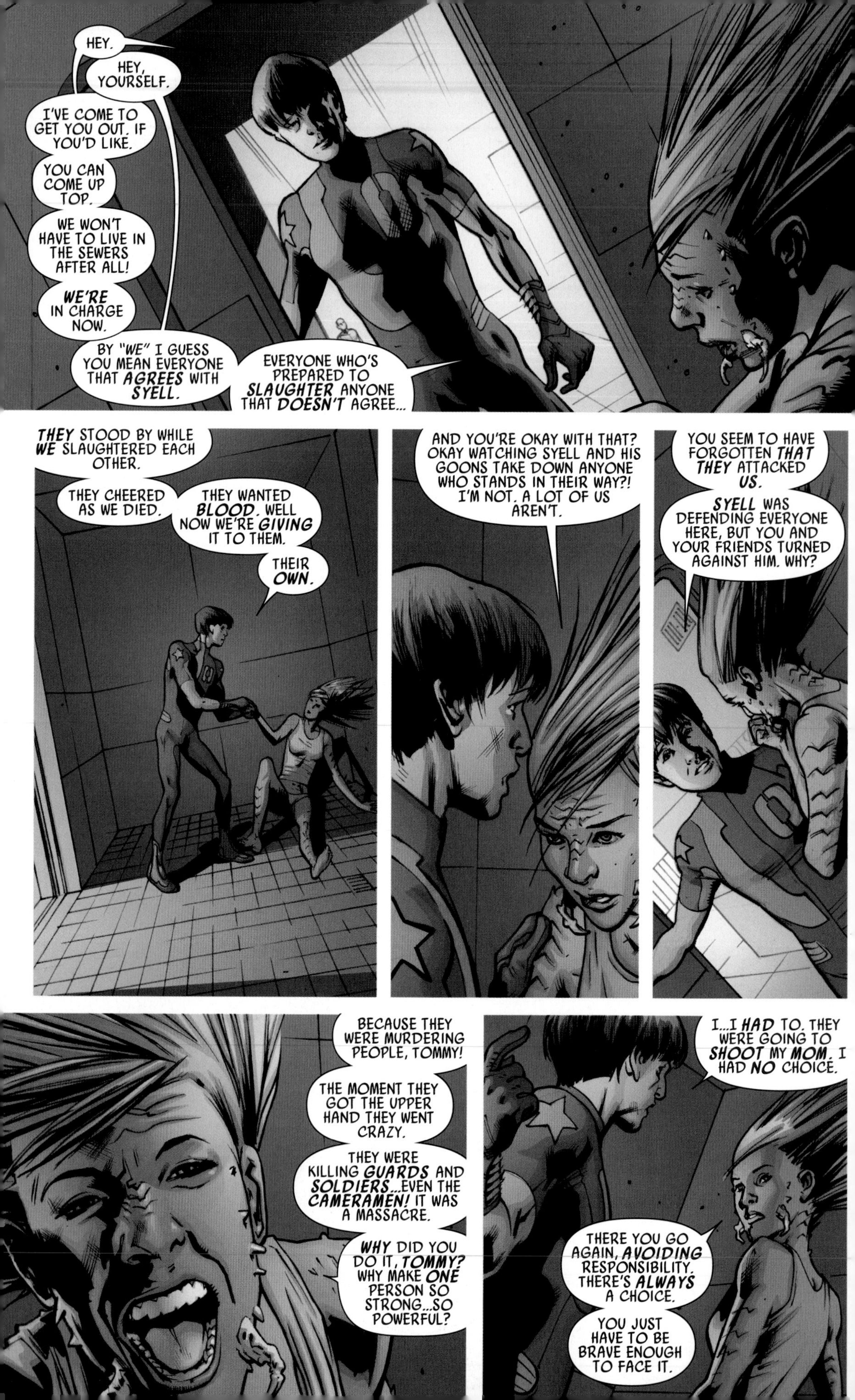
HEY.
HEY, YOURSELF.
I'VE COME TO GET YOU OUT. IF YOU'D LIKE.
YOU CAN COME UP TOP.
WE WON'T HAVE TO LIVE IN THE SEWERS AFTER ALL!
WE'RE IN CHARGE NOW.
BY "WE" I GUESS YOU MEAN EVERYONE THAT AGREES WITH SYELL.
EVERYONE WHO'S PREPARED TO SLAUGHTER ANYONE THAT DOESN'T AGREE...
THEY STOOD BY WHILE WE SLAUGHTERED EACH OTHER.
THEY CHEERED AS WE DIED.
THEY WANTED BLOOD. WELL NOW WE'RE GIVING IT TO THEM.
THEIR OWN.
AND YOU'RE OKAY WITH THAT? OKAY WATCHING SYELL AND HIS GOONS TAKE DOWN ANYONE WHO STANDS IN THEIR WAY?! I'M NOT. A LOT OF US AREN'T.
YOU SEEM TO HAVE FORGOTTEN THAT THEY ATTACKED US.
SYELL WAS DEFENDING EVERYONE HERE, BUT YOU AND YOUR FRIENDS TURNED AGAINST HIM. WHY?
BECAUSE THEY WERE MURDERING PEOPLE, TOMMY!
THE MOMENT THEY GOT THE UPPER HAND THEY WENT CRAZY.
THEY WERE KILLING GUARDS AND SOLDIERS...EVEN THE CAMERAMEN! IT WAS A MASSACRE.
WHY DID YOU DO IT, TOMMY? WHY MAKE ONE PERSON SO STRONG...SO POWERFUL?
I...I HAD TO. THEY WERE GOING TO SHOOT MY MOM. I HAD NO CHOICE.
THERE YOU GO AGAIN, AVOIDING RESPONSIBILITY. THERE'S ALWAYS A CHOICE.
YOU JUST HAVE TO BE BRAVE ENOUGH TO FACE IT.

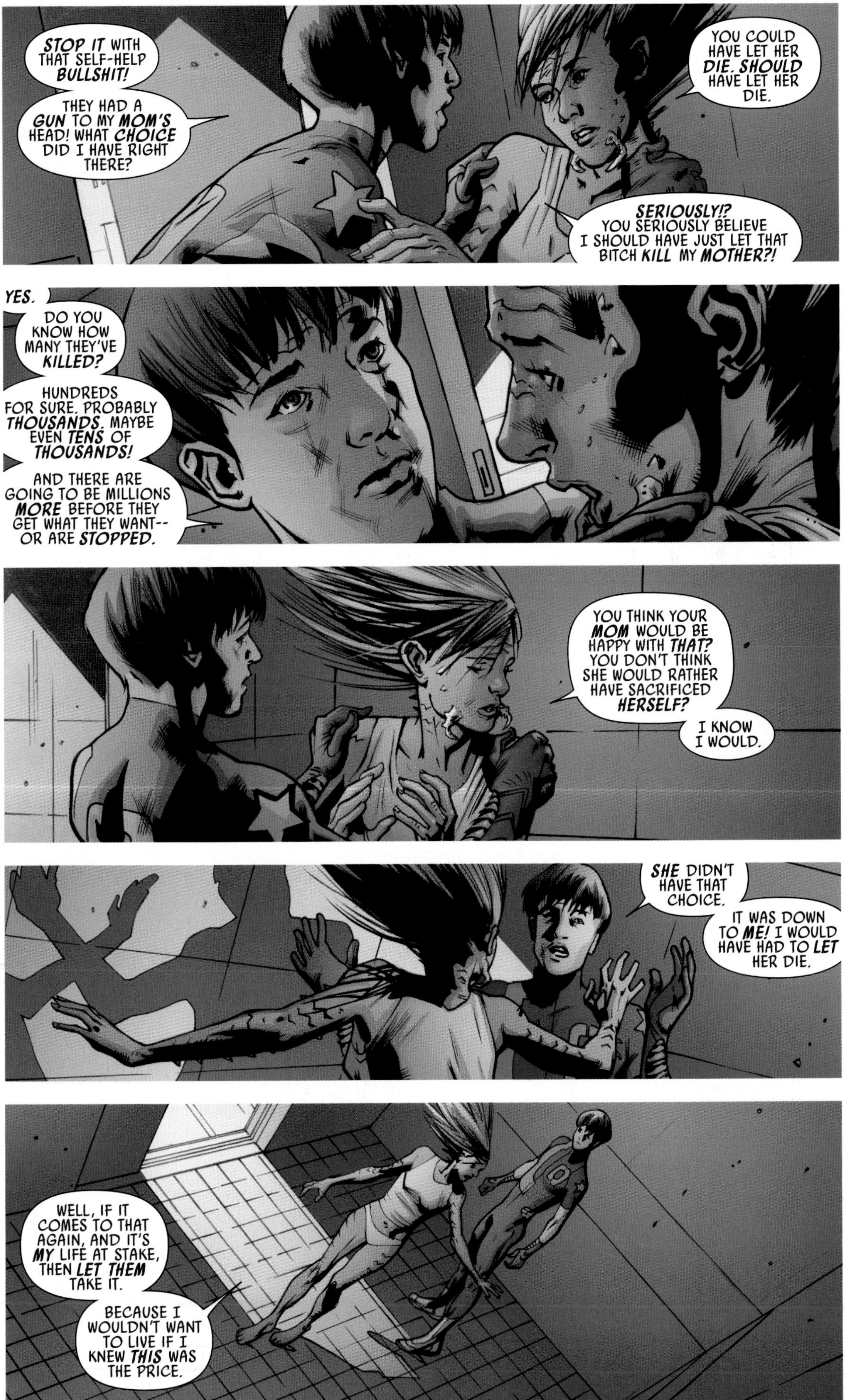

STOP IT WITH THAT SELF-HELP BULLSHIT!
THEY HAD A GUN TO MY MOM'S HEAD! WHAT CHOICE DID I HAVE RIGHT THERE?
YOU COULD HAVE LET HER DIE. SHOULD HAVE LET HER DIE.
SERIOUSLY!? YOU SERIOUSLY BELIEVE I SHOULD HAVE JUST LET THAT BITCH KILL MY MOTHER?!
YES.
DO YOU KNOW HOW MANY THEY'VE KILLED?
HUNDREDS FOR SURE. PROBABLY THOUSANDS. MAYBE EVEN TENS OF THOUSANDS!
AND THERE ARE GOING TO BE MILLIONS MORE BEFORE THEY GET WHAT THEY WANT--OR ARE STOPPED.
YOU THINK YOUR MOM WOULD BE HAPPY WITH THAT? YOU DON'T THINK SHE WOULD RATHER HAVE SACRIFICED HERSELF?
I KNOW I WOULD.
SHE DIDN'T HAVE THAT CHOICE.
IT WAS DOWN TO ME! I WOULD HAVE HAD TO LET HER DIE.
WELL, IF IT COMES TO THAT AGAIN, AND IT'S MY LIFE AT STAKE, THEN LET THEM TAKE IT.
BECAUSE I WOULDN'T WANT TO LIVE IF I KNEW THIS WAS THE PRICE.

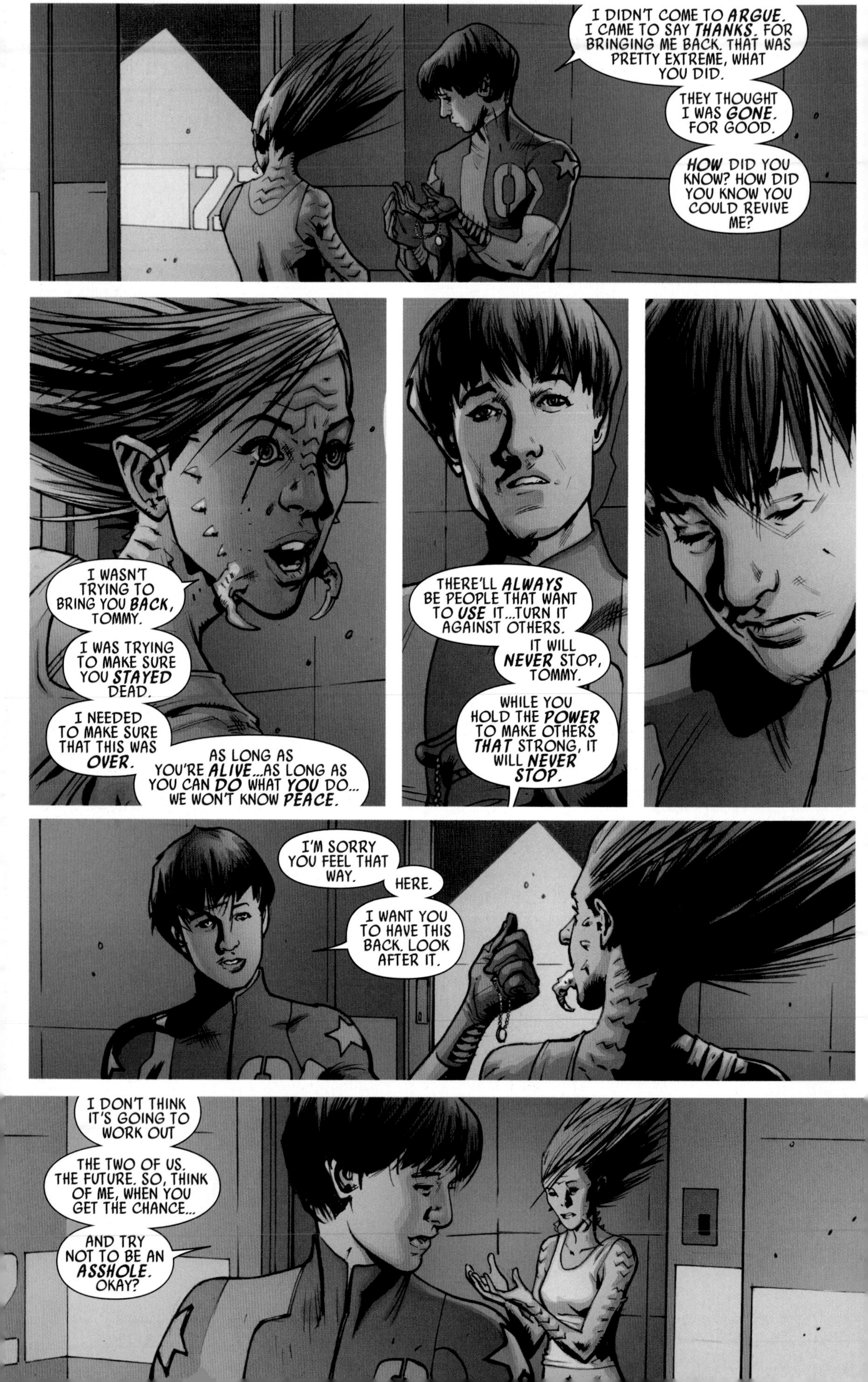
I DIDN'T COME TO ARGUE. I CAME TO SAY THANKS. FOR BRINGING ME BACK. THAT WAS PRETTY EXTREME, WHAT YOU DID.
THEY THOUGHT I WAS GONE. FOR GOOD.
HOW DID YOU KNOW? HOW DID YOU KNOW YOU COULD REVIVE ME?
I WASN'T TRYING TO BRING YOU BACK, TOMMY.
I WAS TRYING TO MAKE SURE YOU STAYED DEAD.
I NEEDED TO MAKE SURE THAT THIS WAS OVER.
AS LONG AS YOU'RE ALIVE...AS LONG AS YOU CAN DO WHAT YOU DO... WE WON'T KNOW PEACE.
THERE'LL ALWAYS BE PEOPLE THAT WANT TO USE IT...TURN IT AGAINST OTHERS.
IT WILL NEVER STOP, TOMMY.
WHILE YOU HOLD THE POWER TO MAKE OTHERS THAT STRONG, IT WILL NEVER STOP.
I'M SORRY YOU FEEL THAT WAY.
HERE.
I WANT YOU TO HAVE THIS BACK. LOOK AFTER IT.
I DON'T THINK IT'S GOING TO WORK OUT
THE TWO OF US. THE FUTURE. SO, THINK OF ME, WHEN YOU GET THE CHANCE...
AND TRY NOT TO BE AN ASSHOLE. OKAY?

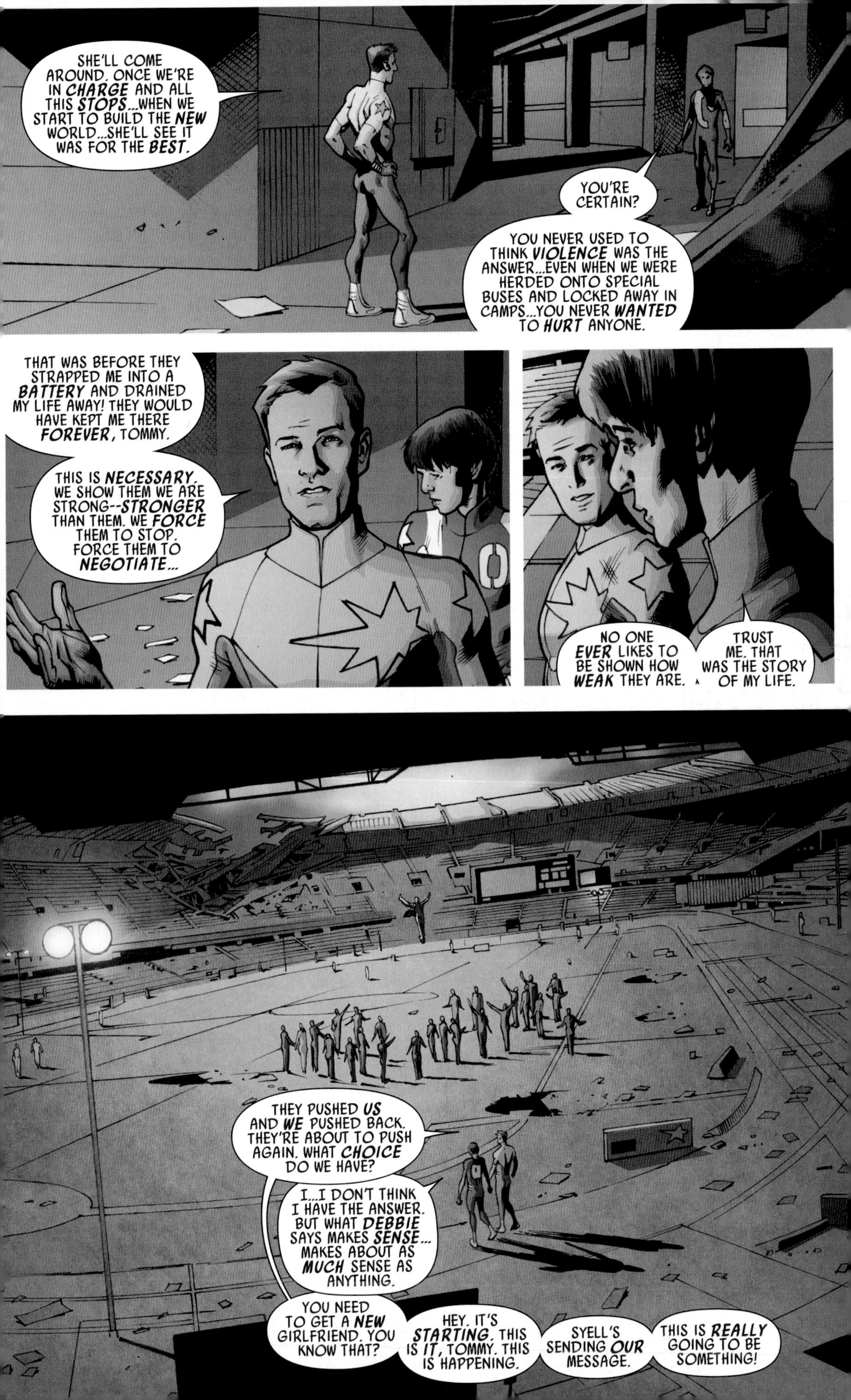
SHE'LL COME AROUND. ONCE WE'RE IN CHARGE AND ALL THIS STOPS...WHEN WE START TO BUILD THE NEW WORLD...SHE'LL SEE IT WAS FOR THE BEST.
YOU'RE CERTAIN?
YOU NEVER USED TO THINK VIOLENCE WAS THE ANSWER...EVEN WHEN WE WERE HERDED ONTO SPECIAL BUSES AND LOCKED AWAY IN CAMPS...YOU NEVER WANTED TO HURT ANYONE.
THAT WAS BEFORE THEY STRAPPED ME INTO A BATTERY AND DRAINED MY LIFE AWAY! THEY WOULD HAVE KEPT ME THERE FOREVER, TOMMY.
THIS IS NECESSARY. WE SHOW THEM WE ARE STRONG--STRONGER THAN THEM. WE FORCE THEM TO STOP. FORCE THEM TO NEGOTIATE...
NO ONE EVER LIKES TO BE SHOWN HOW WEAK THEY ARE.
TRUST ME. THAT WAS THE STORY OF MY LIFE.
THEY PUSHED US AND WE PUSHED BACK. THEY'RE ABOUT TO PUSH AGAIN. WHAT CHOICE DO WE HAVE?
I...I DON'T THINK I HAVE THE ANSWER. BUT WHAT DEBBIE SAYS MAKES SENSE... MAKES ABOUT AS MUCH SENSE AS ANYTHING.
YOU NEED TO GET A NEW GIRLFRIEND. YOU KNOW THAT?
HEY. IT'S STARTING. THIS IS IT, TOMMY. THIS IS HAPPENING.
SYELL'S SENDING OUR MESSAGE.
THIS IS REALLY GOING TO BE SOMETHING!

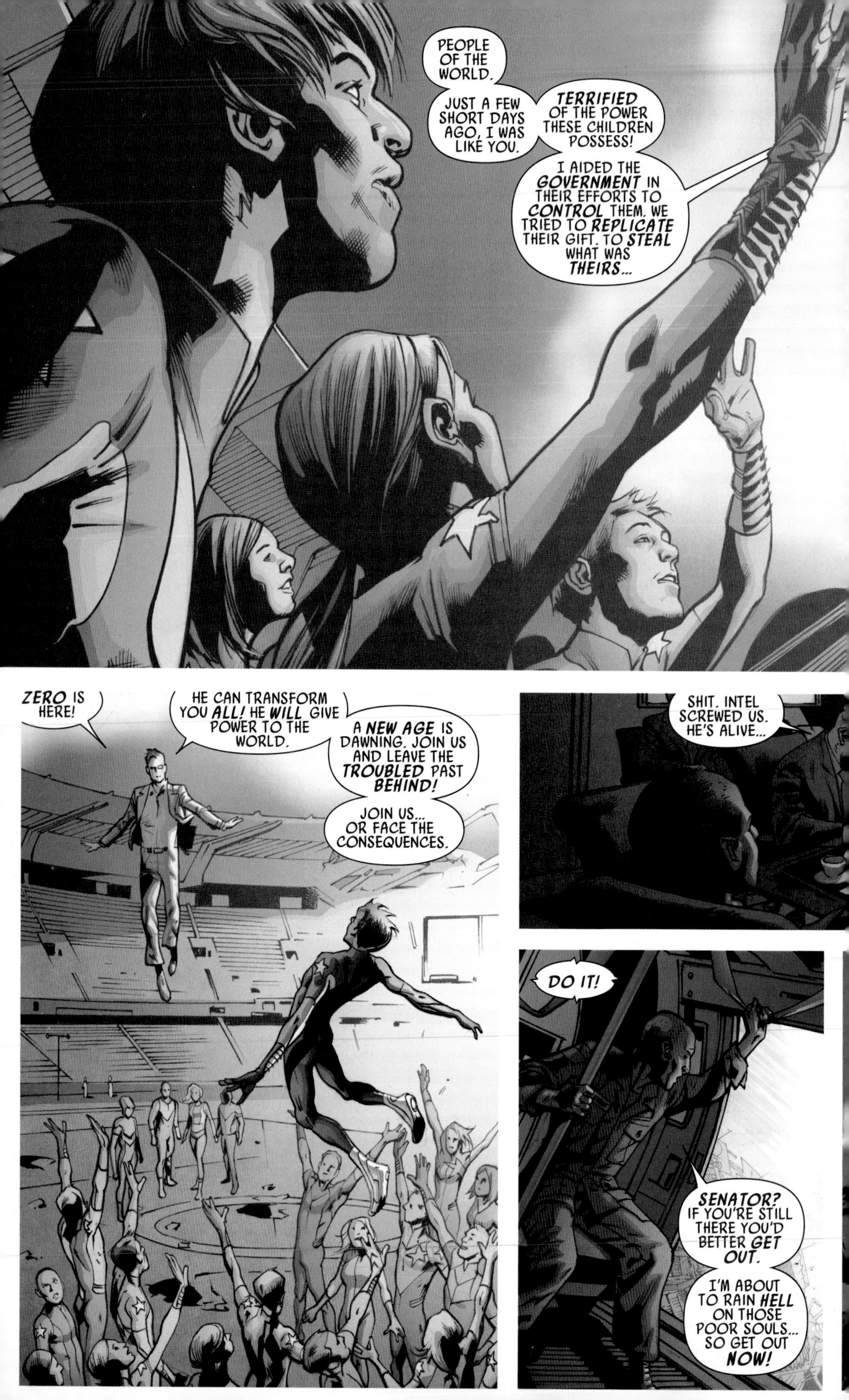
PEOPLE OF THE WORLD.
JUST A FEW SHORT DAYS AGO, I WAS LIKE YOU.
TERRIFIED OF THE POWER THESE CHILDREN POSSESS!
I AIDED THE GOVERNMENT IN THEIR EFFORTS TO CONTROL THEM. WE TRIED TO REPLICATE THEIR GIFT. TO STEAL WHAT WAS THEIRS...
ZERO IS HERE!
HE CAN TRANSFORM YOU ALL! HE WILL GIVE POWER TO THE WORLD.
A NEW AGE IS DAWNING. JOIN US AND LEAVE THE TROUBLED PAST BEHIND!
JOIN US... OR FACE THE CONSEQUENCES.
SHIT. INTEL SCREWED US. HE'S ALIVE...
DO IT!
SENATOR? IF YOU'RE STILL THERE YOU'D BETTER GET OUT.
I'M ABOUT TO RAIN HELL ON THOSE POOR SOULS... SO GET OUT NOW!

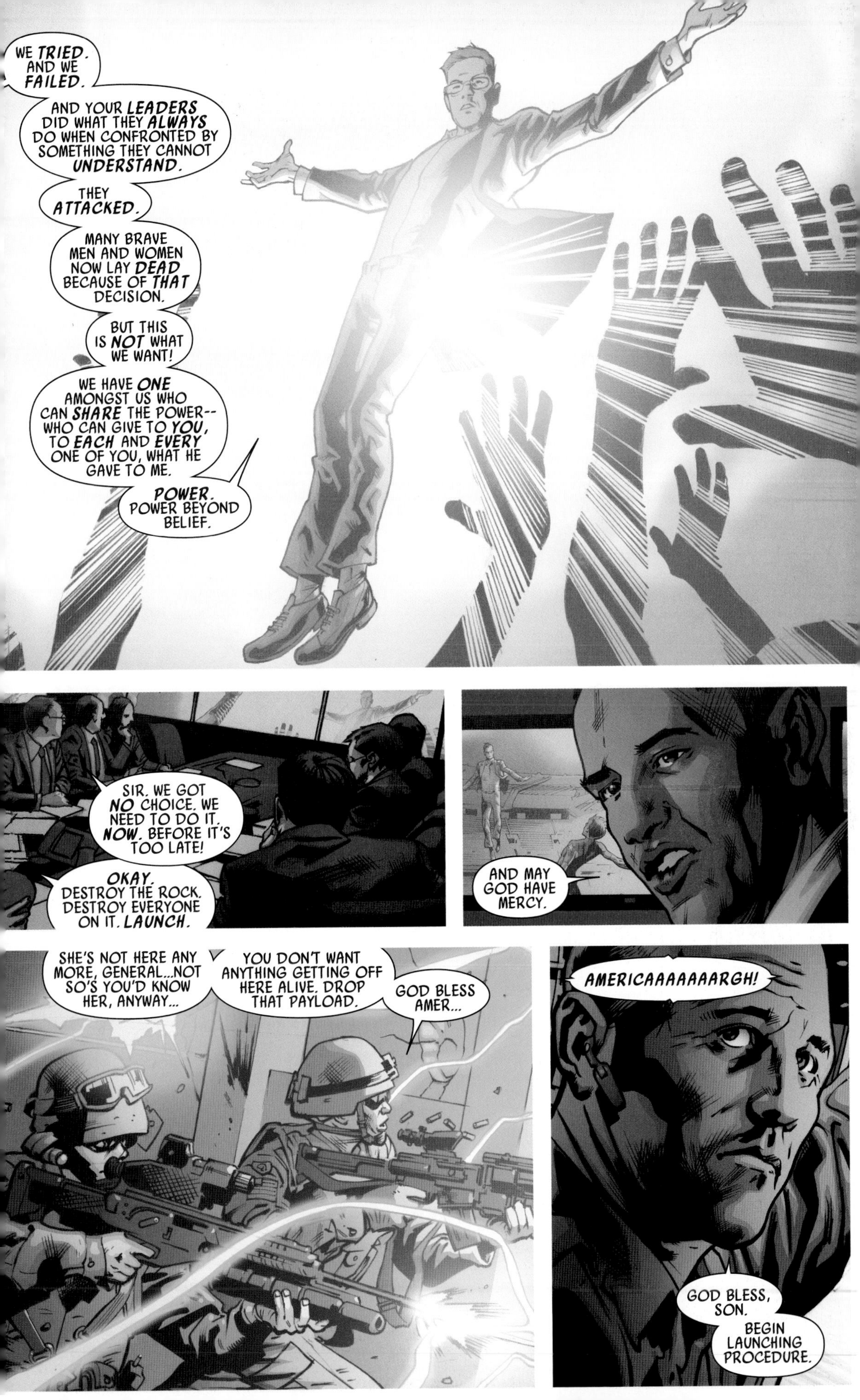
WE TRIED. AND WE FAILED.
AND YOUR LEADERS DID WHAT THEY ALWAYS DO WHEN CONFRONTED BY SOMETHING THEY CANNOT UNDERSTAND.
THEY ATTACKED.
MANY BRAVE MEN AND WOMEN NOW LAY DEAD BECAUSE OF THAT DECISION.
BUT THIS IS NOT WHAT WE WANT!
WE HAVE ONE AMONGST US WHO CAN SHARE THE POWER-- WHO CAN GIVE TO YOU, TO EACH AND EVERY ONE OF YOU, WHAT HE GAVE TO ME.
POWER. POWER BEYOND BELIEF.
SIR, WE GOT NO CHOICE. WE NEED TO DO IT. NOW. BEFORE IT'S TOO LATE!
OKAY. DESTROY THE ROCK. DESTROY EVERYONE ON IT. LAUNCH.
AND MAY GOD HAVE MERCY.
SHE'S NOT HERE ANY MORE, GENERAL...NOT SO'S YOU'D KNOW HER, ANYWAY...
YOU DON'T WANT ANYTHING GETTING OFF HERE ALIVE. DROP THAT PAYLOAD.
GOD BLESS AMER...
AMERICAAAAAAARGH!
GOD BLESS, SON.
BEGIN LAUNCHING PROCEDURE.

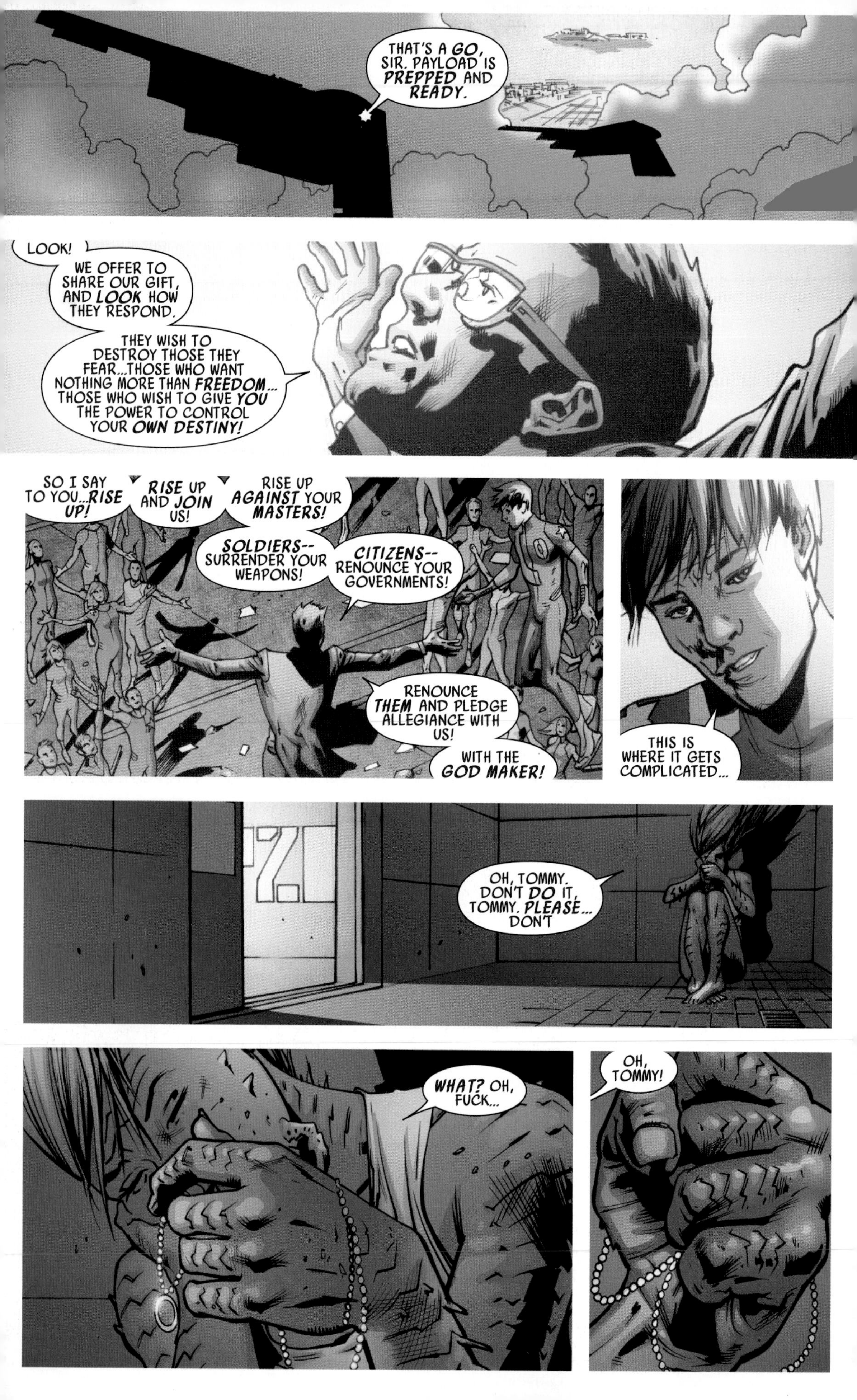
THAT'S A GO, SIR. PAYLOAD IS PREPPED AND READY.
LOOK!
WE OFFER TO SHARE OUR GIFT, AND LOOK HOW THEY RESPOND.
THEY WISH TO DESTROY THOSE THEY FEAR...THOSE WHO WANT NOTHING MORE THAN FREEDOM... THOSE WHO WISH TO GIVE YOU THE POWER TO CONTROL YOUR OWN DESTINY!
SO I SAY TO YOU...RISE UP!
RISE UP AND JOIN US!
RISE UP AGAINST YOUR MASTERS!
SOLDIERS-- SURRENDER YOUR WEAPONS!
CITIZENS-- RENOUNCE YOUR GOVERNMENTS!
RENOUNCE THEM AND PLEDGE ALLEGIANCE WITH US!
WITH THE GOD MAKER!
THIS IS WHERE IT GETS COMPLICATED...
OH, TOMMY. DON'T DO IT, TOMMY. PLEASE... DON'T
WHAT? OH, FUCK...
OH, TOMMY!

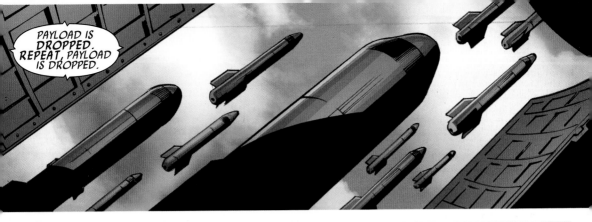

PAYLOAD IS *DROPPED*. REPEAT, PAYLOAD IS *DROPPED*.

GET *OUT* OF THE WAY. GET OUT OF *MY* WAY OR I *WILL* TAKE YOU *DOWN*.

WHATCHA GOING TO DO? *TALK* ME TO DEATH?

GAK!

WE NEED TO GET UP THERE! WE HAVE TO STOP THIS!!

WE DON'T STAND A CHANCE...THEY HAVE AN ARMY!

THEY HAVE TOMMY.

LET *ME* WORRY ABOUT TOMMY. COME ON!

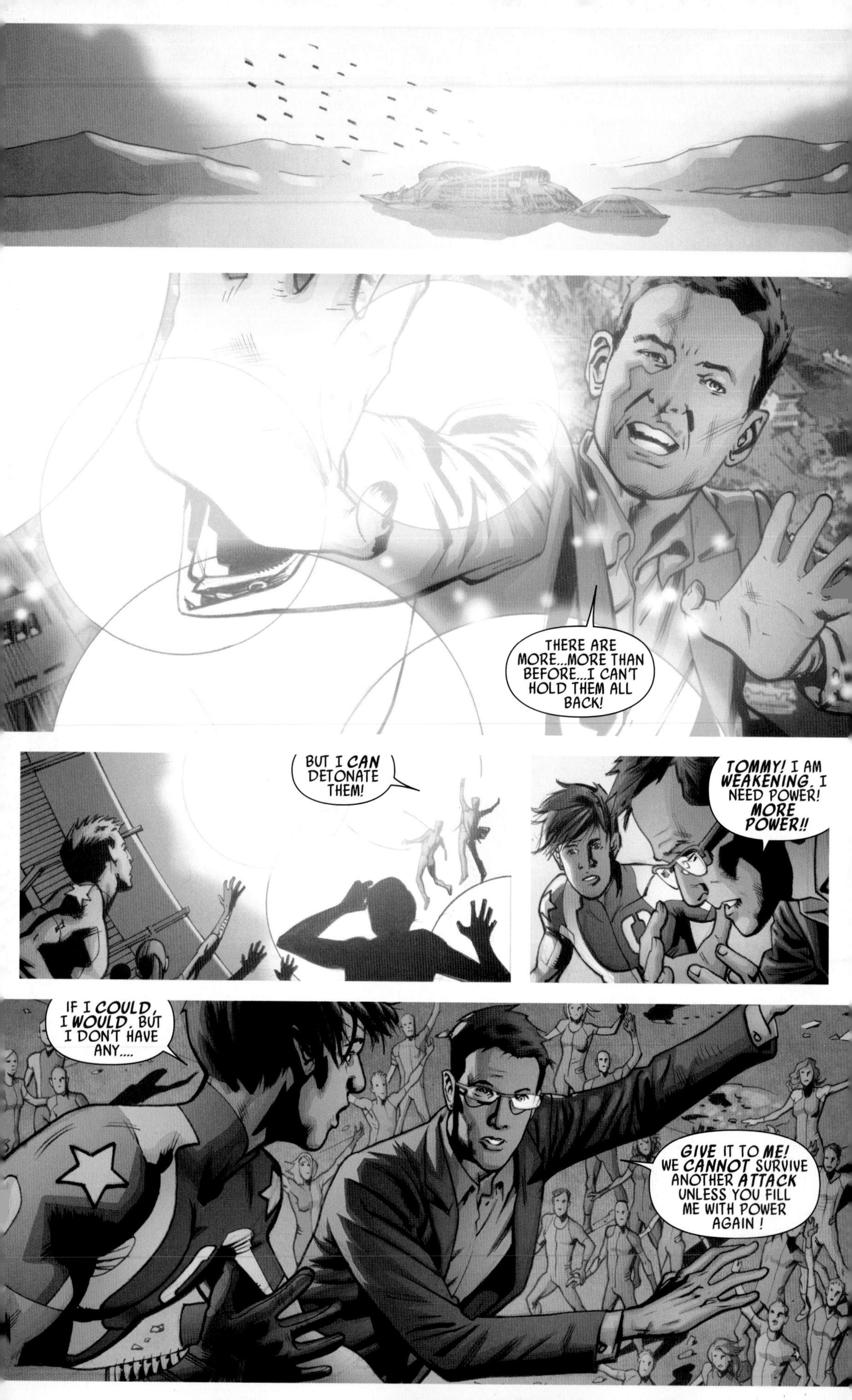

THERE ARE MORE...MORE THAN BEFORE...I CAN'T HOLD THEM ALL BACK!
BUT I CAN DETONATE THEM!
TOMMY! I AM WEAKENING. I NEED POWER! MORE POWER!!
IF I COULD, I WOULD. BUT I DON'T HAVE ANY....
GIVE IT TO ME! WE CANNOT SURVIVE ANOTHER ATTACK UNLESS YOU FILL ME WITH POWER AGAIN !

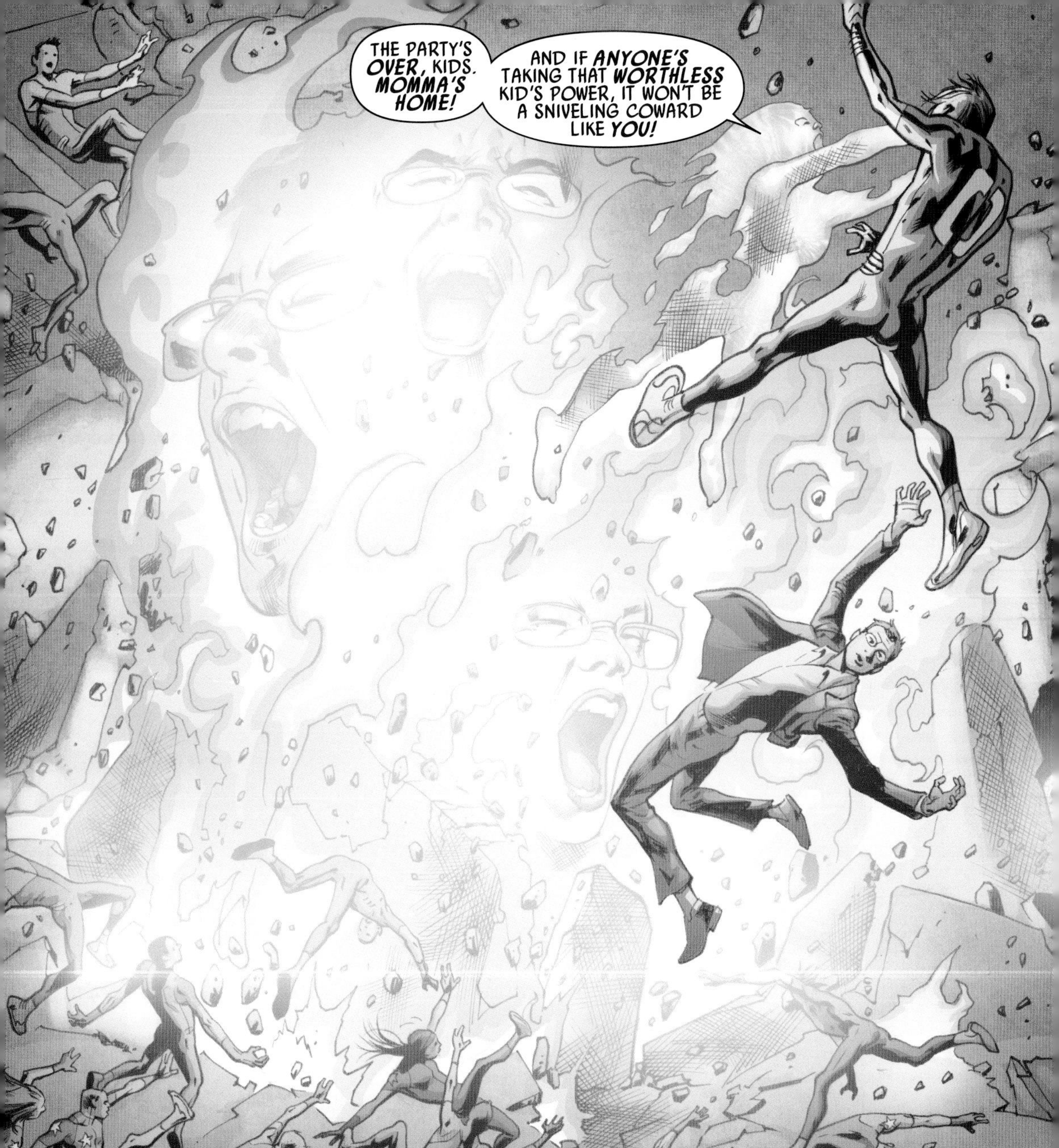
THE PARTY'S OVER, KIDS. MOMMA'S HOME!
AND IF ANYONE'S TAKING THAT WORTHLESS KID'S POWER, IT WON'T BE A SNIVELING COWARD LIKE YOU!

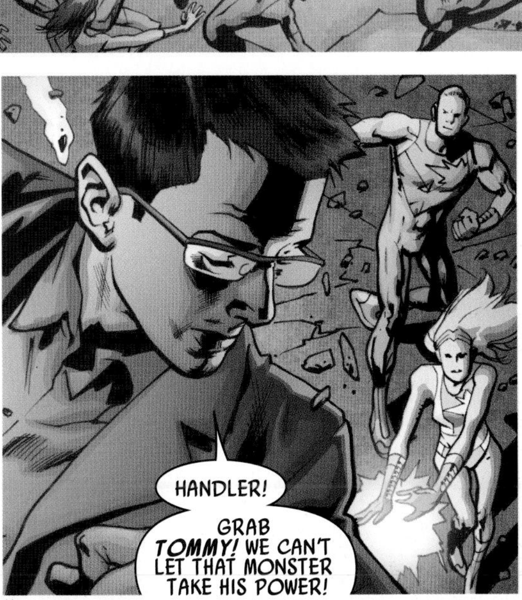
HANDLER!
GRAB TOMMY! WE CAN'T LET THAT MONSTER TAKE HIS POWER!

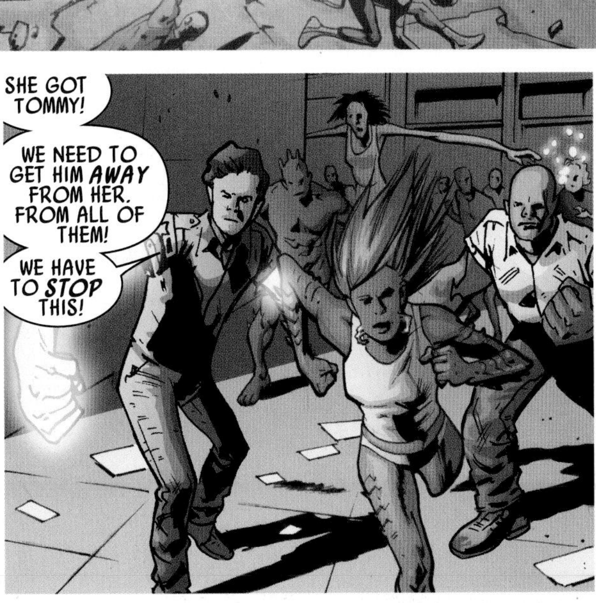
SHE GOT TOMMY!
WE NEED TO GET HIM AWAY FROM HER. FROM ALL OF THEM!
WE HAVE TO STOP THIS!

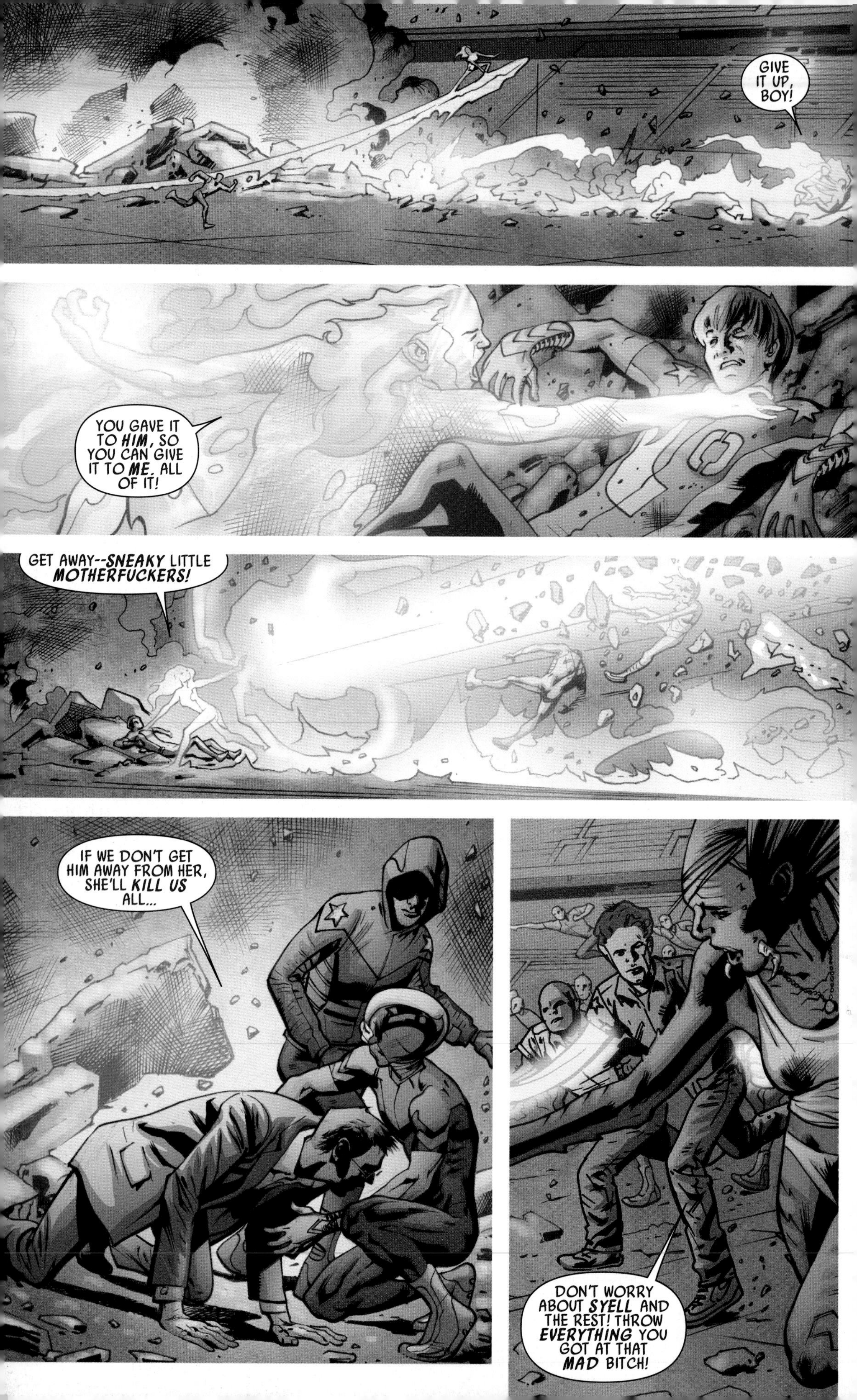
GIVE IT UP, BOY!
YOU GAVE IT TO HIM, SO YOU CAN GIVE IT TO ME. ALL OF IT!
GET AWAY--SNEAKY LITTLE MOTHERFUCKERS!
IF WE DON'T GET HIM AWAY FROM HER, SHE'LL KILL US ALL...
DON'T WORRY ABOUT SYELL AND THE REST! THROW EVERYTHING YOU GOT AT THAT MAD BITCH!

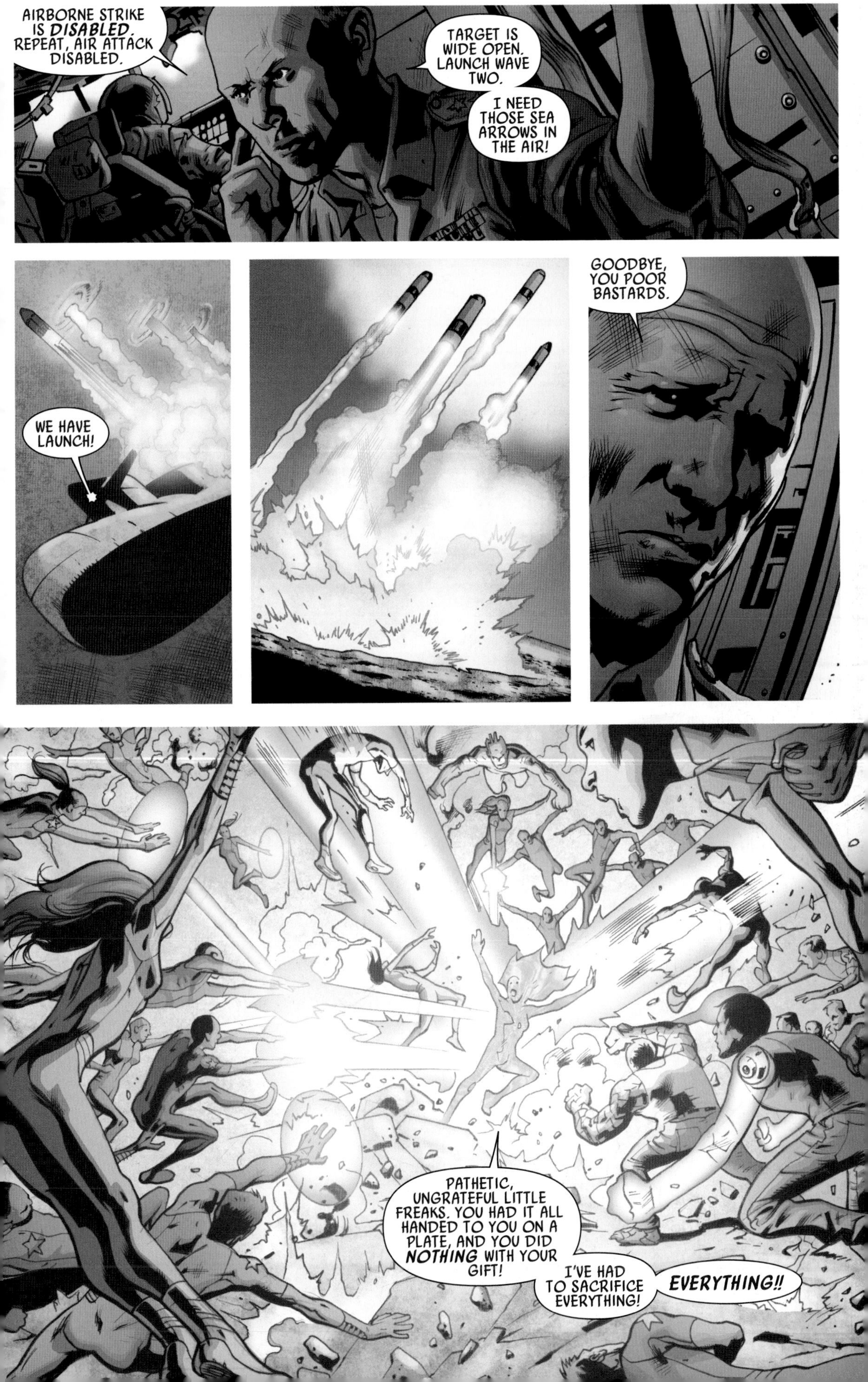
AIRBORNE STRIKE IS DISABLED. REPEAT, AIR ATTACK DISABLED.
TARGET IS WIDE OPEN. LAUNCH WAVE TWO.
I NEED THOSE SEA ARROWS IN THE AIR!
WE HAVE LAUNCH!
GOODBYE, YOU POOR BASTARDS.
PATHETIC, UNGRATEFUL LITTLE FREAKS. YOU HAD IT ALL HANDED TO YOU ON A PLATE, AND YOU DID NOTHING WITH YOUR GIFT!
I'VE HAD TO SACRIFICE EVERYTHING!
EVERYTHING!!

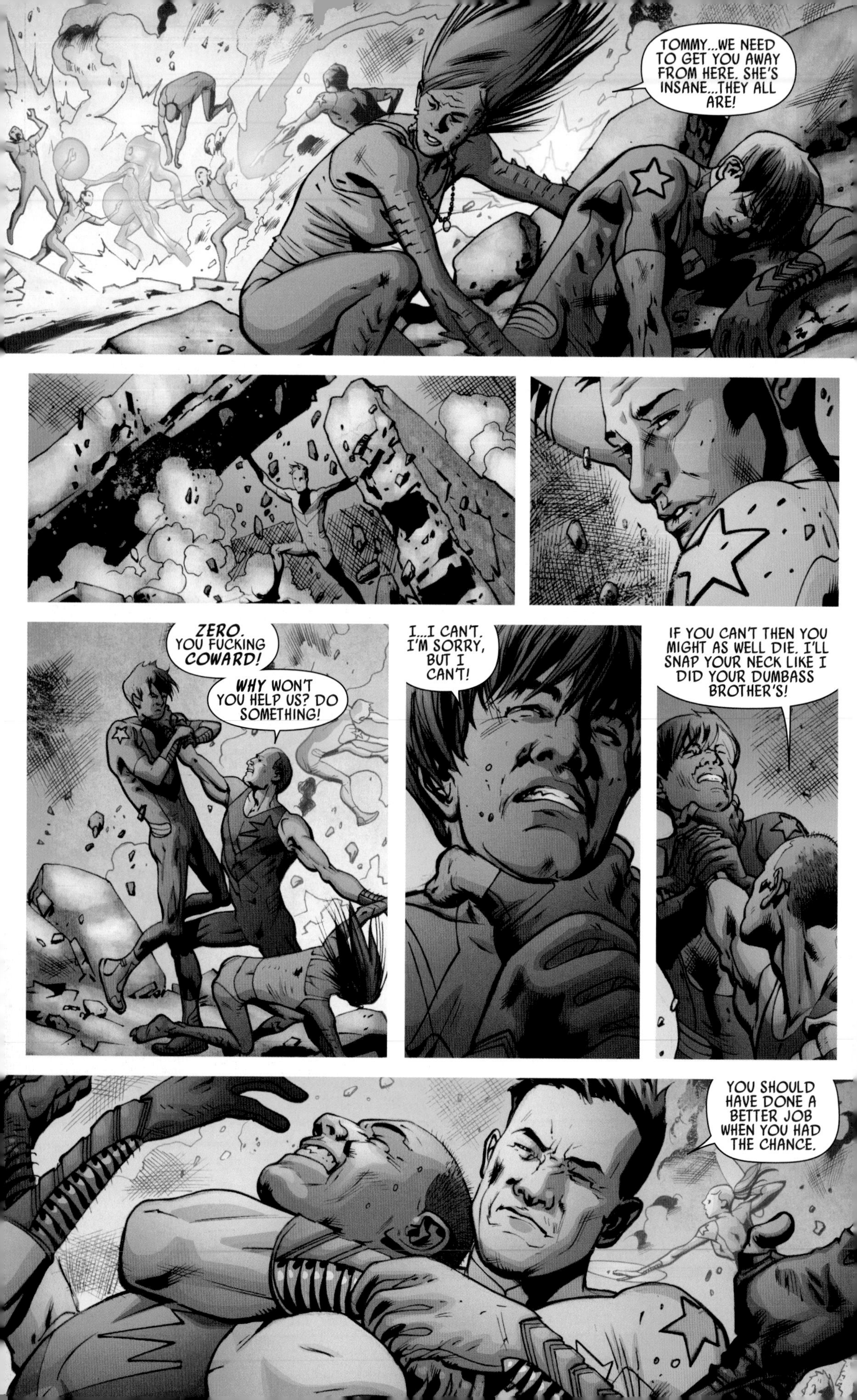
TOMMY...WE NEED TO GET YOU AWAY FROM HERE. SHE'S INSANE...THEY ALL ARE!
ZERO. YOU FUCKING COWARD!
WHY WON'T YOU HELP US? DO SOMETHING!
I...I CAN'T. I'M SORRY, BUT I CAN'T!
IF YOU CAN'T THEN YOU MIGHT AS WELL DIE. I'LL SNAP YOUR NECK LIKE I DID YOUR DUMBASS BROTHER'S!
YOU SHOULD HAVE DONE A BETTER JOB WHEN YOU HAD THE CHANCE.

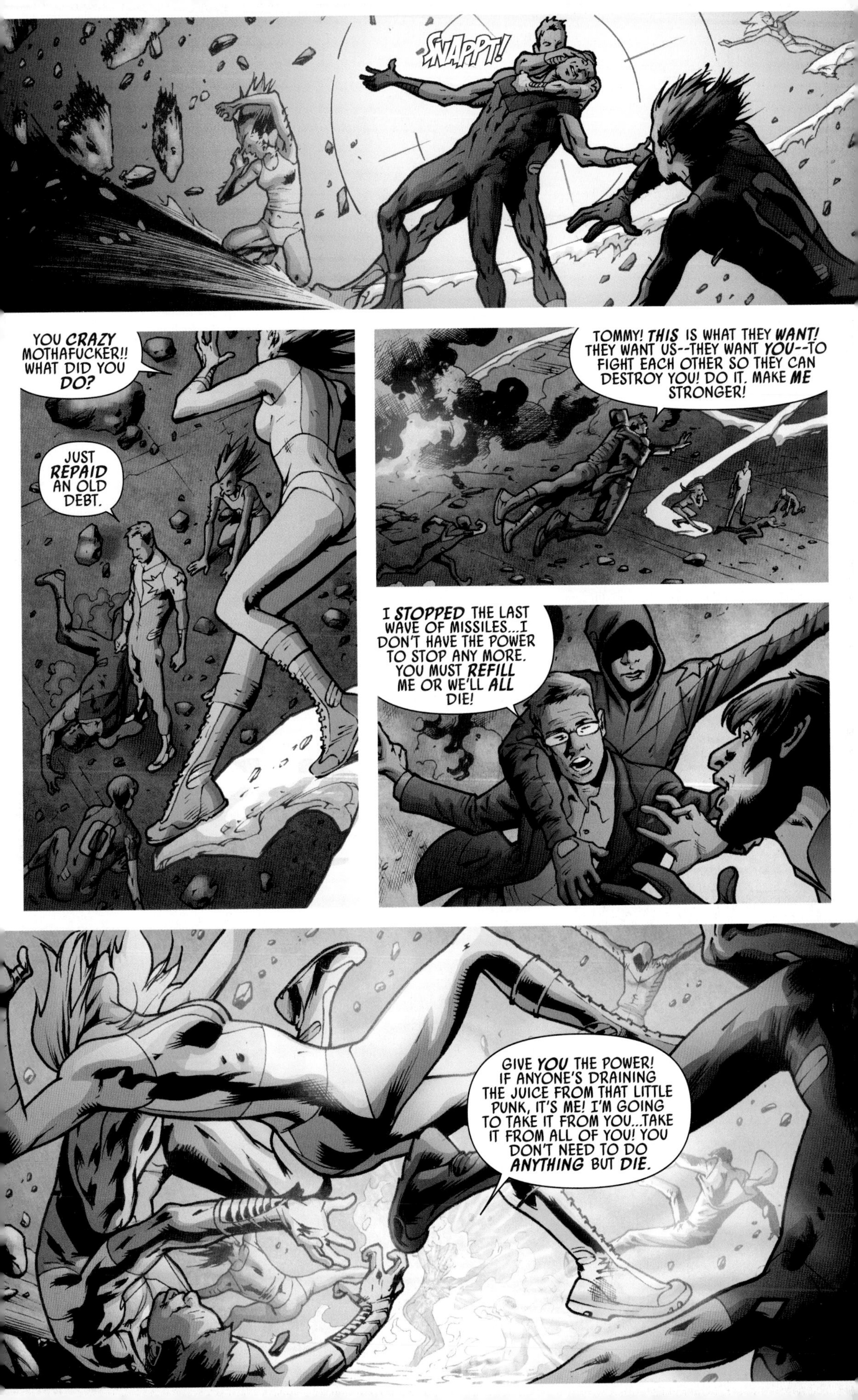
SNAPPT!
YOU CRAZY MOTHAFUCKER!! WHAT DID YOU DO?
JUST REPAID AN OLD DEBT.
TOMMY! THIS IS WHAT THEY WANT! THEY WANT US--THEY WANT YOU--TO FIGHT EACH OTHER SO THEY CAN DESTROY YOU! DO IT. MAKE ME STRONGER!
I STOPPED THE LAST WAVE OF MISSILES...I DON'T HAVE THE POWER TO STOP ANY MORE. YOU MUST REFILL ME OR WE'LL ALL DIE!
GIVE YOU THE POWER! IF ANYONE'S DRAINING THE JUICE FROM THAT LITTLE PUNK, IT'S ME! I'M GOING TO TAKE IT FROM YOU...TAKE IT FROM ALL OF YOU! YOU DON'T NEED TO DO ANYTHING BUT DIE.

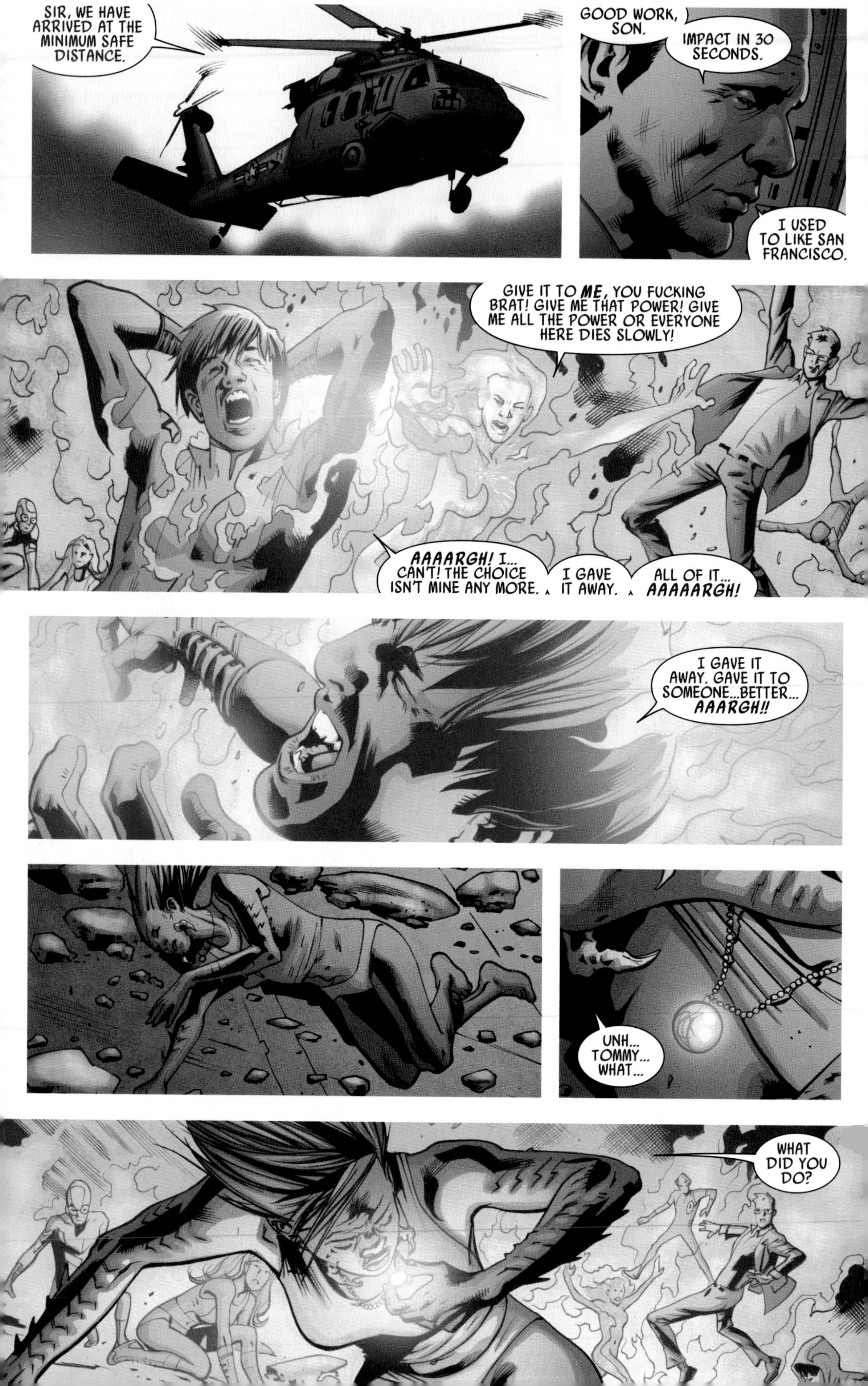
SIR, WE HAVE ARRIVED AT THE MINIMUM SAFE DISTANCE.
GOOD WORK, SON.
IMPACT IN 30 SECONDS.
I USED TO LIKE SAN FRANCISCO.
GIVE IT TO ME, YOU FUCKING BRAT! GIVE ME THAT POWER! GIVE ME ALL THE POWER OR EVERYONE HERE DIES SLOWLY!
AAAARGH! I... CAN'T! THE CHOICE ISN'T MINE ANY MORE.
I GAVE IT AWAY.
ALL OF IT... AAAAARGH!
I GAVE IT AWAY. GAVE IT TO SOMEONE...BETTER... AAARGH!!
UNH... TOMMY... WHAT...
WHAT DID YOU DO?

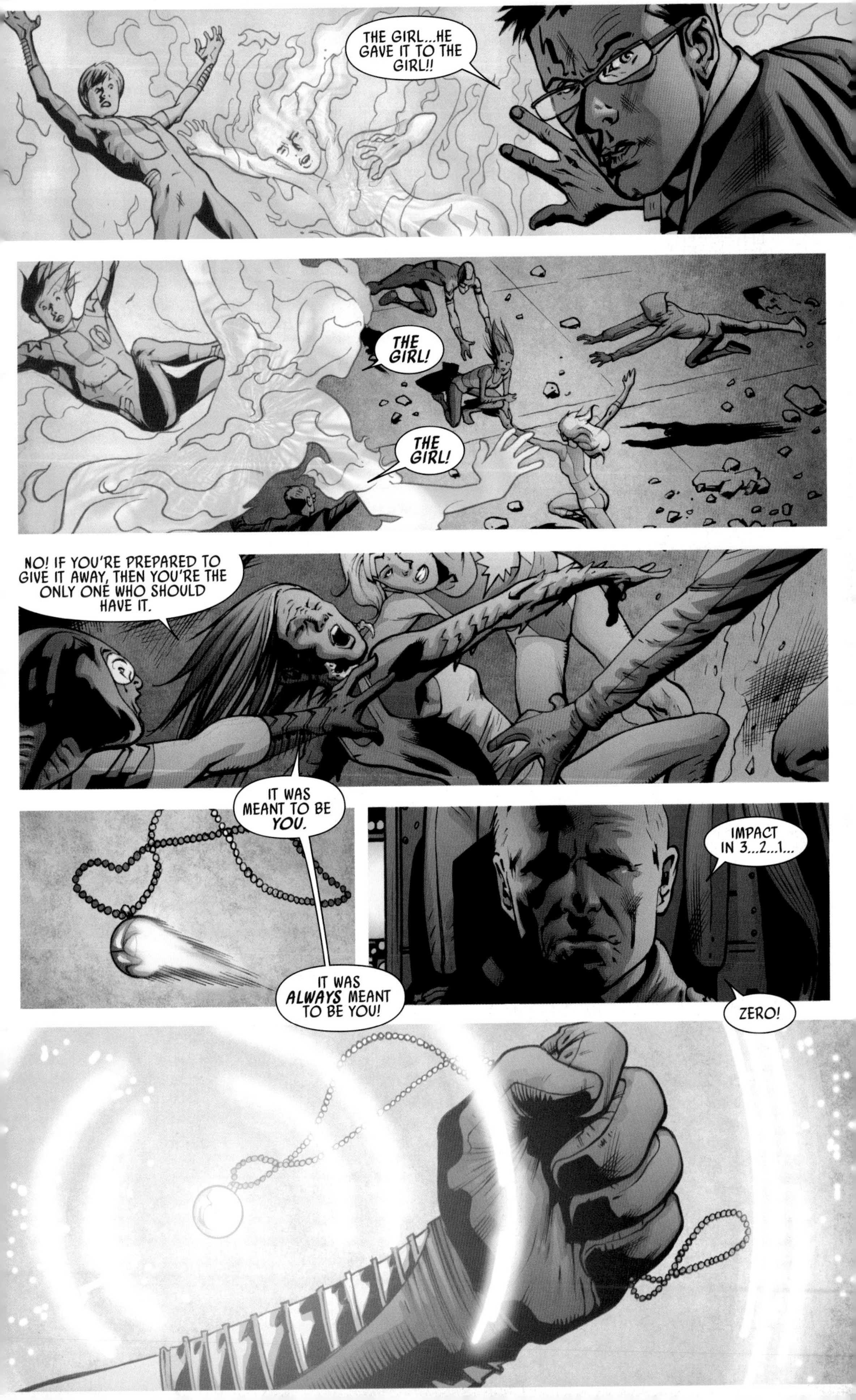
THE GIRL...HE GAVE IT TO THE GIRL!!
THE GIRL!
THE GIRL!
NO! IF YOU'RE PREPARED TO GIVE IT AWAY, THEN YOU'RE THE ONLY ONE WHO SHOULD HAVE IT.
IT WAS MEANT TO BE *YOU.*
IT WAS *ALWAYS* MEANT TO BE YOU!
IMPACT IN 3...2...1...
ZERO!

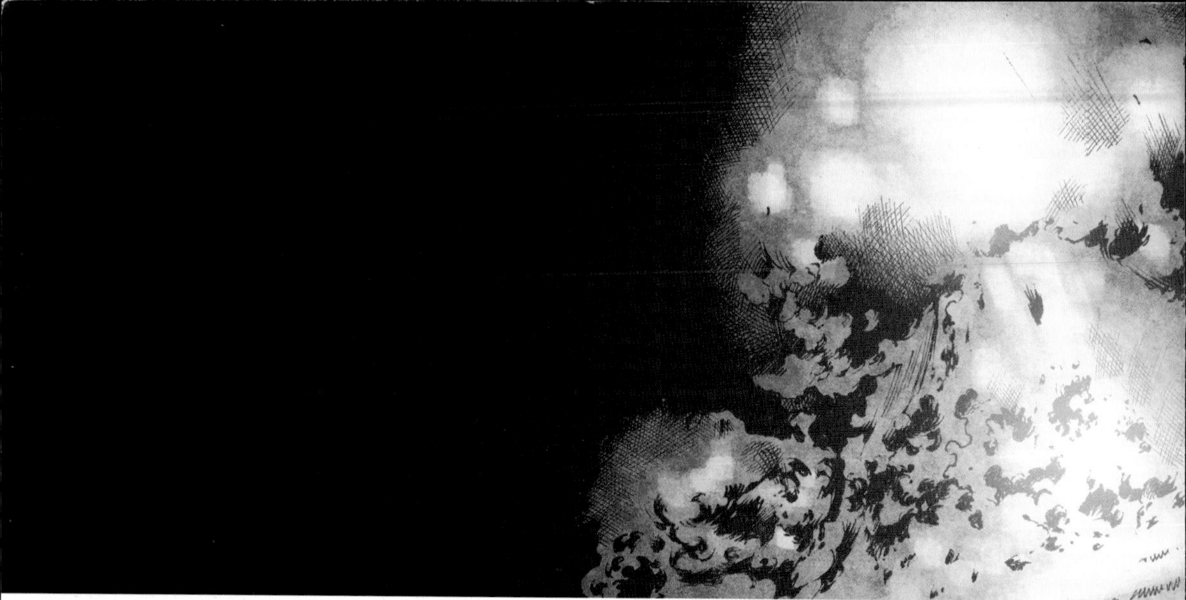

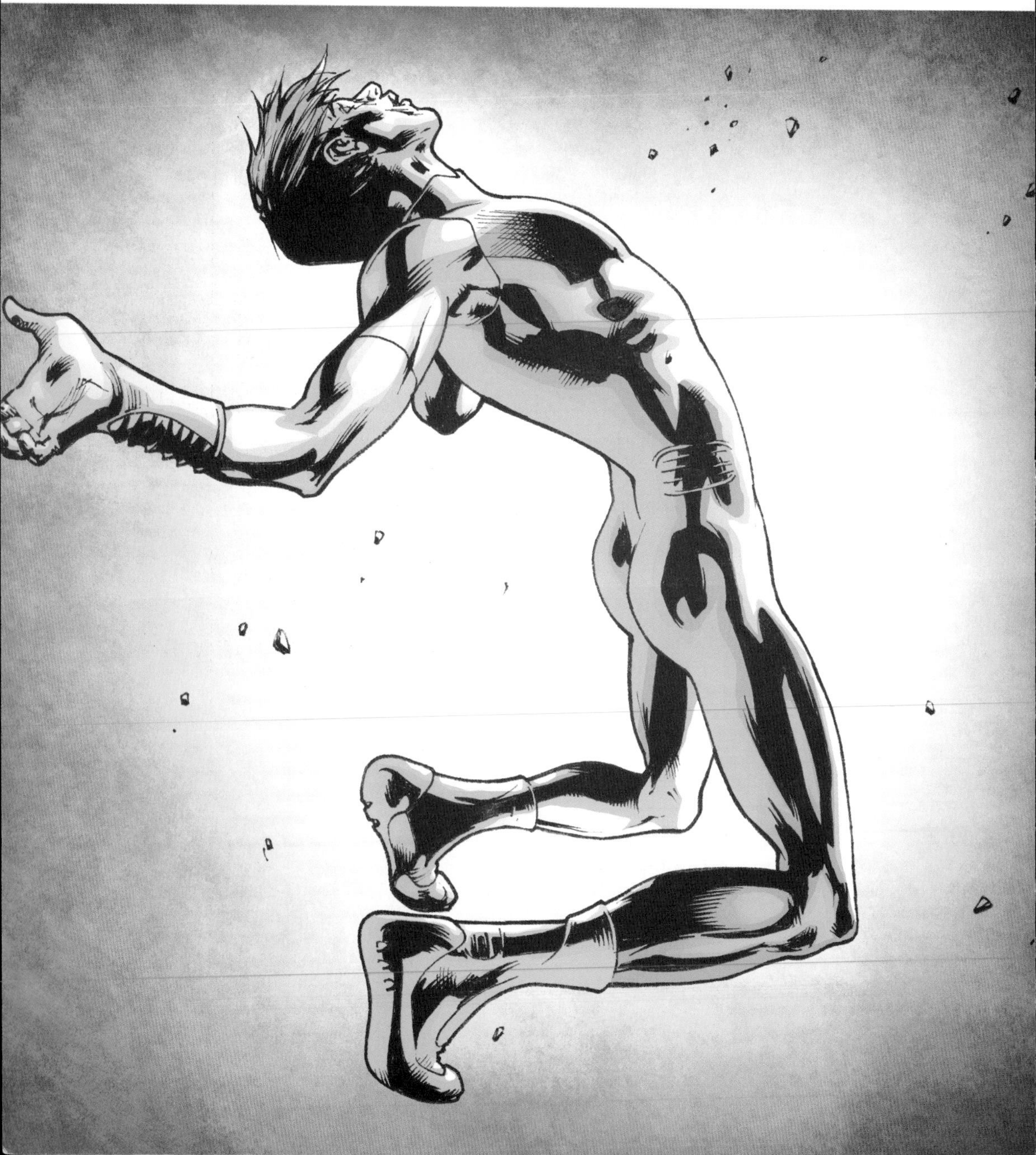

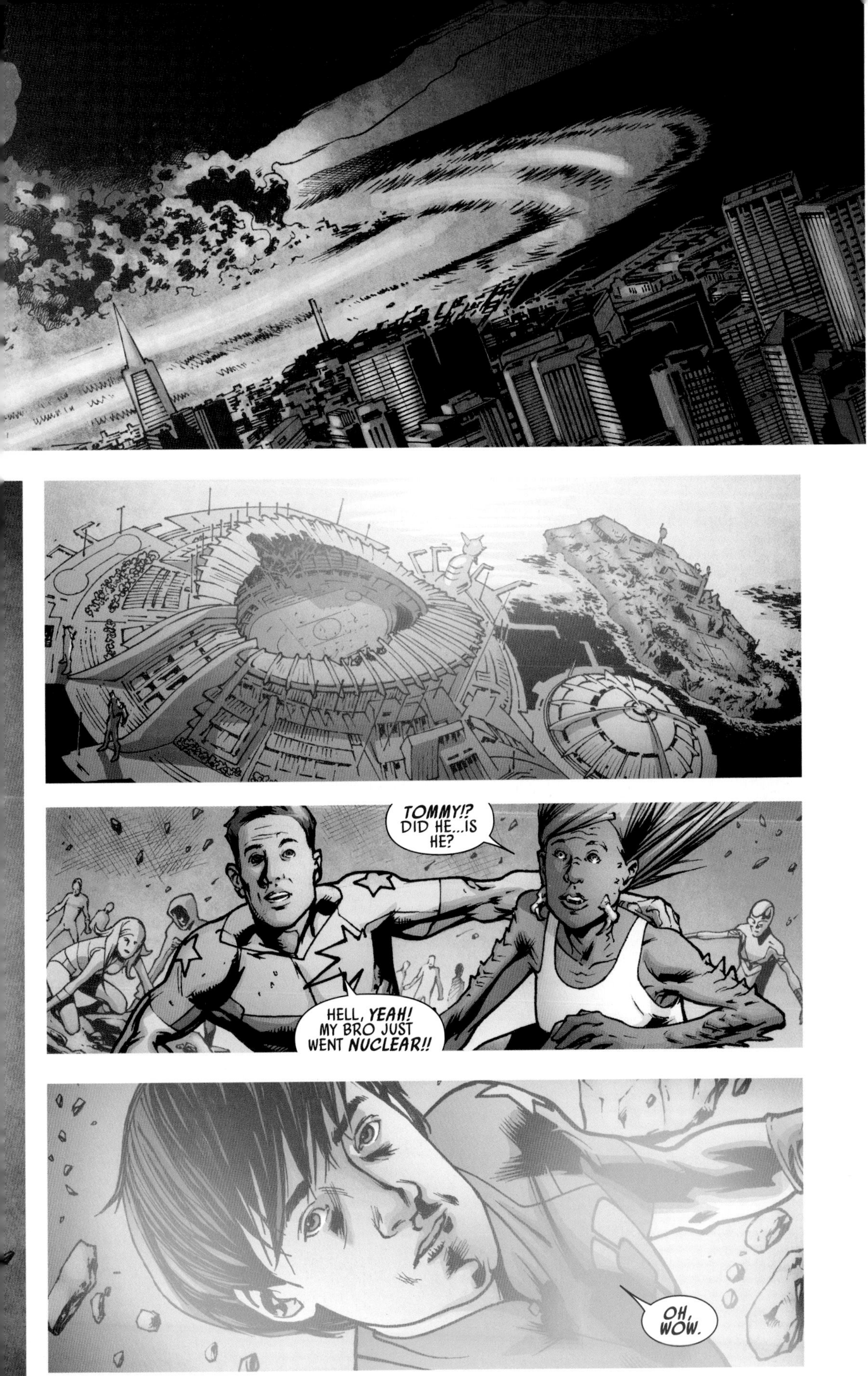
TOMMY!? DID HE...IS HE?
HELL, YEAH! MY BRO JUST WENT NUCLEAR!!
OH, WOW.

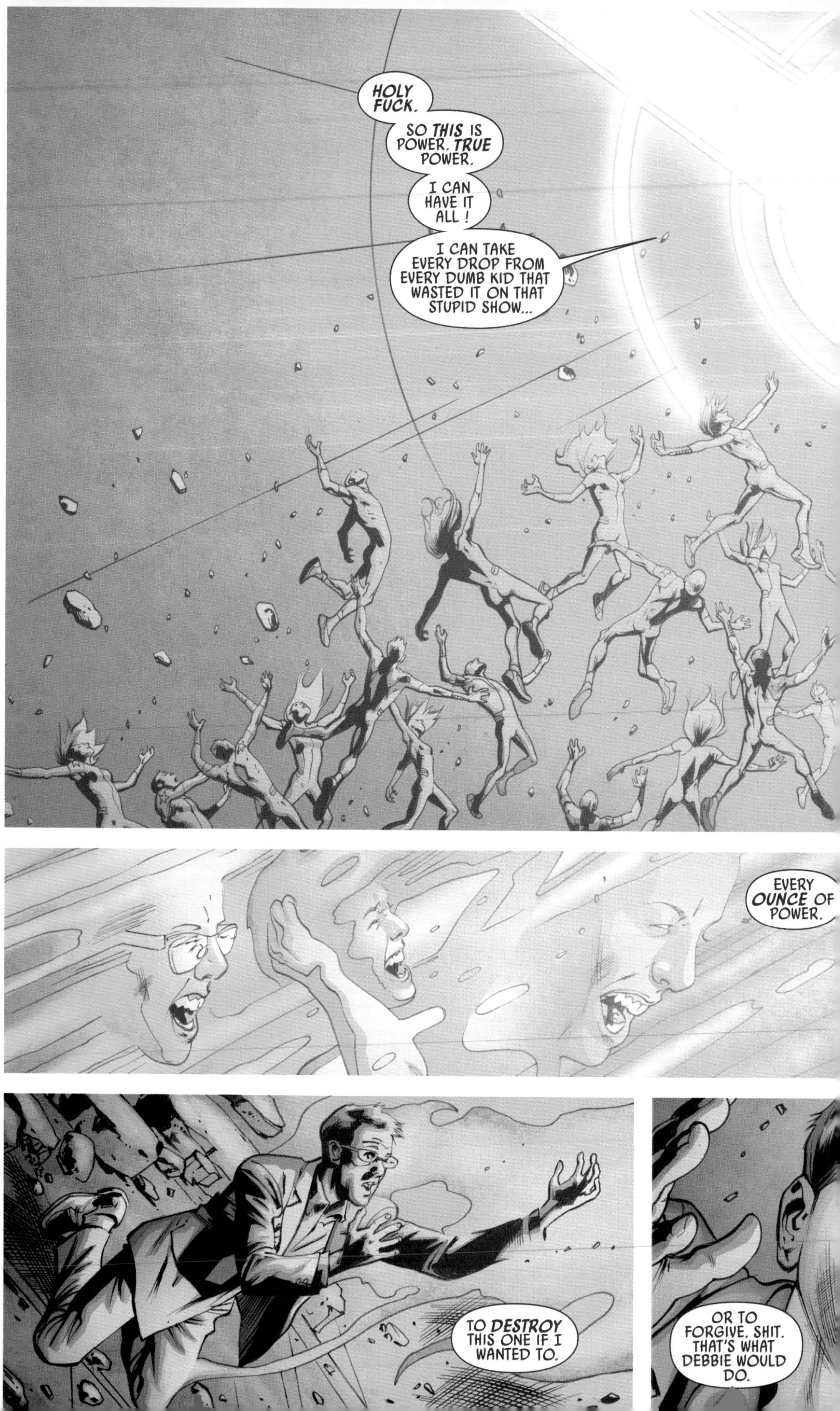
HOLY FUCK.
SO THIS IS POWER. TRUE POWER.
I CAN HAVE IT ALL !
I CAN TAKE EVERY DROP FROM EVERY DUMB KID THAT WASTED IT ON THAT STUPID SHOW...
EVERY OUNCE OF POWER.
TO DESTROY THIS ONE IF I WANTED TO.
OR TO FORGIVE. SHIT. THAT'S WHAT DEBBIE WOULD DO.

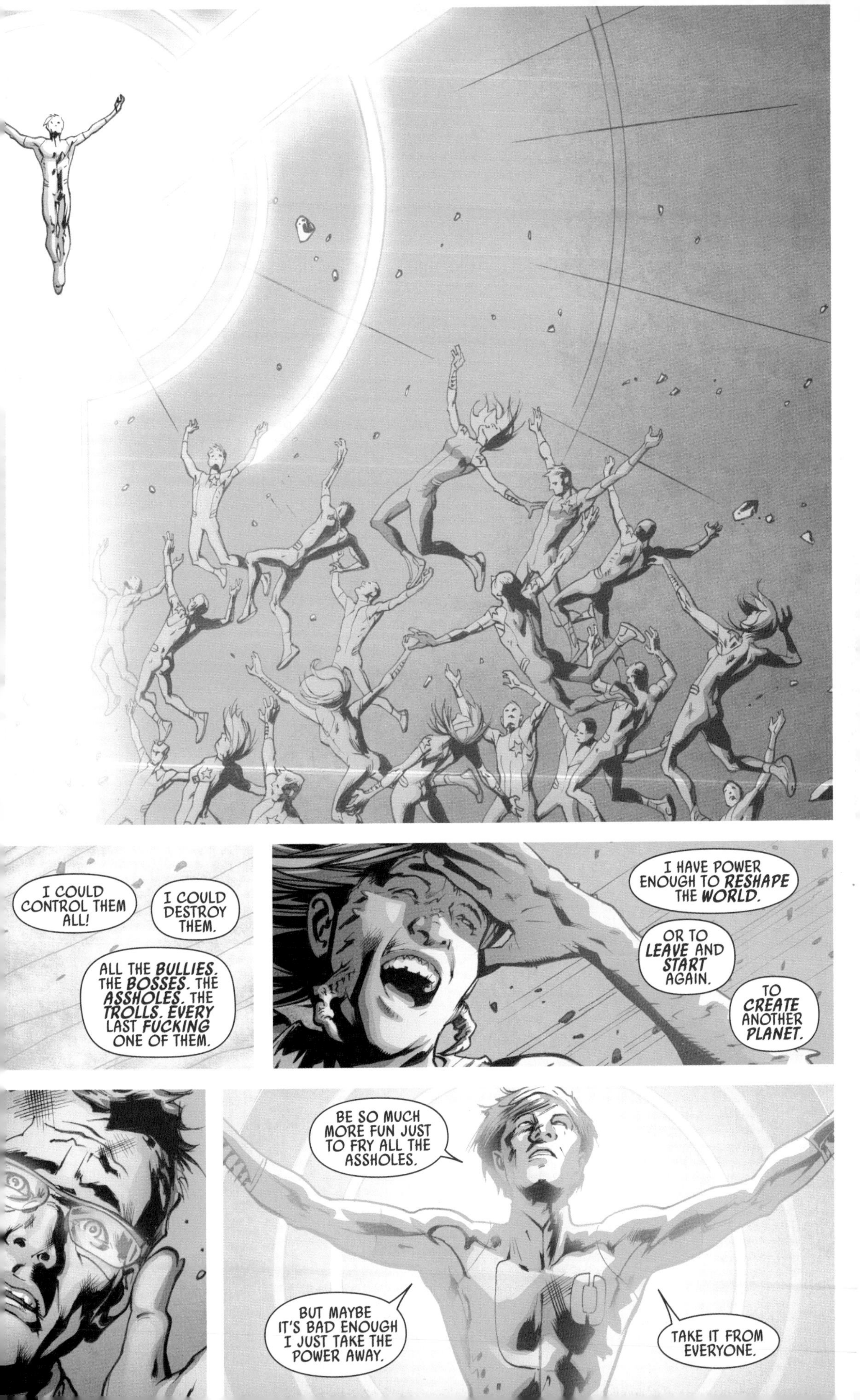

I COULD CONTROL THEM ALL!
I COULD DESTROY THEM.
ALL THE BULLIES. THE BOSSES. THE ASSHOLES. THE TROLLS. EVERY LAST FUCKING ONE OF THEM.
I HAVE POWER ENOUGH TO RESHAPE THE WORLD.
OR TO LEAVE AND START AGAIN.
TO CREATE ANOTHER PLANET.
BE SO MUCH MORE FUN JUST TO FRY ALL THE ASSHOLES.
BUT MAYBE IT'S BAD ENOUGH I JUST TAKE THE POWER AWAY.
TAKE IT FROM EVERYONE.

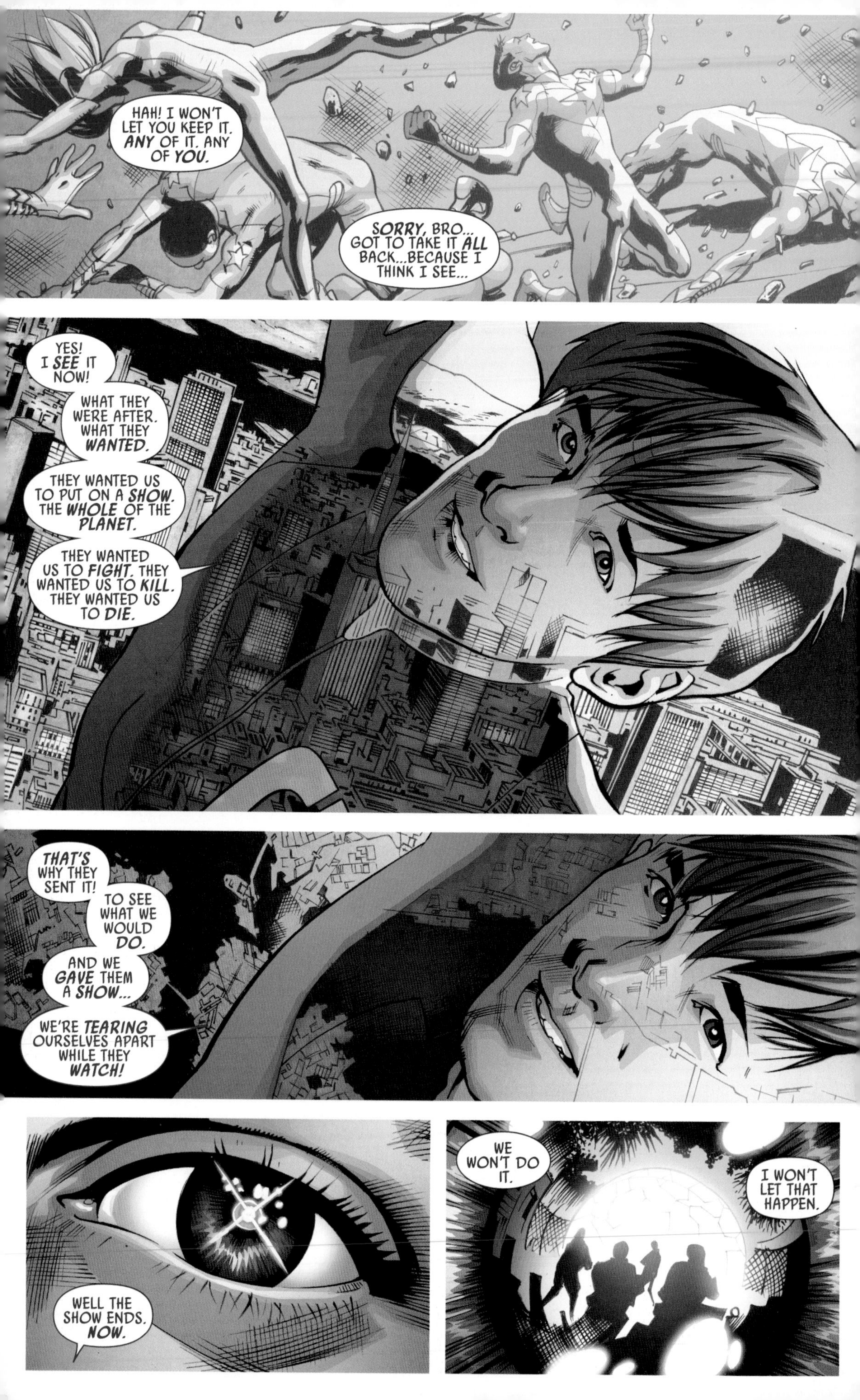
HAH! I WON'T LET YOU KEEP IT. ANY OF IT. ANY OF YOU.
SORRY, BRO... GOT TO TAKE IT ALL BACK...BECAUSE I THINK I SEE...
YES! I SEE IT NOW!
WHAT THEY WERE AFTER. WHAT THEY WANTED.
THEY WANTED US TO PUT ON A SHOW. THE WHOLE OF THE PLANET.
THEY WANTED US TO FIGHT. THEY WANTED US TO KILL. THEY WANTED US TO DIE.
THAT'S WHY THEY SENT IT!
TO SEE WHAT WE WOULD DO.
AND WE GAVE THEM A SHOW...
WE'RE TEARING OURSELVES APART WHILE THEY WATCH!
WELL THE SHOW ENDS. NOW.
WE WON'T DO IT.
I WON'T LET THAT HAPPEN.

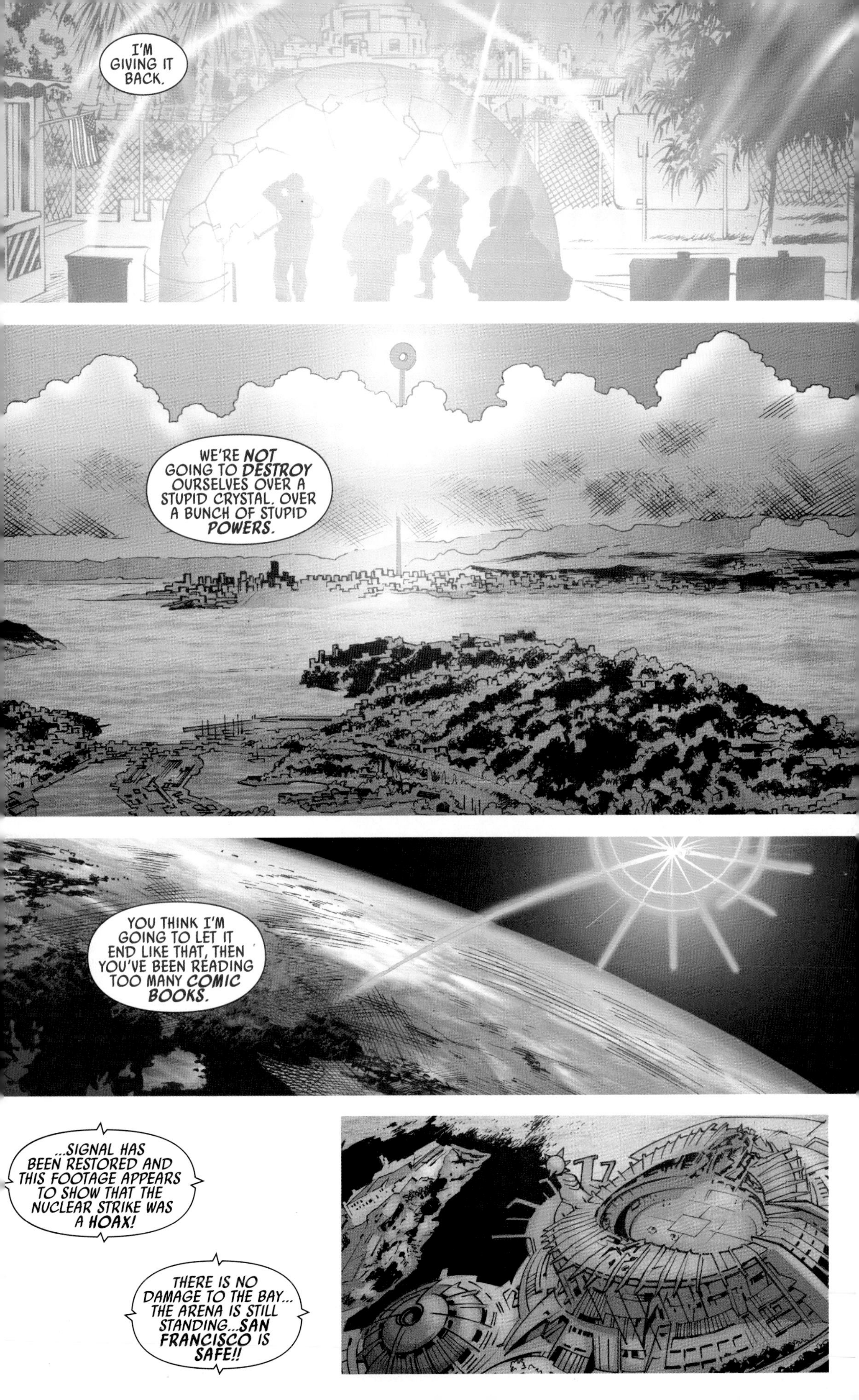

I'M GIVING IT BACK.
WE'RE NOT GOING TO DESTROY OURSELVES OVER A STUPID CRYSTAL. OVER A BUNCH OF STUPID POWERS.
YOU THINK I'M GOING TO LET IT END LIKE THAT, THEN YOU'VE BEEN READING TOO MANY COMIC BOOKS.
...SIGNAL HAS BEEN RESTORED AND THIS FOOTAGE APPEARS TO SHOW THAT THE NUCLEAR STRIKE WAS A HOAX!
THERE IS NO DAMAGE TO THE BAY... THE ARENA IS STILL STANDING...SAN FRANCISCO IS SAFE!!

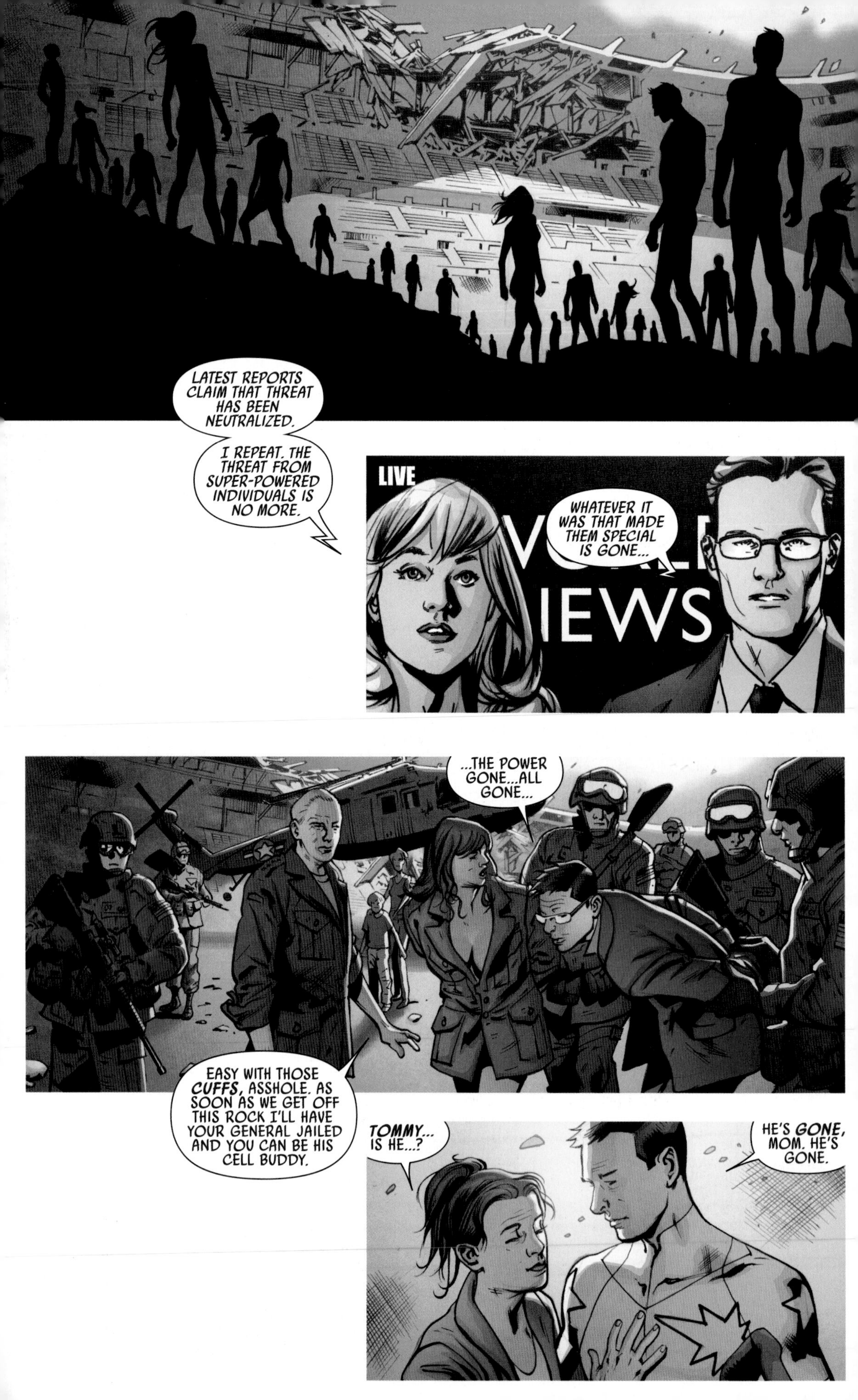
LATEST REPORTS CLAIM THAT THREAT HAS BEEN NEUTRALIZED.
I REPEAT. THE THREAT FROM SUPER-POWERED INDIVIDUALS IS NO MORE.
LIVE
WHATEVER IT WAS THAT MADE THEM SPECIAL IS GONE...
...THE POWER GONE...ALL GONE...
EASY WITH THOSE CUFFS, ASSHOLE. AS SOON AS WE GET OFF THIS ROCK I'LL HAVE YOUR GENERAL JAILED AND YOU CAN BE HIS CELL BUDDY.
TOMMY... IS HE...?
HE'S GONE, MOM. HE'S GONE.

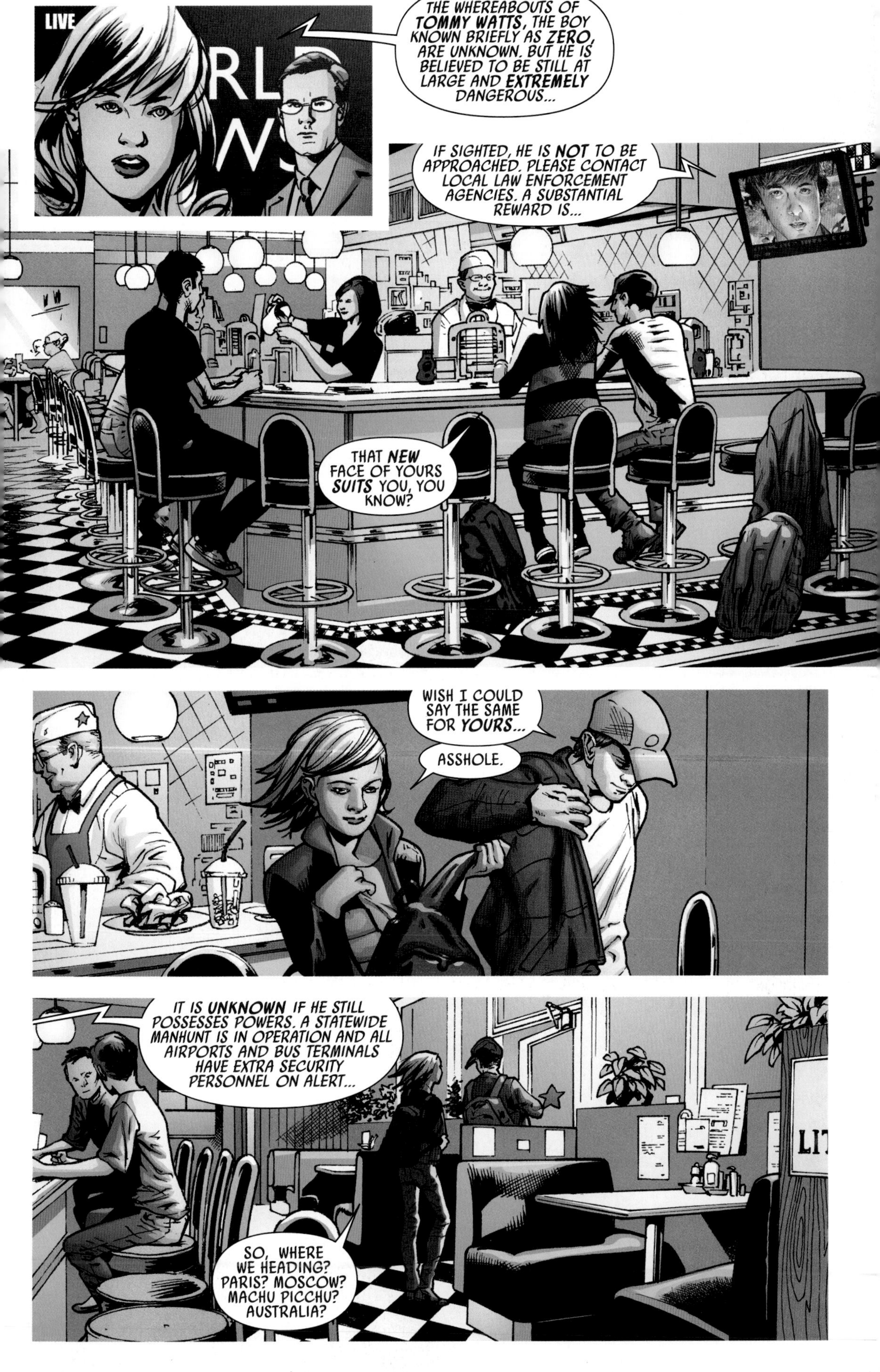
LIVE
THE WHEREABOUTS OF TOMMY WATTS, THE BOY KNOWN BRIEFLY AS ZERO, ARE UNKNOWN. BUT HE IS BELIEVED TO BE STILL AT LARGE AND EXTREMELY DANGEROUS...
IF SIGHTED, HE IS NOT TO BE APPROACHED. PLEASE CONTACT LOCAL LAW ENFORCEMENT AGENCIES. A SUBSTANTIAL REWARD IS...
THAT NEW FACE OF YOURS SUITS YOU, YOU KNOW?
WISH I COULD SAY THE SAME FOR YOURS...
ASSHOLE.
IT IS UNKNOWN IF HE STILL POSSESSES POWERS. A STATEWIDE MANHUNT IS IN OPERATION AND ALL AIRPORTS AND BUS TERMINALS HAVE EXTRA SECURITY PERSONNEL ON ALERT...
SO, WHERE WE HEADING? PARIS? MOSCOW? MACHU PICCHU? AUSTRALIA?

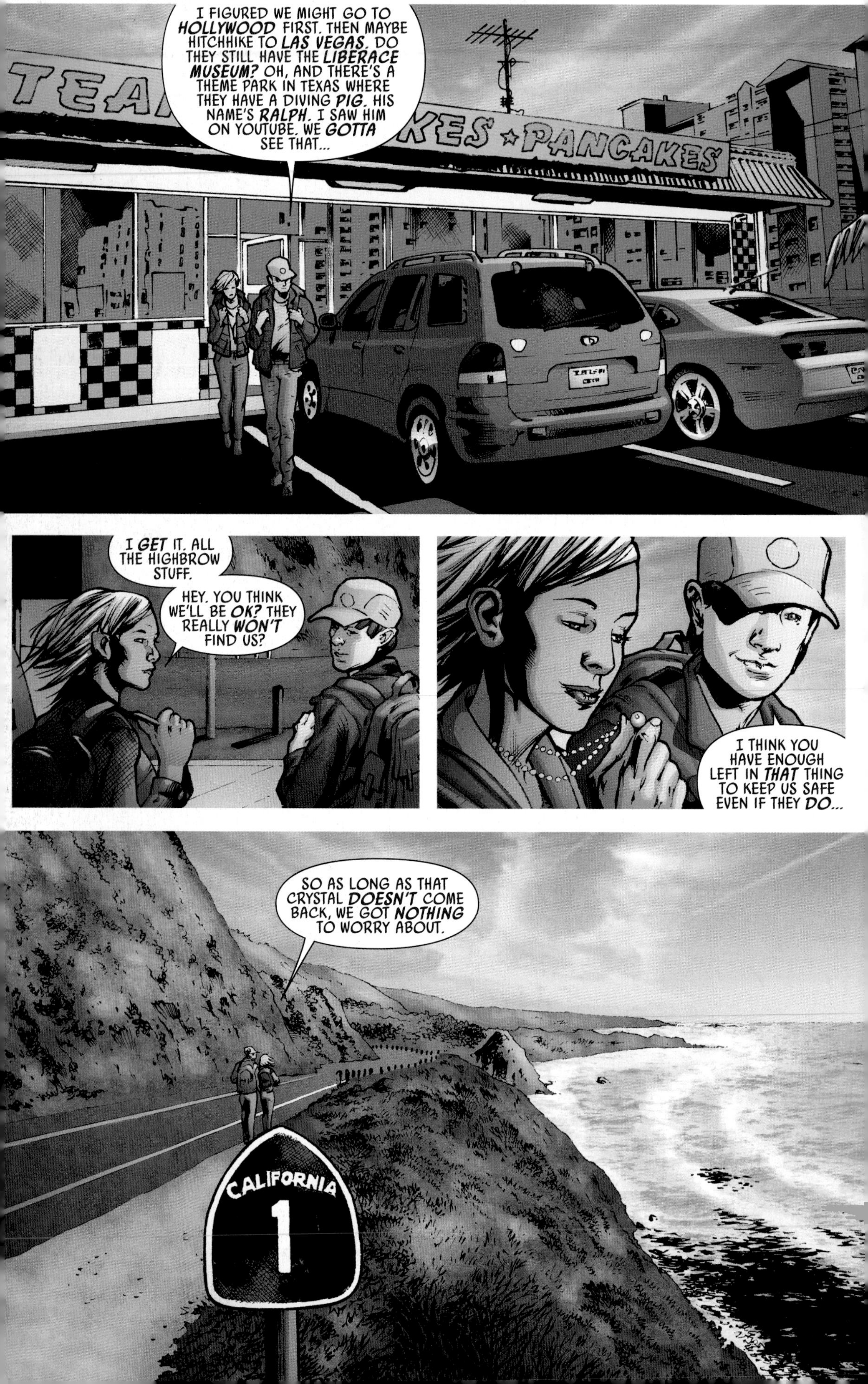

I FIGURED WE MIGHT GO TO HOLLYWOOD FIRST. THEN MAYBE HITCHHIKE TO LAS VEGAS. DO THEY STILL HAVE THE LIBERACE MUSEUM? OH, AND THERE'S A THEME PARK IN TEXAS WHERE THEY HAVE A DIVING PIG. HIS NAME'S RALPH. I SAW HIM ON YOUTUBE. WE GOTTA SEE THAT...
PANCAKES
I GET IT. ALL THE HIGHBROW STUFF.
HEY. YOU THINK WE'LL BE OK? THEY REALLY WON'T FIND US?
I THINK YOU HAVE ENOUGH LEFT IN THAT THING TO KEEP US SAFE EVEN IF THEY DO...
SO AS LONG AS THAT CRYSTAL DOESN'T COME BACK, WE GOT NOTHING TO WORRY ABOUT.
CALIFORNIA
1

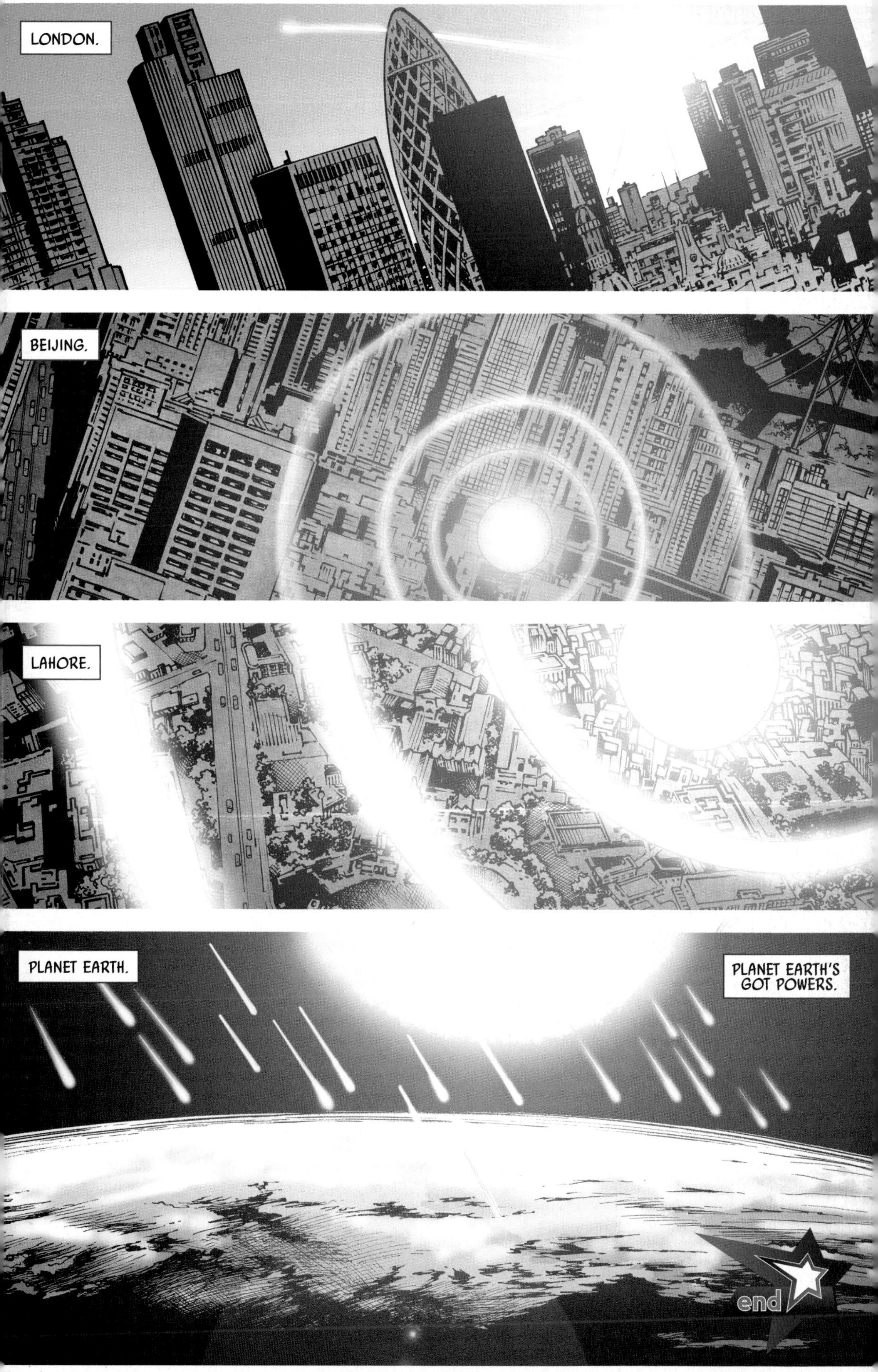
LONDON.
BEIJING.
LAHORE.
PLANET EARTH.
PLANET EARTH'S GOT POWERS.
end